Darach MacDonald has been a professional journalist since 1976, working throughout Ireland, Europe and in Canada and closing his full-time newspaper career as editor of the award-winning *Ulster Herald*. In 2015, he was conferred with a PhD by Ulster University (Magee) for research on a frontier Ulster loyalist marching band, having completed his MA thesis on the Irish Boundary Commission almost forty years previously at University College Dublin. He is the author of four previous books: *The Sons of Levi* (1998); *The Chosen Fews: Exploding Myths in South Armagh* (2000); *Blood & Thunder: Inside an Ulster Protestant Band* (2010); and *Tóchar: Walking Ireland's Ancient Pilgrim Paths* (2013). A native of Clones, a proud father and very soon-to-be grandfather, he now lives in the border city of Derry.

)ate L

Hard Border

Walking through a Century of
Irish Partition

Darach MacDonald

NEW ISLAND

HARD BORDER
First published in 2018 by
New Island Books
16 Priory Hall Office Park
Stillorgan
County Dublin
Republic of Ireland

www.newisland.ie

Print ISBN: 978-1-84840-675-9
Epub ISBN: 978-1-84840-676-6
Mobi ISBN: 978-1-84840-677-3

Typeset by JVR Creative India
Cover design by Kate Gaughran
Printed by TJ International Ltd, Padstow, Cornwall

New Island Books is a member of Publishing Ireland.

Contents

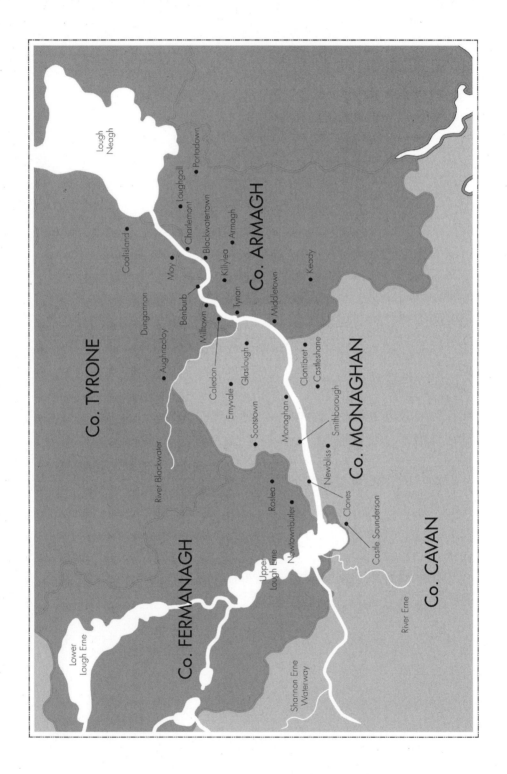

In memory of my 'wee' brother Vincent MacDonald
1965 – 2017
Clones, County Monaghan – Hilltown, County Down

Introduction: Always on Edge

The regatta took place beside the humpbacked bridge at the foot of the brae that we still called Whitehall Street, although the name had been changed officially to MacCurtain Street when Clones was incorporated into the Irish Free State.[1] Our motley fleet of improvised sailing vessels was comprised of rafts made from oil barrels strung together with planks of timber or old doors. One formidable vessel had two huge wooden sleepers, salvaged from the recently abandoned Great Northern Railway that had once made our town the rail hub of Ulster. Now they provided a juggernaut for a crew of young boys on this channel of the Ulster Canal, which spread out before us and stretched off into the distance towards Legarhill, Clonavilla, Glear and the unknown beyond. We were barely aware then that it had once connected Lough Erne with Lough Neagh, and with the Lagan Navigation, reached all the way to Belfast. It had been abandoned about thirty years previously in 1932, when my dad was still a boy, just as our Great Northern Railway connections to Belfast, Dundalk, Cavan and Enniskillen were severed in my early childhood.

Long before its formal demise, the Ulster Canal was dead in the water. An ill-conceived venture of narrow locks and bridges with an insufficient headwater supply, it was built for different barges than those plying the connecting inland waterways. It never attracted the traffic projected by its champions and investors. The link-up of the Erne and the Shannon to create a commercial route encompassing the entire island was too late, and proved an even bigger commercial failure than the Ulster Canal. Barely opened when the railway came to town, our canal was almost immediately outmoded, redundant and cast into a peripheral role. It was neglected at birth, then abandoned as an unwanted orphan of the Georgian era, a relic of pastoral pace shunted into obscurity by the steam, steel and speed of the Industrial Revolution.

Yet the canal still provided recreational diversion during my childhood in the 1950s and 1960s. Apart from the great regatta organised by the Whitehall Street gang, its towpath was a route to distant locations for adventure and exploration. It also provided an alternative border crossing for small-scale smugglers. And when our town was briefly a coarse-fishing Mecca for visitors from the English north and midlands in those times between the Troubles, I recall anglers on the banks. At Halloween, the overgrown channels provided a handy source of bulrushes. We harvested these and soaked their pillowy, dark brown bulbs in paraffin, setting them afire for torchlight Samhain rituals on the steps of the Protestant church that dominated the Diamond in the middle of our town.

I moved away from the town and gave the canal little thought until the rain-soaked summer of 1985, when we spent a week's family holiday in a hired cruiser on the Erne. Local people say the Erne is in Fermanagh for half the year, and, for the other half, Fermanagh is in the Erne. During our holiday, the latter was the case. So day after day, we plied the sodden channels looking for somewhere interesting to berth other than Enniskillen. Near Crum Castle and the cross-border link to Belturbet one day, I saw on the navigation chart that the disused Ulster Canal was a short distance away. If opened, we could have cruised home for tea with my mother. I mentioned it later as a tourism objective. Others did too, and the idea slowly took hold of a campaign for the restoration of the Ulster Canal as the final link in Ireland's inland navigation network.

It seemed feasible. After the Ballinamore-Ballyconnell link of the Erne and Shannon was restored in 1994, my uncle Michael Bowen pointed his boat north from his home on Cork Harbour. His voyage on the inland waterways ended with *Bullfrog's* prow touching the harbour wall in Belleek. He told journalists he would be back when the Ulster Canal was opened and he could navigate all the way to Coleraine, completing his voyage from one end of Ireland to the other. Michael died in 2009, by which time the authorities had been talking about the Ulster Canal project for twenty years and more. Somehow, it always seems to slip down the agenda of funded projects. It has always lacked a champion to point out that it is more than an abandoned navigation for boat enthusiasts. It is a route through many of the places most deeply and persistently afflicted by the conflict of the past century. It is a route that presents another narrative of Ireland's story, one that contradicts the shibboleths on which we build difference and confrontation.

Fifty years ago, *Irish Times* journalist John Healy wrote a series of articles charting the plight of his native Charlestown. These were published in book form as *The Death of an Irish Town*, and republished twenty years later in 1988 as *No One Shouted Stop!* Half a century on, my home town could look with envy at that small Mayo town's tidy shopfronts, its modern road network, its proximity to rail corridors, its tourism economy and its nearby international airport. Clones was left teetering on the brink of ruin by partition. Perched precariously between two states, trade and communications were disrupted. The railway, the main employer in the town, proved bothersome because of its cross-border structure: the line to Cavan crossed the frontier six times within half a dozen miles of the town, just as the near-moribund Ulster Canal crossed it repeatedly before reaching Upper Lough Erne. The canal survived barely ten years of partition before it was abandoned, not that many might have noticed at that time. The railway followed a couple of decades later.

Yet this is not a book about a lost waterway or navigation. One week as the skipper of a rented houseboat on the Erne hardly qualifies me for that. This book is about the places the Ulster Canal's route connects in fewer than 50 miles through five of Ulster's nine counties – Cavan, Fermanagh, Monaghan, Armagh and Tyrone. It is the story of communities divided, split and torn apart by partition, and all that has devolved from Ireland's largest and most intrusive man-made structure, the border. It is about people who are still affected on a daily basis by changes made over the course of a century that made them marginal, left them marooned on the periphery of two states that barely acknowledged each other's existence. It is about people who must constantly negotiate what Gloria Anzaldúa defined as the 'narrow strip along a steep edge'.[2]

These communities are always on edge, their latest anxieties centred on Brexit, the United Kingdom's withdrawal from membership of the European Union. That would elevate the current Irish border into the UK's only land frontier with the EU, at which Britain could end the free movement of goods, services and people. Casual assurances that free movement will continue as normal between both parts of Ireland and Britain seem nonsensical. A 1923 agreement under which free passage was guaranteed is unlikely to prevail with the other twenty-six members of the union, when weighed against the Treaty of Rome. Even that agreement of free movement under the Common Travel Area was modified in the case of Northern Ireland, where up until the 1960s, the unionist government imposed work permits on those who came from the south. That ended when Britain and Ireland joined the European Economic Community at the start of 1973. For the following 25 years, however, the benefits of shared European citizenship with free movement of goods and people were denied to those who lived on the Irish border. It was a militarised frontier of checkpoints, watchtowers, a barrier of threat and fear. The 1998 Good Friday Agreement between politicians representing all sides in Northern Ireland was negotiated with the assistance of the U.S. administration, underwritten by the sovereign governments in London and Dublin, generously funded by the European Union and endorsed by electors throughout Ireland. At last, removing the political and actual roadblocks of the past seemed possible in a shared future. Checkpoints disappeared, severed roads were reopened and, slowly at first, the troublesome and disputed frontier seemed of less consequence. People shopped, worked and socialised with a freedom never enjoyed before. It even promised institutional flexibility as the border that had stultified progress blended into the background. Infrastructural investments spanned frontiers for the first time. There was even an announcement of plans for a cross-border greenway walking and cycling route on the towpath of the Ulster Canal under the aegis of Waterways Ireland, the cross-border agency based at Enniskillen, County Fermanagh.[3]

It now seems like a short, fleeting golden age. On 23 June 2016, the United Kingdom voted to leave the European Union with the effective, yet meaningless slogan that it would 'take back control' of Britain's borders.[4] The only border not rigorously controlled, of course, was the land frontier in Ireland where I started walking shortly after former prime minister David Cameron set the referendum date. I completed the first three stages while the outcome still seemed an inevitable and comfortable remain victory. I resumed in late September when there was still no indication of what the crushing defeat would entail. And I completed the final stages almost a year after starting, as attention turned at last to what might happen in Ireland. I walked through bland assurances that there would be 'no return to the borders of the past' and came to rest on a preliminary but inconclusive agreement all sides claimed as a victory. And still we don't know what the outcome will be. Yet one thing is certain from the evidence of a century of Irish partition, British assurances that free movement will continue as before may have radically different meanings in Westminster, Brussels, Dublin and Stormont. Indeed, the role and nature of the border are subject to radically different perspectives much closer to home.

Northern Ireland's first minister, Arlene Foster, comes from my home parish, but I don't come from hers. She grew up on a farm at Dernawilt in Fermanagh. I grew up in Clones town, about four miles away in County Monaghan. My Catholic parish spilled northwards towards Fivemiletown in County Tyrone, far beyond Dernawilt and St Macartan's chapel of ease at Aghadrumsee. However, a revision of parish boundaries in the Church of Ireland diocese of Clogher created a new Protestant parish of Aghadrumsee, coupled with the adjoining sub-districts of Clogh in Fermanagh and Drumsnatt in Monaghan. It disrupted the ancient and common ecclesiastical boundaries that encompassed our respective home places, and that had us once as fellow parishoners, just as the redrawing of political boundaries consigned us to separate jurisdictions. I mention this because identities are blurred hereabouts, a confusion of history, geography, politics and faith that defies a single perspective. While my world encompassed an Ireland that was whole and indivisible, the world of Ulster loyalism is bounded firmly by defensible frontiers around the narrow ground that must be held by force of arms. So while

Darach MacDonald

the border was an unwelcome presence in my world, it marked the limits of Arlene's. Through my border, I saw family and friends. Beyond hers lurked danger and threat.

Italian scholar Claudio Magris observes that 'A border has two sides to it, it's ambiguous: at one moment it is a bridge on which to meet, at another, a barrier of rejection.'[5] Even that bipartite perspective fails to capture the multiplicity of confounding realities that are inherent in the border that snakes its way out of Carlingford Lough and meanders back to the sea at Lough Foyle. That's a distance of almost 500 kilometres (310 miles), roughly the diagonal length of the entire island, north to south, from Torr Head in Antrim to Mizen Head in Cork. Perhaps it defies explanation beyond the personal experience of living there, or here and there, for there are many differences of location, practice and experience.

A good place to start, however, is to realise that the partition of Ireland did not result in two homogenous jurisdictions diametrically opposed to each other. Indeed, the border was created as a stopgap measure, subject to revision or even removal, under both the Government of Ireland Act (1920) and the Anglo-Irish Treaty of the following year. It wasn't a standard one-size-fits-all international boundary imposed or foisted on the Irish people by a vindictive English colonial garrison. It was an integral part of the negotiated treaty accepted by a majority of Irish voters in 1922, its anomalies and errors to be determined and rectified by a boundary commission. It was made permanent at the behest of William T. Cosgrave's Irish Free State government in the Anglo-Irish Intergovernmental Agreement of December 1925. That forgotten pact amounted to a grubby financial sell-out. The provisional frontier remained as it was, without remedy for the numerous anomalies in social, economic, geographic and political displacement on both sides. In return, the Free State was excused from its share of the Imperial debt from the Great War, estimated at £150 million, although critics of the deal pointed out that this was more than offset by Ireland's £3 billion counter-claim for damage done by Crown forces during the War of Independence.[6]

So the border slipped into place as the rest of Ireland was otherwise engaged. Contrary to the prevailing and mistaken belief that the

6

subsequent civil war was fought over partition, there is strong evidence that the border barely affected daily life in the rest of the nationalist state that tore itself apart over an oath of allegiance and then bedded down behind customs barriers. Since then, historians and other commentators have assiduously avoided a point raised succinctly by Maureen Wall in 1966:

> It is astonishing to find so little attention paid to the Ulster question in the printed reports of the debates which took place in Dáil Éireann between the signing of the Treaty and its adoption by a majority of the Dáil on January 7, 1922. Of 338 pages of debates, nine only are devoted to the subject of partition, and of these nine pages, the deputies for County Monaghan – Blythe, MacEntee and O'Duffy – contributed two-thirds.[7]

Arthur Griffith, who negotiated and signed the Treaty, did not even mention partition in the debates, while his co-signatory Michael Collins proffered direct talks with the unionists, or the boundary commission set out in Article 12, as the best options to replace coercion with goodwill in uniting the country. De Valera, leader of the trenchant opposition, presented his alternative Document No. 2 with the exact same terms on the North as the Treaty.[8] Little wonder that all the IRA's northern forces, apart from Frank Aiken's Fourth Northern Division, backed Collins and the Treaty. Aiken prevaricated, torn between his Armagh roots and his Dundalk stronghold. Among those declaring unequivocally for Collins and the Free State was the IRA's Fifth Northern Division, with its headquarters in Clones.

Yet from the start, the border was used and exploited by both sides as and when it suited them. It was never rectified, yet it was never static. It changed and evolved over a turbulent century in which its very existence was a constant catalyst of conflict. It corralled a sizeable nationalist population into the North, and excluded some 70,000 Ulster unionists in the South from their covenanted brethren – brethren who then appropriated the name 'Ulster' exclusively as their own. It disrupted identity and caused lasting trauma, defined as 'when the very powers that we are convinced will protect us and give us security become our tormentors, when the community of which we considered ourselves members turns against us or when our family is no longer a source of refuge but a site of danger'.[9]

Often there were much stronger ties to those on the other side than those on your own. There were sizeable minorities, people who felt betrayed, unwanted and discounted, people denied a voice in the new dispensations. They languished in that liminal space that all frontiers become, hoping that somebody would notice and make things better. Yet their fate would always be determined by those far away, in the centres of power. Rather than creating a shop window of progressive modernity, the Irish government presented shoddy neglect along its border. It seemed as if notice was taken only when Dublin's security was threatened.

I was a toddler when huge steel girders were driven deep through the road's surface at the Aqueduct Bridge on the Ulster Canal at the edge of town. Other cross-border routes were also 'spiked', including at Kilrooskey, a Fermanagh townland that loops into Monaghan just north of the town, cutting off my uncle Eugene McCabe's farm. I have a memory of him building a small link road through a corner of a field to provide a circuitous escape route to town. He called it the Khyber Pass, in memory of another north-west frontier road. It is still there today, skirting the house where my maternal grandmother settled for her final years between two daughters and their growing families. The house is divided by the border, and that proud County Clare woman relished my dad's cheeky observation that she slept 'with her head in the Free State and her backside in the North'. When Donald, one of my brothers, came home to work in the family drapery business, he moved into the house with his young Dublin wife at a time when the security situation was hot again. Gillian lived in dread of the helicopter swoops and the voices of British squaddies on reconnaissance patrols in the dead of night. They moved into the town as soon as they could.

The spikes circumscribed my childhood world in a ring of steel. They were unnatural barriers between neighbours, friends, family. Like Uncle Eugene, we found ways around them, but they were constant reminders that our freedom of movement was curtailed by a line we could not otherwise see. So from my earliest age, I realised we lived in a frontier town, and these steel impediments marked the border even more forcefully than the customs posts on the Newtownbutler Road where motorists had to have their passbooks checked. Yet there were some marginal benefits of living right on the cusp of another jurisdiction, such as the border shops that offered Opal Fruits, Mars bars, Spangles and other confections unavailable on our side. We had television for a full decade before RTÉ began broadcasting down south. Initially, it was just BBC, but when UTV went on air from Belfast's Havelock House on Halloween 1959, we found a use at last for the rotary channel switch on the Murphy TV set. By then, we were thoroughly immersed in the culture, current affairs and social mores of Britain and its outpost in the north of Ireland. When RTÉ came along, it seemed amateurish, parochial and dated by contrast with Cathy McGowan's *Ready, Steady, Go* on UTV, BBC's *Juke Box Jury* and, of course, *Top of the Pops*. We were there for the gritty start of Granada TV's *Coronation Street* and TV hosts such as David Frost inured us against Gay Byrne's *Late Late Show* from Dublin.

Our cultural influences and sense of the world transcended a line on somebody else's map. We may have been living in a small rural town, but our aspirations were of cosmopolitan sophistication. Even Bobby from Brookeborough, on the fringe of our Fermanagh hinterland in the 1960s, regarded Clones as 'an outpost of American glamour and Sunday freedoms'.[10] While outsiders saw us inhabiting the outer extremity of their world, our parish universe straddled two counties and two states, and we forged from this a common identity as borderers. So we were affronted by the new impediments imposed on our lines of communication. Yet our border was always hard, because it intruded politically in communities that are almost indistinguishable, differentiating people with the same beliefs and allegiances, history and traditions, culture and attitudes. For a century, we were branded as different, corralled into political entities not of our choosing and condemned to peripheral neglect.

This is the part of Ireland through which the Ulster Canal ran, long before the border was even conceived. It is the route through which I have chosen to tell the story of a century of partition. For this is where the border pokes north Monaghan into the soft underbelly of Northern Ireland, a salient that British military strategists dubbed 'the spur'. Its history as a border region began in turmoil a century ago, and it has rarely quietened since. The border lies within 10 kilometres of everyone who lives in this place, intruding in their daily lives, and creating tiny communities that defy the narrative of separate people and places. The passage between Lough Neagh and Lough Erne is also roughly the course that my paternal grandparents took by rail a century ago when they moved to the bustling town of Clones. My grandfather, Owen, had been manager of Hoseys' drapery shop in Portadown, Country Armagh; my grandmother, Catherine, a milliner, had also worked in the drapery business in Portadown, as a floor supervisor in Elliott and Stevenson. They moved to Clones to open their own drapery shop, and raised a family of four. My late father, Eugene, their third child and the family's first 'Free Stater', came into the world on Christmas Day 1922, as the dust settled on the turmoil and strife of the War of Independence, and the 'temporary' frontier was imposed. He was born with the border and we, his family, have been living with it ever since.

1. Border Hopscotch

Castle Saunderson to Clones – 14 km

The contrast in architectural styles could hardly be more striking. One is a low modern building of decorative brick and grey cladding that squats at the far end of a vast car park; the other is a stout Scottish baronial castle being slowly consumed from within and without by vegetation. The first is the new home for Scouting Ireland, and has its fleur-de-lis logo emblazoned on the gable; the second is the former home of the father of Ulster unionism, forever facing north to the Promised Land. They share the Castle Saunderson estate, straddling the ages, the traditions and the border between the Republic of Ireland and the United Kingdom. This is the starting point for a voyage along the Ulster Canal. If current plans for restoration come to fruition, it will be the first port of call for pleasure craft on the Ulster Canal, the final link of an inland navigation system connecting Limerick, Waterford and Dublin to Coleraine and Belfast. Until that happens, the only means of traversing much of the canal's route is on foot.

I set off from the car park along a tree-lined path and soon come upon the cluster of castle buildings that still preside defiantly over the River Finn below. Essentially a large two-storey dwelling, the main house has decorative battlements, corbelled turrets, inlaid coats-of-arms and other features of a bygone age. In the townland of Portagh, County Cavan, it sits on the site of a former castle of the O'Reilly clan of Breffni. Precisely when the Saundersons took up residence is a matter of conjecture. According to a family history,[1] when a plastered-over stone was uncovered it revealed a coat of arms dated 1573. That belied the myth of family origin that had been nurtured for generations, confirming the family was originally named Sanderson and from Scotland, rather than being related to the much grander Saundersons of Saxby, Lincolnshire. The 'u' was added to the name in the mid-eighteenth century in an unsuccessful bid for the discontinued Anglo-Irish title, Viscount of Castleton. Then the discovery of a headstone at Desertcreat churchyard right beside the consecration site of the O'Neills at Tullyhogue in County Tyrone provided a possible ancestor in 'Alexander Sandirson, born in Scotland, a soldier in Belgium, a leader of horse and foot in Poland; in Ireland, a justice of the peace and three times high sheriff of the county' who died in December 1633. The headstone bore the same coat of arms as the stone discovered at Castle Saunderson, which also featured at the home of the Sandersons of Cloverhill, just a few miles away in County Cavan. Whatever their origins, according to the family history, the Sandersons/ Saundersons once commanded an estate that stretched for over 20 miles 'in a straight line' and bounded the equally impressive Upper Lough Erne estates of the Butlers of Lanesborough House and the Crichtons of Crom Castle, both in County Fermanagh.

The family proved staunch defenders of the Protestant crown in south Ulster. So when Richard Talbot, the first earl of Tyrconnell set about raising troops to support the Jacobite cause, Colonel Robert Sanderson assembled his Protestant neighbours and led them in an invasion of Cavan courthouse during the quarter sessions of 1688.

'By whose authority do ye act?' Sanderson demanded.

'By that of his Majesty King James,' the chairman replied.

'We acknowledge no such authority,' Sanderson declared, as he cleared the courthouse.

For this, he was proscribed and a price of £200 put on his head. Having failed to escape to England, he returned to his castle, assembled his Protestant neighbours and prepared for siege when Tyrconnell moved his forces north in 1689, laying siege to Derry and Enniskillen. Sanderson found his route to Enniskillen blocked by the Jacobites led by Lord Mountcashel (Justin MacCarthy), so he marched his men to Coleraine, where the Protestant 'army of the north-east' was mustering.

On his departure, a Jacobite detachment led by Piers Butler (Lord Galmoy) destroyed his castle, drove off his livestock and burned every house and barn on the estate. The family history records:

> This act of destruction was bitterly avenged, for when the Enniskilleners sallied forth and utterly defeated MacCarthy's army at Newtownbutler, four thousand fugitives fled from the battle towards Castle Saunderson. A party of Enniskillen horse, making a forced march, got to Wattlebridge ahead of them; and there under the smouldering ruins of the castle, the whole four thousands were driven into the river and perished, not one man escaping.[2]

There is little evidence now of a bloodbath in the quiet stream separating the Castle Saunderson estate from Derrykerrib Island on the opposite shore, which is in Fermanagh. The island's approximately 500 acres is separated by narrow channels of the Erne and Finn rivers, but connected by a road bridge just west of Wattlebridge. While the original Ulster Canal commercial navigation eschewed Castle Saunderson for a dedicated channel from Derrykerrib Lough, an inlet of Lough Erne, the €2 million excavation recently begun at this end of the canal will redirect it along a channel of the Finn River past the estate. This work, scheduled to be completed in April 2018, is projected as the first phase in the overall project of reopening the Ulster Canal, according to Irish government minister Heather Humphreys when she visited the construction site at Derrykerrib Island.[3]

Back in 1841, it was on Derrykerrib Island that the final phase of the navigation was completed, at a cost of £230,000, far in excess of the original budget. The project had been dogged by false economies from the outset, according to Brian Cassell's pictorial history of the canal.[4] The original proposal presented by John Killaly in 1815 to the Directors General of Inland Navigation was for 35 miles of canal with twenty-two locks costing £223,000. This was revised to a canal with eighteen locks and a cost of £160,050. When Thomas Telford was asked to review the commercial aspects of the plan, he insisted on a new survey, which increased the number of locks to twenty-six, but these were shoehorned into the budget by reducing their width to 12 feet. That was 18 inches smaller than the narrowest locks on the Lagan and Newry canals, meaning cargo would have to be reloaded onto smaller craft. The canal opened in phases from 1838, but it never attracted the projected traffic. When the final and narrowest lock was in place at Derrykerrib – it was only 11 feet and 8 inches wide – the canal was ready to receive the projected traffic from the Shannon-Erne waterway of the Ballinamore-Ballyconnell canal, which was also being completed in the same year, although it would not be navigable until almost twenty years later because of budgetary problems, disputes with millers and fishermen and even labour shortages.[5] But by then, truly, the ship was spoilt for a ha'porth of tar.

Perhaps today's rerouting of the canal so that it passes Castle Saunderson will spur the rediscovery of that place, which should provide an enticing diversion, replete with the history of Ulster. For it was there that Colonel Edward Saunderson entertained house guests who included fellow stalwarts of opposition to home rule in the later decades of the nineteenth century. A former Liberal MP for Cavan, a seat formerly held by his father Colonel Alexander Saunderson, Edward was swept aside in the Parnellite tide of nationalism in the 1880s. However, he was the 'darling of the Orangemen', and he captured the North Armagh seat for the Conservatives in the 1885 election, when many of his electoral divisions achieved a 93 per cent turnout of voters.[6] By the following January, he had organised his fellow Conservatives – who now held sixteen of Ulster's seats against the nationalists' seventeen – into a 'parliamentary Ulster party' that was 'volubly supported' by the prime minister, Lord Salisbury.[7] On the other side, nationalist MPs John Dillon and Timothy Daniel O'Sullivan dismissed them. The latter, remembered primarily as the songwriter who penned the rousing ballad 'God Save Ireland', delivered his put-down lyrically, dubbing the loyalists as 'mere Saundersonian slap-dash, with about as much substance in it as a soap-bubble'. It was a gross underestimation of the colonel nicknamed the 'dancing Dervish', who continued to lead his group of about twenty Ulster unionists until his death in 1906, blocking home rule in the process. He was acknowledged as 'witty and charming' but devoid of business sense and averse to reading legislation with which he disagreed publicly, including the 1896 land bill that would result in the forced division of his own estates.[8] His lasting political legacy, however, was in acting as mentor for the dynamic and precise Edward Carson, who succeeded him as leader of the Irish Unionist Alliance and its Ulster Unionist Council.

Today, Colonel Edward lies in repose in a small and rather nondescript grave in the lee of the chapel, on the estate he inherited from his father in 1857. The headstone epitaph, 'Love Never Faileth', is faded, just like the memory of the man, who should be honoured by those who proclaim the tenets of Ulster resistance to home rule that he initiated and championed during the crisis of the 1880s. The family history printed for private circulation in 1936, in which he is remembered as 'a truly great man' whose 'life is indelibly inscribed in the history of Northern Ireland', includes the observation that he very narrowly missed 'by ten minutes' being appointed as chief secretary of Ireland by Lord Salisbury, pipped at the post by Arthur Balfour.

Most engagingly, Colonel Edward also comes across as an entertaining host much beloved by his extended family. Among his party tricks, he would stand sideways to the billiard table and, putting one foot up on the edge, stand up on it 'without apparent effort'. Another trick was to stand with his back to a door, clasping his hands over the top, and then raise his legs and body quite slowly until he ended up sitting on top of the door. House guests, including comic and romantic songwriter Percy French, loved to stroll in the bog garden created by the colonel's wife, Helena Demoleyns, daughter of the third Lord Ventry. Nor were his guests spared from the challenge of physical feats. An old friend, Thomas Cosby Burrowes, recalled how male house guests were not allowed to go to their beds by the staircase: 'They had to shin up the pillars which supported the landing above! Unless they could accomplish this by no means easy feat there was no bed for them that night.'[9]

Colonel Edward's son Major Somerset Saunderson inherited the estate in 1906 and lived there as a bachelor 'in peace and quiet' until 1914, when 'an outrageous attempt was made … to coerce Ulster into a new scheme of home rule'. The family history records his leading role in 'preparations for defence'. Somerset married late, and his American wife Marie Countess Larrisch spent lavishly on improvements to the castle until the Anglo-Irish Treaty, when Cavan was 'severed from Ulster and all that Ulster meant'. In the family's absence, the castle was raided for arms by IRA Volunteers based in Clones, including many Fermanagh men from the Wattlebridge company. Subsequently, the paramilitary RIC Auxiliaries were garrisoned at the castle. When they left, it was stripped bare of doors, windows, lead from the roof, water pipes and anything else of value. Major Somerset abandoned it to the Free State, and in the process declared poignantly, 'Now I have no country!'

Castle Saunderson lay abandoned and forgotten for decades. When it was acquired in the early 1980s, I visited it as a reporter for the *Sunday Press* newspaper and wrote about the refurbishment and plans for its use. Shortly thereafter, it was raided by Gardaí and a large arms dump was discovered. A short time later, it was engulfed in flames once more. The castle was gutted and destroyed for the final time in that conflagration, although the estate chapel remains a serene resting place for the Saundersons and their role in the history of Ulster and Ireland. Long gone are Castle Saunderson's days of glory, described in 1739 by Rev. Dr William Henry of the Royal Dublin Society and Trinity College:

> The situation of this seat is chosen with both spirit and taste; it stands on the top of a hill, which commands all around, and risen high over the south side of the river; at the bottom of the hill are some plantations; and, from the castle to the skirts all around, the hill descends in a verdant, spacious lawn – here and there interspersed with single large forest trees. The boldness of its aspect makes it naturally a stronghold, and gives it an uncommon air of grandeur; it looks majestically over the river to the north, and a great part of Lough Erne to the west.[10]

Today, not even the shoreline is negotiable until the canal restoration work is completed, so I am forced into a digression along the road. From the estate chapel, the avenue crosses a small stream and runs through an open gate that forms the border between Cavan and Fermanagh; that is, between the Republic of Ireland and the United Kingdom. It is the first of several border crossings on the Ulster Canal route of about 10 kilometres to Clones. Emerging from the historic estate onto the main road almost precisely where it ceases to be the South's N54 and becomes the North's A3 is a shock to the senses. The ornate gates are clamped into a cluster of commercial shopfronts that form the forecourt for P&J Fuels, a service station proclaiming 'LowLowFuels' on its huge green canopy, and offering a fast pump for kerosene heating oil and another shopfront for 'Fireworks'. It's a huckster's welcome to the lakelands county of Fermanagh, a tacky roadside enclave that jostles for space and attention as heavy traffic whizzes by. For the next mile of my walk along the Ulster Canal route, I will hug the hedge, dodging the side mirrors of vans and lorries on the main road connecting the north-east of the island of Ireland with the west coast and midlands.

The plans for the restoration of the canal and its towpath will not encompass this blot on the landscape, and future trekkers and navigators can look forward to a channel quite removed from the interface of Leggykelly, County Cavan, and Drumboganagh Glebe in Fermanagh. Before leaving, however, it is worth pausing to recall one notable death in the recent conflict, that of the first and most senior police officer from the Republic to be killed in the conflict that raged along the border. Garda Inspector Sam Donegan, a native of Ballintampen, Ballymacormack, County Longford, led a detachment of police and army from Cavan to investigate a suspect device left on the road at this very point on 8 June 1972. [11] The booby-trapped device was actually about 30 yards inside Northern Ireland, but Inspector Donegan crossed the border to examine it. In his book about southern border security in the 1970s, *Bombs, Bullets and the Border*, Patrick Mulroe noted that although Inspector Donegan's death caused 'shock in the locality,' it subsequently 'did not receive the same national coverage as other Garda deaths'. [12] Another account described the media coverage as 'pitifully low'. [13] I recall the incident well and the speculation that swirled through the locality in the absence of any arrests or trial coverage. One newspaper incorrectly reported that the blast was detonated by remote control. Unconfirmed reports at the time suggested that the box had the word 'Bomb' painted on its side, perhaps a bizarre suggestion that it was a hoax and this allegedly prompted Inspector Donegan to kick it dismissively. The box actually was connected to a gelignite bomb, and the garda and an Irish Army lieutenant were caught in the blast.[14]

Inspector Donegan was rushed to Cavan Hospital, where he died from his wounds. He was 61 years of age, married and the father of six children. Both the Official and the Provisional wings of the IRA active at that time denied responsibility, but suspicion fell on the latter. It was a huge funeral, presided over by the Catholic Bishop of Kilmore with nine chief superintendents, fifty-three superintendents and 150 other Gardaí leading the cortege, while six Garda inspectors flanked the tricolor-draped coffin and six sergeants acted as the pall-bearers. There was an army guard of honour and Minister for Justice Des O'Malley, Garda Commissioner Michael Wymes and the chairman of Northern Ireland's Police Federation were in attendance.

There had been fewer, less exalted mourners in attendance when 19-year-old Thomas Francis McCann had been buried only a few months previously, in February 1972.[15] Although a Dubliner, like many young working-class Irishmen before him, he joined the British Army's Royal Army Ordnance Corps. Perhaps it was his misfortune to be sent to Fermanagh when he put in a request on compassionate grounds to be nearer his mother so he could visit her regularly in Dublin. He was abducted shortly after one such visit. While nobody claimed the abduction and murder of Private McCann, suspicion in this case fell on the Official IRA, mainly because the Dublin teenager was not included in the Provisionals' admission of responsibility for three similar abductions and killings in which the bodies were dumped on the border. In this case, the hooded remains were left by the roadside here on the border near Newtownbutler, in which direction my Ulster Canal walk now takes me.

To the left as I walk along the twisting route of the A3, the baronial battlements of Castle Saunderson jut above the trees beyond a thin gleaming line of water that snakes its way through the brown and green landscape. A small traditional cottage to the right has a 'for sale' sign attached, but seems to offer little enticement to the heavy traffic trundling by. Behind the cottage, a narrow road veers off in the opposite direction towards Redhills, which enjoyed a few moments in the sunshine during the darkness of the Troubles. In the early 1990s, the tiny Cavan village became the setting for two Hollywood films, both written by Shane Connaughton, who grew up there when his father was the local Garda sergeant. He describes, in his 1995 book *A Border Diary,* his homecoming experience and impressions of a brief period that straddled the momentous announcement of the IRA ceasefire on 31 August 1994.[16] He places Redhills in 'the middle of nowhere', noting that the late English film director Peter Yates described this rolling drumlin terrain as 'buttery country'. I prefer the description of poet Paul Muldoon, who calls it 'curvaceous'.[17] Or Connaughton's observation that the land hereabouts is:

> impervious to maps. What appeared plain on paper was on the ground an orgy of political and geographical confusion. Cavan and Monaghan in the South were locked into Fermanagh in the North, like two dogs trying to cover the one hot bitch.[18]

Connaughton traversed this tripartite terrain trying to remain upright:

> It was all a question of balance. Keeping your feet on the ground. Or landing on them after flight. Learning to walk on edges. The road they were on was a tightrope: Cavan one minute. Fermanagh the next. Customs men lay in wait. Squad cars patrolled ... The closer you were on the ground, the more dangerous it was. Yet danger sharpened the senses.[19]

At a fork in the road a bit further on from the way to Redhills, we veer to the right on the A3. The road less travelled (B533) goes straight ahead to Wattlebridge and Newtownbutler just beyond. That was the main road from Dublin and the South into Fermanagh and south Donegal during much of the recent Troubles, after Aghalane Bridge was demolished by loyalists in 1972 following several IRA attacks, and, at the behest of the British Army, wasn't rebuilt.[20] It wasn't always so quiet.

On 22 October 1972, the IRA ambushed and killed Private Robin Bell at Drumguillagh, just north of Newtownbutler. A 21-year-old part-time British soldier in the Ulster Defence Regiment (UDR), he was also a farmer, travelling with his father and brother to an out-farm. When Robin was shot dead, the other brother – also UDR – returned fire with his pistol, while their wounded father drove off. The IRA ambushers abandoned their vehicle a short distance away, and police said they 'escaped over the border by boat'.[21]

The following day, a military 'brick' patrol from the Argyll and Sutherland Highlanders visited the farm of Michael Naan at Augnnahinch, between Newtownbutler and Wattlebridge. Naan, 31, a prominent member of the Fermanagh Civil Rights Association, was stabbed to death, as was his 23-year-old farm labourer, Andrew Murray, in what would become known as the Pitchfork Murders from early reports that the killers had used a farm implement. During the 1979 investigation of the Yorkshire Ripper murders in England, a former soldier from the Argylls came forward and admitted his part with others who used a Bowie knife in the 'frenzied' murder of the two farmers. Three others were convicted, along with their company commander, who pleaded guilty to covering up the incident, and received a suspended sentence.[22] Since then, further investigation has shown this wasn't the action of a maverick unit of the British Army, and the instigation and cover-up of the murders went all the way to the top of the military command chain in Northern Ireland and beyond.[23]

Local unionist politicians such as John Brooke, son of former Northern Ireland Premier Lord Brookeborough and successor to his title, blamed the violence on Dublin's failure to secure the border, and demanded hot pursuit of suspects by crown forces.[24] The accusations of lax border security dogged Dublin governments from the mid-1970s. A false narrative took hold, fed by selective fact and fiction. It told of a war of 'genocide' along the border, the killing fields of an interface between loyal Ulster and its IRA enemies, a war of attrition aimed at eldest sons of Protestant landowners. At its root, however, was the withdrawal of British regular troops for political reasons and the British policy of 'Ulsterisation', which pushed the RUC and part-time UDR into the front line. Some have argued that 'Ulsterisation' was a military strategy to deal with the 'cell structure' adopted by the IRA after its 1975 ceasefire. However, at a meeting with new Secretary of State Humphrey Atkins in June 1979, British Chief of General Staff Sir Edwin Bramall said the army was 'eager to reduce the number of soldiers deployed in Northern Ireland as the separation from their families was leading men to leave the army'.[25]

Part-time UDR and RUC reservists served on the front line while continuing the regular jobs and routines that made them easy targets, even after they left the security forces. So in the first half of 1980, the deaths in Newtownbutler of Robert Crilly (60) at his garage, Victor Morrow (61) as he waited for a lift to work, and Richard Latimer (39) in his hardware shop, as well as the deaths of two local policemen, sent shockwaves through the loyalist community, which experienced them as 'an assault on the community as a whole', and 'the pathology of violence-induced fear, hate and suspicion ... reached chronic levels in 1979 and 1980 as the Provisionals launched their most intense campaign along the border since the early 1970s'.[26] When Ian Paisley took up the cause of Fermanagh Protestants, he spoke of 'genocide', alleging that the IRA had drawn up 'a list of prominent Protestants to be murdered'. That insinuation gained added traction after the *Impartial Reporter* headline of 1 May 1980: 'It's Plain Genocide'.[27] Church of Ireland Primate Dr John Armstrong was more cautious, saying merely that 'there seemed to be a disturbing pattern in the killings. Sometimes the person killed would be the natural successor to the farm, like the elder son', but 'it is difficult to find evidence of a plan to eliminate Protestants'.[28]

When Richard Latimer's widow Bonnie met the new prime minister in June 1980, she told Margaret Thatcher that while attacks were planned by 'local sympathisers', the gunmen were from the 'safe haven' of the Republic, where Gardaí 'openly admitted to drinking with the IRA in public houses ... unable to arrest them because they did not have the authority to do so from Dublin'. Then on Wednesday, 23 June 1980, Paisley joined Official

Unionist Party leader Jim Molyneaux on the platform of a Newtownbutler rally organised by the Fermanagh United Protestant Action Group for the Defence of Family and Home.[29] He declared that if all cross-border roads were not closed, Protestants would do whatever was necessary to protect themselves. British politicians decided to block the roads once more, although senior security personnel believed that the border could never be sealed effectively and the 'IRA can cross … almost at will'.[30] Shortly thereafter, huge military checkpoints were constructed at Wattlebridge and at Kilturk on the main A34 road to Clones.

This corner of Fermanagh had seen troubles long before the 1970s. In the War of Independence, the Fifth Northern (Monaghan) Division of the Irish Republican Army included an entire company from this district. Among them was Commandant Matt Fitzpatrick, who joined up as a teenage IRA Volunteer after 1916 and was followed into the ranks by three younger brothers – John James, Frank and Patrick. They took part in several major engagements hereabouts, including the February 1920 capture of Shantonagh RIC barracks in County Monaghan, the first such engagement in Ulster.[31] Also involved in that operation were such IRA luminaries as Peadar O'Donnell, Ernie O'Malley and Eoin O'Duffy. In his seminal book about the War of Independence, O'Malley notes that the raid resulted in the capture of 'nine bright carbines, bayonets, revolvers, hand grenades, Verey lights and ammunition'.[32] Over the following two years, the Fitzpatrick brothers were involved in practically every military operation along the new frontier. They were arrested, escaped, wounded, healed and promoted. The family home at Kilgarrow, occupied by their elderly parents, was burnt out in reprisal. Then, on 11 February 1922, after a meteoric rise to acting Commandant of the Fifth Northern Division of the Free State Army, Matt Fitzpatrick was killed by the opening shot of a gun battle that became known as the 'Clones Affray'. He was just 25, and, according to former commanders, a pivotal player in securing the northern divisions in the Treaty split that led to Civil War.

Five and a half years later, on 28 September 1927, Clones solicitor Baldwin Murphy wrote to the Ministry of Defence in Dublin on behalf of his client, Mrs Mary Jane Fitzpatrick of Kilgarrow, County

Fermanagh, enquiring about her pension entitlements as a dependent of the late commandant:

> The last time he was in the family house before his death the deceased gave £10 to his mother. This was out of the pay he was receiving from his military office. Up to the year 1917 the deceased worked ... as a road contractor and while he was at this form of work he lived at home and regularly gave the entire profits therefrom, apart from what it would take to clothe him, to his mother our client. In some years, we are instructed, these profits amounted to up to £50. From 1917 up to the date he was appointed commandant in the Free State Army, he served as a volunteer and during the entire period he was almost entirely engaged on active service and was unable to do any work of a civil character.[33]

A reply to the Clones solicitor signed by 'J.J.H.' for the Army Finance Officer notes that a gratuity of £150 had already been awarded to her husband Edward as a 'final settlement' and payment of a weekly or monthly allowance was made 'only in necessitous or special circumstances'.[34] Evidence showing Fitzpatrick's parents had been left virtually destitute was presented. A letter dated 30 May 1923 from Major General Dan Hogan, GOC of Dublin Command at Collins Barracks and Fitzpatrick's immediate predecessor in charge of the Fifth Northern, certified that they 'suffered very severely financially and must now be in urgent need of substantial compensation'. Then aged 69 and 72, the parents 'dare not return to the County Fermanagh', where their property had been destroyed by crown forces. This meant they had to employ others to work their land while renting a cottage in Clones. As a consequence, they 'have been impoverished and were obliged to borrow a large sum of money to carry on'. General Hogan was backed by a letter from the Office of Garda Commissioner dated 27 February 1924 and signed by Eoin O'Duffy, pointing out 'the exceptional circumstances':

> There were four brothers in the family – Matt who was killed, John James recently released from the [prison ship] *Argenta* broken

down in health, Frank who also did a term of imprisonment and is now, I believe, a military, or an acting military governor of one of the prisons, and Patrick presently a lieutenant in the Intelligence Department stationed at Clones. The four brothers were the backbone of the Wattlebridge Company, Monaghan Brigade – three took part in the taking of Shantonagh Barracks and all four had to fly [sic] from home afterwards. Their home was burned down by the Specials, and a claim for compensation was refused by the judges of the Northern government. The aged parents rented a cottage in County Monaghan and are now pretty destitute. Owing to the part the family took in the pre-truce days, and owing to their loyalty to the present government, it is pitiful to see them in their present humiliation.

Yet those interventions did not sway the Free State decision makers, who stuck by the £150 having been paid in 'full and final settlement'. As I continue my search for evidence of the Ulster Canal's ghost, I wonder that if this was done to friends and supporters, what was that Free State capable of doing to its foes?

The road takes in a huge corner that seems to go full circle in a clockwise direction in the townland of Anaghmore. It almost encompasses an impressive hilltop cottage to my left that faces onto a small, pretty lake below. The Ordnance Survey map tells me it was the rectory for the Church of Ireland parish of Drummully, whose place of worship lies a short distance ahead, but on the other side of the border. The big corner ends in a dip down to a cluster of riverside buildings around the old six-arch stone bridge at Gortnacarrow, spanning the River Finn's channel with lots of allowance for full spate. A stream of traffic trundles across it in convoys of heavy-goods vehicles heading west. I walk across the welcome footpath, veering to the right on the far shore at a small cluster of commercial buildings that includes a home bakery business, and set off on the Drumgramph Road into the Fermanagh townland of Clogher.

Almost immediately, I come upon the first Ulster Canal stores of my trek. These distinctive cut-stone buildings were the nodes of the inland navigation system, the collection points where barges took farm produce on board and where their clients collected coal and other cargoes for local distribution. A centre of commerce at one time, the building is now derelict, its open windows barred, upper and bottom doors barricaded against intrusion. Through one open window of the top floor, a gaping hole is visible in the slated roof. Slightly recessed to the side, the former store manager's house is also derelict and overshadowed by the grey steel walls of the modern industrial building next door used by Gortnacarrow Tyres.

Today's commercial hub is just a couple of hundred metres down the road in a large gravel-covered open space with an equally expansive car park… but only on Saturdays. Then this isolated location is transformed into Clogher Market, a tented city bazaar of stalls and chip vans. Clothing and tools abound between outlets selling pictures and statues, bikes and balloons, toilet tissue and laundry powder, curtain fabrics and curiosities, crockery and lampshades, toys and trinkets. Row upon row of striped awnings are interspersed with vans, lorries and cars from which traders haul their wares onto makeshift counters or clothes rails, or simply strew them on the ground. Some are equipped with huge trays of neatly arranged merchandise; others make do with disintegrating cardboard boxes. Several stalls offering duvets and fabric-and-foam pet beds simply pile them at the edge of the walkways where early-bird customers scan what is on offer. Although they vary in age, the clients seem a more uniform bunch than the traders, who range from the decidedly local to a strong representation with roots in the Indian sub-continent. Huddled in anoraks and hooded jackets, the latter have the routine of regular attendance at this or similar markets.

With the aroma of frying burgers and onions in the morning air, some quaff from Styrofoam beakers of tea or coffee and the stallholders hunker down for the day. The backdrop of one unattended stall is a large Irish tricolor of green, white and orange, emblazoned with an Easter lily republican crest with Dublin's General Post Office in the background and the words, 'Irish Republican Army 1916 Undefeated 2016'. Amid the jumble of plastic containers, boxes and a pile of other merchandise yet to be arranged, sits an incongruous Union Jack mug. As W.B. Yeats might observe, Clogher Market is focused clearly on fumbling in the greasy till and adding the ha'pence to the pence.

This is one of a series of established border markets that have drawn customers from the far reaches of the midlands and south of Ireland, dipping their toes tentatively into Northern Ireland to secure a bargain, but seldom venturing beyond the market sites here or in Jonesborough, County Armagh. It thrives on its precarious location between two jurisdictions, and the reluctance of law-enforcement agencies to ensure that nothing untoward is afoot.

Shane Connaughton described it more than twenty years ago as 'higglers, hucksters, tinkers and shopkeepers from all over Ulster', who 'gather here to sell their wares to thousands of bargain hunters, buying anything from third-hand tools to vegetables, bread clothes and holy pictures'.[35] He noted then that the RUC didn't venture this far for fear of IRA attacks, but that there was a British army checkpoint 'over the hills along the Enniskillen road', where the soldiers rarely leave their post except to return to their base by helicopter. The checkpoint at Wattlebridge is long gone, along with all those squaddies once consigned to duty on the fringe of the precarious north-west frontier.

The RUC has gone too, replaced in 2001 by the Police Service of Northern Ireland (PSNI) under the new dispensation of the 1998 Good Friday Agreement and the subsequent St Andrews Agreement that prompted Sinn Féin to support the new policing structures. In November 2011, the PSNI mounted a large raid on Clogher Market, arresting nine stallholders on a combined 118 charges of selling fake products and infringing copyright on brands including Nike, Adidas, Audi, Canterbury, Ralph Lauren, Hollister and Tiffany.[36] Those arrested were from Longford, Leitrim, Lurgan, Omagh, Lisnaskea and Newtownbutler. There had been a similar raid in 2007 when the police seized £1.5 million worth of fake goods. On that occasion, Inspector Roy Robinson warned that these peddlers of fake goods were paying no taxes and hurting their neighbours 'who are working in legitimate businesses'.[37]

As I wander around taking occasional photographs, I come under suspicion when I point my camera down a walkway bordered by an array of used tools and farm equipment. A voice from behind calls my attention.

'You're not allowed to take pictures here.'

'They're just for myself,' I explain.

'Doesn't matter, the stallholders don't want their pictures taken. You were taking them inside a stall over there.'

'I took one picture from inside the stall but the camera was pointing out.'

We quibble briefly, me insisting I was just photographing the wares and the general scene, he adamant that any photography was 'against the rules'. I have already sated my curiosity about Clogher Market, however. Relieved that I'm not confronted by a demand to delete what I have taken, I decide to retreat. In any case, I still have an Ulster Canal to locate and walk.

I find it a short ways back towards Gortnacarrow Bridge, where a laneway veers off the Drumgramph Road towards a newly built house. Just past the house, a gateway allows access to the very first part of the towpath I have seen so far on my odyssey from Lough Erne to Lough Neagh. After the decaying splendour of Castle Saunderson, the incessant bustle of the busy main road and distraction of the market, there is a wonderful sense of liberation in striding along the rough laneway next to a clearly discernible canal. Yet the canal is just there in the form of a densely overgrown but uniform channel stretching off into the distance in a straight line. It contrasts with everything else in this locality where roads, lanes, fields and especially the border itself twist and turn back in a serpentine jumble of jurisdictions. For, already, I have left Fermanagh, and the United Kingdom of Great Britain and Northern Ireland, and I'm back into the Republic of Ireland, and now in County Monaghan.

Two large craggy rocks rest against each other on the soft, grass-covered towpath, and just ahead, somebody has gathered branches, twigs and other driftwood into a large pyre in the former channel, amid clumps of green rushes denoting soggy land below. In the early spring afternoon, the trees and bushes are still without foliage, yet the sun shines in a clear sky as a harbinger of better days to come. Through a gate, the towpath changes once more, this time into a rough country road comprising a wide grass-covered median with gravelly surfaces on either side. An electric fence now delineates the channel as another gradual corner sweeps me into a small country road. A small green mail van passes by, its side emblazoned with the logo of An Post. I trudge along happily, taking in the wide vistas of Drummully district and wishing that this towpath road might last forever. While there is no discernible water in the channel to my left, the canal now has an economic value in providing a fenced-in paddock for a small shaggy brown pony, which prances over in great expectation of favours. All I can offer are a few gentle strokes to his head and forelocks before proceeding on my way.

The vista is surprisingly flat for drumlin country, a point that was noted sharply when Lieutenant Edward Durnford of Ordnance Survey came this way on 20 November 1835. In a report, he remarked:

> Nothing could be more uninteresting than the general appearance of this parish [Drummully], flat wet bogs with round hills or hillocks about them. The only exceptions are the small portion about Carra House which is clothed with fine trees, and the neighbourhood of Wattle Bridge where Lough Erne and the woods of Castle Saunderson on the Cavan side of the lough change the appearance and the scenery much for the better.[38]

Lieutenant Durnford's report provides a wealth of information about the conditions of this locality just before the Great Hunger of the 1840s, when the potato crops failed. People lived in families of five or six in thatched mud cottages and, Durnford wrote, those 'in the bogs are most wretched hovels', with the residents subsisting on meal, potatoes and milk. They had an abundance of peat turf for fuel, but their 'dress in general is very bad'. Emigration was rife, especially in the spring when the land was still extensively flooded by the Finn and the Erne, when the migration path takes them to Belfast and thence to Canada and the United States. Yet 'even with these disadvantages they live to a great age', and one man in Clontask townland is 'above 100 years old and able to walk about'. Durnford notes that the introduction of the new National Schools had improved the 'moral habits of the people', and 'generally speaking, they appear anxious for information and knowledge'.

Of particular interest as I follow the overgrown course of the abandoned Ulster Canal is the following passage:

The Ulster Canal connecting Lough Neagh with Upper Lough Erne is not yet commenced in the parish of Drummully, through which it will pass longitudinally, dividing the parish into two very nearly equal parts … Great expectations have been raised in this district of the advantages to be derived from this canal, but it remains to be seen whether they will be realised. The inhabitants complain about want of markets for their produce, which the construction of this canal ought in a great measure to remove, as it will give them the means of cheap conveyance to some very large markets.[39]

The Ulster Canal has come and gone, leaving little in its wake except the towpath I am walking and a visible, but overgrown channel. To my left and north, however, stands St Mary's Church, a prim wee place of worship for Drummully, and now part of an amalgamated parish encompassing Newtownbutler and Sallaghy up near Lisnaskea. Closer to the southern shore in the place known as the Connons is the Catholic chapel of St Alphonsus, which is one portion of the three-part Clones parish, with the town and its immediate hinterland, and then the sprawling Aghadrumsee district in Fermanagh completing the trio. The chapel squats out of sight of the main road. I also know that unseen to my right and south near the River Finn stands Ballyhoebridge Presbyterian church. All three draw congregations from both sides of the border, and road closures during periods of unrest from the 1920s until recent times have caused particular difficulties and distress when worshippers were unable to attend services, and children could not get to schools.

The first two churches sit quite near the canal that dissects the district, a huge chunk of Monaghan ballooning north in the townlands of Clonooney, Drumgarn, Clonagore, Clonoula, Clonkeelan, Corvaghan, Derrybeg and Coleman Island. Like the town of Clones (Cluain Eois) ahead, many of the place names are rooted in the Gaelic word '*cluain*', meaning 'meadow'. It is a familiar theme hereabouts. To the south of the canal lie Clontask, Clonsloe, Clonrye, Clonshanvo, Clonestin and Annagraw, the final townland formed at the narrowing – to a gullet's width of mere metres – where the Drummully salient meets the Finn River on its tiny link by water with the rest of the Irish Republic. During the early 1970s, the Garda Síochána had to wade across the river here to conduct their policing duties. Subsequently helicopters became available for patrol. By then, however, an accommodation had been reached with the British authorities whereby Southern police officers drove through Northern Ireland, then donned their tunics and caps for checkpoint patrols.

Earlier, it would seem, the area had been regarded as a front-line barrier against invasion. Ordnance maps show that the area immediately below the isthmus of Annagraw contains ancient remains of the Black Pig's Dyke in the townlands of Fastry and Cornapaste, County Monaghan. The name of the latter townland is from the Gaelic 'Cor na Péiste', meaning 'Worm's Ditch', another name for the deep trench and ramparts, which legend attributes variously to the track of a gigantic worm or of a giant pig. This is one of several such emplacements in the parish of Currin, which centres on Scotshouse village to the east. Widely regarded as part of a line of ancient defences for Ulster, they comprise a wide bank of about 9 metres with a 6-metre ditch on both sides. Excavations and radiocarbon dating in this area revealed that the original construction in the period 390–370 BCE included a substantial timber palisade at the external ditch. The dating also confirmed that these defences were in place long before the Roman fortifications in north Britain.[40]

Issues of territorial integrity after partition figured in a dispute between neighbours in this locality over an alleged trespass, which was heard by Judge Devitt KC at Monaghan Circuit Court on 29 April 1925. William Tate of Hermitage, County Fermanagh, was suing John James Gillespie of Fastry for damages of £5, but his solicitor John G. McGrath said he would settle for a shilling if the court could determine the issue, since it would 'almost take the Boundary Commission to settle the matter'. The defendant, it turned out, went to sleep with 'his head in the Free State and his feet in Northern Ireland' since his house was largely in County Monaghan and liable for rates there. However, his land and the alleged trespass were in Fermanagh. When the judge pointed out that he could only deal with land in the Free State, the solicitor said the County Court in Enniskillen could not serve a summons outside its jurisdiction.

Judge Devitt then helpfully pointed out that if Gillespie did indeed sleep with his feet in Fermanagh, why not serve his feet with the summons?[41]

The utter confusion of place presented by the Drummully salient provided the backdrop for Sean O'Faolain's atmospheric short story, 'No Country for Old Men'.[42] Although the protagonists are a middle-aged corset manufacturer and his accountant from County Louth, the terrain in which they search for the boss's fugitive son and his IRA compatriot after a raid on the fictional Carnduff police station is clearly the Drummully salient, with the pinchers of Fermanagh that enfold it. The father says:

> Did you see the lights of a car away there to the north? It may only be a private car on the main road from Newtownbutler to Clones, but if we are still in the north they may be police or B Specials trying to cut us off. Damnation! I wish I knew to hell where exactly our wandering border is tonight.

The fugitives are equally nonplussed. The wounded one remarks: 'We're in the South now. But this bloody border loops all over the place. Any road we take, if we take it far enough, might take us back into trouble again.' The son is found and sent home as the industrialist and his accomplice take the other IRA man, now dead, to the graveyard beside Drummully church. In the final denouement, they head off too weary to check the direction of the sunrise, and run straight into a police patrol.

The glaring anomaly of the Drummully salient should have been rectified in 1925 by the Boundary Commission when it set about determining the wishes of residents so far as they were 'compatible with economic and geographic conditions'.[43] That didn't happen because of a number of factors, not least the determination of the Dublin government and its nationalist supporters in the North to press for the wholesale transfer of counties Fermanagh and Tyrone, rather than considering piecemeal adjustments. The latter, however, turned out to be the primary concern of the other parties involved in the process. Nonetheless, individuals and local statutory agencies, including the Clones rural councils covering the town's Monaghan and Fermanagh hinterlands, did make their cases for specific localities such as Drummully, which was almost completely cut off from the town and the rest of Monaghan and the Free State by the Fermanagh districts of Clonkeelan and Derrysteaton.[44] The roads across the new border were frequently sealed off; customs checkpoints affected people in both jurisdictions; and memories of the recent Troubles were fresh in local minds when the Commission held its hearings in Enniskillen.

Council chairman Bernard Flynn presented the case for the restoration of the town's natural hinterland, including Drummully, stating that Clones was the natural market town for the parishes of Roslea, Newtownbutler, Coonian and three-quarters of Lisnaskea parish. He produced testimonies from people adjacent to the town who were now forced to shop in Newtownbutler and Lisnaskea. While nationalist Drummully residents wanted enough of Fermanagh moved to the Free State to restore them to their town, they rather despondently added that, failing this, Drummully should be transferred to Northern Ireland. Similarly, Drummully unionists who made a counter-submission to the Boundary Commission for the transfer north of the sixteen Monaghan townlands of the district said they would favour any end to the anomaly by being placed entirely on one side or the other. As members of the Church of Ireland, their primary concern was that their church and school were now in the Free State and their children, though Northern Ireland Protestants, would be compelled to learn Irish and would be 'cast adrift to the tender mercies of republicans'.[45] A petition was organised by Drummully rector Reverend John Robert Meara, who at a commission hearing in Enniskillen on 4 May 1925 said: 'We never thought about the difference between one county and another before that change was made.'[46] Their world had now been turned upside down and such was the confusion after partition that no marriages conducted in the Drummully parish church situated in County Monaghan had been properly registered with the Dublin authorities, according to Fermanagh County Council's Mr H. Kirkpatrick, who had testified on 29 April.[47]

The Drummully unionists asserted that since Protestants owned most of the land in the Monaghan salient, their votes should count for more. Of the sixty-three farmers registered, thirty-eight were Protestant and the other twenty-five had holdings of as little as four acres. However, the census showed that the 263 Catholics were the majority of the population of 449. Protestant farmer James Garland pointed out:

My father and myself have cottages on our land and there are twelve votes in these cottages, whereas our own votes number only four. The consequence of this is that our unionist votes are outnumbered on our own property by eight, and by our own dependents.[48]

In its report, the Boundary Commission recommended transfer to the Free State of Fermanagh districts immediately adjacent to Clones town.[49] In all, it would have moved 6,120 residents of east Fermanagh, just over 1,000 of these Protestants, into the Free State. Only the townland of Coleman Island in the extreme northern end of the Drummully salient was to be transferred north, with thirteen Catholics and thirty-eight Protestants. The report was suppressed, however, with a deal for no border changes in exchange for Free State relief of Imperial debt after the *Morning Post* newspaper disclosed its main findings. Dublin's Minister for Justice, Kevin O'Higgins, negotiated a financial deal – 'the best day's work I have ever done'. Executive President W.T. Cosgrave presented it to the Dáil, which passed it on a vote of 71 to 20, with 14 abstentions and the non-participation in the vote of the 48 Sinn Féin deputies who refused to take their seats. Elected representatives from the six counties were refused entry to the debate, yet Cahir Healy, MP for South Fermanagh, noted, 'John Redmond was driven from office for accepting partition for five years: Our present leaders have accepted it forever.' It was a dead end of hope for those who had banked their hopes on the Boundary Commission and the promise of a rectified border.[50]

Just beyond Drumsloe Lough and a pretty yet deserted traditional farm cottage and outbuildings, I come to my own dead end. The towpath ends abruptly in the townland of Clonlura, where the canal seems to disappear in a muddy pool under a stone bridge. That leaves no alternative but to head north a short distance and then east on the main N54 Cavan-to-Clones road and follow the canal from a distance. At least the road is open now. Unluckily for one resident, carpenter James McElroy of Clonlura, the road through the landlocked salient was opened just as the Boundary Commission arrived. He was stopped by the first patrol of Civic Guards into Drummully who demanded to see the customs pass for his motorbike.

McElroy didn't possess such a document since, as solicitor M.E. Knight pointed out on his behalf, he was 'living for all intents and purposes in County Fermanagh' in the North, and had never encountered Free State regulations, since his home area had been blockaded off from the rest of the Free State more than two years previously. The Clones District Court judge hearing the case pointed out that ignorance of the law was not a defence, but imposed the minimum fine of £20.[51]

The Ordnance Survey map shows that the canal ahead is confined to a few landlocked channels. However, an open gateway into a field offers a glimpse of the canal, with a striking house ruin on the far bank. In his book, Brian Cassells identifies this derelict building as the home of the Ulster Canal manager.[52] He also relates the following story from May Blair's book, *Once Upon the Lagan*:[53] George Lynch, an incumbent of this house and the post that went with it, got the job of superintendent of the Lagan Navigation in 1909. He loaded all his belongings onto a barge and headed east through Clones, on to the Blackwater River and Lough Neagh, entering the Lagan Canal at Ellis Gut and continuing on to Sprucefield, outside Lisburn, County Antrim. At Halliday's Bridge, near Moira, County Down, canal-bank ranger Hughie Bann hopped aboard the barge. Bann accompanied his new boss all the way to Lynch's new home in Sprucefield, to help him unload. It was a gesture that Lynch surely remembered and rewarded. The forsaken Ulster Canal manager's house at Tievegarrow on the Ulster Canal, meanwhile, might well have been deserted since Lynch undertook that voyage to Sprucefield. Its walls are crumbling and full bushes of ivy sprout from its windows, gables and red corrugated roof.

Back on the main road, I slip out of Monaghan and back into Fermanagh on the A3, and into the townland of Rabbit Island, where a small, neatly thatched cottage sits on a little side road. A short distance ahead, shielded just below the road, sits an even more picturesque thatched cottage, which once featured in a postcard image as the prettiest home in Fermanagh. My late father always remarked proudly on that, and my sons tell me that I have kept up the practice. Some things don't change in border country.

After the Boundary Commission of 1925, the border remained where it was, an intrusive, inconvenient and anomalous impediment in the lives of all those in Drummully and far beyond. The two governments' failure to deal with glaring frontier anomalies would become an acute problem during the Troubles. From its deployment in 1969, the British Army was intent in sealing the frontier. It partially closed them in 1970, cratering or blocking fifty-one 'unapproved' roads, but resistance from 'enraged locals and IRA sympathisers, which included the use of explosives, was so fierce that the operation was abandoned and the blockages removed'.[54] Not for long, however, as British commanders on the ground succumbed to the demands of James Chichester-Clarke's unionist regime in Stormont for tighter border security, ignoring the strenuous advice of Defence Secretary Lord Carrington and the British ambassador in Dublin, Sir John Peck, that the 'spikes, craters or elephant pits, are totally counter-productive … and are a standing invitation to the population to tear them down or fill them in'.[55] From a local point of view, the closures were sheer provocation:

> Blowing up the roads was … a stupid idea. It served no purpose whatsoever, because if the IRA wanted to come across the border, they come across anyway. There was a million roads they could go; they would go a lane way or go the fields, or come in with a bomb and hijack a vehicle and blow it up, which they did do. So really, they blew up roads and done a lot of damage to property, a lot of damage to roads, for years, and it was serving no purpose whatsoever. It was only annoying the local people and the IRA were only laughing at it.[56]

Already coping with the violent urban backlash from the introduction of internment without trial in August 1971, the British army cut off eighty-nine cross-border roads, including several in the Drummully salient. By the end of November, fifty-two of those had been reopened by local people. In one instance, at Munnilly Bridge in 1971, a garda officer from Clones drove his car onto a stretch of road that British troops from the Royal Engineers had mined with explosives and remained there for two hours until the military backed down and removed the charges.[57] Military strategists continued to try to close the border to some extent, though, concentrating their efforts on blocking eighty-five routes. This led to a virulent cat-and-mouse game and frequent violent clashes between local residents and British troops with 'no local knowledge and, at times, scant regard for local sensitivities', throughout the early 1970s.[58]

Yet commanders on the ground were deeply committed to pursuing the 'low-intensity' counter-insurgency operations promulgated by Brigadier Frank Kitson, whose army career had begun with the brutal suppression of the Mau Mau uprising in Kenya, where he was awarded the Military Cross.[59] Among Britain's terrorist tactics in Kenya had been the use of pseudo-gangs to carry out covert operations aimed at flushing out and capturing insurgents.[60] It did the same thing in Northern Ireland in the early 1970s, with a pseudo-gang known as the Military Reaction Force, and its successor, the Force Research Unit.[61] British military commanders did not stop their operations at the border, either. From August 1969, there was an annual average of forty ground incursions into the South, rising to a peak of 108 border incursions recorded by the Irish Army over five months in the latter half of 1972.[62]

In the early hours of 25 May 1973, Gardaí in Clones stopped a van and discovered four fully armed British soldiers in the back. The driver and front-seat passenger were in civilian clothes. They reported the incident up the line, and, by 3:45 a.m., an 'agitated' Foreign Affairs Minister Garret FitzGerald was on the phone to British Ambassador Sir Arthur Galsworthy seeking an assurance that this was a mistake, so that the soldiers could be taken to the border and released.[63] According to the ambassador, FitzGerald conceded that the border was 'impossibly difficult at that particular point'.[64] Obligingly, army headquarters at Lisburn said the soldiers had been dispatched to set up a vehicle checkpoint on the border and had strayed into Clones. The civilian disguise of the pair in front was explained as a precaution against the risk of IRA ambush. The soldiers were released forthwith. It later transpired that the soldiers had gone to the Drummully townland of Derrybeg, where they had tried to raid a house that was bisected by the border and arrest the owner, who was suspected of being a leading member of the Provisional IRA, according to FitzGerald's autobiography. He wrote that the 'British security forces had real problems patrolling this particularly complicated section of the border', adding, however, that this incident 'though trivial in itself, was symptomatic of the problems that we experienced with security forces in Northern Ireland, which clearly could not be relied upon to be frank with our police'.[65] Having failed in the mission, the patrol commander 'exceeded his instructions', and brought his men into the town centre of Clones, creating what the British ambassador described as 'another famous event to which the Irish will be prone to refer and which they may well magnify in so doing'.[66] Incursions by armed British soldiers in disguise were a frequent occurrence from this time onwards, and, according to Fianna Fáil TD Bill Loughnane, the Military Reaction Force was implicated in kidnappings and brutal killings along the border. Subsequent episodes showed that undercover British military agents were operating as far as Dublin, trying to provoke a situation that would force the government there to start interning members of the IRA.[67]

The canal reappears at MacEntees Cross in the Fermanagh townland of Clonfad, just past the remains of a humpbacked bridge. Now equipped with gateways on both sides, the bridge serves as a temporary shelter for horses and other livestock. Across the small road leading to Munnilly Bridge and the Monaghan townland of Cloncallick beyond, the outline of the canal can be seen once more, stretching towards Clones town. Just beyond that small neck of Monaghan, Annies Bridge bestrides the River Finn and the border once more. Annies Bridge is not named for a person, but for the townland of Na hEanaigh (The Marshes), which nestles into the splendour of the demesne of Hilton Park, the stately home of the Madden family. Unlike many other landed families, including the Saundersons, who abandoned this part of the country after partition, the Maddens were deeply involved in providing leadership under the new dispensation. Colonel J.C.W. Madden was an officer of the Royal Irish Fusiliers, a leading member of the Ulster Unionist Council, deputy grand master of the Grand Orange Lodge of Ireland, the former commanding officer of the 2nd Monaghan Battalion of the Ulster Volunteer Force, and a director of the Great Northern Railway. According to one historical account, he was known to nationalists by the nickname 'Dirty Buttons'.[68]

In the seventeenth century, the Maddens of Maddenton, County Kildare, had relocated northwards when John Madden, an attorney of His Majesty's Court of Castle Chamber, married Elizabeth, daughter and co-heiress of Charles Waterhouse of Manor Waterhouse in County Fermanagh in 1635.[69] Their second son, Dr John Madden, married Mary, daughter of Samuel Molyneaux of Castle Dillon in Armagh, and their son was Dr Samuel 'Premium' Madden, one of the most fascinating Irish characters of the eighteenth century.[70] As rector of Drummully Parish, he endowed Trinity College and was co-founder (with Thomas Prior) of the Royal Dublin Society. He was an ardent patriot in the manner of Dean Jonathan Swift, his contemporary. One of Madden's plays, *Themistocles: the Lover of His Country*, was performed in London to some acclaim; another, *Reflections and Resolutions Proper to the Gentlemen of Ireland*, was a well-received polemic describing the impoverished condition of the country. Dr Samuel Johnson wrote of Madden that 'His was a name that Ireland ought to honour.' However, Madden's *Memoirs of the Twentieth Century*, written in 1733 and dedicated to his former pupil, Frederick, prince of Wales, incurred some official disfavour. Madden took it from the London printers and had it destroyed, only a couple of copies surviving, one of them in the family library at Hilton Park.

That stately home was gutted by fire in 1804, and the Maddens were reduced to living in the servants' quarters for a few decades before they could afford to rebuild. A series of John Maddens succeeded to the family fortune, most of whom served in the military, and several of whom were members of parliament. Of these, one was dismissed as deputy lieutenant for Monaghan and justice of the peace in 1869 for contravening the Party Processions Act and 'using language of studied insult to the government of the Queen'. He was described as a 'semi-madman' by the Countess of Dartrey.[71] He also briefly espoused home rule and contested the 1874 election unsuccessfully on that platform.[72] His son, also John C.W. Madden, was the aforementioned Orange and unionist stalwart; Colonel Madden was shocked but undaunted by the summary ejection by the Ulster Covenanters of the three abandoned counties. As the crisis deepened after that 1920 Unionist Convention in Belfast's Ulster Hall, he drew on his military training to put Hilton Park on a defensive footing, with armed guards. His most significant brush with the IRA occurred when he returned from a Great Northern Railway meeting in Belfast and was told by staff at Clones station that his car had been commandeered by General Eoin O'Duffy, forcing him to walk the 4 miles home to Hilton Park. He wrote to O'Duffy asking him if his government wished people like him to leave the country. The family history records that 'The reply was non-committal, non-apologetic and cited national business.' Subsequently, Colonel Madden immersed himself in local affairs as a founder of the Protestant Association, which became the political vehicle of the rejected Ulster unionists in Monaghan. He was elected to Monaghan County Council on three occasions after partition, almost topping the poll in the Clones electoral district in 1934, the year before his death.

His successor, Major John Madden, was a war hero credited with having an 'Irish sixth sense' after he saved the lives of fellow officers by warning them of imminent danger when he was wounded himself in shelling and lost a leg during the Battle of Normandy in 1944.[73] I remember him best as the imposing chairman of the Clones Agricultural and Horse Show, which dominated the local farm and town calendar each September of my childhood until the conflict in the early 1970s forced its discontinuation. The showgrounds at the edge of town straddled the border, and, when there was an outbreak of foot-and-mouth disease in Britain in 1967, livestock entries had to be presented in their own jurisdictions, separated by a rope barrier. I seem to recall that Major Madden scooped top awards for his magnificent Hereford cattle. His son Johnny Madden returned to Hilton Park when his ageing parents moved to join family in England in 1983. With his wife, Lucy, Johnny transformed the estate, opening the grand house as sumptuous accommodation in the Hidden Ireland chain of stately guesthouses. An accomplished food writer, Lucy's culinary exploits have delighted a series of guests that has included the retinues that descended on the locality for the filming of works by Shane Connaughton and Patrick McCabe. The latter local novelist was more intimately involved in Hilton Park when he and the son-in-law of Johnny and Lucy Madden, Welsh film director Kevin Allen, launched the Flat Lake Festival on the estate in 2007. It ran for several years, to growing acclaim, but then ran out of steam or money, or both. It never did run out of eclectic and sometimes bizarre line-ups, ranging from Shane McGowan and Lily Allen (Kevin's niece) to country-music acts and local Orange bands, and a formidable line-up of Ulster poets including Seamus Heaney, Michael Longley and Paul Muldoon, to most of Ireland's top writers. It fully deserved *NthWORD* magazine's description as a 'cheap, off-beat, anarchic weekend that is hard to beat'.[74]

Hilton Park is quieter these days, and the stately home accommodation is now run by Freddie Madden, a chef, and his wife Joanna. Johnny and Lucy have taken up residence in the orchard home after Kevin Allen separated from their daughter Laura. Also a film producer, Laura was among the first women to help the *New York Times* expose the predatory sexual behavior of Holywood film mogul Harvey Weinstein.[75] Her father Johnny has maintained the family interest in local history and the deep and adverse effects of partition. He believes firmly that the 'social, familial and economic orientation' of Clones is 'less to the rest of County Monaghan but to the north and west towards Fermanagh', leaving it 'a Fermanagh town, although it's in Monaghan'. Until the Troubles erupted, he says, Clones people 'shopped, traded and used services in Enniskillen, some twenty-eight miles from the town, as frequently as – and possibly more frequently than – in Monaghan, which is only twelve miles distant'.[76]

I take a break from my trek to call in with my brother Frank, who lives just inside Fermanagh, but still safely ensconced in the parish of Clones. Frank interrupts his work in the bicycle sales and repair business that he operates from his garage to make tea, and we talk about the canal, which will run past his garden and would be a big boost for his small business, Clonfad Cycles. Frank has been anticipating the restoration of the canal since he and Evelyn built their home and started their family. His eldest is now off at university, and Frank is more relaxed about the project now. If it comes, it will come, but he's not holding his breath.

Frank suggests that I should retrieve my car from the car park at Castle Saunderson immediately, before the Scouting Ireland centre closes for the day. So we pile into his work van and drive out there.

Then I drive all the way back into Clones, leave the car at the Ulster Canal Stores, and drive back out to resume my walk. Frank has another suggestion. Since the towpath is heavily overgrown and blocked further along, I should walk along the 'old Cavan road', which runs parallel to the A3 and rejoins it on the edge of the town, about 1 kilometre away. So I skirt around the back of The Noble Grape, more commonly known as 'MacEntee's off-licence', and take a sharp right into a virtually forgotten thoroughfare. The off-licence now occupies the forecourt shop of what was once a busy service station back when motor fuels were cheaper in the North. About 100 metres further towards the town, McQuaid's service station is now an auto-parts shop and used-car dealership. When the fuel prices flip-flopped in the mid-1990s, Johnny McQuaid built an alternative service station on the Monaghan Road, just on other side of Clones town. With a rival new station built across the road by another local businessman, this immediately filled the gap left in Fermanagh on the Cavan Road. Such price fluctuations have an immediate impact on border towns. It pays to move quickly and decisively.

Small roads and ancient laneways like the one I am now on have played a crucial role in the local economy as smuggling trails, of course. Bounded by high banks with thick hedgerows, this one follows the crest of a hill that at various points offers good views over the world below on both sides. Today it soon transforms into a soft surface of new grass, but in times past it was a rutted thoroughfare along which herds of cattle and vehicles carrying contraband goods could penetrate the frontier and evade the customs and police patrols on the main roads. Now it is deserted as traffic whizzes along on the A3 below, allowing me time to admire the rolling drumlin landscape and sheer beauty of the bare trees in early spring. With Clones town visible as I ascend the ridge, a gate gives way onto the banks of the Lackey River known hereabouts as the Wee River. In a few paces I am back on the main road just at the Aqueduct Bridge where the installation of 'spikes' in my early childhood informed me that I lived on the border. A few metres to the west, a road sign greets motorists with the news that 'Fermanagh welcomes you, naturally'. I am crossing the border for the final time today.

Where the A3 becomes the N57 again, I turn right at the eastern end of the bridge through another gateway and onto a path where the Lackey widens into a lagoon as it enters twin caverns at the base of the aqueduct that carries the canal over the river. Now bursting with bushes and ivy, the cut-stone structure doesn't quite conceal the congealed mass of flotsam and jetsam gathering at the base. A path leads up and over the structure and I am back on the towpath for the final couple of hundred metres into the town. Ahead, the Canal House, a handsome stone cottage, nestles snugly beside the final bridge as the canal channel winds gently to the Ulster Canal Stores. Back in the days when Clones was still a transport hub, scores of horses clip-clopped across this bridge and on through the centre of the town to the railway's Ulster Yard in the early morning. At that time, the MacEntees who own the Canal House had a contract to supply the Belgian army with Irish horses. Though they were probably destined for the military menu, the town held on to the illusion that the Belgians still had cavalcades of cavalry in the early 1950s.

Opposite the bridge, the Mullanamoy Lane veers off towards the Newtownbutler Road, and an avenue with a white-railed metal fence and ornate lampposts sweeps up to Clonboy House. Diagonally opposite, Crossmoyle House is its twin. These were formerly the homes of the Pringle and Parke families, the most notable of whom was James Cecil Parke (1881–1946), Ireland's greatest-ever sportsman. Having won his first tennis trophy at Clones Lawn Tennis Club in 1900, Parke achieved the pinnacles of success in international tennis, rugby and golf, as well as representing his hometown in chess when he was only 9 years old.[77] The Pringles and Parkes were noted locally for skating on the canal's frozen channel during winter freeze-ups.

On the left, a road sign proclaims that County Monaghan is twinned with Prince Edward Island, Canada. On the right, another welcomes me bilingually to County Monaghan as I come to my first major destination, and enter the Ulster Canal Stores for food and rest, with a vantage of where a major marina is planned for future pleasure craft.

2. Cheek by Jowl: Clones

Twelve-year-old Patrick Shea's train pulled into Clones, its journey from Dundalk having been punctuated at every stop with gunshots fired by a man in the adjoining carriage. The gunman had disembarked before the final stage, however, and when Shea stepped down from the train into the normally 'wide, busy station', it was at first deserted. Then Shea's father, commander of the town's Royal Irish Constabulary, stepped from the station-master's office, and armed police appeared from every nook and cranny in the station. They had heard reports of a gun battle on the train. 'It's that bastard Fitz,' the chief exclaimed when the culprit was described. Fitz was a Black and Tan, who, 'much to his [Inspector Shea's] relief', had just been transferred from Clones to Ballybay.[1] It was 1920, and Patrick Shea had arrived just in time to witness the transformation of his new home into a border town, his father having been transferred north. And what a wonderful town Patrick found, 'busy, thriving, with electric lights hanging over the middle of the streets, the first public electric lighting I had seen'. He noted that nearly all the townspeople wore wooden clogs, crafted locally. The clogs clattered in the early morning and late at night, competing with the clip-clop of horses going to the railway station, in which trade the entire town seemed to be involved.

It was a time of change for the area:

The border which had been drawn around the six counties of Northern Ireland ran close to the northern edge of the town. Five minutes walk from the Diamond was a border road-post manned by members of the Ulster Special Constabulary, some of whom were Clones men.

The Ulster Special Constabulary was a quasi-military reserve force of armed police established in October 1920 and divided into A, B and C classes. The A Specials were on full-time duty, especially along the northern side of the newly emerging border. Specials in nearby Newtownbutler, in County Fermanagh, patrolled in their lorries 'right to where the town ended'. Shea, who later became the highest-ranking Catholic public servant in Northern Ireland, recalls going to Mass in Clones as Specials fired shots across the border at the spire, chipped stone raining down on worshippers when their bullets struck it. Sometimes they encroached further, as on the night when the barracks in Clones was aroused by the frantic knocking of a local publican known as 'Black Jack', who reported that the IRA was raiding his premises at the foot of Fermanagh Street. The police rushed to the scene, called on the raiders to surrender and were fired upon. A gun battle ensued for several minutes until the raiders surrendered. They turned out to be Special Constabulary from Newtownbutler on a looting expedition. One of the raiders was killed, and another seriously wounded. The captured Specials were tried and 'almost all of them given terms of imprisonment'.

According to Shea's memoir, the Clones police numbered about twenty, of whom half were Black and Tans, usually of shorter stature and with English accents, but dressed in regulation uniforms. Their barracks on the Diamond had a sandbag porch with small openings for sentries, and all the windows had steel shutters, from one of which the 'muzzle of a machine-gun' poked out towards the shop of a man who was 'important in Sinn Féin'. The police Auxiliaries based at Castle Saunderson drove into town on summer evenings dressed in their distinctive uniforms of Glengarry caps, riding britches and leggings, some of them sporting revolvers 'slung, cowboy style, from their hips'. They sat on the Diamond in their Crossley Tenders singing and drinking beer fetched to them by the 'boots' at the Lennard Arms Hotel. Before returning to the castle, they stocked up at Peter Carron's pub on Cara Street. The King's Royal Rifles were based at the workhouse, from which lorry-loads of people had been evacuated and sent waving cheerily 'on the most exciting journey of their lives' to the Monaghan workhouse. The squaddies had a good football team that competed locally and 'an excellent band which on Sunday afternoons played in the Diamond under the baton of the elegant Bandmaster Dunne'. Townspeople, at first reticent, soon occupied the chairs provided, and the alfresco concerts became very popular, part of the town's lively social life, for which 'political loyalties were overlooked'.

Not everyone was in tune of course. The district was alive with skirmishes, arms raids, kidnappings, shootings, ambushes and more. Under Eoin O'Duffy, who had 'no great reputation as a guerilla leader', according to Shea, and was 'thought of as a chocolate soldier', the IRA was deeply embedded and backed up by republican courts. They also had civilian accomplices, including Davy Levinson, who owned a general merchants business on the Diamond. Police suspected Levinson of providing vehicles for IRA operations, so they visited his premises each evening, and removed vital parts from each car. They did not monitor his neighbours as closely. McHenry & Maguire, Hardware Merchants on the Diamond, received a consignment of thirty-six hand grenades and revolvers in February 1920, and these were collected by John McGonnell, captain of Newbliss IRA company.[2] He also collected 50 pounds of gelignite from Miss R. Tumman of the Hibernian Hotel in Erne Square, and brought it on his bicycle carrier to John Donnelly's house in Killeevan, where they defrosted it in boiling water. The weapons and explosives were used in the attack led by Ernie O'Malley on Ballytrain RIC barracks, an operation planned at Tom Cosgrove's home on Newtownbutler Road, Clones.

When the Troubles intensified in early 1921, the attention of the Fifth Northern Division was focused on the Special Constabulary forces massing on the fledgling border between Newtownbutler and Roslea, and on enforcing the Belfast Boycott. Truce and Treaty between Dublin and London followed, with sighs of relief and hopes of better times. Yet the Troubles for Clones were all ahead. In early 1922, the King's Royal Rifles departed after a special ceremony at Clones Town Hall where Mrs M.E. Knight presented a clarinet to Colonel Willan 'on behalf of the loyalists of Clones'.[3] The new National Army moved into the old workhouse, a motley crew of country boys in improvised uniforms who spent their evenings strolling past the shop windows. They were augmented by men released from the internment camp at Ballykinlar, County Down. Patrick Rooney, a local veteran of both the Great War and the recent Troubles donned an officer's uniform and took charge of drilling.[4]

Clones then became the pivot of operations for a shadowy new body called the Ulster Council. It was established in January 1922 by Michael Collins in his clandestine role as president of the Irish Republican Brotherhood Supreme Council, even as the new Free State government was being set up in Dublin.[5] The Ulster Council took charge of IRA operations along the border to prevent the unionist regime gaining hegemony over the six counties. Collins was joined by his IRB colleagues Minister for Defence Richard Mulcahy and IRA Chief of Staff Eoin O'Duffy. Fourth Northern Division Commander Frank Aiken recalled O'Duffy telling northern IRA officers in Clones early in 1922 that the Treaty was 'only a trick' to obtain arms and supplies to fight the British.[6] For the next six months, the Ulster Council harried the border.

Meanwhile, the Clones garrison of the new National Army was first to be outfitted with new uniforms at Beggar's Bush Barracks in Dublin. The arms issued from British Army stocks were diverted to southern divisions of the IRA commanded by Liam Lynch, in exchange for older weapons that could not be traced if captured in cross-border forays. The fortifications were removed from the Clones police barracks on the Diamond and the ominous machine-gun muzzle turned out to be a piece of iron spouting. The republican judge at whose house it was pointed, Owen Conlan, now took the courthouse seat 'vacated by His Majesty's resident magistrate'.[7]

As riots erupted and the Northern state seemed on the verge of collapse, refugees from Belfast were sheltered at Clones in a long wooden building on the Newtownbutler Road where the armed forces of two states faced off against each other. Then on 14 January 1922, ten armed men, six with Clones addresses, were arrested by the A Specials constabulary at Dromore, County Tyrone. Among them was IRA Divisional Commandant Dan Hogan and his senior staff officers. They were on their way to Derry, ostensibly for the Ulster Football Final, but actually to rescue two prisoners on death watch in Derry Gaol. The IRA retaliated by kidnapping three A Specials at Cookstown. Then when talks between Premier William Craig and Michael Collins representing the two Irish governments broke down on 2 February, the IRA launched cross-border swoops, kidnapping dozens of prominent unionists.[8] The same day, Clones detachments of the IRA/ National Army engaged in ambush gun battles with Special Constabulary at Wattlebridge, Newtownbutler, Roslea and elsewhere, taking prisoners, hostages, weapons and armoured vehicles, with reports of many deaths.[9] Strong barricades of carts and mowing machines remained for weeks as evidence of those gun battles.[10] Raids and reprisals were carried out on the homes of men from the Clones district serving in the Special Constabulary. A pork buyer for Lipton & Company called Maywood was taken hostage in Clones and interned at Ballybay with about seventy others from across the border. Rowland Beatty, a farmer from Kilcorran, just outside Roslea on the Monaghan side, was hauled from his car in Clones when found to have a revolver and ammunition. He was subsequently released, but a rifle and ammunition were seized from his home. Some internees at Ballybay were Clones Protestants. They were then released as others arrived and raids continued even after loyalists began to trench roads and fell trees along the border. The Northern Ireland Home Office dispatched an extra 5,000 A and B Specials to the border, and gun battles raged along Monaghan's county line. The *Northern Standard* reported that 'from Clones to Newtownbutler, a male member of almost every household and, in some cases two, have been kidnapped'.[11]

Into this maelstrom, on Saturday 11 February 1922, the 5:15 p.m. Belfast train arrived at Clones, where three other trains were already waiting. Passengers mingled until 5:30 p.m., when Lieutenant Patrick Rooney received a message at the workhouse barracks that a large party of armed RIC men were in the station. Rooney told his commandant, Matt Fitzpatrick, who had just arrived at the workhouse with other officers. They climbed into garrison vehicles with all the available armed soldiers and sped off through the town, klaxon horns blaring. Fitzpatrick told the stationmaster to hold the Enniskillen train. His men took up positions. With Vice Commandant Joseph McCarville alongside him, Fitzpatrick then strode towards the rear of the train, where two

A Specials were standing at a carriage door. Lieutenant Rooney and John McGonnell followed with a fully loaded Thompson machine gun. Fitzpatrick told the Specials to raise their hands. They complied, but a single shot rang out from inside the carriage. Fitzpatrick fell. Rooney emptied his revolver into the carriage, then dived for cover. McGonnell also raked the carriages occupied by A Specials and bullets also sprayed the stationmaster's officer, where a clerk had a narrow escape. A battle raged. Screaming passengers threw themselves to the floor, fled, or crammed into waiting rooms. Some Specials who clambered from the train's buffet car set off running down the tracks towards the nearby border. Others who got off the train were forced back at gunpoint.[12] One Specials constable managed to escape the station, discard his tunic and cap and run up Fermanagh Street to the RIC barracks on the Diamond.

In a few minutes, the battle ended and the station fell silent. A doctor examined Fitzpatrick, pronouncing him dead from a head wound. He was given the last rites and taken to the workhouse chapel. The bodies of Special Sergeant William Dougherty and Constables Joseph Abraham, James Lewis and Robert McMahon were taken to the RIC barracks. Three others who were badly wounded, including Special Constable David Morton from Belturbet, were rushed to Monaghan Infirmary. Former nationalist MP for South Fermanagh Patrick Crumley was also wounded in the hand. Four Specials were taken prisoner as the Enniskillen train departed with their wounded comrades. It stopped at Lisbellaw, where news of the Clones incident spread like wildfire. A riot ensued, and all Catholic families were driven from the village. Word also reached Belfast, sparking fresh riots that lasted four days with a total of thirty-one deaths.[13]

Clones waited for the reprisal. IRA reinforcements were rushed in from Fermanagh, Cavan and other parts of Monaghan. Young Patrick Shea noted the town was filled with marching feet and sharp military orders, public lights were switched off, shops and homes were ordered to 'black out', and the telephone and wire services were out of commission for several hours. The next morning (Sunday), General O'Duffy arrived from Dublin with an armed guard. He ordered heavy patrols and banned all Fermanagh Protestants from coming into the town. However, the fugitive A Special was sneaked from the RIC barracks across the border in a borrowed delivery van. Four blanket-covered stretchers were also placed in a large furniture lorry, driven down Fermanagh Street and out the Newtown Road.[14]

On Monday, 13 February, Lord Chancellor Birkenhead informed Westminster that the IRA in Monaghan had been 'entirely out of hand' for some weeks, and the Dublin government couldn't control them. Evacuation of crown forces from the Free State was put on hold. The following day, five captured Specials – four in uniform and the other in a grey shower-proof coat buttoned to the neck – were marched between two files of armed men to the inquest in Clones courthouse. The liaison officer for Monaghan, Commandant Con Ward, confirmed that there was no official notification that armed police would be passing through. The coroner ruled that Fitzpatrick's death was murder, and the jurors, half of them Protestants, extended sympathy to relatives of all the dead and to Fitzpatrick's comrades.

Fitzpatrick was buried on Wednesday, 15 February. Hundreds of motor cars and even more bicycles brought an estimated 3,000 IRA Volunteers from throughout Monaghan, Tyrone, Armagh, Fermanagh and Cavan. Chief Requiem Mass celebrant Canon McMeel described them as 'the finest and cleanest body of men in the world'. They then marched 13 miles by a circuitous route avoiding Fermanagh to Drumalee Cemetery near Castle Saunderson. O'Duffy delivered the graveside oration for Fitzpatrick, saying 'when his country called him, he laid down his hurley for the rifle' and had a momentous career, including his escape from Monaghan Infirmary after he was captured, one of the 'greatest achievements' of the war: 'Would to God that the people of Ireland shall unite so that the blood of this brave man and of others shall not have been shed in vain.'[15]

As the hero was buried, Special Constable John James Cummins from Strabane had his leg amputated in Enniskillen because of injuries he had sustained in the Clones battle. And regular soldiers from the West Kent Regiment were deployed along the border to bolster security as Winston Churchill reported great apprehension over large numbers of the IRA 'accumulating and concentrating in the villages of County Monaghan' and the prospect of an all-out attack, while 'considerable movement of armed constables', gave rise to 'similar apprehensions' in Monaghan. He refused Craig's demand for 5,000 troops to cross the border and occupy the Clones area until all kidnapped loyalists were released.[16] However, he gave Craig twenty extra mobile platoons of A Specials and 2,000 additional B Specials. Churchill also proposed 'two impartial commissions' to maintain constant communication to 'allay suspicions', saying both sides had already agreed. Over the following days, the hostages and the 'Monaghan footballers' were released. The latter travelled to Clones via a 250-mile detour to avoid crossing the border.[17] That avoided a meeting with Craig, who was touring the border 'to visit and encourage the Specials' now redeployed with extra battalions of British troops on standby to reinforce the frontier. The A Specials now had more than 4,000 full-time members in forty mobile platoons operating from big houses commandeered in the border areas.[18]

The new north-south commissions only operated until the end of March 1922, but in that time, they quelled much of the unrest.[19] The two sides differed over the status of 'refugees'. While the Free State guaranteed non-interference with an estimated fifty refugees from Clones in Newtownbutler, the northern authorities said many refugees who fled south were fugitives and Northern Home Affairs Minister Dawson Bates said he would not have IRA men 'coming in and out of the Northern area as they see fit'.[20] In a report to Collins, border liaison officer Commandant Ward said Sir Basil Brooke, commandant of the Special Constabulary at that time and later Northern Ireland premier, gave him the names of a dozen B Specials who feared returning home to Clones and, without reciprocal arrangements, the south withdrew its guarantee of safety.[21]

The sides were drawn and, increasingly, the line was fixed. Civilians were caught in the crossfire. In early March 1922, Clones youth James Mulligan was shot in the leg at Castle Saunderson. He was the helper on a bread delivery van that came upon a Specials patrol. The driver, John McPhillips, was too scared to stop. Mulligan was treated by Dr E. Tierney, but had to be sent down to Dublin for surgery. Van drivers then collectively refused to serve Fermanagh customers, forcing Clones businessman Edward Brady to get behind the wheel himself.[22]

The focus shifted momentarily with the passage of the Civil Authorities (Special Powers) Act, providing draconian measures for the unionist government to deal with nationalist dissent and civil unrest, and leading to widespread violence and sixty-one deaths. The Specials remained at their checkpoints to 'boldly define' the border in case of an IRA invasion, and the *Northern Standard* reported that Fermanagh farmers who formerly patronised Clones were starting a market at Newtownbutler, only 4 miles away.[23] By the middle of March, 'North and South were to all intents and purposes openly at war', with 'roads and bridges ... blown up or blocked by both sides, and fighting and outrages became common occurrences through the six counties'.[24] In the Clones area, cars belonging to Fermanagh Protestants were being seized. Royal Mail, still an all-island delivery service, was disrupted between Clones and Roslea, where the postman had to unharness his horse at Aghafin, cross a big trench, then get a Special Constabulary escort into the village.

While negotiating peace, Collins was arguing that Sinn Féin pursue the setting up of the boundary commission and then take tariff action against districts remaining outside the state. He was also sending arms north, so that even anti-Treaty forces remained loyal to him.[25] Clones was virtually sealed off, with a huge force of Specials garrisoned at Loughkillygreen Orange Hall on the Newtownbutler Road just at the apex of the Drumully salient. Lackey Bridge on the Clones-to-Fivemiletown road was blown up on St Patrick's Day. Two days later, the Specials felled trees at Knockballymore in a bid to seal off the only remaining road into the town from that direction. There was widespread panic in Clones on Wednesday, 22 March, with reports of a large force advancing on Carra Bridge. Armed men were sent at high speed and the Specials withdrew. Next day, the *Northern Standard* reported, three Protestants were expelled from Clones – a postman, a driver and a bakery delivery man.

The Craig-Collins pact of 30 March 1922 amounted to 'de facto' recognition of partition, but the overwhelming IRA majority in Ulster continued to have confidence in Collins even after the formal split at the IRA convention.[26] While IRA divisions elsewhere were riven by allegiance to the republic, the northern forces were held together by Ulster Council plans for a major offensive. On 11 April, there were reports of IRA massing in Clones, and all Specials in Fermanagh were put on full-time duty; one B Special was wounded in an incident near Newtownbutler.[27] Atrocities were committed against Protestants in far-off west Cork, and sectarian attacks continued on the border.[28] Drum Orange Hall and Drumully Protestant school were destroyed and a notice warned Monaghan Orangemen that for every Catholic killed in Belfast, two would be 'similarly dealt with locally'.[29] When a curfew was imposed throughout the North in May, many nationalists fled into Clones, but Cahir Healy MP and Fermanagh Council Secretary Thomas Corrigan were arrested under the Special Powers Act and interned on the *Argenta* prison ship in Belfast Lough.[30]

Using weapons secretly supplied by Collins, the IRA pushed into west Fermanagh capturing the Belleek-Pettigo Triangle.[31] The *Northern Standard* reported on 9 June 1922 that all roads from Clones into Fermanagh were closed by Specials firing their weapons, and refugees were in temporary accommodation, including solicitor Henry Murphy, who couldn't get to his home just across the border in Fermanagh. By the time the insurgents were driven from Belleek in a huge counter-offensive by the Specials and British Army, civil war had erupted with the shelling by the National Army of the Four Courts in Dublin, where anti-Treaty forces were garrisoned on 27 June. The Provisional Government succumbed to British pressure to stamp out attacks on the North.[32] The major offensive planned by the Ulster Council for late June was called off. IRA Volunteers headed south to join the two sides in the Civil War, leaving the North an armed camp of 50,000 police (including Specials) and sixteen full British battalions.[33] Partition slipped off the agenda until southern hostilities ended.

With the end of Civil War, it was expected that attention would turn northwards once more. It did, but not as expected. The Free State continued to share levies and duties collected by HM Customs and Excise.[34] However, on 3 March 1923, Dublin announced its intention to impose customs duties from 1 April in a 'remarkable and an anomalous example of a phase of boundary administration actually predating the final boundary delimitation'.[35] In Belfast, Craig could hardly believe his luck as Cosgrave established a fiscal frontier and scuppered the economic foundations of his government's case for a major shift in the boundary. He noted that it would 'make the South and not the North responsible for partition' by imposing 'a barrier' that left the

North firmly inside the British customs union.[36] Calling it 'a great error of judgment,' Craig told the Belfast Wholesale Merchant and Manufacturers' Association that 'partition was nothing; there was no such thing as partition if they (Dublin) did not erect a customs barrier between North and South'.[37] Belfast nationalist leader Joe Devlin MP agreed that it would result in 'stereotyping the existing boundary'.[38]

So on Sunday morning, 1 April 1923, Clones awoke to a new world order. All but one road crossing into Fermanagh was deemed 'unapproved'. All traffic was channelled towards Clontivrin on the Newtownbutler road. The Great Northern Railway also had to 'come to terms with operating as an international railway', since 'its lines crossed the newly established border in seventeen places, six of them between Clones and Cavan'.[39] There were delays, confusion and frustration, which increased on the second day as many headed off to a holiday race meeting in Enniskillen. That week's *Northern Standard* quoted customs officials saying that they would 'take things easy at first till the people get into the routine and the screw will then become tighter'.[40] Free State customs and excise set up frontier posts on approved routes and at railway stations, as well as customs stations in Clones, Monaghan and Castleblayney. In contrast to the British customs officers' gold-braided uniforms, the *Northern Standard* noted that the Free State officers lacked uniforms. However, some borrowed peaked caps from GNR railway and bus services and took up duty in huts and tents, under sheltering roadside trees and in the third-class waiting rooms of stations, where chalk directions were scrawled on the platforms. Their primary task initially would be educating people on the 'new system of legal barriers in place to control their movement'.[41]

One immediate problem was the disruption of bread deliveries, with northern bakeries shut out of the Free State. Farmers also complained of the 1.5 lb limit on tea, and they were in a quandary over creamery deliveries. When regulations were clarified, they required a bundle of paperwork, fuelling a belief among farmers that the authorities were just trying to find out their income.[42] Clones shopkeepers opened small stores across the frontier; one bought land for a warehouse to comply with customs regulations; and a special meeting of Clones council extended an invitation to the Imperial Tobacco Company to build a factory at the Fair Green, thereby avoiding heavy duties on tobacco.[43] It wasn't taken up. Customs officers felt that the simple designation of a road as 'unapproved' was ineffective, so they rendered many of these impassable.[44] When Annies Bridge on the River Finn near Scotshouse was barricaded in February 1924, the *Frontier Sentinel* pointed out that people were separated from turbary plots in both Fermanagh and Monaghan.[45] The newspaper noted that the 'Six County government refused to do anything about the barrier, despite the inconvenience to both Catholics and Protestants'.

The first customs officers in Clones were Free State soldiers who had fought a bitter civil war and were now regarded as the primary threat with the arrival of peace and penury.[46] They were organised into the Military Customs Brigade to save the state from bankruptcy. Cosgrave told the Dáil on 13 April 1923, 'The Free State has become an independent fiscal entity, and its taxes are being collected by its own officers.'[47] He then announced that customs revenue would be tripled from the £2.5 million received the previous year, and excise duties would more than double to £16.5 million, more than twice the £8.1 million raised in income tax and more than half the £28.1 million total tax yield. As well as duties on tobacco, alcohol, tea and sugar to raise revenue, the great majority of levies were protectionist, and the Free State extended its list of tariffs throughout the 1920s. They included 'symbolic' tariffs on Rosary beads, but also duties on footwear and clothing.[48] Yet what was keeping the Free State in business was causing 'hopeless confusion' in border areas and was 'most detrimental generally to business' leading to 'further serious unemployment'.[49]

Even as Cosgrave's Free State government was ratcheting up the fiscal border, local minister Ernest Blythe insisted that all would be well as soon as the Boundary Commission was established.[50] The Dublin government appointed a high-powered North Eastern Boundary Bureau under Omagh-born solicitor Kevin O'Shiel to prepare the case for transfer of all Fermanagh and Tyrone, south Armagh and Newry, as well as Derry City. But when the Boundary Commission was finally set up in 1924, chairman Richard Feetham focused on rectifying anomalies. He was supported and encouraged by J.R. Fisher, who had been appointed by Westminster to represent Northern

Ireland. The Free State's commissioner, Eoin MacNeill, was minister for education and only involved part-time in the border determinations. The commission's report on Clones notes its wide reputation as a market centre possessing unusually good rail communications that drew buyers from as far away as Derry. It concluded that the market and station were designed to serve at least a 10-mile radius, 'while now, the frontier is less than a mile away', and the adjoining Fermanagh districts were beyond a customs barrier. Chief technical assistant Major R.A. Boger estimated the market area of Clones extended west to a point between Newtownbutler and Lisnaskea and to the north past Roslea to Coonian and Moan's Cross.[51] That was the context for Clones Urban Council submitting a separate claim from the Free State government for the transfer of Clones Rural District Number 2. Chairman Bernard Flynn said Clones was the natural market town for the parishes of Roslea, Newtownbutler, Coonian and three-quarters of Lisnaskea parish and produced testimonies from people now forced to shop in Newtownbutler and Lisnaskea, which 'were only recently being used for purchases'.[52] Businessman Edward Brady claimed that over half his trade had been with Fermanagh people. Now the 'trade of Clones was … greatly diminished by placing the frontier on its doorstep'.

As tensions rose over the border, Brady was also involved in a remarkable power-sharing deal with Monaghan Orange Grand Master Michael Knight, a Clones solicitor, to avoid fractious elections to the urban district council. At a meeting chaired by Catholic curate Father James O'Daly, Knight proposed a three-way split of the nine seats, between his Protestant candidates, Brady's Catholics and Independent Labour.[53] Labour decided to contest and won a seat at the expense of former unionist Victor Bright.[54] However, Knight's group took three of the seven Clones-area seats on Monaghan County Council with himself, William Carson and Colonel J.C.W. Madden proclaiming they were no longer 'Ulster unionists', but non-political candidates for 'economy and efficiency'.[55]

Brady took the UDC chair, declaring Clones a 'shining example of a non-sectarian municipality'. He was contradicted when a convoluted case was heard at Clones District Court in August 1925.[56] Edward Carroll had gone with the Clones Orange contingent to the Twelfth celebrations out in Newbliss and came home to his lodgings 'cursing the Pope' and calling his landlady, Mary O'Dwyer, a 'Fenian bitch from Tipperary'. He claimed she called him an 'Orange bastard', and that Edward Purdy came out of her house and punched him, confining him to bed for two days. It transpired, however, that Carroll was a Catholic who had gone to the Twelfth in hopes of getting a house under political patronage, and got drunk toasting King Billy. He was fined 15 shillings for disturbing the peace and causing an affray, while Purdy was fined half that and Mrs O'Dwyer was cautioned.

As expectations for the Boundary Commission report rose, military reinforcements arrived in Clones on 19 October 1925, on the last train from Dundalk.[57] On the other side of the border, the entire part-time force of B Specials and C Specials was on stand-by.[58] The *Daily Mail* reported that Scotland Yard's Special Branch had a round-the-clock guard on the Boundary Commission papers, amid fears of an IRA raid, adding that Free State Civic Guards were set to occupy barracks in Fermanagh and Armagh.[59]

The *Morning Post*'s publication of leaked details from the Boundary Commission report on 7 November 1925 threw everyone into a frenzy. Alarmed at the prospect of losing a tiny bit of territory at Coleman Island between Clones and Newtownbutler, as well as Mullyash Mountain near Castleblayney, Monaghan County Council warned Belfast to keep its hands off, even while Colonel Madden insisted it was all just 'press rumour'.[60]

MacNeill's resignation from the Boundary Commission and then the government confirmed the rumour, and a deal was hammered out to maintain the border status quo. Suddenly it was all over bar the shouting. The bookkeeper head of the new Free State pointed with pride to the 'cancellation of any liability for a share of the British national debt'.[61] Justice Minister Kevin O'Higgins hoped that would 'deaden in the twenty-six counties the echo of the outcry of the Catholics in north-east Ulster', and Free State Executive President W.T. Cosgrave hailed it as a 'damned good bargain'.[62] Cosgrave sought no guarantees for northern Catholics, even declining a British offer to have nationalist leader Joseph Devlin as his political agent in the north to allay Catholic fears.[63] While protest was muted, the deal 'appalled all sections of Irish opinion from the most moderate to the most extreme', because it 'struck at the axiomatic national loathing of partition, now legalised in a formal document by Irish representatives for the first time in history'.[64] However, Cosgrave expressed satisfaction that he had escaped at last from 'this barren question of the boundary'.[65]

So the border remained, with all its quirks and anomalies. Initially, Clones was probably more preoccupied with the case of two Belfast men stopped on the Diamond by Guard Jeremiah Lyons, who discovered they were transporting a corpse in their Ford car.[66] Mary Anne Brown was en route for burial in her native Cavan, but her son couldn't get an undertaker to transport the remains for under £19. He borrowed his employer's car and set off with his friend late one evening, arriving in Clones at 1 a.m. Guard Lyons allowed them to proceed on condition they call into Clones barracks on their return. They did so, and were promptly detained. At their trial, District Justice Hannan said the charges were proven, but he issued a dismissal, sending them back to Belfast to explain to their boss that his car had been impounded by customs.

Tales of smuggling and amusing foibles became standard on the frontier. Yet entire communities on both sides were grappling with the imposition of a border where none had ever existed, a boundary at variance with prevailing social, cultural, economic and geographic conditions. Along its entire length, the border 'cut through complex local microgeographies of ethnic, political and religious difference, regional agricultural and economic networks, and senses of collective regional identity'.[67] While deploring the sectarian state in the North, Dublin assiduously ignored the emergence of its own. Cosgrave's government allied itself with the Catholic Church during the Civil War, and afterwards sought and complied with the hierarchy's advice on morality, education and social justice.[68] With the change of government in 1932, Catholic hierarchy reservations about the religious fervour of the new regime were 'more than dispelled' by Fianna Fáil's embrace of the Eucharistic Congress, an 'organisational triumph for the state no less than the Church'.[69] In a state that promulgated an exclusively Catholic nationalist version of Irishness, Orange traditions continued quietly in Clones and elsewhere along the border with sizeable populations of Protestants. Taoiseach Eamon de Valera called these Protestants an 'alien garrison', representing 'only English interests' who should 'give way to the majority'.[70] The 1937 constitution accorded a 'special position' to the Catholic Church, which Dev regarded as synonymous with the Irish nation, a 'binding force' central to its ideology.[71] The South was a 'cold house' for Protestants, and many moved north across the border.

Other cross-border traffic was more restricted, as the economies grew further apart. Even up to 1931, it was 'still possible to speak of one Irish economy' in agriculture, industry and fiscal policy.[72] However, the global Great Depression and De Valera's 'Economic War' involving the withholding from the British exchequer of land annuities owed for the purchase and sale of Irish landed estates to the tenant farmers meant the 'two parts of the island began to move more rapidly apart'. In its first budget in May 1932, Fianna Fáil introduced forty-three new tariffs, along with tax increases, to end the 'evils' of free trade.[73] An *Irish Times* report found that this was a huge boost to smuggling, as 'virtually every article brought from North to South across the border is now dutiable'. Although couched in the comic style so beloved in smuggling stories, the report describes the responses of 'harassed but obliging' Southern customs preventive officers on the labyrinthine regulations that were strangling border towns. With Britain's reciprocal import duties of 20 per cent on Irish imports, trade was devastated.

The Great Northern Railway had been excluded from the Free State railway amalgamation in January 1925.[74] Now with livestock and coal hit hardest by tariffs, cross-border trade slowed to a trickle at the Ulster Yard goods depot in Clones during the 1930s. It became worse when rail workers went on strike in sympathy with Northern Ireland colleagues seeking a pay raise, according to former GNR man Dan Kerr, who recalls snow on the ground during a time of great hardship in Clones when he was a child.[75] He recalls when a station-bound fruit lorry was stopped at a picket and its cargo thrown over the hedge to be salvaged happily by Dan and other children. The strike began in January and was settled in the North in late March or early April but that left the 'Free State men suffering'. Even when services resumed in Clones, many union activists were not recalled and Dan names several family men who were unemployed for years. For some, it wasn't until the onset of the Second World War that they got back and only then 'because a lot of the Protestants on the railway went off to join the British Army'. Dan found temporary work and then a full-time job. It also provided a reprieve, if temporary, for the town. As Dan observes, 'Only for the war, the railway was gone.'

During the 1930s, nothing defined partition more clearly than the chain of customs posts along the frontier. The border had become a fiscal matter for Dublin, and its Customs and Excise operated static posts and mobile patrols. British customs officers staffed frontier stations in Northern Ireland, maintaining London's control. Since the border was primarily a security concern for Belfast, RUC officers conducted patrols on behalf of HM Customs and Excise until 1951.[76] Just outside Clones, Sarah McManus received £2 twice a year for having a British customs post on her land at Clontivrin.[77] Some southern customs cars were provided by the Revenue Commissioners at the end of 1934, 24-hp Ford Saloons for patrols and for supervisory visits by chief preventive officers to frontier posts. New instructions emphasised the importance of co-operating with the Gardaí, sharing intelligence and mounting joint night-time patrols.[78]

Border posts were little more than huts from which lone customs men were expected to patrol, sometimes on foot and sometimes on bicycle. Their instructions, updated in 1940, said:

> Each patrol preventive man is to watch, not so much the actual frontier line, as the area within the limits of his patrol station. Special directions may be given to him from time to time... Generally speaking, the patrol work should be carried out by surprise visits to selected unapproved roads and other parts of the station ... and not by regular perambulation of the whole station or of the frontier line... Patrol preventive men should learn local habits in the matter of traffic, and they should keep in constant touch with their preventive offices and with the preventive men at frontier posts in the same or adjacent stations.[79]

Charged with these responsibilities, the resources of the customs service in Clones and elsewhere 'were not commensurate with the relative importance of import duties to the national exchequer. With the imposition of customs duties on imports, private and commercial smuggling became a way of life, not only in the frontier zone area.'[80]

While the cross-border trade in livestock was sharply curtailed during the 1930s, there was still a thriving trade in cheap labour. Like other market towns across Ulster, Clones had two annual hiring fairs, in May and November, as described by Roslea singer and farmer John Maguire in his recollections, published in 1973.[81] These had much bigger crowds than the monthly fair, and were colourful events with 'a lot of trick o' the loops and wheels of fortune men about the Diamond in Clones'. With few opportunities and very big families, there might be as many as 'five out of one house would be hiring'. Those seeking work presented themselves outside the Market House, where prospective employers would survey who was on offer. Contract details were agreed, often in a public house over a 'couple of drinks', between the employer and a father or neighbour acting for the jobseeker. On payment of earnest money of a few shillings, terms were agreed:

> There was a lot of variations in the wages… Some had six pounds for the six months only, and others had seven and eight and nine pound. It was according to the place they were working and who they were working with. Some would have more to do than others, a lot more stock about the place and a lot more farming to be done, more crop and potatoes and corn and everything else.[82]

Hiring girls was somewhat different, according to Reverend Victor Forster, Church of Ireland rector of Aghalurcher, who grew up in Roslea:

> It still pains me today when I remember mothers standing on the footpath with two or three daughters, and farmers, roughly dressed, peaked caps over their ears and ash plants in the hands, looked at these girls as if they were cattle – in other words trying to make up their minds if they were capable of doing the

work they wanted them to do. But mothers were really more concerned, not with the wages they would get – which was six pounds for six months – but that they would have a clean bed, reasonable food and that they could get off for Sunday morning worship. Many of them were farmers'… daughters from the mountain farms between Fivemiletown and Roslea. It was thickly populated and families on the whole were large.[83]

For a border town of diminishing fortunes and limited scope, the Second World War was a godsend. Even as Britain battened down the hatches of its island redoubt, cross-border passenger rail traffic picked up in Ireland, and Clones became a Mecca for bargain hunters. Smuggling became a popular wartime pursuit as ordinary folk played off shortages and rationing on one side, against plenty and surplus on the other. So, for instance, tea poured south and sugar and butter went north.

For Dan Kerr, it was a frantic and fun-filled period. As well as working as a young railway porter, he stood on the front line lest crown forces attempt to invade the poorly armed Free State, to prevent Germany from doing so first as a step towards an invasion of Britain. There had been no regular military garrison in Clones since the 27th Battalion garrison was moved south with the December 1925 border agreement. When Dev declared the Emergency, Dan joined the Local Defence Force (LDF) with other young men from the town, including my own father, Eugene. Dan recalls:

> We all had to do our training. You know, you were called out at night for mock battles and suchlike. We were fully qualified as soldiers, but we were all just on rations [rather than wages]. As far as I remember, there was a half ounce of tea per person and you got brown bread. And other things, like cigarettes, were rationed. You never saw bananas or fruit or anything at all like that.

Clothing from my granddad's drapery shop was also rationed and, throughout this period, Dan's dressmaker sister Annie Kerr was very busy 'turning' coats to make them appear new. Yet that didn't stop shoppers pouring in from Belfast and elsewhere north of the border on two weekly 'mystery trains'. These were advertised in Belfast city cinemas, where regulars could determine the 'mystery' destination from the train fare. Clones was popular, Dan observes, at least until local cafés started taking advantage by 'charging 1/6d for a cup of tea that you'd get in Monaghan for a shilling'. But the mystery train passengers were still drawn by the fact that they could get butter, meat and cigarettes without rationing restrictions:

> So it was like an Ulster (Gaelic Football) Final coming out of that station, trampling each other to get up the town. And then they'd all come back and you could see them bulging with all the stuff they'd bought hidden inside their coats. And when they'd go back on the train to Monaghan where the customs boarded, all the stuff would be taken off them. There used to be more yarns told about what was going on. Like this lady who sat down and the customs man says, "You're very big, what have you got in there?" and she says, "Come back in three months and I'll tell you."

Dan recalls being put on full alert when British soldiers from Derry strayed across the Donegal border, sparking fears of an imminent incursion. He also recalls carriage-loads of confused Belfast children being deposited on the platforms of the Clones railway station in the spring of 1941, when German warplanes were blitzing Belfast. One of those child evacuees on his way to Fermanagh was Robert Harbison, who describes how he and the others reacted to the disclosure that they were crossing the border:

> Of course, none of us believed it. A train-load of us Protestant children being taken across the border into the Free State to be massacred? Things had not quite come to that, even if all the German spies that ever existed were hiding down in Dublin.[84]

Being the most 'worldly-wise' of the children, having 'already been in four of Ulster's six counties', Harbison eventually gives his 'considered opinion' that this was not the border: 'Where, I asked, were the battlemented walls, the moats and the vast palings with cruel spikes which must separate the dirty Free State from our clean and righteous Ulster? It could not be.'

While the child evacuees did not get spiked walls on their cross-border trek to Fermanagh, they did get sandwiches, refreshments and an almost exclusive enclosure in the passenger terminal, according to Dan Kerr. The Red Cross operation was overseen by a formidable woman known locally as 'Mrs Win-the-War' for her zealous support of the Allied effort. Having instructed the railway staff to ensure the poor wee Belfast children were undisturbed, she fussed around making sure they had enough to eat. Dan says she was especially solicitous of one bedraggled boy stuffing himself with all the food on offer. 'So where do you come from, son?' asked Mrs Win-the-War, expecting he was from the hardest hit Docks area of Belfast. 'From O'Neill Park,' replied the waif, pointing a sandwich to the relatively new housing estate on the crest of a hill beside the station.

Despite the Free State's neutrality in the war, the sides were drawn in Clones between formidable ladies who battled for the hearts and minds of any who might stray towards or from the Allies ensconced just across the border. When a major Christmas fundraising concert was organised for the LDF and Red Cross, 'Mrs Win-the-War' suggested it should also be staged for British troops stationed at Crom Castle, just on the other side of Newtownbutler. This was vigorously opposed by republican-minded Mrs McGilly and her ally Mrs Coffey, who made it clear 'there was no crossing that line', Dan Kerr recalls. However, as well as singing in the concert chorus, and playing in the local brass band, Dan, his brother John and several others had a small dance band and they agreed to play in Newtownbutler at a New Year's Eve dance for the soldiers:

> It was the Seaforth Highlanders and, God, they were a lovely regiment. During the dances, they were all drinking and carrying on, but I remember this fellow came in walking up the dance floor and he had his false teeth in one hand and a sandwich in the other and him eating away at it, or making out he was. Anyhow, when the dance was over there were some had been

drinking whisky and fell asleep about the place. Then this big blond military policeman, Big Bob they called him, came in. He had a blackthorn stick with a head on it was like a shovel and he was shouting, "Get up outta that. C'mon get up outta that." He hit them and hit them. It was vicious and then they carried them out and threw them in the back of vans. They were shipped out for the front a day or so later and we heard they were torpedoed by their own, by the British Navy, when they were going in to land. It only came out later. But those Seaforth Highlanders were very popular about here and some of the Newtown and Clones girls used to go out with them and all. It was terrible what happened them.

Then the Americans set up base in Crom Castle. They caused huge excitement as they roamed the countryside:

They were a great crowd. I remember them coming in (on the train to Clones) and they'd always give you Camel cigarettes. They'd come in and they'd buy bars of chocolate, bottles of whiskey and they'd go in and have a feed in the hotels.

Dan's sister Molly was a waitress in the Hibernian Hotel beside the railway station, where she encountered the Americans:

She says an officer used to come in and take three or four eggs with a big mixed grill, a feed that she said you would never see a man ate before. Then some of the publicans started to sell whiskey with water in it but they got fly for that. They used to come on the train to Clones, a lot of them in uniform unlike the British soldiers. I think they used to come in about half seven or eight o'clock and then back out on the 10 o'clock. Apart from that, some could come into the border in Jeeps and then walk the rest of the way.

Traffic went both ways:

They used to have dances in Crom Castle. And they used to send a big tender, as we called it, and anyone here in the town who wanted to go out, the girls and the boys, could get on and go out there and then be left back to the border again when the dance was over. It was very popular.

Then one day, the Americans didn't come into town, and Clones knew D-Day was dawning. Dan had an early insight into the great embarkation that would lead to the end of war:

> I was a porter, so I was on the platform when these empty wagons started to come in. Honest to God, nearly cattle wagons they were that bad – no corridors at all – and they had to be swept out, and the toilets filled with water and cleaned up a bit. Then all them empty carriages went out to Newtown to lift all the soldiers from Crom Castle or anywhere else and they went on around the other way into Derry or Belfast to ship them out. Then the empty wagons came back to Clones the next day and we had to clean them out again and there was boxes of stuff left in them – caps and hats, sometimes a rifle and then the Guards would have to be notified. There used to be a lot of these wee boxes full of tablets, y'know pills. I think they could put them into seawater so they could drink or make tea with it. Some would be nervous or scared and leave all this stuff behind. Half of them were drunk, I suppose. Och, they had to be pitied not knowing what they were going off to.

Dan recalls being told that 'hundreds and hundreds of bikes all in a row' were stacked at Newtownbutler's military aerodrome when the Americans left. They had been abandoned and some people came along to sell them, but before bidding started, a steamroller came along the entire line 'crushing them because they wouldn't let them be sold'. Other salvage from the D-Day departure *was* sold, however, by Clones opportunists including former railway worker Martin Carroll, Kerr recalled:

He bought all these Nissen Huts and sold them to people all round the country for dancehalls. He was a great salesman, give him his due. He could sell anything. There were these bomb boxes that would be fitted into planes with three bombs in them. Carroll got them for nothing, or maybe he was even paid to take them away. He used to advertise them for sale in the *Irish Independent* every Monday as chicken troughs. They sold all over because they looked like the real thing, you know, with three hollows in them and a place where the chickens could stand and drink away for themselves. He also bought these officers' beds, terrific steel beds with a spring for the mattress and you could snap it down like a trestle table, the legs would go under and then you could throw it under your own beds and pull it out when visitors came. Anyway, they used to come in a (railway) wagon, about 300 to a wagon, and I was supposed to check all these. But you could never check them because you could hardly see anything, just beds and beds, hundreds of them, so I'd just send them on down to Dublin where there was some shop that used to sell them. Anyway, I says to Martin, 'I could do with one of them', and he says, 'Aye Dan, I'll give you one for two pounds.' Then I saw them advertised in the paper, these special beds for sale … at five pounds apiece.

The canny Martin Carroll was not the only one profiting from the post-war economy, especially with the strict rationing of many items in Northern Ireland. Everybody along the border did their bit, and in her memoir, *Not a Leg to Stand On*, double amputee Mary O'Brien describes a shopping trip to Clones as one of the highlights of her Aunt Kitty's annual visits home to Fivemiletown, County Tyrone.[85] Mary was the only child from her large family included in the group that set off across the border by taxi. They stocked up on tobacco, sugar, tea and stockings, all still 'easily available in Clones'. Then, before heading back, the contraband was stuffed inside Mary's hollow prosthetic legs. She thought it was a 'great game', as she looked up innocently at the customs officer at Clontivrin who asked if they had 'anything to declare'.

There was a brief post-war boom in passenger traffic on the Great Northern Railway, but this was to be the last hurrah for Clones as the rail hub of Ulster. The Ulster Transport Authority (UTA), founded in 1948 to formulate transportation policy for Northern Ireland, was given powers over the financially ailing GNR.[86] In December 1950, the UTA's chairman, Major F.A. Pope, announced the complete closure of the GNR, with the wind-up beginning in the New Year. The governments intervened, but this was only a temporary reprieve, because the UTA and Stormont clearly favoured road transport over rail. Clones was on borrowed time. It ran out when Stormont 'unilaterally' scrapped the GNR connections in the North for an annual saving of £14,000, forcing Dublin to abandon the 'stump lines'.[87] The Clones-to-Omagh service was discontinued on 30 September 1957.[88] When the final scheduled passenger train left Clones for Monaghan in that same year, I was on board with my dad and brothers Eoin and Donald, and many others from the town. The lines remained open for goods traffic for another year because businesses such as McCaldin's Bakery and Pattons Hardware in Monaghan had contracts for deliveries. Then, in September 1958, Derry played Dublin in the All-Ireland Football Final and a huge crowd travelled south to support the Ulster champions. Buses brought fans to Clones and they travelled to Dublin and back on the last passenger trains at the station. The Great Northern Railway's board was dissolved on 1 October 1958.

To this day, the closure of the railway is identified by most townspeople as the worst blow inflicted on Clones. It provided the backdrop of local writer Patrick McCabe's novel *Carn*:

> The night the railway closed. That was the night the clock stopped in the town of Carn, half a mile from the Irish border. For over a hundred years, the black steam engines with their tails of smog had hissed into the depot at the edge of the town. It was inconceivable that it would ever be any other way.[89]

Yet, from the time the border had been put in place, railway closure had been inevitable. Its impact was immediate and very visible. Scores of 'railway families' left the town. They headed for Glasgow, Birmingham, Toronto and other far-flung destinations. In one memorable instance, an extended 'railway' family paraded from the Diamond down Fermanagh Street to one of the final train departures, their luggage stacked on handcarts. In some instances, fathers set off alone, leaving broods behind holding out for brief annual visits. In a few worst-case scenarios, fathers simply disappeared. Even beyond the town, the GNR closure had a huge impact in the cross-border district. In 2015, in her first interview as Northern Ireland's first minister, Arlene Foster described how her mother Georgina, from Belfast's Sandy Row, 'married and came to Fermanagh by train to Clones Junction in 1957. Then the train was taken off and my mother was more or less stranded in Fermanagh for a while'.[90]

The railway's closure left a huge hole in the fabric of the town, a hole illustrated by the dismantling of the railway buildings themselves. They were stripped bare, their finer embellishments sold off as scrap. Dan Kerr was still working in the station on Erne Square and recalls some huge pitch-pine timber joists:

> They were about four or five feet in circumference, big beams, and we had to get two flat (railway) wagons to put them in once they came down. They were all shipped away to Limerick, all the pitch pine. And the stones were all bought by some man up above Scotshouse. Clones never got a penny for any of it, whatever way that worked. They just said to take it down and they never said anything about prices or anything. I could see them coming down and you know, I cried to see all that stuff going away out of Clones.

The railway closure came against the background of more border trouble. Fired by post-war rhetoric and alarmed by the drift of partition, republicans set out to destabilise Stormont in a 'campaign of destruction' codenamed Operation Harvest. IRA Director of Operations Seán Cronin planned to 'liberate' areas along the border with majority nationalist populations.[91] Flying columns, based on the model used in 1919–21, would be composed of local volunteers, supplemented by four further columns from further south. While the IRA was still planning, however, it was upstaged by the breakaway Saor Uladh, which attacked the Roslea RUC barracks on Saturday, 26 November 1955. In a frantic gun battle, Sergeant William Morrow shot Derry man Connie Green in the chest and arm and drove the raiding party back into County Monaghan, where Green died.[92] Although dismissed by the IRA as a 'sentimental or microscopic' organisation, Saor Uladh's campaign became almost a template for Operation Harvest, which began in December 1956. Far from a major uprising, it became an 'irritation to the unionist government', and during the following year the IRA was only active 'with any consistency' along a 'twenty-mile stretch of the Fermanagh/Monaghan frontier', where two IRA men were killed and almost twenty arrested; fifty were interned in Belfast's Crumlin Road Jail.[93]

Clones was the centre of that theatre of operations, with tragic consequences for a local young man who joined the North Monaghan Unit of Saor Uladh.[94] In the early hours of 2 July 1958, the RUC shot dead 20-year-old Aloysius (Alo) Hand from O'Neill Park and seriously wounded 25-year-old Patrick Trainor. Earlier, Hand had left his girlfriend to Newtownbutler, returned home and told his sister Cecilia he was going out to 'snare rabbits'. With a five-man Saor Uladh unit, he'd then gone on foot along the railway lines, where they met the police at Clontivrin. A brief gun battle ensued. Hand was killed instantly, and Trainor was wounded and captured; his leg was later amputated. Flares lit up the skies around the town, but the other Saor Uladh men escaped. Hand's family – he was one of nine children – was shocked when they were informed by a garda at 5 a.m. of his violent death. People verbally abused his mother and brother when they attended the inquest in Enniskillen, where Coroner J.R. Hanna instructed the jury to return a verdict of 'justifiable homicide'.

With the railway gone and roads 'spiked', Clones was effectively sealed off. Just past the British customs posts on the Newtownbutler Road, the B Specials maintained a near nightly checkpoint at Clontivrin Cross, which dissuaded many from travelling that way. I have vivid childhood memories of my uncle Gerry Magee from Irvinestown urgently coaxing my Auntie Etta to come home, 'C'mon Etta, the Specials will be out the road.' It is a beckoning refrain still echoed in my family more than fifty years on. Even when the spikes were dismantled, tight control was exercised through regulations and procedures for border crossings. In 1962, the Automobile Association's handbook provided six pages of guidance for motorists planning to cross the land frontier between Northern Ireland and the Republic.[95] For a start, it lists eighteen approved roads with customs posts. Four of these were in County Monaghan: Clones to Newtownbutler; Moy Bridge to Augnacloy; Tyholland to Middletown; and Tullynagrow to Carnagh. Goods not declared were contraband and liable to seizure, with the smuggler prosecuted. The handbook also warns motorists that their vehicles were also liable for both customs duty and purchase tax on entering Northern Ireland, requiring them to 'lodge large sums of money at the frontier' or avoid doing so by presenting a British 'triptyque' passbook for stamping at the frontier post. Northern vehicles entering Monaghan were also subject to duty, but private owners could 'temporarily import' their own cars and motorcycles 'under cover of a permit … issued free of charge' and valid for a year for multiple entries and exits. The AA advice on crossing the border ended in a bold warning that a motorist crossing by unapproved routes is 'liable to very severe penalties, including confiscation of his car'. However, a further inconvenience was that customs posts had limited opening hours and late-night crossings were subject to a special fee of 2 shillings (10p), usually paid in advance. The Clones-Newtownbutler crossing operated from 7 a.m. to midnight.

In practice, the procedures relaxed as the 1960s progressed and relations thawed between Dublin and Belfast. Yet the contrast between the two sides of the border became starker as Stormont invested in infrastructure. New roads opened to Enniskillen and Omagh and others got smooth asphalt surfaces in contrast to the South's rutted and potholed thoroughfares. Fermanagh town centres began to take on the uniform look of places we saw on telly. Even the pink-and-yellow pebble-dash was different. New schools with fully funded education and school dinners, better public transport, free health services and a range of cradle-to-grave benefits left us lagging behind neighbours even within the parish. In high summer, the contrast was accentuated by red, white and blue bunting and Union flags wafting from the dreary steeples in Newtown, Lisbellaw and other towns and villages, reminding us to stay on our own side.

For a child in Clones, difference was a matter of sweet delights. An array of confectionery was openly on sale out there, yet unavailable on our side. So while Fivemiletown butter became the mothers' choice of contraband, we stocked up on Mars and Milky Bars, Spangles and teeth-destroying 'penny chews' of hard toffee. Our calorific addiction was serviced by an array of border shops less than a mile from the town on five of our eight outward routes.

We had attractions on our side, too. There were Ulster GAA Football Finals, especially those involving emerging Down superstars who swaggered to All-Ireland glory. The town buzzed and burst at the seams on Ulster Final days, as did our house, with callers. It was standing-room only once more when the All-Ireland Fleadh came to town twice. The first in 1964 surfed the crest of the great international folk music wave, and it brought many street performers soon to become household names: Luke Kelly and Barney McKenna of the Dubliners, Christy Moore and Andy Irvine of Planxty, Tommy Makem and the Clancy Brothers. I like to recall that our second All-Ireland Fleadh in 1968 was wedged between the 'Summer of Love' and Woodstock. So while the first was a triumph of Irish tradition and contemporary fashion, the second was a harbinger of great rock festivals to come, with all the colourful energy of 1960s youth culture on our small-town streets. It seemed anything was possible.

Yet as barriers came crashing down elsewhere, Clones was mired 'always on the vulnerable brink of a borderline existence'.[96] Indeed, its reality became the landscape of imagination for authors such as Maurice Leitch, in his *Poor Lazarus*, an award-wining novel banned in the Republic. That evocative tale of emotional displacement and stultifying isolation is set on the Armagh border in a town called 'Slaney', yet it is unmistakably Clones, from the hotel on 'Erne Square' with a long wall opposite painted with a named 'monumental works' and a café on the corner.[97] The 'erratic main street' rises to the Square with a canopied fountain dedicated to Queen Victoria, which is dominated by the towering Church of Ireland rising in the 'centre of an old grey town'.[98] The cinema is even called the 'Luxor'.[99] In the eyes of an outsider, this is 'no man's land. Only recently the spikes marking the line between North and South have been removed, ripped out like teeth from the tarmacadam. Blotchy scars remain. Great smuggling country ...'[100]

From the skeletal remains of the railway station, a new textile company emerged. Ernetex opened its modern factory where the former passenger platforms stood in 1962, combining and expanding on two smaller workshops on Whitehall Street and Jubilee Road. By 1963, it was churning out jersey fabric for export, and I had secured my first paid job – picking up litter on its expansive lawns for a weekly wage of half a crown (2/6d). The shareholders and directors were local, with the sole exception of the magically named Zigmund Starczynowski, who came in as general manager. Yet the initial wave of confidence soon crashed against the harsh reality of a border zone. By 1967, Ernetex had gone and the haemorrhage of jobs and hopes resumed. Fortuitously, fresh hope soon arrived with the meat-processing plant set up by Hugh Tunney in the old workhouse. Originally from Trillick in County Tyrone, Tunney soon acquired the former homes of the Pringles and Parkes on Cara Street, beside the old disused Ulster Canal Stores. Within ten years, Tunney Meat Packers had become Ireland's premier beef processor, with plants in Clones, Enniskillen, Belfast and Omagh, and a string of associated businesses on both sides of the border, including Dublin's Gresham Hotel. Yet it was far from plain sailing for Tunney's rapid expansion. A cloud of suspicion hung over some early Troubles-related incidents – a bomb attack on the main plant before installation of a new boning hall that brought in a huge contract for the US armed forces in Europe; or the bomb that destroyed the fat-rendering plant at Lackey Bridge, just outside the town.

There was no hint of internal wrongdoing, however, in the most chillingly awful incident, which claimed my old Clones schoolmate Larry Potter in March 1977.[101] Just 25 years old, and the father of two small children, Larry was the driver for a crew of fellow meat-boners dispatched to Tunney's plant in Whiteabbey, Belfast. A UVF bomb had been attached to the driveshaft of their vehicle by a piece of fishing line, which detonated the device as the van drove off. Big strong Larry died from his injuries two days later. The other boners from Clones, Newtownbutler and Roslea survived because he took the brunt of the blast.

It was inevitable that Clones would be sucked into the conflict on its doorstep. When the Dublin government responded to local defence committees in Belfast and elsewhere during the mayhem of the late 1960s, 'substantial funds' were lodged by the cabinet sub-committee 'to be accessed by republicans' from a Bank of Ireland account in Clones.[102] 'That was the birth of the Belfast Fund for the Relief of Distress,' according to Irish Army intelligence officer Captain James Kelly.[103] An initial £5,000 was lodged in the Clones account, held in the names of politicians Paddy Devlin and Paddy Kennedy, and west Belfast solicitor Paddy McGrory, all three of whom Finance Minister Charles Haughey vouched for as 'reputable men', according to Mary Murphy of the Irish Red Cross Society.[104] Two further lodgments of £5,000 were made by Haughey's personal secretary, Anthony Fagan. Sums of £2,000 were withdrawn on four dates in October and November 1969, and 'a significant portion found its way into the hands of the IRA'.[105] Shortly thereafter, the remaining funds in the Clones account were transferred to an account in Captain Kelly's name at a bank in Dublin.[106]

The influx of refugees and growing numbers of IRA men on the run created a 'febrile atmosphere' in border towns during the early 1970s.[107] Clones was regarded by many as too close to the border for comfort. It had been blasted a few times. In 1972, the town centre was wrecked and the Luxor Cinema doors blown open during one of many explosion scenes in *A Fistful of Dynamite*, starring James Coburn as a fugitive IRA explosives expert.[108] There were near misses, evacuations for hoax bombs, and one viable device on Fermanagh Street was defused by a customer who emerged from a nearby pub, re-entered after making the device safe and then fled out the back. Several people were injured by bombings over the years, including local grocer Eugene Cumaskey, who suffered serious wounds from a bomb in the Butter Yard.

Other families were affected by arrests for offences related to the conflict. Five young Clones men were given life sentences for the murder of Senator Billy Fox, who was shot during a raid a short distance from the town. By then, the very fabric of the town had been ripped asunder by the spillover of conflict. Minor yet despicable incidents of intimidation, or simply fear, prompted an exodus of Protestant families after Derry's Bloody Sunday. They moved north, and to Canada, depleting further the natural diversity of the town and its attraction to Protestant customers. More sinister influences played a role, too. I recall vividly a harrowing scene when a highly valued Protestant customer from the Clogher Valley called in to my dad one Sunday evening to tell him he could no longer frequent our drapery shop after a gunpoint warning from loyalist paramilitaries. Between sobs, this successful businessman spoke of his personal shame that he could no longer support a business that had helped his family when he was growing up in Clones.

With the loss of Protestant pupils from neighbouring Fermanagh, Clones High School had closed. Protestants from the town then crossed the border. Other Protestants who had once frequented the town stopped coming, especially after Douglas Deering, 52, a father-of-three shopkeeper from Roslea and member of the Brethren Assembly that worshipped at the Gospel Hall on the Jubilee Road in Clones, was shot dead in 1977.[109] The number of Protestant-owned businesses declined by two-thirds, according to a subsequent survey.[110] The Orange Hall was sold, as well as the last surviving Methodist chapel in a town that once boasted two thriving Wesleyan congregations. It closed its doors in 1982. The Presbyterian congregation on the Monaghan Brae was depleted, and the pews in St Tighernach's Church of Ireland were nearly empty; the Protestant Hall, the Meeting Rooms and other institutions began a slide to dereliction.[111]

As the conflict intensified across the border, Margaret Thatcher's government bowed to loyalist pressure to seal border roads. That meant practically every access road to Clones was cratered and sealed with massive steel spikes in reinforced concrete. A permanent checkpoint was set up at Kilturk, on the main road to Newtownbutler. Just beyond Lackey Bridge, a similar checkpoint was set up, even though the bridge itself had been blasted to impassability. The closure of the roads and the sense of utter abandonment by the Southern authorities exacerbated a bad situation, heightening suspicion and alienation. When a delegation from the town met Minister for Foreign Affairs Gerry Collins in the 1980s, he assured them he knew what it was like to live in a 'border town' because he was from the 'border' of Limerick and Kerry!

In all the doom and gloom of the 1980s, there was a brief period of golden sunshine, a time when a community that straddled the border bestrode the globe in a featherweight colossus. Boxer Barry McGuigan encapsulated hope for so many on both sides of the bitter divide, as the embodiment of a new Ulster. He was the Clones Cyclone to the core, exemplifying so many of the anomalies of our place – a Catholic married to a Protestant, living on the cusp of a 'southern' town but in the North, an Irish-born British champion who flew no flag and entered the ring to the strains of his showbusiness dad Pat singing 'Oh, Danny Boy'. Through a few short years, we rode the crest of his success, travelling by coach from Clones to the Ulster Hall and King's Hall in Belfast and win after win after win. All the way to Loftus Road stadium in London for the title bout against Eusebio Pedroza on 8 June 1985, we flew the banner of our town and came back as world champions. Clones was the toast and was packed with well-wishers and the simply curious, who wondered how it had languished alone for so long.

When the cheers subsided, Clones was all but forgotten in the harsh embrace of craters, concrete and life-choking checkpoints. Yet hope persisted, not least in elaborate plans to build the town's future on its rich past, as well as modern leisure centred on a Drumlin Heritage Centre. Professor Alan Rogers of the University of Ulster (Magee) in Derry convened a group of townspeople in December 1984, suggesting they conduct a survey of the needs of Clones. Published the following year, it provided a comprehensive assessment of all aspects of social, economic and cultural life, and plans for wider community action. Its many recommendations included using the canal buildings and towpaths for walking routes. In a 'personal note' at the end of the document, Rogers wrote:

> this has been the most exciting group I have worked with over
> many years in adult education. I have never met with such an

enthusiastic, committed and hardworking group; they have produced more work over the last few months than any other group, and I have at times found it hard to keep up with them.

Professor Rogers ended with the observation that:

Clones has many friends scattered throughout the rich society in which it stands; and in addition there are many others who are willing, like God, to help local communities who help themselves. Clones can call on all these resources to get things done.

The survey document was presented to the authorities, but apart from the formation of a dynamic Clones Development Society, it came to naught. The 'many friends' simply shook their heads and said 'Poor Clones.' The decline continued, with the loss of 80 per cent of retail businesses amid growing dereliction and depression.

Belfast journalist and raconteur Sam McAughtry found 'steep, narrow streets' in the 'home town of Barry McGuigan'; it was a 'friendly enough little town', he noted, 'but there's a certain apathetic air to it. It could be doing with a haircut and shave, and yet it's nice up there on its hill.'[112] Wexford-born Colm Tóibín remarked that:

If any town in Ireland deserved a hero it was the border town of Clones … Signs of former prosperity were everywhere … the old railway buildings, for example, the market house or the banks on the Diamond. The town was important as a place where rail lines crossed, a northern version of Limerick junction, an Irish version of Crewe. The northern railways were closed in 1959. Clones was also cut off from the North, its hinterland; the road was cut at Lackey Bridge on the border. It was a town which had gone to sleep.

He noted, pointedly, that 'it was also a town in which three or four hundred copies of the Provos' newspaper *An Phoblacht* were sold every week'.[113] Colm joined my uncle, local writer Eugene McCabe, and other family members, including me, to watch Barry McGuigan defend his world title against Steve Cruz. He describes in excruciating detail our reactions as, blow after blow, round after round, we watched Barry lose in Las Vegas. He followed with an allegorical pounding for a has-been champ's home town that could have been a contender.

Next day, Colm walked down to Lackey Bridge with my aunt Margôt, musing about Eugene's literary attempts to explain the situation in his Victims border trilogy. Unfortunately, he omitted two of the volumes and latched onto *Heritage*, which presented the Fermanagh loyalist perspective. It supported his view of what had happened here over the previous fifteen years:

> Some called it genocide, believing that Protestants were being picked off because they were only sons, and a farm might then fall into Catholic hands. Everyone knew that the IRA had an information network which was effective and local, which could trace the movement of people they wanted to kill. Protestants had good reason to suspect their Catholic neighbours.[114]

Colm wasn't alone. That view of genocidal and wholesale slaughter perpetrated by local Catholics against Protestants was promulgated widely, drip-fed from Paisley's first sweeping reference and the headline: 'Campaign of Genocide against Protestants'.[115] It echoed through the Third Force show of loyalist paramilitary strength. Alarmed by that paramilitarism, Orangeism launched its Committee for the Defence of Democracy, highlighting the plight of border Protestants, led by local Church of Ireland rector Reverend Alwys Kille, who affirmed 'the army and police are our tool of security'.[116]

Even those who didn't approve of Paisley's paramilitarism, subscribed to the alarmist view that Protestants were being systematically wiped out in an area where they 'make up about 20 per cent of the population … in this strife-torn part of Ulster'.[117] Each IRA attack on the security forces along the border was portrayed as an atavistic sectarian assault on Protestant neighbours, a cold-blooded terrorist land grab. Among those targeted in the Clones area was RUC Reservist and farmer John Kelly of Dernawilt. Shot in the head as he tended cattle, he crawled home with blood streaming down his face. He survived and his family subsequently moved from the area, including his young daughter, future DUP leader and Northern Ireland first minister Arlene Foster.[118]

As blanket security failed to stop IRA killings, resentment and suspicion grew. Yet little heed was paid to others who lived in fear and trepidation on the border – those whose lives were circumscribed by checkpoints, by neighbours in the security forces brandishing lethal weapons who felt that Catholics should not be trusted. Even amidst the stark fault lines of Northern Ireland, this border area stood out, David McKittrick, northern editor of the *Irish Times*, wrote:

> One of the most striking features of Newtownbutler and the surrounding district is just how many of the able-bodied Protestant men are members of the security forces, either the Ulster Defence Regiment or the RUC Reserve. There appears to be hardly any, in fact, who are not present or former members of some section of the security forces. It is a throwback to the time of the B Specials.[119]

And it was also a time of sectarian assassinations by loyalist gangs armed with weapons purloined from UDR armouries. A time when vivid memories of the Pitchfork Murders pervaded the community. While the *Irish Times* northern editor could describe the UDR men of south-east Fermanagh as 'sitting ducks', they certainly were not alone on the shooting gallery.

By 1992, senior British military instructors were drawing comparisons between Fermanagh and Bosnia. Patrick Darting, lecturer at the British Army's Staff College in Camberley, Surrey, suggested that assassinations and intimidatory acts to encourage Protestants to leave were a success for the IRA's 'long war' strategy.[120] The term 'ethnic cleansing' supplanted 'genocide', because it had 'an emotional truth for border Protestants as the continuing attacks and killings struck at their community's morale and sense of security'.[121] Among those using it to highlight the vulnerability of Fermanagh Protestants around Clones was Arlene Foster, then secretary of an organisation called FEAR (Fear Encouraged Abandoning Roots), formed in 1995.[122]

Ceasefires and peace promised relief at last, and a chance to rebuild the fortunes of Clones. Roads were reopened, permanent checkpoints disappeared, the siege lifted, life resumed. Yet Clones resembled a ghost town, its main thoroughfares a series of boarded up shopfronts interspersed with the walled-off dereliction of bombed sites. The cinema was gone. A total of forty-five once-thriving businesses – including my family's – were starved beyond endurance. Pubs once sustained by Sunday trade from the Sabbatarian North and big football matches had shut forever. The town changed as shoppers found new outlets. With a ranking of 9 out of a possible 10 in the socio-economic deprivation profile, Clones had become 'in effect, a microcosm of the conflict, exhibiting in sharp relief the experience of the southern border communities as a whole: loss of its hinterland; waves of economic decline; disinvestment by the state; the effects of physical violence, tension arising from the militarisation of the surrounding area; the fractured social connections arising from the road closures; Protestant exodus'.[123]

Yet there was still life in this community, which had managed to endure since Saint Tiernach founded a monastic city here in AD 500. An early highlight of peace was the 1996 filming of *The Butcher Boy,* based on local writer Patrick McCabe's novel of the same name. Local wags, many of them extras in the movie, observed that the set designers had an easy job preparing for the apocalyptic ravages of the climax. And director Neil Jordan wryly observed that 'If I want to quantify anything, I measure it against Clones. There is nothing you will ever encounter in life that you haven't seen in some form in Clones.'[124] *The Butcher Boy* still inspires the annual Clones Film Festival, billed as 'Ireland's biggest little film festival', where statuettes shaped as pigs' snouts are called 'Francies' after the film's main character.

Meanwhile, after an embarrassing hiatus of two years (2005–6), when 'increased capacity' was cited for using Dublin's Croke Park, the Ulster Football Final returned to Clones. Although it was refurbished in the early 1990s, the province's premier stadium has languished in neglect since then, and the Ulster GAA Council has shown unseemly haste in trying to shake Clones' dust from its feet. Plans announced in 2012 for a huge and costly stadium at Casement Park in Belfast have run the gamut of planning and safety concerns rooted in the insistence on crowd capacity greater than Clones. In what has become a costly embarrassment racking up more than £9 million before construction even begins, the Ulster GAA continues to seek planning permission for Casement while its Clones stadium declines further.[125]

However important links were re-established under the EU peace programmes in the Clones Erne East Partnership that restores Clones to the centre of its hinterland. A singular achievement has been the Peace Link, a state-of-the-art sports facility and home for Magheraveely FC (Div. 3, Fermanagh and Western League), the only venue in the Republic for matches played under the Irish Football Association. Unfortunately, a less successful venture of the Clones Erne/East Blackwater Project has been reopening the Ulster Canal. Even after all this time, the town awaits its arrival. That glimmer of light in the prospect of the canal, and all the achievements of EU assistance, an open border and restored respect for the town and its people now hang by a thread under the threat of Brexit.

3. Cloak and Dagger

Clones to Smithborough – 10 km (13.8 km via Analore)

It can be very hard to leave your hometown, as I find out shortly after resuming my walk along the Ulster Canal. It begins auspiciously on a bright spring morning. I climb down the bank at the Ulster Canal Stores and reach the towpath opposite by simply walking across the dried-out channel. Then it's an early morning amble past the proposed site for a wonderful new marina and the play-park beyond. In the background is a decapitated ninth-century round tower presiding over a graveyard where an ancient sarcophagus is reputed to hold the remains of Saint Tiarnach. Further into the background, the elegant steeple of the church named in Tiarnach's honour presides over my decaying birthplace. Yet all is fine until I reach what was once the Whitehall Street bridge, scene of our childhood regatta. The towpath of the Ulster Canal is inaccessible. On the opposite bank, however, a sturdy pathway runs as far as I can see. I choose that path more travelled, until it ends at the town's waste-water treatment plant. Sidling around the fence, I gain access to the canal's north bank past an improvised animal shelter constructed from waste materials, including road signs for Enniskillen and Cavan.

After negotiating the muddy bank for another few hundred metres, I reach an impassable side channel. I trudge back dejectedly. Beyond the waste-water plant, an in-filled section of the canal has muddy hoofmarks. I make my way onto the towpath where an old mile-stone is tilted slightly in the soft earth, its surface weathered and partly overgrown with moss. Its now indecipherable chiselled characters would have said it's 7 miles to

Smithborough, 13 to Monaghan, 24 to Caledon and 39 to Charlemont and the end of the Ulster Canal. Yet I am getting nowhere fast. So I set off, aware that I will have to improvise a path where the canal has been obliterated further ahead near Scarvey Bridge. I am overly confident for, having walked more than a kilometre, once again I find the canal had been cut into drainage channels, making further progress impossible. Anxiously, I trudge back as the klaxon from the meat plant at Teehill screeches that another steer has gone to the slaughter.

The factory squats above a muddy field: white steel walls, a giant reservoir tank, twin chimney stacks in the background and a post with twin lamps in the foreground. It occupies the site of a building that served a number of public functions before it was absorbed into beef baron Hugh Tunney's factory in the late 1960s, and then obliterated by the redevelopment of rival beef baron Larry Goodman. Prior to that, it was the local technical school, and before that, the part-time garrison of the Local Defence Force was billeted there during the Emergency. It was the town's scout centre in my dad's boyhood, and the headquarters for the Fifth Northern Division garrison following the Anglo-Irish Treaty, just after it was vacated by the British Army's King's Royal Rifles. Most significantly, however, it had been the workhouse, with accommodation for 600 people in the Clones Poor Law Union, which included eight electoral districts in counties Fermanagh and Monaghan.[1] It was also closely linked in time and space with the Ulster Canal, opening in 1842, just as the canal's final stage reached Lough Erne.

The workhouse proved a bigger draw than the new trade route, as successive potato-crop failures struck with devastating impact.[2] Thirty-eight per cent of the poor law union's entire population – 17,000 people – was lost. Thousands perished from starvation and disease, an estimated 12,500 of them buried in mass graves in the Bully Acre behind the workhouse. Others gathered what resources they could and fled, leaving behind 'an awful loneliness as silence fell over the countryside'. The catastrophe in this district of south Ulster fell with non-sectarian devastation on Catholics and Protestants. It was on a par with the more widely recognised devastation of Skibbereen in west Cork, or the Westport district of Mayo. Yet as my brother Brian's painstakingly detailed account *A Time of Desolation* (2000) noted, that memory was all but obliterated because it didn't fit the popular narrative of a disaster striking the impoverished Catholics of the west and south.

Clones was chosen as the third official venue for National Famine Commemoration Day in 2011. The date of the ceremony was shifted from May to October, avoiding a possible clash with the first official visit of Queen Elizabeth II to Dublin.[3] In the event, the autumn ceremony was the last major public function of President Mary McAleese in her home province of Ulster, yet it was largely unrecorded by the media, compared with the first two national commemorations. Another poignant ceremony took place a year later when the final part of the workhouse, the fever hospital, was demolished. It was noteworthy perhaps that the sizeable crowd that day included ministers from the local Presbyterian and Church of Ireland congregations, but no Catholic clergy.

Both the horror of the Great Famine and the trauma of partition centred to a large extent on that workhouse building. The evacuation of crown forces undermined the very identity of local loyalists. Their place was taken by the IRA's Fifth Northern Division, and their Clones headquarters was the nerve centre for the strategy of Michael Collins to frustrate the establishment of the Northern Ireland state through arms raids, kidnappings, property burning, summary executions and other confrontations.[4] Caught in the hybridity of their changing status from insurgents to National Army, the Clones soldiers were unequivocally loyal to Collins. Yet their ambivalent role and their border war was superceded by events further south, where an oath outweighed partition in the split of the Treaty. A British Pathé newsreel illustrates this. *IRA Guard the Northern Border* was filmed entirely within the precincts of Clones workhouse.[5] It opens with an armed IRA sentry in signature trench coat, wide-brimmed fedora hat and Sam Brown belt patrolling a lane at the side of the ivy-covered building, then it switches to a group of six uniformed Free State army officers walking past the workhouse gates and a thatched cottage, and then it switches to an armed group of uniformed soldiers, all smoking cigarettes casually as they search a car approaching from Comber Bridge on the Scotshouse Road. The newsreel was issued to cinemas on 23 February 1922, just eleven days after the railway-station gun battle.

Having turned from the truncated towpath, I am back on MacCurtain/ Whitehall Street and trying to re-engage with the Ulster Canal. A handy back route takes me through Beech Grove, where the ruins of a former brewery have been replaced by neat homes. I emerge on Analore Street and, walking along the elegant curve of Legar Crescent, I pass the bungalow Garda station on the other side. During the worst days of the Troubles, it housed a revolving garrison of about four dozen gardaí. Many were young and inexperienced, packed off for a compulsory stint of border duty on completion of training. Few, if any, lived in the town or even attempted to become part of the community. They knew little of the torn allegiances and scrambled identities of border people. They were outsiders and behaved accordingly. So relatively minor encounters often became confrontations. In his *Border Diary*, Shane Connaughton relayed the view of a garda stationed on the border for twenty years, half of that in Clones: 'Strange place, that. The people are different. That's my opinion … You'd go into a pub for a drink and they'd know you were a policeman. And they'd bang their glasses on the bar until you left. Politics, you see.' Connaughton adds, 'Along the border, feelings are hidden only when they have to be.'[6] Yet what that policeman found in Clones was the result of gradual change in which outside influences played no small part. Central to it was the work of the British Foreign and Commonwealth Office, the British Army, the Northern Ireland Office (NIO), the RUC and the British embassy in Dublin.

Documents uncovered in the British National Archives at Kew reveal an obsession with Garda operations in Clones during the early 1970s under the supervision of Sergeant Pascal McArdle.[7] While the 'charges' are barely specified in secret correspondence between the Foreign Office, the Dublin embassy, NIO and army authorities, they variously accuse McArdle of 'spying on the British Army in Northern Ireland' at the behest of the Fianna Fáil government, being a close ally of former minister Neil Blaney, and of being too friendly with local members of the Provisional IRA. The context is provided by a document described as 'Annex A', dated 14 December 1973, ascribed to 'British Army HQ 3 INF BGE' and entitled 'Garda Locations and Personalities'. It lists those above the rank of sergeant at every border station from Donegal's

Finn Valley to north County Louth. Listed for the County Monaghan stations are Chief Supt Cotterell, Supt McDonagh and fifteen others in Monaghan town, and for Clones, Sgt McArdle, Sgt Kelly and Sgt Padden. In all, seventy-seven gardaí are named. The document does not disclose the source of this highly sensitive information in the possession of the British Army's Third Brigade, based in Portadown and covering the Armagh, Fermanagh and Tyrone border with County Monaghan.

The interest in Garda deployment was not new, of course. A month before this document was filed, a letter dated 16 November 1973 was written by Kelvin White, head of the Foreign Office's Republic of Ireland Desk, to Colonel Charles Huxtable in the Ministry of Defence (MOD). It drew attention to a telegram from Ambassador Arthur Galsworthy highlighting a 'Border Report' from the Third Brigade saying it was 'still fuming about Sergeant McArdle' in Clones. White suggests that specific examples were needed 'which point either to active cooperation between Sergeant McArdle and the IRA, or to an unconvincingly passive attitude to the IRA'. He adds, 'We would be glad to have as thick a dossier as can be produced.' Six days later, on 21 November 1973, Huxtable of the MOD quotes the army's original 'Border Report' remarking that McArdle 'continues to exert a continuing disruptive influence in the Clones area'. This document names an agent, Mark Coe, who visited the Fermanagh military base covering the Clones area, then staffed by 1st Battalion Royal Tank Regiment. Coe briefed an Adrian Hill 'on his return', made it clear that specific complaints were needed 'if we are to have any chance of achieving Sgt McArdle's removal' and noted that this would be difficult since, after previous complaints, the sergeant was 'now taking care not to appear overtly sympathetic to the IRA'. A paragraph points out that McArdle had been stationed in Clones for sixteen or seventeen years, making him more of a 'village copper than … the young, ambitious police officer keen to enforce law and order in a situation of terrorism which we would prefer'. It adds that therefore, 'his sympathy could well be to his "local friends" rather than to the "IRA cause"'. The letter then goes on to allude to the 'predicament facing Dublin', which would need strong evidence for McArdle's removal on 'disciplinary' or 'administrative' grounds. To rectify this 'area of weakness in cooperation', it suggests that the 'simplest way out for them would be to promote Sgt McArdle and move him to an area away from the border!' A final paragraph points out that 'the level of co-operation' in the Clones area 'still lags behind others and presumably we can only wait either for the Irish to act or for Sgt McArdle to play into our hands'. However, at the top of the official and 'confidential' MOD letter, in what appears to be another handwriting style to the signature of Charles Huxtable, there is a note, dated the following day, 22 November, which says, 'I think we must try to rub Irish noses in the problems Sgt McArdle creates for his parishoners [*sic*], as opportunity arises.'

A telegram to the British Embassy in Dublin on the same day purports to offer evidence of McArdle's transgressions, pointing out that he 'has earned the reputation of being the most uncooperative Gardaí [*sic*] officer along the length of our border'. Transgression number one occurred on 10 May 1973 in the aftermath of the premature explosion of a landmine on the border at Roslea that killed Anthony Ahern, a 17-year-old IRA volunteer from Cork. McArdle arrived and met RUC Chief Inspector Currie, giving the latter 'the impression that he was in possession of detailed information concerning the background of the incident which he was not prepared to divulge'. To the RUC and army (16/5 Lancers) present, this 'indicated that his information came from those involved in this explosion, i.e. the Provisional IRA'. And 'in spite of RUC suspicions that further booby traps might still be deployed', McArdle's attempt to take away the young man's body, gave the 'impression that he was acting on behalf of Provisional IRA comrades of the deceased'.

The second transgression outlined in the 22 November telegram concerned a house at the Four Ash Trees, a colloquial name for the crossroads at Legnakelly, just outside Clones. The RUC had informed McArdle that it was 'being used as an HQ by local Provisionals'. The telegram says McArdle was 'seen to visit Four Ash Trees frequently but when pressed always replied that there was nothing of interest there', adding, 'it should be remembered that a well-known Provisional, Thornberry, was caught in that house by so-called loyalists on 10 Nov. 1973'. The telegram concludes that RUC M divisional command 'believes that he (McArdle) was employed by the Fianna Fáil government and had close links with Neil Blaney'.

What appears to be a briefing note, also dated 22 November, repeats the link with Blaney, who had long since been removed from the government after being implicated in the Arms Trial, the 1970 political scandal that resulted in his dismissal as a minister along with fellow cabinet member Charles Haughey for alleged IRA gun-running. Contradicting the observation that he had been stationed there for up to seventeen years, this document says it is 'understood' McArdle was posted to Clones on the orders of Lynch's government elected in 1966:

> with the object of making out a report on the border situation and it is believed that they also tasked him to travel privately into Ulster and assess the situation there. Whilst carrying out the latter task he developed considerable antipathy for the British Army.

It further alleges that he developed a 'close association with PIRA activists', naming one friend as Kevin McCooey, owner of the 'well-known PIRA meeting house' at the Four Ash Trees, where McArdle 'stayed for considerable periods of time'. Added to his lack of cooperation with the British security forces in apprehending 'insurgents', it cites his failure to 'pass on any useful information', which 'is not the case with most of the other border Garda representatives'. On that 'evidence', the commander of the Lancers had asked his Third Infantry Brigade commander to request McArdle's removal from the border on 19 May 1973.

Recording the renewed push to have McArdle removed six months later, the small cache from the National Archive turns up one further missive, a confidential cypher dated 28 November and signed 'Allan'. It instructs the Dublin embassy that it 'should not repeat not pursue' the McArdle case with Dublin's Foreign Affairs officials, because the RUC's Head of Special Branch Johnston and his deputy, Millar, were in Dublin that day and the case for removal of the senior Garda from Clones would be 'more effective coming from RUC' rather than the army.

I played alongside Pascal McArdle on the Clones Gaelic football team, and he is named on the Monaghan GAA Roll of Honour for his part in the county's 1956 All-Ireland Junior Football triumph.[8] He is remembered locally from a 1963 story of a Fermanagh punter who presented falsified betting slips at a Clones bookies, and then tried to break for the border when detected. Sergeant McArdle pursued him at a steady running pace and collared him right on the edge of his jurisdiction. A report of the subsequent court case remarked: 'He (the punter) won when he should have lost; and lost when he should have won!'[9] Obviously, McArdle's football prowess paid off in fitness. In the history of the Clones GAA club, he is pictured smiling with teammates in the 1965 Junior Championship.[10] He was an affable and well-integrated local policeman, so I am rather puzzled by the fixation on removing someone they could only accuse of truculence and an unwillingness to provide information about his community to a foreign security service. Yet clearly, it became a central concern of British policy in Northern Ireland during this period. So also did their determination to shut down the border. When Tory MP David Howell visited the area, he found the cooperation of Gardaí and Irish Army with the British security forces 'at best patchy', and he was told that 'co-operation from the police at Clones was lukewarm although Clones has as many bad men in it as Dundalk'.[11] Apparently, this view of the town was supported by the RUC and British Army.[12]

There can be little wonder at the disaffection of local communities from the policies being pursued by the British security forces. By January 1972, most of the 160 unapproved border roads had been rendered impassable during what was described in Dáil Éireann as 'lunatic' operations, when British troops openly 'challenged the Garda authority', 'hurled insults' at gardaí on the ground, and even crossed the border outside Clones, where they 'assaulted many locals'.[13] In what Irish Finance Minister George Colley called a 'provocative and dangerous' incident on 23 January 1972, for instance, British troops fired CS gas and rubber bullets at local people attempting to fill a cratered road at Aghafin, between Clones and Roslea. When uniformed gardaí tried to de-escalate tensions, they were 'deliberately targeted' by the soldiers and sustained 'minor CS gas related injuries'.[14]

Elsewhere, the British desire for closer security links was paying off, with the change from Jack Lynch's Fianna Fáil to Liam Cosgrave's Fine Gael-Labour coalition. The new government was regarded as tougher on security. In May 1973, British Ambassador Galsworthy told the Foreign Office that Justice Minister Patrick Cooney 'had instructed the Garda to cooperate with the Northern security forces in the suppression of criminal activities across the border', and 'all Garda superintendents in border areas knew that this was government policy'.[15] However, that very month, the 'Clones Incident' occurred. A van containing armed British soldiers was stopped by gardaí on the Diamond. The official British response was lies and obfuscation, contradicted by facts on the ground and naturally raising suspicion and distrust. Local Fianna Fáil politician Jimmy Leonard TD pointed out that the soldiers were caught only yards from where bombs had injured several innocent people, while his colleague Noel Lemass TD accused the British Army of bombing border towns and killing and dumping victims on border roads.[16] Foreign Affairs Minister Garret FitzGerald remarked that the 'security forces in Northern Ireland … clearly could not be relied upon to be frank with our police'. Little wonder then that Sgt McArdle distrusted his counterparts in Fermanagh.

Today, the Garda station is a shadow of its former self, an outpost with a sergeant and a few guards that operates until 5 p.m., when business transfers to Monaghan town and mobile patrol cars. The border has all but disappeared, but as Brexit looms in all its uncertainty, the lifeblood has been sucked from the home town I finally forsake by walking out Analore Road past a house that my parents built as their first home. They called it Corbiére after a lighthouse on Jersey in the Channel Islands where they honeymooned. I was their second child and I lived in it for only six months. My granddad's sudden illness prompted a flit to the home above our drapery shop on the Diamond, the first of many moves in my life.

Just beyond the town precincts where the level crossing of the Dundalk rail line once was, a small road to the right goes to the scenic Scarvy Bridge. That was my objective almost an hour ago on the towpath. Where the canal once ran are feedlots and silos built from the ruins of Clonavilla House, sadly demolished in yet another legacy of the Tunney beef barony. I had been given a newspaper cutting by Dan Kerr, whose mother sometimes worked there as a servant. Headlined 'Historic Clones House', the column is undated but it carries the byline of E.P. Sherry, once the local correspondent for the *Northern Standard*. It was an interview with Harford FitzGerald, then 73 and the last occupant of a house that had stood here for 400 years, surrounded by a hundred fertile acres. Prominent members of the Church of Ireland, the family also had a grand house at Clontask, where they donated land to the Catholic parish for the construction of the Connons chapel in Drumully. In a couple of paragraphs of the cutting, Harford FitzGerald describes 'a big freeze-up of about sixty-five years ago, when thick ice brought the canal transport to a standstill'. Three barges were marooned at Clonavilla. They provided a wonderful playground for Harford and his brother Marshall FitzGerald until ice-breaking barges with steel blades fitted on their sides reopened the channel after three days. The column adds, 'It was during this winter that a remarkable ice-skating competition was held from Clones to Monaghan on the canal which was illuminated with oil lanterns for the occasion and the winner was awarded a cup and £5.'

A less enchanting image of Clonavilla is provided in a book by a Canadian member of the FitzGerald clan.[17] James FitzGerald laments that 'three ageing sons of William, all sworn bachelors' with pretension of gentry, allowed the grand house to 'slowly rot' as they 'lived in collective lassitude and pigheadedness' while 'indulging in persecutory delusions of grandeur'. Then Harford, the last of eight family owners, sold it 'for a pittance' to the 'nouveau riche' tycoon Tunney, who set it ablaze in late 1974, 'laughing heartlessly as old Harford watched from the roadside, dumbstruck'.[18] The book adds that 'Harford died a sad and embittered man in 1980 at age 87', which suggests, incidentally, that my undated newspaper cutting was from 1966.

Immediately beyond the silos and feedlots at Clonavilla, giant pillars rise like twin colossuses from the middle of a field where once they supported the GNR line from Dundalk and Dublin. This was the south-eastern approach to the four-way rail junction through the level crossing, then a deep cutting and over the Red Bridge on the Monaghan Road, all landmarks of my childhood. A flat road has now replaced the humpbacked canal crossing once known as Mary Slowey's bridge after the woman who lived in the now derelict white cottage right beside it. Dan Kerr recalls a 'big iron sign' on this bridge that said 'Ulster Canal Company', but that sign is long gone. A gate on the left side gives access to the towpath. I resume my trek along the Ulster Canal and recall a voyage of trivial proportions commemorated in epic terms in a local song, 'Shipwreck on the Clones Canal':

Come all ye noble sailors and listen to my song,
Which I now will relate to you, and I'll not detain you long.
It's all about a ship and crew that never sailed at all,
Until the night they got a row on the Clones Grand Canal.

Chorus
The town was in a dreadful state, it being on a market day,
Whitehall Street was crowded from the hotel down to the quay;
To see us going on to board, sure it was a pleasant sight,
But later we thought we were going to the bottom that very night.

Our captain's name was Frank on the good ship *Mary Ann*
With divil a crew I ever knew that ever sailed from land.
There was a crate of wine and porter, and all things of that sort,
And James McElroy of the Connons Bog had twenty clamps of turf.

When we came to the Legar Mountain the wind began to roar,
Our captain he got up on deck and we all down below.
With a spyglass in his hand, 'Japers boys', he said,
'We'd best roll up our trousers and make a shape for land.'

When we came to Mary Slowey's bridge, there rose a terrible frost
And a wire from Killeevan said one hundred men are lost.
We thought of wives and children we never would see more,
When Billy Ramsey threw his scarf and he pulled us all ashore.

Quite near the site of Mary Slowey's bridge, a small area of thick woodland obscures the view of Bishopscourt, a stately home built here in the townland of Altertate Glebe in the early nineteenth century as the rectory for Clones parish. It was the home initially of Reverend Roper and his family, descendants of King Charles II and related to the earl of Sussex, whose Lennard family were principal landlords of Clones after the Plantation of Ulster. In the mid-nineteenth century, it was the home of Reverend Thomas Hand and his wife, Cassandra, who introduced crochet lacemaking to the area during the Great Famine; this variation on Venetian point lace, with unique motifs and a distinctive 'Clones knot', spawned a huge and once-thriving cottage industry that sustained many families through hard times. In a conciliatory address to an Irish conference on Brexit in Killarney, Arlene Foster illustrated the strong cross-border trading relations by recalling that her own grandmother used to cycle the few miles into Clones to sell the crochet lace she had made.[19] According to big-house historian Turtle Bunbury, the rectory was renamed as Bishopscourt at the turn of the twentieth century by the incumbent, Dr Charles Frederick D'Arcy, who had been elevated to bishop of Clogher and subsequently to archbishop of Armagh and primate of all Ireland.[20]

After the departure of Archbishop D'Arcy, Bishopscourt was acquired by the Mealiff family, later in-laws of Barry McGuigan, and the top portion was rented as a flat for some years by local solicitor Baldwin Murphy and his wife Judith. Then it passed through several ownerships as it faded and decayed. By the 1960s, the grand house was quite derelict, and its owners were living in Britain, when local Fianna Fáil politician Erskine Childers, who was soon to be president, suggested that it be used to house a garrison of the Irish Army after another car-bomb explosion blasted Clones during Christmas week of 1972.[21] An army spokesman confirmed that although troops were already stationed at Castleblayney and Cootehill, Clones was 'closer to the border and vulnerable to car bombers'. The garrison never arrived, but around that time, refurbishment work started on the mansion. Many of those involved as painters and decorators came from north Armagh and, it was said, at least adopted the guise of being 'on the run'. The house was then bought in the 1980s by Monaghan County Surgeon Archie Moore and his wife Miriam, who set about restoring it as a family home.

Back on the towpath of the Ulster Canal, there is water in the channel here, but certainly not to any navigable degree. And it is choked with reeds, grass and bulrushes, creating a wonderful habitat for a profusion of wildlife. The path is grass-covered but perfect for walking, and I stride along past Bishop's Lough to my right, where a lone swan glides along the glass-like surface. Beyond the lake, a couple of horses stand proudly on a hillside before shaking their heads in unison and galloping off. Apart from a bag of household rubbish dumped in the brush where a laneway cuts through the course of the canal for farm access, it is an idyllic walking route. It holds all the promise of a fully restored Ulster Canal. And the crowning glory of this section comes in the townland of Glear, with two impressive but overgrown canal locks, the sturdy ruins of the lock-keeper's cottage and, just beyond, a perfectly constructed humpbacked bridge.

The familiar Ulster Canal cottage has a distinctive semi-circular front, with windows affording views to the west, north and east so that the lock-keeper can spring to duty on arrival of a barge. The roof has deteriorated badly since I last saw it about fifteen years ago, and inside the rooms are open to the elements. The walls and woodwork are peeling, and discarded chairs and a Formica-topped table are slowly disintegrating together. This tiny but neatly built dwelling was once the home of the Reihill family, alive with the sounds of about a dozen children. One of them, John, a very well-known Clones character, lived here until 1994, when he passed away quietly in the thronged Bursted Sofa pub during a televised viewing of the Ireland v. Italy match in Giants Stadium in New Jersey, during the World Cup. The story goes that as the dearly departed John sat smiling as usual from a window seat while awaiting an ambulance, customers bought him another bottle of stout. John's boast had been that he was the 'richest man in Clones' because he lived 'on the bank … the canal bank'.

Over the bridge, through another gate and I'm back on the towpath and setting off through the townland of Creevleagh, where the canal curves gently along for a few hundred metres until, once again, the passage is obstructed by a huge overgrowth of impenetrable bushes and thicket. My attempts to find a way through arouse the curiosity of a herd of about a dozen young steers. They amble out of the field that opens off to the right. Resigning myself to yet another retreat, I trace my way back to the bridge at Glear, with the young cattle following me. I go through and then secure the farm gate. Sitting on the bridge for a moment, I look back at those big, expectant bovine eyes framed by bright yellow ear tags. I can sense their disappointment in me.

To my right, the little country road leads to the main N54 route between Clones and Monaghan, emerging just at the Four Ash Trees crossroads that once preoccupied Her Majesty's security personnel. To my left, the road soon rejoins the Clones-to-Newbliss route, and that will allow me to cross the River Finn and then track the canal route from a distance. I opt for new horizons on the far side of the Finn, and soon emerge onto the R183 road at Annaghkilly. A short distance ahead, the road takes a sharp left, then a sharp right on the picturesque Analore Bridge, its graceful cut-stone arches linking Clones to Killeevan parish. I can name the families that lived in the cluster of bridge houses – Keatings on the Clones side, Lynns and McAdoos on the Killeevan shore, the latters' house tucked in neatly just above the riverbank. Where the road turns sharply left once more, a small patch has been tended and planted with spring flowers, a colourful foreground for the small road ahead known as the Shades of Analore. It is a local beauty spot where beech trees arch gracefully over a short stretch along the riverbank. Around the next corner, on the main road, a parkland field resplendent with flowers sweeps up to a beautiful old stone cottage.

Another sharp left a few hundred metres along takes me back onto a parallel route, with the overgrown Ulster Canal towpath about a kilometre to its south. At a junction ahead, the road to the left leads to Stone Bridge, another crossing of the Finn and another boundary interface with Roslea parish, which is also divided in two by the border. In between, there is a small canal bridge with an attractive cottage. Local lore has it that a letter once landed at Clones Post Office addressed vaguely to 'something like fish, near Clones'; it was delivered here correctly to the McKerels!

I know that wee bridge and the road dip on this side, however, as the scene where my mother almost perished during severe winter flooding in 2013. Her car stalled and started filling rapidly with water. She used her mobile phone to summon the emergency services, and the operator asked her repeatedly for the road's reference number (it's L2140), which few, if anybody, would have known at the time. Luckily, guided by her directions, the local voluntary fire brigade from Clones arrived and winched my then 83-year-old parent from her vehicle before she succumbed to the flood or the numbing cold.

Back at my crossroads, a racing channel of water is neatly enclosed in sturdy banks as it hurtles headlong to the Finn. In pursuit of another channel, the canal, I walk straight ahead on the small country road that follows the townland boundaries of Annamakiff to the north and Drumcaw to the south. It is picturesque drumlin country of sharp bends and small steep hills, with modest houses tucked neatly into the folds. Once it was the hub of a thriving linen industry – flax-growing, beetling, scutching, hackling, spinning and weaving – a prosperous rural economy of small mills and cottage enterprises bound inextricably by road, rail and canal links to Belfast along the watersheds of Ulster's two great inland water systems, the Erne and Lough Neagh. Lines of communication along these valleys were conduits for commerce and radical politics.

In the 1790s, the 'Mighty Wave' of United Irish Society politics swept west from Belfast to Monaghan – and beyond, into Cavan and Fermanagh – through distribution of the *Northern Star* newspaper and other radical literature. As William Mayne, agent for the Clones estate, remarked to his employer Lady Dacre on 16 July 1792, local Presbyterians were 'inclined much to [Thomas] Paine's principles' and had 'imbibed a dangerous democratic spirit'.[22] A sharp rise in sectarian tensions in south Ulster brought harsh suppression of United Irish sentiment. That spurred the first inroads of Orangeism and by 12 July 1796, the Orange Lodges of Monaghan and Fermanagh were strong enough to hold their first walk at Drum, County Monaghan.[23] Yet the spirit of revolution persisted among the largely Presbyterian population in the area. By May 1797, hundreds of people carrying white flags and singing republican songs were going throughout the district around Newbliss doing farm work for imprisoned neighbours. Local landlord Alexander Ker of Newbliss raised his yeomanry and, with a party of North Lowland Fencibles, attacked people setting potatoes at Leysborough, now Annaghmakerrig.[24] Eleven were killed, many wounded, more arrested.[25] Thus began a wave of terror that quelled the republican spirit and restored loyalist hegemony in the district.

Despite opposition from some Monaghan and Armagh Orange lodges, who feared it would bring Catholic emancipation, the Act of Union came into force in 1801, having been moved in the House of Lords by Lord Cremorne. His family, the Dawsons, later became earls of Dartrey after the west Monaghan barony encompassing Clones, Newbliss, Rockcorry and points between. What republican sentiment survived among local Protestants was diluted further in the great migration from south Ulster in the economic depression that followed the Napoleonic Wars. Among those who departed were the McCullum family from Radeerpark and the Corbetts of Analore. They settled in Miramachi in New Brunswick, and their direct descendant Mary Baldasaro became my great friend and a wonderful day-carer for my two young sons when I was a lone parent far from home in Canada. Her ancestors probably left Killeevan parish because of the collapse of the cottage linen trade because of competition from the steam-powered textile mills in the big towns and cities.[26]

Even with the exodus of so many Protestants from south Ulster, the union held strong, apart from a slight waver when Monaghan in 1826 voted for Henry Westenra, the third Lord Rossmore, who favoured Catholic emancipation. Belfast journalist 'Honest' Jack Lawless hailed Daniel O'Connell's 'invasion of Ulster' and declared that he would enter Ballybay, an 'almost exclusively Presbyterian' town at that time, for a rally. That prompted 8,000 'determined' Orangemen armed with muskets, swords, bayonets, pitchforks, scythes and other weapons to gather and force Lawless and his supporters to divert to Rockcorry by a 'circuitous route'.[27] That settled the tussle for the area and loyalism was back comfortably in the driving seat when another Lord Rossmore (the fifth) led thousands of Monaghan Orangemen to Roslea to prevent a Parnellite meeting in the Fermanagh village in October 1883. Over the following thirty-five-year home rule crisis, the loyalists of Dartrey proved their mettle. When the Ulster Defence Union was formed after the second home rule bill in 1893, and each constituency allocated delegates to its ruling council in proportion to unionist electorate, North Monaghan had thirteen, the same as South Down and Mid-Tyrone, while South Monaghan had six.

Sitting comfortably within the fold of Ulster on the map of Ireland, Monaghan's demographic and political profile was virtually indistinguishable from neighbouring districts of Fermanagh, Tyrone and Armagh. Indeed, Monaghan loyalists were among the first to rally to the cause of Ulster unionism during the great mobilisation of the 1912 home rule bill. Long before the much-vaunted Carson Trail of rallies leading to Ulster's Solemn League and Covenant, a huge demonstration was held in Omagh at the very beginning of January 1912. It drew 30,000, with strong contingents arriving on special trains from Clones, Newbliss, Castleblayney, Smithborough, Monaghan and Glaslough.[28]

By September 1912, there was strong support for the Covenant in Monaghan, as evidenced by 10,000 signatures, and this was then reflected in two battalions of Ulster Volunteers, comprising well over 2,000 men at arms. The Monaghan regiment's 2nd UVF Battalion, based at Clones under the command of Colonel Madden, enlisted more than 1,000 men at its peak, in an area extending to Ballybay, with main drill areas at Drum, which included Scotshouse; Clones, including Stonebridge and Drumully; and Ballybay. Newbliss had its own section, with an additional UVF nursing brigade for the county under the command of a Miss Murray-Ker. The UVF companies gathered in Newbliss for inspection when Sir Edward Carson came in August 1913 to visit the 'outposts of Ulster'.[29] He found ranks of trained men under a strong, structured officer corps determined 'to ensure the regiment was militarily ready for any eventuality', according to the popular historian of loyalism Quincey Dougan.[30] In early 1914, the Monaghan and Fermanagh UVF organised a 'war camp' at Lord Erne's

Knockballymore House, just outside Clones in County Fermanagh.[31] Three hundred men spent the weekend under instruction in drill, firearms and other martial skills. Such was the scale and intensity that London's *Daily Sketch* and other newspapers had extensive coverage, including front-page photos of local men and officers, such as Colonel J.C. Madden, in motorbike squadrons and simulated attacks.

Home rule was put on hold for the duration of the First World War, but Ulster's resolve to stand alone was demonstrated in the 36th Ulster Division of Kitchener's new army in which the UVF was allowed to retain its formations and officers in thirteen additional battalions for existing Ulster regiments. Monaghan men joined up through their UVF units and were enlisted in the Armagh-based Royal Irish Fusiliers. They took part in major engagements, including Suvla Bay. What is less widely known is that the RIF fought in Dublin during the 1916 Rising, and among them was Joseph Clarke from Newbliss, who had emigrated to Canada briefly and returned to 'do his duty'.[32] Two of Joseph's comrades were killed in Dublin and six wounded. Then Joseph's brother William, also of Newbliss, died from wounds he sustained at the Somme on 1 July 1916. He'd been shot in the left leg and stomach, and had also lost his right eye.

In that same year, a convention at Trinity College Dublin began formulating a settlement of the home rule question on whether to exclude Ulster, or part of it. Over the course of its deliberations, the unionists of Monaghan, Cavan and Donegal were prevailed upon to set aside their demands for the duration of the war. Their concession came back to haunt them in 1920 when, in an egregious renunciation of Ulster's Solemn League and Covenant 'to stand by one another', representatives from the three counties were shown the door of the unionist convention in Belfast's Ulster Hall, and told they were superfluous to need. The rhetoric became more dismissively shrill in the House of Commons, when Captain Charles Craig, brother of the imminent Northern Ireland premier, declared that 'no sane man would undertake to carry on a parliament' with an extra 70,000 unionists, who would bring 'some 260,000 Sinn Féiners and nationalists' with them.[33]

The breach of Covenant with those Ulster unionists from the 'lost counties' consigned to the Free State was particularly hurtful to the almost 50,000 Presbyterians among them.[34] Their sense of utter betrayal by fellow Covenanters, their crisis of identity in being 'in Ulster but not of Ulster', in the words of Reverend Waterson of Aghabog, was pervasive and persistent. It more than matched the sense of vulnerability felt by Catholic nationalists marooned in the new Northern Ireland and forsaken by their erstwhile compatriots in the Free State. Rubbing salt in the wound was the persistence of the new Northern Ireland government and unionist spokesmen in using the term 'Ulster' to denote only the six counties. This exacerbated the confusion for the Ulster Protestants of Monaghan, Cavan and Donegal. Canon Given of Dartrey remarked:

> Our position is a very curious one. We are not in Ulster, according to the new law. I wonder where we are. Neither are we in the South. We are the buffers between the North and the South. Ulster, or rather six counties of it, has adopted home rule in its own way. We in the other three counties are outside of home rule …

For loyalists on the wrong side of the border, the 'pragmatic policy' adopted by Carson and Craig constituted both a 'callous betrayal and a repudiation of the very essence of unionism'.[35]

Many Protestants in this area of north Monaghan also experienced a strong sense of abandonment by Britain with the Anglo-Irish Treaty in 1921, but kept their hopes alive until 1925 that the Boundary Commission would 'put them back on the right side of the border'.[36] Others decided to put themselves on their chosen side, and moved across the new border. Many did so with help from the Clogher Fund, which was established under the aegis of the Orange Order to facilitate Protestants moving to Fermanagh, where the population was finely balanced but favoured nationalists. In 1925, a private census was presented to the Boundary Commission by the Enniskillen law firm of James Cooper MP, listing 2,117 Protestants from the Free State who had taken up residence in Fermanagh since 1920.[37] Most of those were from neighbouring counties and did not relocate any great distance. Some were retired couples and individuals, but many were young families. From Killeevan parish, for instance, there were the Corbetts and the

McClellands, both families with eight children. From Newbliss, there were the Scotts, with seven children, and the Knoxes, with four. Samuel Hicks, his wife and eight children moved into Fermanagh from Drum; the Halls and Johnstons moved from Smithborough, both families with six children; the Fergusons from Stonebridge moved with five; and the Sheridans from Clones with four.

When the Boundary Commission hearings convened in Enniskillen, two significant submissions were made for the transfer from the Free State of Protestants in the Clones area. Church of Ireland Protestants between Clones and Smithborough who attended Clough church beside Roslea cited compulsory Irish when presenting their case for transfer to Northern Ireland.[38] Meanwhile, the influential owner/editor of the *Impartial Reporter* in Enniskillen, William Copeland-Trimble, urged the transfer to Northern Ireland of a large 'unionist' area comprising Drummully, Currin, Killeevan and Aghabog parishes to the south and west of Clones, with territorial compensation for the Free State in Roslea and the mountainous district to its north.[39] Neither of these proposed transfers of Protestant districts was adopted in the shelved report of the Boundary Commission, but the transfer of Roslea and the Sliabh Beagh district was included.

In those early years, according to historian David Fitzpatrick:

Loyalists were less concerned about the border than about survival, few being free from the fear of murder, arson and intimidation. The reiterated destruction of the sites of the Protestant community, such as churches, Orange halls and Masonic halls, surely reinforced the very fraternal bonds which such outrages were designed to snap ... Though systematic anti-loyalist campaigns occurred even in remote Cork, the Ulster border counties were the site of the most intense sectarian violence outside Belfast.[40]

Eoin O'Duffy, appointed as the first commissioner of An Garda Síochána, was charged with protecting loyalists, yet during his leadership of the IRA in Monaghan and throughout Ulster, he had ordered frequent raids on Protestant homes, and made repeated references to the 'robber gang of Drum'. That sentiment was reciprocated in the almost exclusively Protestant village, where he was 'celebrated' in a local song:

> Just after dark another squad come in from Clones town
> In command of Eoin O'Duffy the village to surround
> But like their other leaders he is just another bum,
> For he left his comrades to their fate in the famous town of Drum.[41]

There was a widespread conviction that unionist households throughout Monaghan were well armed with legal firearms as well as covert caches of military weapons from the days of the UVF mobilisation. Quincey Dougan says it is clear that the Monaghan UVF had been engaged in its own gun-running activities prior to the general landings of April 1914, but it also took part in the Donaghadee gun-running, and secured a consignment of Swiss-made Vetterli rifles from that. Dougan says that in the 'ratio of man to weapon', Monaghan 'was the most well-armed unit of the UVF following the gun-running', with 'an incredible 1,678 rifles for its 2,095 men'.[42]

That certainly became an issue for the even more plentiful force of some 5,000 National Volunteers who metamorphosed into the IRA in the War of Independence. In the general raid for arms of September 1920, Protestant homes were specifically targeted. Former volunteer John McKenna recalled:

> In [the] Newbliss area, about 50 per cent of the population were unionist. Some of the unionist young men did armed duty on the roads at night. On one occasion William Quigley, Drumbrain, a Volunteer in the Newbliss company of the IRA, was fired on and wounded by a party of unionists.[43]

The Newbliss IRA company 'raided all the unionist houses'. In the adjoining district of Aghabog, an IRA volunteer in the local company 'was wounded during an exchange of fire in raiding a unionist house and, as a result, lost one of his eyes'; in the Rockcorry area, 'a Volunteer named Reilly was shot dead during an exchange of fire in the raid on a unionist house'. The IRA got virtually nothing of value in these raids. Moreover, such testimony and the disclosure that O'Duffy found refuge on the night of the Shantonagh RIC barracks raid in the 'residence of the Parish priest of Killevan' illustrates the overtly sectarian nature of the campaign he conducted.

Republican violence in Monaghan was 'inevitably more sectarian than much of the rest of the country', according to Fearghal McGarry of Queen's University Belfast, who notes that the pattern of violence against Protestants in Monaghan was 'little different' from that highlighted in Peter Hart's research on Cork, where more than two hundred civilians were killed. 'The main target group was the Protestant minority, followed by ex-soldiers, tinkers and tramps and others seen as social or political deviants.'[44] However, he adds, 'If O'Duffy was responsible for some of the questionable murders which took place under his command, he was also responsible for the relative restraint demonstrated by the IRA during this period.' O'Duffy's role in the Roslea atrocities, he argues, provided 'the exception rather than the rule'.

On 5 February 1921, Special Constable George Lester received a 'threatening' letter in relation to the Belfast Boycott, and then, using a weapon, he confronted the wife of a neighbour who was active in Sinn Féin. On 21 February, Lester was shot and wounded as he opened his shop in Roslea village, his brother driving off the IRA gunman whose weapon then misfired.[45] A large force of police, Specials and military took over Flynns' pub in the village. Fearing reprisals, local Catholics began to evacuate their homes. That night, the Specials burnt out many of the Catholic homes in the village. Among the houses attacked was the home of a Catholic priest beside the police barracks. In that case, however, a rifle butt used to ram the priest's door discharged a bullet in the breach and wounded one of the attackers.[46] The Burning of Roslea is commemorated in a local rebel song:

They roamed through the town like a pack of wild boars,
They broke all the windows and hammered the doors,

They pillaged and looted and carried away,
The stuff of poor Catholics, ri-tor-al-aye-ay.[47]

According to John James Connolly, captain of the Roslea IRA company and subsequently a Garda officer, all the officers of the 5th Northern Division attended a meeting at Derryhinlish, heavily guarded by the IRA. The door burst open and the man who strode in turned out to be Frank Aiken, commander of the 4th Northern Division (later, IRA chief of staff and a senior Fianna Fáil government minister). At first Aiken opposed reprisals, but when O'Duffy assured him that the Specials would not retaliate if they 'hit them hard', he said, 'Well burn them and their houses.'[48] A list of approximately twenty-one houses was drawn up, and O'Duffy assigned between eight and ten men, including scouts, to attack each one. Company commanders James McKenna and Matt Fitzpatrick took joint charge of the operation.

About sixteen of the targeted houses were attacked on the night. In one vicious incident, Special Sergeant Samuel Nixon was caught in bed and shot twice.[49] He got up and returned fire until loss of blood and his wife's pleas made him surrender. He handed over his rifle and was shot dead. Ironically, his house was not burnt because the IRA attackers did not want to leave his large family homeless.[50] His neighbour, Special Constable William Gordon, returned fire and wounded an IRA man. A bomb was thrown through the window and Gordon was killed. Both men are commemorated on a local Orange Lodge banner. Loyalists claimed that a third man, who was not a member of the Specials, was dragged from his house and beaten, dying later from his injuries. Four more houses were burnt and arms taken, while two IRA men were reported killed and five wounded.[51] One of the wounded was Matt Fitzpatrick.

John McGonnell, captain of the IRA's Newbliss company, was at Aghafin, on the Clones side of Roslea village, where Matt Fitzpatrick of the Wattlebridge company was wounded in the attack on the home of a 'unionist named Magwood'.[52] McGonnell recalls how they got a pony and trap from a man called McQuaid at Drumadraney, Stonebridge, and carried Fitzpatrick to Joseph O'Duffy's house at Annagoes, Newbliss. There he was tended to by Dr Canning of Rockcorry and subsequently by Dr May Kearns of Glynch House, Newbliss. Fearing that Fitzpatrick's location was becoming too widely known, the IRA then moved him to Joseph Beggan's house in the same locality. However, when Benny McMahon, captain of the Clones company, called to see him, he was stopped and arrested as he cycled home and the military and police then followed his wet cycle track all the way back to Beggan's house, where they found Fitzpatrick badly wounded.

In his memoir, Patrick Shea said that the Black and Tans wanted to finish him off there and then, but his RIC Head Constable father sent them into Clones for an ambulance and had Fitzpatrick conveyed under guard to Monaghan Infirmary, whence he escaped after a brief recovery. He later thanked the former head constable for saving his life.[53] By that time, Inspector Shea had been relieved of duty as the RIC awaited disbandment and the instatement of the new Civic Guard (Garda Síochána). For his part, the ill-fated Fitzpatrick had become acting commandant of the Fifth Northern Division of the new National Army after the Treaty.

In 1923, when the only Twelfth parade south of the new border was scheduled for Clones, Ernest Blythe stepped in as the Free State's only Protestant minister to recommend that the Civic Guards and military take 'special, but unostentatious precautions, to ensure that no unpleasantness occurred'.[54] An estimated fifty lodges marched two miles from the station to the Killygoonagh field, just across Analore Bridge. They were greeted by Grand Master Michael Knight, and he especially welcomed brethren from County Cavan, who had 'also passed through deep water and through troublous times'.[55] The guards subsequently reported that 'everything passed off very quietly' except for four arrests following the seizure of a 'large quantity of intoxicating liquor' on the public road.[56]

Yet the pervasive sense of peril, bitterness, displacement and abandonment persisted for the remainder of the century, as Protestants were fed anecdotal folklore of atrocities during and after the time of partition. Their fear was manifest and expressed in various ways. Walter Keating of Corkish, Drum, told of raids on Protestant homes and his grandfather burying his precious Orange Lodge banner in the bog for three or four years for fears of it being seized and burned.[57] On the other side, animosity was fuelled by the sweeping justification that Protestants were unionists and disloyal to the new state. There were frequent atrocities as late as mid-1925, when Gardaí were investigating the abduction of Humphrey Mitchell from his Aughnamullan home by armed men who 'tried' him before a kangaroo court and ordered him to pay £15 in two weeks or be burnt out.[58]

Nevertheless, annual parades of the loyal institutions continued in the district over the following years, encouraging the Protestant communities in Cavan and Leitrim to hold parades too, according to David Fitzpatrick of Trinity College Dublin. In July 1931, however, an all-out attack on Orangemen parading in Leitrim by armed men thought to be IRA was followed in August by an equally 'ferocious attack' on a parade in Cootehill of Monaghan and Cavan Royal Black Presbyteries, whose ornate banners with biblical themes were seized. The following year, the guards gave assurances that there would be 'no interference' with the county Orange demonstration planned for Clones, so the Monaghan Grand Lodge declined invitations to parade with their brethren across the border. However, in late June, the grand master received intelligence from a 'very reliable source that arms were being distributed by the same party who had caused all the trouble at Cootehill, with the object of interfering with our July demonstration' as a reprisal for 'attacks which have been made on Roman Catholics recently in the six counties'.[59] The Clones parade was abandoned without dissent, and no further county demonstrations took place.

Small church parades by Orange Lodges, and annual 'picnics' in Drum and adjacent strongholds, became the social mainstay of rural Protestantism through the succeeding decades. Yet Monaghan Orangeism continued to thrive through mutual support and the close proximity of brethren in Fermanagh, Tyrone, Armagh and Cavan. In 1935, Michael Knight put at 1,000 the number of active Orangemen in the county's forty-eight lodges.[60] Forty of those lodges were still active thirty years later, with an estimated 700 members, while Cavan had forty-three lodges (down from seventy-six), and Donegal brethren mustered at about 300 in 1965, affiliated to only seventeen lodges, according to Grand

Orange Lodge of Ireland reports. The figures show that almost half a century after partition, the Orange culture and tradition in Monaghan was almost indistinguishable from neighbouring counties in Northern Ireland. More than 10 per cent of the entire non-Catholic population – a third of all Protestant men – were Orangemen, according to Trinity's David Fitzpatrick. The Troubles along the border led to a subsequent decline in membership, he noted.[61]

The border Protestant distrust of the Free State authorities since the early years of partition also extended to the unionist establishment in Belfast. 'Since partition, we are totally alienated from government, we distrust unionists; we distrust politicians; you name it we distrust them and we have every reason to distrust them,' said Angela Graham from Drum. 'We have a sense of righteous betrayal about our forefathers and mothers signing the Ulster Covenant and the (women's) Declaration. We were just kicked into touch' and 'became very disillusioned people …'[62] As for interaction with Catholic neighbours, Protestants in Monaghan were generally noted for 'keeping their heads down and their mouths shut'.[63]

After a considerable loop and a gentle climb at Bouhill, I join the 'main road' from Killeevan to Smithborough and resume a course parallel to the Ulster Canal. A pretty hilltop copse in the townland of Bessbrook enfolds the site of a megalithic tomb known hereabouts as the Giant's Grave. I recall an historical walk about twenty years ago with the Killeevan Historical society when we made our way along a tiny winding road in this locality and learned that a small stream once powered nine flax and corn mills as it coursed its way to the River Finn. At the time, the landscape was dotted with small derelict homes, the evidence of migration over the decades away from a forgotten frontier zone. Today the houses that remain are mostly modern, comfortable dwellings, some with adjoining farm buildings testifying to the strong agribusiness economy of this region, based on dairy, poultry and mushroom production. In an economy dominated by intensive farm production, food processing, light agricultural engineering and other agribusiness ventures, there are real fears that Brexit would be economically disastrous as well as presenting huge security implications in a district not long recovered from a traumatic legacy.

As the road rises further to the east, the view presents a vista to the north where the River Finn flows south from the Sliabh Beagh hills above Roslea. Then between the main N54 road and the Ulster Canal, it veers off sharply to the west and Lough Erne, as if recoiling from the townland of Tircooney. That was the scene of an atrocity that encapsulated Protestant fears in this district during the modern Troubles. On the night of 11 March 1974, this was the quiet rural setting of one of the most notorious events of the Troubles. What happened is the subject of fear-driven recollection, conjecture, speculation and rumour, lots and lots of rumour.[64] Yet the outcome was starkly real; a young, vibrant and deeply committed political representative was found dead in a ditch and five young men from Clones would spend decades in prison as a result. Less palpable was the lasting impact of the murder of Senator Billy Fox on all the strands of the wider community.

For those who recall this incident from the crowded catalogue of horrors of those times, there is a vaguely familiar narrative. On that Monday night in March 1974, a gang of about a dozen masked gunmen burst into the mobile home of farmer George Coulson, his wife Audrey and their two young children. The raiders demanded arms. They tied George's hands behind his back and took him to the adjacent house, where they ordered his father Richard, his mother, a retired teacher and his sister Marjorie to lie on the floor. George was then forced to show them around the property, which they ransacked in a futile search for a weapons cache. In an act of provocative desecration, one raider threw the family Bible into the blazing fireplace. While this was happening, Billy Fox drove into the lane, coming home from Dublin to visit his girlfriend, Marjorie, a senior nurse at a Belfast hospital. Fox was forced from his car at gunpoint, but in the darkness, he managed to run away from the armed gang. They fired and the senator disappeared from view. The gang forced the Coulsons outside, set fire to the house and mobile home, and then dispersed.[65]

Gardaí at Aghafin, a short distance away near Roslea, came to investigate a red glow in the night sky. They met George Coulson in the laneway. He alerted them to the missing senator. Even before Billy Fox's body was discovered, however, two young men were already in custody at Clones garda station. After the raiding party broke up, they had flagged down a car on the main road to Clones, and found that it was an unmarked garda car. The pair had a shotgun, which they explained by saying they had been hunting, an excuse not believed by the gardaí. Despite several searches by gardaí and army, it was not until 9:30 a.m. that Fox was found dead in a field about a quarter mile from the house. His inquest in May 1974 was told he was shot in the chest and foot and also had scratches and a bruise on his head, as well as abrasions and lacerations. That same month, five Clones men, who refused to recognise the court, were convicted of murder and sentenced to penal servitude for life.[66]

From those agreed details the narrative becomes less coherent in the absence of a full trial, with testimony and details of the investigation. Gaps are filled by disjointed episodes that now seem bizarre twists. For instance, in the immediate aftermath, the IRA issued a statement:

> The IRA was not involved in any way in the activities which resulted in the death of Senator Billy Fox. We have repeatedly drawn attention to the murderous acts of a group of former B Specials from County Fermanagh. This group is led by serving officers of the British Army. Mr Fox was known personally to a number of the leadership of the republican movement.[67]

A parallel statement of innocence from Sinn Féin President Ruairi Ó Brádaigh pointed out that Fox had actively protested with republicans. A phone call to an Enniskillen newspaper from a 'Captain Wilson' of the Ulster Freedom Fighters claimed responsibility for Fox's death, saying he resisted when questioned and it was 'regrettable' that he was Protestant, but 'he had been watched by the UFF who believed he had links with the IRA'.[68] And even between the crime and the trial, a man in court for IRA membership identified himself as a senior member of the East Tyrone battalion, and said he was the first to raise the alarm when he was driving past, stating 'categorically that neither he nor anyone connected with him had anything to do with the shooting of Senator Billy Fox'. Furthermore, there was an alleged unsworn trial statement from one of the accused, disassociating himself and his co-accused from the murder and arson, saying they 'profoundly regret the death of Senator Fox', and suggesting that he was killed by one of the unidentified 'north men' who instigated and led the raid.

Meanwhile the rumour mill was running, with speculation that Fox confronted the gang, ripping the balaclava off one man and remarking that he recognised him; that he was riddled by nine bullets, the raiders standing over him for the fatal shots; that it was planned as a general 'message to Protestants' but went wrong; that it was a specific plan to get Billy Fox and nothing to do with the Coulsons. The claims and disclaimers certainly fuelled one line of thought: that Billy Fox was slain because of his political activities.

The young politician had been dogged by taunts from 'both sides of the fence'. In 1969, soon after he had won a parliamentary seat on his second attempt, the young Fine Gael deputy for Monaghan was accused in the Dáil chamber by a senior Fianna Fáil minister of being a member of the B Specials. According to a parliamentary sketch by John Healy published on 4 March 1970, Local Government Minister Kevin Boland withdrew the charge in a 'rare personal statement' a week later, even though it was not included in the official record.[69] The erroneous charge persisted, however, as it did for other Protestants living south of the border.[70] Posters appeared in Fox's Monaghan constituency advertising 'Vacancies for B Specials – Apply to Billy Fox'.[71]

Fox was never in the B Specials, but he was certainly involved in highlighting the plight of border communities due to the closure of roads. As a former activist in the Irish Farmers' Association, he had an understanding of the difficulties faced by the rural communities, and he was catapulted to the forefront of efforts to keep the roads open. It cost him politically when in December 1971, he was ejected from the Dáil chamber for producing two rubber bullets and a CS gas canister that had been fired into the South during a road-filling altercation at Aghafin, outside Clones. Despite being loudly heckled by Fianna Fáil deputies, Fox had stood his ground until Foreign Affairs Minister

Patrick Hillery was forced to admit that the British were pursing a 'lunatic policy' on the border.[72] Fox's photo with the projectiles in question was on the front page of the *Irish Independent* the following day.[73] Despite the misgivings of many Protestants, Fox kept harrying the government on the road closures. His main concern, however, was that residents would not be left alone to confront the British Army on road cratering being carried out illegally in the southern jurisdiction. To this end, he wanted a permanent Irish Army presence on the border.[74]

Yet the impact on his electoral base was catastrophic, and political friends on the ground estimated that it cost him his seat in the 1973 election. Peadar McElroy and Packie Boyle reckon that there were between 6,000 and 7,000 votes in Monaghan that were strongly influenced by the Protestant Association, a registration, electoral and lobbying body set up under the aegis of the Orange Lodge shortly after partition. In 1969, Fox grabbed the lion's share of these votes. In the subsequent election, he 'didn't get half a dozen' though he did pick up republican votes in north Monaghan. Protestant electors on the doorstep called him 'Bogside Billy' because of his apparent alliance with republicans on the border-roads issue.[75] So while he pulled in more first-preference votes than the second Fianna Fáil candidate, he lost the third seat because of a dearth of transfers from fellow Protestant candidate Erskine Childers.[76] He was consigned to the Senate, and then passed over for Brendan Toal as the Fine Gael candidate in the November 1973 Monaghan by-election caused by Childers' accession to the Irish presidency. On that occasion, Fox's party recaptured the Dáil seat.[77] From a bright political future at the start of the Troubles, Fox was consigned to the wings. Then he became a political martyr, extolled by his political peers and mourned by friends, notably Minister for Justice Paddy Cooney, who was 'deeply affected' by the atrocity.[78]

Security policy in the North was driven from the outset by military men, and they were never dissuaded from trying to seal the border, a policy strongly supported by unionists. Ignoring ambassadorial advice and lessons of experience that provocation increased risk, they blasted away when they could. Even as the Sunningdale accord was ratified in December 1973, making way for a power-sharing executive in Stormont, the army pursued its policy of 'selective canalisation of terrorist routes closing all but the socially essential crossings', blasting roads on the Donegal-Tyrone border and setting about doing the same to others on the Monaghan-Fermanagh frontier.[79] They desisted only when Foreign Affairs Minister Garret FitzGerald threatened to make it an issue at his next meeting with British Secretary of State William Whitelaw, causing a rift in Anglo-Irish relations.[80] British demands for direct army-to-army contact also continued, despite the reasonable and oft-repeated explanation from Dublin that its army was deployed solely as an aid to the Garda, which had primacy in security.

Indeed, Dublin was pumping up Garda numbers in border posts, with the deployment during one fortnight of February of two inspectors, forty-two sergeants and 197 other gardaí, including armed officers and army back-up for checkpoints, searches and pursuits.[81] In a major redeployment of extra gardaí to border stations after the Billy Fox atrocity, Pascal McArdle was transferred to a new post far from the frontier, in north County Dublin. And the Irish Army garrison that Billy Fox had sought for the border came in December 1976, when Taoiseach Liam Cosgrave opened a new barracks in Monaghan town.

Many other consequences and speculations flowed from the violent death of Senator Billy Fox. One appeared in an obscure book, *Monaghan: County of Intrigue* by Michael Cunningham, son of Patrick Cunningham MP, who represented Fermanagh-Tyrone during the 1930s and 1940s.[82] This tells of a sandy-haired Protestant man called McClean from Ballinode who appeared in Monaghan Circuit Criminal Court on charges relating to cars stolen in Northern Ireland. He was acquitted on the direction of Judge Noel Ryan, who indicated that certain witnesses before him were lying. A short time later, McClean was abducted in a dramatic incident at a Monaghan town hotel, and interrogated by the IRA in a house close to the border. Under threats, the man admitted to being a member of a loyalist paramilitary group and named the Coulson farm as the local headquarters. He was released and subsequently told a 'prominent member of the Fine Gael party' that he had told his abductors a 'bundle of lies'. This account says the IRA Army Council explicitly refused permission to raid Coulsons' or other Protestant homes in the border area: 'When a raid did eventually take place it was done without authority and with harmful results for the IRA.'[83]

One thing is certain about the killing of Billy Fox, however. According to George Coulson, 'It left a lot of the community very afraid at the time, because they thought they were next.'[84] Already strongly depleted, notably by incidents of intimidation following Bloody Sunday in Derry, the Protestant population of the wider district withdrew further from Clones. When Angela Graham, a Free Presbyterian from Drum, applied for a job on the Peace and Reconciliation programme in Clones, it presented a major problem:

> The big issue was about going to work in Clones because in our Protestant community in Drum it is perceived as being a republican town and it was hugely scary and challenging to even consider that … I went in trepidation.[85]

After the Good Friday Agreement, I had a conversation with a young Protestant man from the Annaghmakerrig area of Newbliss, a conversation which turned to where he and his friends went for nights out. He mentioned Cootehill, Cavan and Monaghan. I asked if he ever went to Clones. He looked aghast: 'God no, that's a rebel town.'

Yet fear and trepidation were already widespread in the community before that fateful night in March 1974. Clones had been bombed several times, along with other border towns including Belturbet and Pettigo with fatalities and injuries attributed to Fermanagh-based loyalist gangs.[86] Clones Urban District Council estimated 1972 bomb damage in the town at £368,000; it also reported £10,880 in damage caused by road cratering on the Monaghan side of the border, and a further £391,000 outstanding for other cross-border incidents in the locality.[87]

Just before midnight on Saturday, 10 October 1973, the small cottage at the Four Ash Trees was blown to smithereens. Eight men in two cars were involved in this cross-border raid on the dwelling where 30-year-old Noel Thornbury, a Provo from north Armagh, was staying with his wife Stephanie. As she was taken upstairs, the four male occupants were ordered outside at gunpoint. Fearing they would be killed on the spot, Thornbury shouted to the others and made a break for it. Shots fired by the raiders wounded him in the chest, but he managed to get to a neighbour's house, where he collapsed. The raiders in the house planted a bomb and fled in the cars, and Stephanie Thornbury just managed to get out before the explosion.[88] One of the men later convicted of Billy Fox's murder, Sean Kinsella, emerged from his home across the road and fired a shotgun at the fleeing bombers. He was charged with illegally discharging the firearm, but never prosecuted. It was the only charge proffered in the case. Then in late February 1974, Kinsella's mother, Agnes, suffered a heart attack in a neighbour's home during a subsequent raid by Gardaí backed up by troops during a huge sweep of the Clones area, possibly prompted by British demands. During the raids, British helicopters hovered on the border, monitoring progress. An organisation called Unity protested at Mrs Kinsella's treatment and other Garda searches, including claims that a pregnant woman was 'terrorised' with 'serious consequences'.[89]

I walk along my north-easterly course, on the road from Killeevan to Smithborough. Over neatly trimmed hedgerows, I see the Ulster Canal again on my left, wending its way from Tircooney through well-tended farmland. Soon I am approaching Magherarney chapel, the Catholic place of worship in the Monaghan portion of Roslea parish. When the canal builders reached here from the opposite direction, they had to construct three locks at the crest of the navigation. From the third lock, it will be downhill all the way to Lough Neagh. While they were busy building locks and the small bridge that is now marooned at a fork in the road, the canal workers also helped to construct the chapel. On the orders of William Dargan, each of the masons delivered a cartload of stone to the church site at the end of each day, on pain of losing their jobs.[90] Similar stories are cited for the Church of Ireland back at Drummully, showing that the honourable gentleman showed no sectarian favour. Perhaps the instruction at Magherarney explains why the canal sweeps sharply to that point, having given a wide berth to Smithborough village. Could the coincidence of canal locks and the former bridge on the road to Killeevan have been a diversion to shorten those daily cart journeys? In any case, the navigation curves south in a couple of loops before settling into its north-eastly course alongside the N54.

It would be remiss, however, to give a wide berth to the recent political legacies of Smithborough. By 1977, the political fallout of Billy Fox's death had been consigned to memory in the politics of the latest atrocity. Cavan and Monaghan were rolled into a single Dáil constituency of five seats, one fewer than the status quo that had prevailed since partition. Fine Gael's Brendan Toal, of the Smithborough dynasty, who had been presented as the by-election candidate in place of Fox, lost out. However, his near neighbour Jimmy Leonard was swept home for the second time in a landslide victory for Fianna Fáil. With one brief hiatus during the election that coincided with the H-Block hunger strikes, Leonard held the seat until his 1997 retirement, when his daughter Anne came up short in her effort to put the family stamp on the seat for another generation.

As it happens, the Leonard homestead is just at this juncture of the canal and Magherarney amid a cluster of buildings that includes rows of black polytunnels, the ubiquitous evidence of intensive mushroom production. The canal channel has been obliterated and one of the carefully constructed locks sits like a beached dry-dock in a carefully groomed lawn. About 20 metres away, a small, squat functional building with a steel-barred gate and a warning sign on the door is the water-treatment plant for Smithborough. It features a plaque with the flag of the European Union proclaiming that this facility was 'officially opened by Mr Pat The Cope Gallagher TD, Minister of State at the Department of the Environment, Heritage and Local Government on Monday, 17 November 2003'. I might well be wrong, but on close examination of the beached lock, the bridge and the projected course of the former channel, I'm fairly sure that the ministerial plant now sits on the Ulster Canal. At least it is something to ponder as I amble on past the chapel and rejoin the main road for the final short leg into Smithborough village and an excellent cup of freshly brewed coffee at Toals' shop – yes, the same family.

4. At the Summit

Smithborough to Monaghan – 10 kms

Two local men were walking down the stairs at Smithborough Presbyterian Church hall, having just attended a public meeting to establish an Ulster Canal branch of the Inland Waterways Association of Ireland. The main speaker, Brian Cassells, had emphasised that £100 million was a reasonable cost for opening the final link of the island's inland navigation system. The budget would be borne by two governments and costed over five to seven years. So it really wasn't a lot given the impact the scheme would have on the local economy of this cross-border region. I had remarked that before any millions came on stream, it would help if the wider public was made aware that an accessible walking route could connect Ulster's two major water systems and five contiguous counties. That could be achieved by asserting the right of way along the towpath that is now impassable because of brambles and other growth. One of the men descending the stairs remarked to the other, 'So, do you think they'll get the canal open?' The other replied, 'They'll not even cut the fucking bushes.'

Such cynicism is born of a lifetime of neglect and the absence of 'joined-up' thinking by the central governments when it comes to border issues. Economic policies and strategic planning on both sides have served to entrench the boundary, not blur it. An excuse is usually found to deny or renege on funding for major capital projects that straddle the line. The political view persists that funds should only be spent where they have a cohesive electoral impact for the benefactors. In the end, that was what did for the railway that once trundled through this village on its way from Belfast to Clones and beyond. It is what has impeded the upgrading of the N2/A5 route from Dublin to Derry and the north-west, the only corner of the island not served by a controlled-access highway or rail network.

However, since it preceded the border, such myopic thinking does not explain why the canal looped south of Smithborough village and made my walk more complicated than necessary. Given the lack of towpath access, I decide to follow the road and pick up the canal along the way. So I head off for Monaghan town on the footpath, which only takes me a short distance beyond the village to where the old Bog Road is the route to Scotstown. That road runs past Eldron Cottage, the first of the homes recalled by Christopher Fitz-Simon in his memoir of childhood, *Eleven Houses*. In the book, he describes Smithborough in the 1930s as a village with two shops, owned by Mr Kerr and Mr Toal.[1] His grand-aunt Zane favoured Kerr's because they were Protestants, indeed 'somewhat superior Protestants for they were members of the Church of Ireland parish of Drumsnat', rather than the 'unassuming Presbyterian church' that Zane attended in the centre of the village. While the Kerrs drove off to Sunday Matins in their smart pony-and-trap, Christopher and his aunt walked the half-mile from Eldron Cottage into Smithborough for hymn singing and lengthy ad-lib prayers made up by Reverend Andrew Alexander. On the way home, they would meet and greet the more plentiful Mass-goers coming from Magherarney chapel. Christopher's world then was a community rooted in plain Ulster-Scots descriptives like 'communion table', never 'altar'; where the Enniskillen edition of the *Belfast Telegraph* was dropped off from the passing trains; where local Orangemen set off on the excursion train to the Fermanagh Twelfth and came back 'rather the worse for wear'; yet where the annual and much anticipated Orange Tea commenced with a rendition of 'O God, Our Help in Ages Past' and the only alternative drink to tea was cocoa. Loyalties were clear. A visiting Reverend Dunwoody, 'who had travelled all the way from Newbliss', declared in Smithborough that 'in spite of the way things had gone over the past number of years they would always remain loyal and nothing would ever put a stop to their singing "God Save the King" with heart and mind and voice. Then they sang "God Save the King", not all together or with all the right notes, because there was no organ or piano to get them going.'[2]

Life was not always so tranquil for Smithborough's loyalists. When Eoin O'Duffy ordered IRA reprisals for the burning of Roslea in 1921, the targeted homes covered an area that extended over the fledgling border into Monaghan. Philip Marron, commander of the IRA in Monaghan town, was assigned to Smithborough. 'Each of these districts selected for reprisals contained large unionist populations where all young unionists were armed and trained in the use of arms,' Marron subsequently stated. He led his men to Thornhill House, home of a family called McLean, 'extensive farmers' who dealt in horses, where at least four brothers living at home had been British officers in the Great War. Someone had informed the IRA that they had been seen on 'local roads armed and carrying out their duties as members of the Special Constabulary'. The IRA party made up of Smithborough, Threemilehouse and Corcaghan volunteers, approached the house at 1 a.m. with a horse and cart carrying 'petrol' for the arson, by an avenue from the main road. However, a large locked gate, high walls and impregnable outbuildings prevented them from getting into the back. Marron and a volunteer called Paddy McCarron knocked on the front door but there was no response, so they let all the horses out of the stables. Noticing a lamp in one of the top windows, they tried the hall door again, and shouted a warning that they would force entry. A volley of shots rang out from the house in reply, and a gun battle ensued for about half an hour, with the house's defenders keeping up steady fire from the front and gable ends. The IRA then tried to set the barn alight by soaking the hayloft with the petrol, which turned out to be paraffin oil. They set it alight anyhow and moved back to the main road, but the fire was smothered because they had forgotten to open the barn windows for air. By this time, sounds of shooting were coming from all directions, since 'the area surrounding the McLeans' house was a unionist stronghold', and this was 'a defence plan to give the alarm to other unionist houses'. Deciding they were dealing with 'well-armed opposition' in a 'veritable stronghold', the IRA abandoned the raid.[3]

Fifty years later, another Protestant family was not so fortunate in protecting its home from armed raiders. On 26 July 1972, four armed IRA men visited the farmhouse of John McElwaine at Tattymore, a Roslea townland that juts into County Monaghan. He, his wife and four children were forced to stand against a wall in their farmyard while they were robbed of valuables, and then watch as the raiders threw petrol bombs into their home, destroyed a car and a tractor, and burnt down the hay shed. The same night another Protestant farmer in the Roslea area had his house petrol-bombed.[4] Yet such incidents were exceptional. Many Protestant farmers continued to live unmolested close to the border on both sides. Moreover, such acts of sectarian vandalism and intimidation were roundly condemned by the wider community, as shown in the views of the Catholic neighbour who acquired the land in Tattymore when the McElwaines sold it. Brendan the neighbor remembers the 'general bedlam' of the night, when Mrs McElwaine came to their house 'just a hundred yards away'.[5] She was 'frantic and in an awful state and said to come on quick, that they were being burned out. We arrived on the scene, myself and my brother and we'd phoned the security forces and the fire brigade and stuff like that, to come along and it was pure pandemonium at the time.' There was a 'lot of shock' about this and other acts of intimidation at the other end of the village where some other Protestants moved out, but most were not interfered with and stayed. The McElwaines moved to Lisnaskea and put the land at Tattymore up for sale a few years later. Brendan bought it by private treaty using a Protestant middleman, because the Orange Order vigorously opposed the sale of Protestant land to Catholics and usually intervened. The middleman came under pressure and tried to break the sale, but Brendan got possession in the end.

Even then, it was difficult to live on the land because the British Army built two huge checkpoints, creating what Brendan called 'pure hardship':

if you had to go to Roslea from where I was living, you used to have to go through a checkpoint, and when you went to the checkpoint there was already three or four cars in front of you, and there was an hour wait at least at times. Going to Mass on Sunday, it was pure hassle. The same thing with the kids when they were growing up, going through checkpoints, buses being stopped and even through the bus had passed two minutes before to lift the children up the road a bit, when he came back he still had to show his licence again … You were in an area where you couldn't go across the border on the southern side (because of the Finn River) and you had to go through a checkpoint on the northern side, so you were in a cul-de-sac, hemmed in.[6]

In his memoir, Christopher Fitz-Simon also mentions his encounter with a turkey at a house in Keenogue townland, just north of the village. It may have been an ancestor of the millions of turkeys that passed that way to Grove Farms, for many years the turkey-processing centre of Ireland. Founded by the Cosgrove brothers, the plant has passed through several hands since. It was most recently acquired by the 2 Sisters Food Group, owned by Ranjit Singh.[7] Its contract supplier network, on both sides of the border, was part of the agribusiness revolution in this part of Ireland, providing a chance for many smallholders to turn poor and marginal land into profitable enterprises though hard work and intensive production. By the mid-1980s, when I was agriculture correspondent for the *Irish Press* newspaper group in Dublin, it was reckoned by An Foras Talúntais (Agricultural Institute) that Monaghan farmers – such as those supplying Grove – had the highest farm incomes per hectare in the Republic of Ireland. It could not have come soon enough for those living on the outer margins of the state, particularly since the advent of the European Economic Community (later, the EU) brought the removal of customs barriers (except for livestock and bulk commodities), which eliminated one alternative source of income.

Many previously had resorted to small-scale smuggling to supplement or simply stretch household incomes. In this locality, it would have been preposterous to do otherwise, for as Margaret Thatcher's former Tory minister of state for Northern Ireland, Lord Gowrie (September 1981–June 1983), remarked, 'The border is an economic nonsense;

anyone with initiative can laugh all the way to the bank.'[8] There was plenty of enterprise, if limited opportunity in the district. Yet today, the border is barely noticeable along the R187, which runs just north of Smithborough village in a westerly direction into Fermanagh. Once there was a Southern customs checkpoint at Inishammon and clear road markings. Today, only the skeletal remains of a bombed-out UK customs post stand guard, and there isn't a single trace of the huge former British military checkpoint that nestled beside Unshinagh Lough in the Fermanagh townland of Annaghmartin, one of three in close proximity on Fermanagh's eastern frontier. That is just outside the village that provides the name and nominal centre of the parish, with Magherarney, Smithborough and surrounding districts from the Monaghan half. So a single Irish Catholic parish encompasses two villages of roughly similar size, two counties and again the two secular jurisdictions on the island.

This part of the border between Fermanagh, Tyrone and Monaghan is a labyrinth of small mountainy roads renowned in the past for small-scale smuggling. It was carried out by people who 'had no well-paid jobs, no unemployment money from the government and no factories', and who conveyed their contraband by 'walking, donkeys and bicycles', according to Joe Goodwin of Roslea.[9] In this area, he noted, smuggling eggs in cases and baskets was most popular, 'as there was a ready market in England for fresh eggs', and families depended on this line of business to merely exist, although some more professional smugglers did well from the transactions:

> It was never plain sailing because there was always the dread of meeting a customs patrol along the winding roads that straddled the border. I can well remember the most popular topic being discussed, such and such a person was caught smuggling cattle, pigs, eggs and whatever. There was also the local law cases each month, usually in the (Roslea) market house cum courthouse for the day. This was where the resident magistrate would decide the penalty for the unfortunate smuggler. The local newspaper gave great coverage to these events and sometimes commended the defending solicitors on winning court cases. I can remember vividly each smuggler when apprehended would make a

particular choice of solicitor to defend their particular cases, for example, Lennon of Armagh was renowned as first-class to defend cattle smuggling.

From Smithborough, the border sweeps away north towards Sliabh Beagh and the little pucker in its brow just beyond Barritatoppy that is known as the 'three counties hollow', the place where Fermanagh and Monaghan meet Tyrone in the confluence of the three parishes of Roslea, Tydavnet and Clogher. It is where the raparee or tory called Sean Bearna took refuge in the 1840s and set up his camp in the shallow caves at a rocky outcrop beside the Three Counties Lough in a place still known by local people as Sean Bearna's Stables. It is where hardy souls or pilgrims from the three parishes and counties have gathered once a year to meet and socialise when other modes of contact were severed by road closures and checkpoints. Back down a short distance into County Monaghan, a small hotel and community resource centre promotes recreational walking along the border in this remote district of Knockatallen. It is a tough slog, for this is where the resolute determination of community meets the harsh challenge of poor land and political indifference. At a small crossroads adjacent to the hotel, there is an imposing monument recalling a modern-day raparee who roamed these hills. His name was Seamus McElwain and while he is clearly a man glorified among his own people, he is vilified by the North's first minister, Arlene Foster, who identifies him as the terrorist who tried to murder her father, RUC Reserve Constable John Kelly, in 1979.[10]

Born in the townland of Knockacullion, one of eight children, Seamus McElwain became active in the IRA as soon as he could, reportedly turning down a chance to study in the USA so 'no one will ever be able to accuse me of running away'.[11] Active from 16, by 19 he was commanding the IRA in Fermanagh, and little more than a year later he had been captured in an SAS ambush and convicted of the murder of two off-duty members of the security forces – UDR Corporal Aubrey Abercrombie at Kinawley, near Fermanagh's border with Cavan, and RUC Reserve Constable Ernie Johnston just across the border from Clones – and sentenced to serve thirty years.[12] While in prison on remand, he stood as a candidate in the Irish general election of February 1982 and received almost 4,000 first-preference votes.[13] Then he escaped from the maximum security Maze Prison with almost forty other IRA prisoners the following year in Europe's biggest prison break since the Second World War.[14] While many were quickly recaptured, McElwain is said to have led a band of fellow escapees on foot to safety in south Armagh. Eschewing another offer of safe passage to America, he was soon back on active service on the Fermanagh-Monaghan border. A leading republican figure who also escaped has credited McElwain for the success of the operation, due to his meticulous approach to planning and his orienteering skills, honed on the mountainy roads and bog fields of Monaghan and Fermanagh. IRA veteran Bik McFarlane called him 'exceptional': 'His wealth of experience from operating in country lanes and hedgerows was to prove vital for the survival of the small unit of eight volunteers who took to the fields with him that Sunday night.'[15]

In *A Secret History of the IRA*, author Ed Moloney argues that Seamus McElwain was in a group of Monaghan-based IRA dissidents who rejected moves towards peace talks and political primacy over the military struggle in the republican movement. The nub of his argument centres on a secret meeting of these dissident volunteers in McElwain's family home at Knockacullion, at which 'seven or eight' dissidents were present in the 'spring of 1987'.[16] Moloney cites an 'interview with former Tyrone IRA member, April 2000' as his source for this meeting.[17] However McElwain himself was already dead by the time the meeting took place, having been summarily executed as he lay wounded on the ground, in an SAS ambush near Roslea in April 1986.[18] He and Sean Lynch had gone to inspect a landmine at Mullaghglass, near Roslea. In the ambush, Lynch was severely wounded but escaped execution by hiding in a ditch, and he then went on to become the influential commanding officer of IRA prisoners in the Maze Prison, credited with swinging opinion in favour of the peace process. He and others vehemently deny the contention that McElwain was at loggerheads with the IRA peace strategy, pointing to McElwain's own words, delivered to the Fermanagh Easter Commemoration of 1985:

We call on all republicans to unite, to put petty bickering and old grudges behind them and we emphasise that no one has the right to carry on campaigns of vilification or division ... We call on all who class themselves as republicans to vote for the candidates put forward by the Republican Movement – that is to vote solidly for the Sinn Féin candidates in every area and not to be misled by smooth-talking politicians who claim to be republicans and make loud noises when it suits, but who resist organised republicanism and pursue an independent course in furthering simply their own career.[19]

These words resonated with those who elevated McElwain's memory to a legend within republican circles, and his funeral was 'massive', with crowds turning out in Clones and Smithborough as his remains were brought home for a tense funeral at Urbleshanny chapel in Scotstown, where 150 gardaí in riot gear stood at the ready as Martin McGuinness delivered the graveside oration of 'an Irish freedom fighter' who was 'murdered by British terrorists'.[20]

If Seamus McElwain's bloody death in a field near Roslea means he had no central role in moving the IRA towards a ceasefire, another who did play a key part lived quietly for much of the Troubles in the small Mulladuff housing estate in Smithborough village. Perhaps Kevin McKenna's facility in keeping a low profile is hinted at by his introduction in Moloney's history of the IRA, where McKenna is first described as a 'taciturn, guarded figure', and later as 'a pleasant man to talk to, thoughtful, hospitable and affable' and also as 'avuncular', 'tolerant and understanding'.[21] Raised on a small border farm near Aughnacloy, County Tyrone, McKenna had joined the IRA but emigrated to Canada just before the Troubles erupted in 1969. He returned when internment was introduced in 1971 and helped form an IRA active-service unit operating in south-east Tyrone. A year later he became commander of the Tyrone Brigade. He was then in his mid-20s.

He moved over the border permanently after he was allegedly involved in the shooting death of a UDR soldier in 1973.[22] Yet when he was subsequently arrested, McKenna was interned without trial and released from Long Kesh in early 1975, whence he returned to Monaghan and reassumed control of IRA operations in Tyrone. He soon took control of all of the IRA's Northern Command, encompassing Northern Ireland and the border counties of the Republic.

Regarded as a strictly military, non-political operator, McKenna was then chosen as the IRA's chief of staff in 1984, when Belfast's Ivor Bell was remanded in custody on charges brought as a result of testimony by one of his senior officers, who later recanted.[23] McKenna's base was pivotal to IRA operations, especially outside Belfast and Derry city. County Monaghan has been described by British military strategists as the 'spur' sticking into the soft underbelly of Northern Ireland. From his Smithborough home, McKenna could easily reach into Fermanagh, Armagh, Tyrone and even beyond into south Derry, a huge vantage described as the IRA's 'most important and active operational area outside of south Armagh'.[24] The IRA always recognised the strategic value of this area. In the 1922 spring offensive organised by Michael Collins, the Ulster Council was established in Clones and directed from there. In the 1950s, the IRA launched and directed its Operation Harvest from the district also. On the first night, the three leaders – director of operations Seán Cronin, chief of staff Tony Magan and adjutant general Charlie Murphy – coordinated a series of military attacks from 'a farmhouse near Knockatallen'.[25]

Stepping into the same role thirty years later, Kevin McKenna was a hands-on IRA leader, even allegedly rolling up his sleeves in August 1985 to help his young volunteers unload 10 tonnes of arms from the *Casamara* on a Wicklow beach, the first of four arms shipments procured from Libya on his watch.[26] Through crises such as the 1986 split with the Continuity IRA, the 1987 ambush death of eight IRA volunteers at Loughgall, the SAS killing of three IRA volunteers in Gibraltar the following year, and IRA atrocities including the 1987 Remembrance Day bombing in Enniskillen and the 1990 death in Derry of Patsy Gillespie, who was forced to drive a bomb into a border checkpoint, McKenna provided the gel that held the IRA together. He was also the chief of staff who led it into the 1994 ceasefire that opened the way to peace talks and the Good Friday Agreement. Yet he rarely features in Moloney's book, *A Secret History of the IRA*, except in relation to a feud he had with tentative IRA dissidents such as the East Tyrone Brigade's Padraig McKearney and Jim Lynagh, who were both killed by the SAS in the 1987 Loughgall ambush.[27] More recently, Moloney has claimed in a 21 February 2011 post on his blog *The Broken Elbow*, that McKenna had serious differences with Martin McGuinness, and that the two had a 'vicious feud' that 'simmered beneath the surface' – although there is no corroboration for this.[28]

However, in the two IRA conventions of 1996 and 1997 that allowed the Republican Movement to abandon its armed struggle in favour of the Good Friday Agreement, McKenna was a central player. In the first, he set the tone with his opening salvo in the chief of staff's report. He commended the recent double car-bomb attack on Lisburn's Thiepval Barracks, the hub of British army operations in the North, and promising more of the same. That meant McKenna had stolen the offensive strategy of the dissident hawks on the IRA Executive led by Michael McKevitt. He also ensured that the convention was chaired by Clones man Pat Treanor, who steered the agenda of more than 130 motions to procedural qualifications that nullified any adverse motions that were adopted.[29] In the 1997 convention, McKenna organised the timing of delegate arrivals, ensuring that the dissidents were present only after the others had been warned of their coup plan, which was then strategically defeated.[30]

McKenna's tenure as IRA chief of staff ended at that October 1997 IRA convention, and so did the armed struggle he had led for more than a dozen years. While Moloney finally paints him as a pitiful character who was 'discarded' when no longer useful, McKenna became quartermaster general under the new chief of staff.[31] That was a crucial position in ensuring that as much as possible of the IRA arsenal was kept intact for eventual decommissioning, and out of the hands of the former incumbent of that position, dissident leader McKevitt. However, the fact that he led the IRA for fourteen crucial years in a century during which about forty others held the position, usually for very short durations due to death, detention or ouster, is surely proof of his forceful character. He brought the organisation through some of the most difficult patches of its history. Yet there is only one known grainy photograph of this enigmatic character, who was regarded as quiet and unassuming by most of his neighbours while he was living in relative obscurity in a very modest Smithborough council house. He has been barely noticed by media commentators, and that was the secret of his success as leader of an underground guerrilla army in the world's most enduring military struggle.

From the crossroads just outside Smithborough village, I walk along the main road, trying to reconnect with the canal. Just past a small abandoned gate lodge on the right is an avenue for Thornhill House, the scene of that comically thwarted 1921 IRA raid for arms. A small farmhouse across the road is fronted by a wooden fence brightly coloured in red, white and blue, with just a splotch of pink and yellow, all packed into a small space that looks like the leftovers from a miniature gymkhana. Further along this road, which is treacherous for walkers, are the park fields of Thornhill House, with a couple of striking weeping willows displaying their leafless limbs in the foreground. The roadside view provides a peek of the squat rectangular steeple of St Molua's church, just behind the sturdy manor house with its semicircular frontage. Another crossroads in the dip between two small drumlins, with a flashing traffic-control sign ahead, is well signposted. On the left, pointing north, an imposing fixed sign points to Hollywood Park. That Californian enticement probably grabs the attention of most passers-by, who fail to see the much smaller fingerposts on the other side, just visible to east-bound traffic. The topmost sign points to the small village of 'Three Mile House' (or Threemilehouse). Below it and fairly certain to be missed by the passing traffic is another fingerpost, pointing to:

Drumsnatt Church of Ireland
burial place of
Oscar Wilde's sisters

I divert to the right, of course, and walk a short distance past another entrance for Thornhill House, and then sharp right up the lane to the crest and a strong iron gate and wall. Beyond them looms St Molua's, a tall grey pebble-dash building with three vaulted stained-glass windows surmounted by the sturdy stone steeple with corner spires and vaulted shuttered windows matching those below. Unseen, but present nonetheless, the Ulster Canal towpath is just to the left at the bottom of the hill. There is nothing to indicate the origins of the church on the site of the first monastery founded by Saint Molua, born around AD 554 and a student and friend of Saint Comgall of Bangor. The church at the main gates of the Stormont Parliament buildings in Belfast is also named in Molua's honour, though it doesn't have Drumsnatt's direct connection with the saint. Nor does Stormont have Drumsnatt's connection with the earliest written record of Ulster's literary culture, the 'Táin Bó Cúailnge' ('Cattle Raid of Cooley'), which was first transcribed from the oral vernacular at the monasteries of Bangor and Drumsnatt in the eighth century.[32]

Nor is there much evidence of the churchyard's prime attraction through the spiked gate. However, a thorough search of the churchyard reveals a small, almost nondescript grave tucked into the hedge at the far side of the church. It has twin headstones of modest granite, one a newer version of the original, with the inscription:

> In memory of
> Two loving and beloved sisters
> Emily Wilde aged 24
> And
> Mary Wilde aged 22
> Who lost their lives by accident
> In this parish in Novr 1871.
> They were lovely and pleasant in
> Their lives and in their death they
> Were not divided
> (II Samuel Chap. I, v 23).

While almost indecipherable on the original because of wear, the epitaph is followed on the replacement headstone with the information that it was 'Erected by the Oscar Wilde Society and Drumsnatt Parish Church'.

An easy-to-miss road sign and a hard-to-find gravestone, however, are the most obvious evidence of the mystery that lies behind the deaths of these two young women.

An investigation was carried out by local historian Theo McMahon based on available accounts and extremely scant evidence included in the coroner's inquisition book for County Monaghan covering the period.[33] Although the entries by Coroner Alexander Charles Waddell are sketchy and even give the family name as 'Wylie', in what has since been taken as an obvious bid to spare from embarrassment Sir William Wilde (also identified as 'Wylie'), a narrative emerges from the thicket of obfuscation and confusion. The half-sisters of Oscar by his father and an 'unknown woman' attended a social event at Drumaconnor House, which was owned by Alexander N. Reid, a short distance from Drumsnatt, in the neighbouring parish of Kilmore. The event took place on 31 October 1871, which neither the coroner, the historian nor others, has identified as Halloween. In what was said to be a final dance of the evening, one of the sisters was swept past the fireplace by the host and her crinoline dress was set alight, causing the other sister to rush to her aid and also be consumed in the flames. One or both may have been carried out and down the fourteen steps to the lawn – or 'rolled down' as one account has it – where they were covered in overcoats to extinguish the flames. However, they succumbed to the burns, Mary on 8 November and Emma (or Emily) on 21 November. Both were cared for in the house where the accident occurred. A death notice appeared in the *Northern Standard* on 25 November 1871:

DIED

At Drumaconnor, on the 8th inst., Mary Wilde.[34]

At Drumaconnor, on the 21st inst., Emma Wilde.

The parish records at Drumsnatt offer only a few details. The burials book lists them as numbers 189 and 190, their name as 'Wilde' (without first names) and their abodes and ages as 'not given'. It states that the funeral ceremony was performed by Rev. Thomas Le B. Kennedy, officiating minister. He was the rector at the neighbouring Kilmore parish at that time, while Drumsnatt's rector was Rev. John Edward Henry Simpson, then aged 81. One account has the sisters staying at Drumsnatt rectory, where they were being educated prior to the tragedy.[35] There is also a footnote reference to their uncle and guardian, former 'perpetual curate' at Portglenone, County Antrim, Rev. Ralph Wilde, living in County Monaghan at the time of the deaths of 'the two illegitimate daughters of this brother … at a country Christmas ball'.[36]

There was no notice or coverage of the tragedy anywhere else until 1942, when Sir William Wilde's biographer, T.G. Wilson, gave a brief account of the tragedy. Wilson did not include names in his recounting of how, during Christmas festivities at the country mansion of a local bank manager, 'drink flowed freely' and tragedy struck, with the host taking his dance partner outside and rolling her in the snow.[37] A subsequent account in *The Replay*, a Corcaghan parish history published in 1984 also mentions snow, but not Christmas.[38] That account has the unnamed host wrapping both girls in his coat and says he 'rolled them down the steps in front of the house into the snow'.

In his memoir, Christopher Fitz-Simon, places the social event on New Year's Eve, and suggests that it could not have been a ball because 'Drumaconnor isn't big enough'.[39] His mother mentions the tragedy as they view a house called Aughnamala, just across the road and the Ulster Canal from Drumaconnor House:

> Snow was on the ground, drifting against the ditches, so they walked round by the road (from Drumsnatt) instead of along the towpath of the canal. There was dancing. One of the girls twirled too close to the chimney-piece and a spark caught her dress. It was made of some kind of flimsy stuff, muslin perhaps, and immediately caught fire. Her sister rushed to try to put out the flames by beating her with a cushion but her dress caught fire too. Apparently, there was a lot of screaming while people went to the kitchen to get jugs of water to throw over them but a sensible man shouted to someone to open the hall door and he and other young men carried the girls out and rolled them in the snow.

However, weather readings from the archives of Armagh Observatory, only 20 miles from Drumaconnor, show that there was no snow recorded that Halloween, when the night-time temperature was 48.7 degrees Fahrenheit (9.3 degrees Celsius) and the moon was 'bright but hazy'.[40]

In Christopher Fitz-simon's mother's anecdotal account, the young men are burnt 'but only slightly', and it was lucky the house didn't catch fire. Other details are that the 'two young girls from Dublin' had been staying with their uncle and aunt at Drumsnatt rectory. However, from Theo McMahon's investigation in the *Clogher Record* we know that, while Rev. Ralph Wilde officiated at three Drumsnatt christenings in December 1871, the month following the burial of his two nieces, there is no record of him in the parish prior to that.[41] His wife Pricilla, moreover, died in June 1860 at the parsonage in Dudley, England; he was not attached to Drumsnatt; and he 'does not appear to have had a fixed curé between the ending of his curacy at Portglenone, County Antrim, in 1862 and his commencement as curate of Bridgenhall, Derby, England, in 1874'.[42] Furthermore, there is no documentation of his alleged guardianship of his two nieces.

One might expect the coroner's report to shed some light on the event. However, following the notification from Constable Williamson of Smithborough a full nine days after the event, Mr Waddell received a letter from 'Sir Wm. Wylie', asking him to set aside the inquest arranged in Carrickmacross as it might have 'fatal consequence' for the deceased Mary's sister, who was 'dangerously ill from severe burns'. The coroner asked Constable Williamson to arrange a 'few respectable gentlemen' to meet him at Drumaconnor to hear the account of the owner, with whom 'some friends' had been 'spending time' when the accident occurred. Those 'respectable gentlemen' included Reverend Le Bon Kennedy, who performed the burial service, two other clergymen from neighbouring Tydavnet and Monaghan parishes, and two others, identified possibly by Theo McMahon as a gardener at Rossmore Castle and a witness at his [gardener's] marriage.[43] So instead of a formal inquest at Carrickmacross, as far as possible from the scene yet still within the county coroner's jurisdiction, inquiries were made of the householder at the scene itself, where the surviving sister was dangerously ill and at risk from formal inquiries into the event.

In the case of the second sister, the date of the accident is confirmed as 31 October. From 'all the circumstances of the case' supplied by the homeowner, Coroner Waddell did not consider 'anything further necessary than a careful inquiry into the facts, which showed that everything possible was done to preserve the life of the deceased'. Again the names of father and daughters are entered as 'Wylie'. Although the daughters had not been given names in the first report, this time they were identified by the initials 'L.' and 'M'. And that was it, apart from the headstone in Drumsnatt and local talk of a 'lady in black' who came by train from Dublin to visit the graveside. She was reported by the sexton to have said of the sisters 'they were very dear to me'.[44]

However, the *Clogher Record* account adds an intriguing passage from Hesketh Pearson's 1998 biography of Oscar Wilde, in which he talks of his mother's tolerance of his father's 'constant infidelities'. It describes a 'woman dressed in black and closely veiled' who came to their house in Merrion Square, Dublin, and sat at the head of his dying father's bed all day 'without ever speaking a word or once raising her veil'.[45]

Still pondering the mystery of the Wilde women, I walk back to the main road and over the brow of the hill, with its flashing speed-warning sign and a small broken-down, derelict tin shed with rotting bales of hay. The townland of Drumaconnor spreads off to the right or south, measuring just shy of 140 acres, and touching the main road and the Ulster Canal where the R183 branches off to Roslea. Drumaconnor House has long since passed from the owners at the time of the tragedy, and Theo McMahon describes his visit when James and Madge Treanor were operating it as a B & B. They showed him around the extensively renovated property, and he describes the room where the social event took place as of 'moderate size' and 'not of the category of the stately ballroom' suggested in some accounts.[46]

Just around the corner from Drumaconnor, the ordnance map shows a serrated line running along the boundary of the townlands of Aghalisk and Kilnahaltar, labelled 'Quig Lough Feeder'. This is the channel that once fed the Ulster Canal at its highest point, or that was supposed to do so. According to Brian Cassels, the ongoing problems of the Ulster Canal were 'lack of water and too much weed'.[47] The water problem was sourced right back to Quig Lough, as was discovered by the Dundalk Steam Packet Company, which bought the Ulster Canal navigation from William Dargan in 1857. In January of the following year, the new owners were embroiled in a court case brought by a Mr Cargill, owner of a flax mill in the village of Ballinode, which straddles the Ulster Blackwater river just north of Quig Lough and its water supply.* The miller wanted a court prohibition on the canal company diverting water from the river to supplement the canal. At the heart of his case was the Act of Parliament setting up the navigation, which permitted supplementary water supplies only between the months of November and April, and not, as climate and logic would dictate, during the summer months, when the canal was low. The court costs racked up, as did the running costs of the canal, and the chairman of the Dundalk Steam Packet Company, Major Jocelyn, told the shareholders that the Ulster Canal would continue to be 'a thorn in their side ... until they got rid of it', which they did, but not until 1865; it had been costing them 'in the region of £2,000 a year'.[48]

By then, drainage works carried out by the Board of Works had exacerbated the water shortage. That, plus declining canal traffic, weeds and poor maintenance, as well the arrival of the railway, was proving 'an intolerable burden'. The Board of Works took over the canal and closed it for eight years to carry out improvements costing £22,000, but just a year after the reopening in 1873, the Quig Lough reservoir was dry.[49] The problems persisted, despite the opening of the Ballinamore-to-Ballyconnell link with the Shannon navigation, and the anticipated increase in traffic that that would bring. It didn't, and fared even worse than the Ulster Canal, which in 1878 saw only forty boats go up to the Blackwater navigation channel from the Ulster Canal into Lough Neagh, with no through traffic recorded going from the canal into the Erne. Despite that, the Lagan Navigation Company, which linked Lough Neagh to Belfast, took it over, spending about £12,700 on

---

* Two separate rivers in this region are known as the Ulster Blackwater, this one flowing from Sliabh Beagh, the other from Murley Mountain on the other side of Tyrone's Clogher Valley. See Chapter 7, Oriel Affairs.

improvements, and increasing tolls. Traffic picked up briefly, but any profits were eaten up by maintenance costs. In 1905, the new owners sought permission to close it down.[50]

There is a plentiful supply of water in Quig Lough now, and the sturdy stone building to control the sluice gates still stands in a parkland setting, waiting to go back into service if needed. Nor is there any impediment to supplementing the supply from the nearby river, since Ballinode's three water-powered flax mills have long gone. So too has the 'enormous acreage of glasshouses, most of them shattered and broken down' that Colm Tóibín noted on the road to Ballinode in the mid-1980s.[51] The glasshouse farm was owned by Dudgeons, one of the pioneering local agribusinesses of former times. Ballinode has now given way to a proliferation of black poly-tunnels all over the district where the mushroom industry has, well, mushroomed since then. Shattered glass aside, Tóibín noted approvingly how well-kept Ballinode was, attributing that to the 'legacy of Monaghan's Protestant heritage'.

The implication that the depletion in the Protestant population of north Monaghan was the result of personal and institutional sectarianism is contested strongly, even by those who left their home village. Carol, who grew up in Ballinode, said the exodus into Northern Ireland was a matter of 'economic necessity' for Protestant families, not least because of the 'availability of free health care and education and unemployment and child benefit in the North'.[52] Moreover, Belfast was more accessible from north Monaghan than Dublin was, and with much better roads until recently. That is why Carol, who wanted to come home at weekends, opted for a job in Belfast. Her sense of community at home had been 'cushioned' by sufficient Protestant numbers for schools and social events from any 'stark difference' with the majority Catholic population, and this fostered mutual accord across the sectarian divide.[53] On moving north, she actually found that sense of belonging disrupted. Her sense of being distinctly Protestant, Monaghan-based and Irish was connected to neighbouring Fermanagh, Tyrone and Armagh, but 'different from the North', and this was compounded in the 1960s by the requirement for her on moving north of the border to get an annual work permit, which made her 'feel like an alien despite her family connections there'.[54]

While Colm Toibín was impressed by Protestant Ballinode, he was less kind to neighbouring Scotstown, describing it as 'sleepy and unkempt'.[55] He describes ominously the 'dead silence' when he went into one local pub, the stares, then the loud remark of one customer about 'strangers wanting to know his business', forcing Toibín to leave. He describes the wire-covered windows of the local Garda station and the entrance intercom, and somebody watching him as he walked down the main street. All that was missing was menacing music as he entered Moynas' pub! I was in Moynas and around Scotstown village around the same time as his visit, and Scotstown could hardly be described as sleepy then. Mind you, that was the night in 1985 that the Monaghan senior football team brought home the National Football League trophy. The Scotstown fans set their sights on the All-Ireland Football championship in that year when Monaghan ran the eventual champions Kerry to a replay in the semi-final. Where else would I have been that night but in the village that was the powerhouse of county pride and football prowess?

But aside from mentioning that Tommy Moyna and his twin Mackie had been county footballers in the 1950s, Tóibín's interest in sport was set aside in favour of observations on their family's links to then SDLP Deputy Leader Seamus Mallon, and a bugging incident involving Gardaí, as well as explosives charges on which a young member of the Scotstown family was subsequently acquitted. Tóibín wanted to know about the Protestant exodus from Ballinode. Where had they gone? He discussed the various translations of place names for Scotstown in Irish, hiring fairs of the past, its republican pedigree and Seamus McElwain's funeral. All civil and generous before the visiting writer was treated to 'a big fry-up and loads of hot tea' in the family kitchen. He latched on, however, to a nasty remark about unionist politicians by a 'man at the bar', before accepting a lift from the same man out to the McElwain home in Knockatallen with a brief tour of the destruction caused by British Army road cratering: 'The whole place was desolate now, depopulated, lonely; there wasn't much need for these small roads.'

At the McElwain family home, Tóibín was treated hospitably, and plied with even more tea and freshly made chicken sandwiches. He had his harsh observations about hiring fairs challenged by the host's accurate remark that many of those hired by Protestant farmers were treated well and some even inherited the farms. He also heard in detail the family's view on the cold-blooded killing of Seamus, and how they were treated by the Gardaí. When the father left briefly, clearly to check the identity of the unexpected stranger who was interrogating them about their son, he returned and then deliberately confused Colm's name with the actor Niall Tóibín, remarking that he also was a 'bit of an actor': 'His eyes fixed on me, half amused, half ferocious. He grinned at me.' Little wonder, many readers might observe.

What remains of the Ulster Canal now hugs the N54 on the approach to Monaghan town. Clambering over a fence beside a small bridge and down an incline, I gain access once more to the towpath, a strange overgrown landscape of gnarled trees and bushes, beside wide lagoons of dark water covered in green lichens. Running parallel, another trench, dry this time, seems to mimic the canal channel, or even the road just beyond. Yet the most striking aspect of this abandoned walkway is the silence that reigns on this spring morning, a silence interspersed with occasional shrill bird calls, or the sound of a car whizzing by. These noises leave in their wake an even more noticeable absence of sound.

I negotiate a path through the mud and over dead branches and boughs that are strewn like obstacles to deter intruders. Ahead, two old donkeys amble in from an adjoining field and fall into step beside me, as if expecting me to guide them from their enchanted imprisonment. After a few hundred metres, I climb over a small fence and down and up from a trench and the donkeys are imprisoned once more, regarding me forlornly as I trudge ahead. Through the cover of trees and vegetation, I can see the road clearly now and a row of four derelict cottages that have been decaying as long as I can remember on the far side of the main road in the townland of Tullybryan. To my right meanwhile, a wooded hillside is alive with birdsong, the mating calls of springtime on a bright but damp day. Finally, my path comes to a halt at Carson's bridge, which straddles the canal in elegant twin arches, now decaying and ivy-clad. Beneath the nearer arch, the channel is blocked and the cavern is impassable. Again with difficulty, I clamber up and out from the towpath and resume my walk along the busy N54 with an almost immediate reminder of the danger in a roadside shrine to Damien 'Bicy' McCabe of Newtownbutler. Beneath a wooden cross with a metal crucifix draped in rosary beads, a picture shows Damien astride a powerful motorbike and holding a newborn baby. Beneath it, a brass plaque says:

In loving memory of
DAMIEN WHO DIED ON THIS SPOT
ON SUNDAY EVENING 16 AUGUST 1998
AGED 29 YEARS
Gone but not forgotten

Bright yellow flowers have been placed at both sides and a bottle of (holy?) water and a corked flask rest on the concrete plinth that supports the shrine. Similar shrines are dotted along the roads hereabouts, where there is a strong culture of motorbike clubs and gangs.

Indeed, the phrase 'Gone but not forgotten' is combined with the word 'bikers' in an annual memorial service that began in 2003 as a Mass of remembrance celebrated by the 'biker' priest Father John Kearns for some of his fellow motorbike enthusiasts from Monaghan, Fermanagh and Cavan in the Catholic chapel at Aghadrumsee, in the Fermanagh end of Clones parish. The event grew quickly as the word spread, and now it attracts an attendance of about 1,500 from all over Ireland, north and south. It has been moved to the Sacred Heart church in Clones and has become an ecumenical matter, with the early participation of local Church of Ireland rector, Rev. Helen Steed. The religious service is followed by a cavalcade of hundreds of bikers through the town. A website set up by members of a committee also has a roll of honour that has been growing year on year, with the names and details of bikers killed in road accidents all over Ireland. However, a disproportionate number of them originate from this border region. That may be because of the popularity of fast motorcycles and impromptu road racing where hot pursuit is frustrated by different jurisdictions, or it may be down to poor road conditions. Yet if anything is a cautionary warning to those who favour two wheels and high speeds, it is roadside memorials and that annual church commemoration.

Moving along at a brisk walking pace now, I'm anxious to get off the road and back on the towpath. I find a way on the final bend before the traffic-calming speed-limit signs for Monaghan town, when I enter a field in the townland of Cornacassa Demesne, once part of the extensive estate of the Hamiltons that spread over 7,300 acres in the 1870s.[56] There is little evidence of it now, apart from the townland name. The townland actually covers an area once more commonly known as Hollands' Hill, an expanse of parkland that was the venue for cross-country and track athletics when I was a teenage competitor. The great house, which the Irish Georgian Society notes as a 'dignified smaller classical house with a lower service wing', was described by Samuel Lewis in *A Topographical Dictionary of Ireland* (1837) as 'pleasantly situated in a highly cultivated and well-planted demesne'. It was demolished, and the library contents were sold off by auction in 1922, the year the border came into existence.

Also demolished since then was Rossmore Castle, which once presided majestically over this approach to Monaghan town. The castle was built in 1827 by Warner William Westenra, the second Lord Rossmore, around the time he and others – including the marquis of Donegall, the marquis of Downshire, Sir James Stronge and Sir Arthur Chichester – were engaging Thomas Telford to check out the commercial prospects of the proposed Ulster Canal.[57] His castle was designed by William Vitruvius Morrison and built in the Gothic style. It was extended in Scottish Baronial style in 1858 and, according to accounts, it also had its drawing room extended no fewer than five times as the Rossmores vied with the Shirleys, a landed family in south Monaghan, for the largest room in the county. With such vanities are the aristocracy consumed. In any case, the castle had 117 windows in fifty-three different sizes and styles when it was found to have dry rot after the Second World War. The sixth Lord Rossmore moved to Camla Vale, a large house on the family estate. The castle roof was removed so rates would not have to be paid. It fell into ruin and the seventh Lord Rossmore, William Warner Westenra, had it demolished in 1974. That was around the time he was engaged to 1960s British pop singer Marianne Faithfull, more than twenty years his junior and former girlfriend of Mick Jagger of the Rolling Stones!

The Rossmores didn't always keep such bohemian company, of course. The fifth Lord Rossmore, Derrick Warner William Westenra, was grand master of the Monaghan County Orange Lodge at the start of the home rule crisis in the 1880s when he led a reported 8,000 Orangemen into battle at Roslea, where the Irish National League (INL) was holding a political rally. The rally was one of many staged in the follow-up to the victory of Timothy Healy MP in the 1883 Monaghan by-election. Healy and the INL were backed by Clogher's Catholic Bishop James Donnelly, prompting talk of another 'invasion of Ulster'. There were many confrontations at the time, of course, but the most serious of the near affrays occurred in October 1883, when Lord Rossmore organised the Roslea counter-demonstration, which was described by Thomas MacKnight, editor of the *Northern Whig* newspaper:

> Lord Rossmore … was represented as saying that the nationalists on the hill were rebels and scavengers, whom the Orangemen could easily vanquish, and that the Brethren could also, if they thought fit, eat up the handful of soldiers in a few seconds.[58]

Insults and shots were exchanged, but the sides were kept apart.

Rossmore had rejected a request from fellow magistrate Hugh McTernan, a Catholic, to reroute his procession of 'belligerent Orangemen' away from the nationalist meeting to avoid conflict. McTernan later reported Rossmore's conduct to the undersecretary at Dublin Castle, and Rossmore told the subsequent inquiry that the Orange campaign was justified 'to stamp out revolutionary nationalism in the north', in accordance with the call made by Prime Minister William Gladstone in a speech in Leeds two years earlier.[59] Not surprisingly, the government stripped Rossmore of his position as magistrate. That led to Orange outrage, and Rossmore was hailed as a hero of the emerging Ulster unionist faction. There were lengthy and heated debates in the British parliament.[60] As well as lengthy correspondence in newspapers such as the *Times* of London, Rossmore co-authored a book with Rev. J. Wallace Taylor on the affair, setting out his side of the argument through correspondence and other documents.[61] And if that wasn't enough, readers of the *Northern Standard* could buy for 4 shillings each from W.J. Hunter & Co., photographers in Armagh, souvenir photos of Lord Rossmore being served with the writ depriving him of his office as magistrate. The advertisement for the photo featured cameo appearances by Colonel Edward Saunderson and Captain Somerset Maxwell. Enthusiasts could also purchase for 2 shillings a 'photo of his Lordship wearing collar as deputy grand master'.[62]

My improvised route along the towpath comes to an abrupt end at Gortakeegan, where the R189 road takes off for Newbliss, Threemilehouse and the entrance to Rossmore Park. It is also where a sports ground with floodlights and a big blue covered stand for spectators is emblazoned with the name and logo of Monaghan United Football Club. Before I reach it, however, the final part of my path is a deep tangle of bushes making it impossible to get out onto the road. So I hop down from the towpath and set off across the corner of a large field towards the gate in the nearest corner. As I'm securing the gate properly, a van pulls up and the driver asks if I'm 'all right'. I reply that I am and thank him for his concern, whereupon I'm informed that I have been trespassing on private land. I explain my predicament of needing to cut through a small corner of the field because the right of way on the towpath has been blocked. A brief exchange follows about property rights, public access and the integrity of the right of way on the Ulster Canal north and south of the border. We finally agree that the next time I find myself caught in that corner of his field, I'll give him a call before crossing.

But back to Gortakeegan and the Monaghan United Football Club. Founded in 1979 when they played at Belgium Park, a small ground beside a housing estate of the same name built to host Belgian refugees in the Great War, Monaghan United joined the First Division of the League of Ireland in 1985. With the exception of two short periods when it was elevated to the Premier Division, it played in the First for about twenty-five years. That is, until halfway through the 2012 season, when it suddenly dropped out of the competition for 'mainly but not only financial reasons', according to club chairman Jim McGlone on 18 June 2012.[63] At the time, it still owed considerable loan payments to the league.[64] A major portion of those borrowings was for development of facilities at the Gortakeegan stadium, capacity 5,000, after the club moved in 1987. A new stand seating 800 and the floodlights were added in 1995, and the following year Gortakeegan was officially opened by the Republic of Ireland national football team's manager, Mick McCarthy.[65] Yet Monaghan United has never attracted the crowds that would make Gortakeegan viable, even with the financial backing of a major local industry, Kingspan Century Homes, which is based just on the other side of the Ulster Canal.

Soccer, or association football, has become a sharp indicator of identity in Ireland. That is because it has been partitioned since the border was established, unlike every other sport in which Irish teams compete internationally. Sports such as rugby, golf, cricket, badminton, hockey and boxing are organised on a provincial and all-Ireland basis. Yet having two international football teams has brought a muddle of confusion. Until partition, the Irish Football Association (IFA), founded in Belfast in 1880, governed the game throughout the island. With the foundation of the Free State, the breakaway Football Association of Ireland (FAI) was established in Dublin. Both associations fielded 'national' sides called 'Ireland', often comprising some of the same players. Finally, in the 1950s, the football world governing body, FIFA, ruled that Irish players could not compete for both teams as no fewer than thirty-two had already done until then.[66] However, even with a FIFA directive on the names that the two sides would use for competition, confusion still arose because of the IFA's use of the name Ireland for the British Home Championship.

Yet the muddle and duplication over soccer did not end there, and certainly not along the border, where players could be affiliated to different football codes and play for teams on both sides of the border. That is because football competitions in Northern Ireland are played on Saturdays, while in the south, competitive matches are on Sunday. Many players could, and did, compete for teams across the border, teams such as Lisbellaw in Fermanagh and Darkley in Armagh, and then return to their home clubs in Clones or Monaghan for Sunday competitions. Many even managed to dodge the notorious ban on 'foreign games' imposed from 1905 until 1971 by the Gaelic Athletic Association by playing Saturday and Sunday soccer as well as Sunday Gaelic. It was hardly surprising, therefore, that the first waves in the tide that would sweep away the Rule 27 'ban' at the 1971 GAA congress began in Monaghan, when two separate clubs put forward motions to have it deleted at the 1970 county board convention.[67]

Across the road from the sports ground, meanwhile, a grand entrance with pictorial noticeboards welcomes walkers and cyclists to the Ulster Canal Greenway, an elaborately restored towpath wending its way into the centre of the town and out the other side. Having negotiated the obstacle course and endured the blockages of the towpath thus far, it is a wonderful relief to lope along without a care in the world as the pathway forges ahead through the fringe of the Rossmore estate, along the side of the Clones road, through the Mullaghmatt and Cortalvin housing district, and past a beautifully restored lock-keeper's cottage, avoiding the dangers of an abandoned lock before descending down into the grounds of the Convent of St Louis, where an unseen ancient *crannóg* was probably the first place of habitation in what grew into the county town.

Yet there is something about this development that makes me uneasy, and nervous about future plans to extend the greenway. The pathway is fenced in on the channel side and where any danger might lurk from watery perils or ghostly nuns, it is fenced in with stiff steel mesh barriers that restrict any deviation and even obscure the view. I am reminded forcefully of a section of the other greenway path I walked recently through the fringes of Westport in County Mayo. The design is exactly the same, as are the style of fencing, the notices and all the other furniture of a carefully constructed 'wildlife habitat and nature trail' in a 'linear park' along what was once a commercial and recreational thoroughfare for navigation and other access, running alongside a canal channel teeming with life and wonder. It is as if the entire project has been taken over by health-and-safety officers who will suck up all available funding in over-elaborate measures to guard against all eventualities. As I complete this leg of my journey at the Glen Road and head up into the town for a coffee break, I feel a pang of regret. For while the H&S crowd is in control, there will never be a chance of a makeshift regatta on the canal for the youngsters of the future.

5. County Town: Monaghan

Sam McAughtry's early memories of Monaghan were of a 'shanty town with nothing going for it but the fact that it had stayed out of the war'.[1] Yet Belfast Protestants flocked there to buy things rationed in the North, contending with 'bullying customs men storming through trains and the railway line littered with rolls of wallpaper and packets of butter, as the word spread that they were contraband'. It was a town of local people 'standing at street corners staring, as the deprived Northerners hit town, rushing into the cafés to tear into bacon and eggs, and into the bars to lower bottles of stout with one-third off'. On his return in the mid-1980s, McAughtry noted the similarity of accent, a feeling of home, the kinship and blunt honesty of Northerners, the absence of 'significant support' for Sinn Féin, and the cohesion of a Protestant vote. That last aspect puzzles him as he ventures into a state where Protestants are said to be 'fully integrated'. He is not won over by the reassurances of Alan Crawford, town council chairman, headmaster and representative of the Independent Protestant Association, that the 'instinct' to come together for voting purposes began in the 1920s when Protestants felt 'threatened by the new Free State' and, over time, it had become 'very low-key'.[2]

The early threat was real and, apart from the house raids, kidnappings, intimidation and constant 'othering' of local Protestants during the early years of partition, one episode in particular had a huge and lasting negative impact. In Dáil Éireann on 6 August 1920, Monaghan South TD Sean MacEntee presented a petition drawn up by Sinn Féin members of Belfast Corporation 'and many others' in the city, appealing for help against the 'war of extermination being waged against us' in pogroms and workplace expulsions.[3] The petition called for a boycott of Belfast goods and withdrawal of funds from Belfast-based banks. The North Monaghan TD Ernest Blythe totally opposed this petition for a blockade, describing it as the 'worst possible step to take', since it would 'destroy forever the possibility of any union'.[4] He said the basis of 'every trouble in the North was sectarian' and that that 'made possible the fury of the anti-Catholic forces there', but the Dáil, acting as a government, 'could not afford to range any section of the citizens against them'. Blythe was supported by Countess Markievicz, who noted that 'a blockade would be playing into the hands of the enemy and giving them a good excuse for partition'. She wondered if it was a 'trap on the part of the English government to cut off trade with Belfast and so make Ireland into two trading centres'. The Dáil's acting president, Arthur Griffith, intervened to support action, saying that 'twelve or thirteen million pounds was paid annually into Belfast banks from Leinster, Munster and Connacht', and 'that could be cut off' in order to 'bring the unionist gentlemen to their senses'. Others, including Michael Collins of Cork South, spoke of the impact of a boycott in Belfast, and protested the attempt of 'two deputies from the North of Ireland to inflame the passions of members' because 'there was no Ulster question'.[5] An amended motion backing a boycott was then put and carried.

Nobody mentioned in the debate that the boycott would put Monaghan on a fast track to the economic siding where it remains to this day. North Monaghan, in particular, was wholly connected to Belfast for markets, supplies and jobs. Since the city's emergence as the commercial capital of Ireland, virtually everything went to and came from there on the GNR rail network. Because of that, Monaghan was chosen as the focus for the Belfast Boycott. The clampdown was quick and it was ominous. Travelling salesmen for Belfast firms were warned not to return; shopkeepers were cautioned not to deal with Belfast; and the general public was told not to enter shops supplied from Belfast.[6] On 19 August 1920, four delegates of a new committee of Catholic traders visited all the shops in Monaghan town with a declaration to be signed pledging not to deal 'directly or indirectly with Belfast unionist firms'. All the Catholics signed. Protestants shopkeepers protested about the added cost of sourcing supplies and had IRA pickets placed on their premises. Described as 'friendly persuasion', the pickets convinced many customers not to enter for fear of 'becoming marked'.[7] Meanwhile,

Catholic traders in Monaghan and Clones withdrew their accounts from Belfast-based banks. According to the *Northern Standard* on 4 September 1920, this resulted in 'very slack' business and temporary redundancies.

Whatever the intention of the organisers, the Belfast Boycott in Monaghan was seen as utterly sectarian, and unionists held a meeting to protest the 'boycott of Protestant traders'.[8] As the months progressed, tensions rose even further, and the friendly persuasion became outright intimidation. When McCaldin's bakery refused to honour the boycott, five of its bread vans were burnt out in April 1921. Elsewhere in the county, a list was circulated of twenty-one Castleblayney merchants who were allegedly still trading with Belfast. Only three of those were Catholic, and documents show that Monaghan's Sinn Féin courts in 1921 were dealing predominantly with cases of those who 'purchased Belfast goods in Protestant shops'.[9] Another blacklist was compiled by the 2nd Brigade of the Fifth Northern Division, naming eleven businesses in Castleblayney and six in Ballybay. Letters were sent to those businessmen saying their names would be removed if they signed guarantees not to offend again, returned all Belfast goods and paid whatever fine the IRA imposed. Eoin O'Duffy reported that 'several merchants, including unionists, have fallen in with our wishes and paid stiff fines to have their names removed from the blacklist'.[10]

When some traders still refused to bow to picketing and fines, the IRA tried to prevent entry of Belfast goods by road and rail. On 4 March 1921 at Inniskeen, a train was raided by armed men and a wagon with sugar, bacon, bread and hardware was emptied out and burned. In April, a mail and goods train was halted at Glaslough by IRA volunteers with several wagons full of foodstuffs and other goods targeted under the Belfast Boycott. John McGonnell took part in the raid:

> We took the train crew off, collected such mails as we considered necessary, then sprinkled the train with petrol from the engine back to the guard's van at the rear of the train and set the petrol alight. Dan Hogan then mounted the footplate of the engine and started the train going on towards Clones. Hogan then stepped down from the engine when it had properly started.

The train proceeded on its way burning fiercely, and when near Monaghan town stopped – probably for want of water in the boiler – and had by then practically burned itself out.[11]

O'Duffy noted that the Glaslough train raid was very important because the IRA seized railway invoices and mail revealing names of businesses still dealing with Belfast, and action against these businesses had the 'desired effect'.[12]

But information about breaches of the Belfast Boycott was not all that O'Duffy was seeking. After Glaslough, McGonnell was ordered to carry out a raid on Clones Post Office as the mail bags were delivered from the railway station. With about seven of his men, they overpowered the Post Office staff, seized the mail and brought it by car to Latton, where O'Duffy and his staff examined it. A further raid in January 1921 was carried out on Clones Post office, and the mail was delivered to O'Duffy:

Information obtained in one of these raids resulted in the execution of two British spies – Kitty Carrol from near Scotstown and Arthur Treanor from Tydavnet direction. In both of these cases I heard that cheques were actually enclosed in letters in payment for services rendered. I know for a fact that both of those people were executed as a result of information got in raids on mails which left no doubt as to their guilt. After Kitty Carroll was shot, Prime Minister Lloyd George made a statement in the British House of Commons in connection with the execution and the press reports said he wept when he described the callous disregard which the IRA displayed for the niceties of civilised warfare in executing a woman.[13]

Around the same time, two other suspected informers were executed at Latnamard, Aghabog, off the Monaghan-to-Newbliss road. One had broken under interrogation in Belfast, and the other had divulged information to two IRA volunteers dressed in RIC uniforms.

Meanwhile, the Belfast Boycott in Monaghan town raised surprises, such as the invoice for goods delivered from a firm on the boycott list addressed to the chairman of the town's boycott committee. It was found in the Glaslough train raid. Philip Marron, commander of the town's IRA battalion, said:

> This man's case was taken to the Sinn Féin court and he had, as a consequence, to pay a substantial fine. This particular case received wide local publicity and its sequel provided an effective warning to others who were inclined to ignore the boycott regulations.[14]

Enforcement of the boycott included a 'constant watch on all conveyances using the public roads'. Large firms with headquarters in Monaghan town specialised in selling Belfast goods: 'We had to keep a watch on these firms and maintain a constant check on their deliveries, and where we found them abusing the boycott regulations, we destroyed the goods.'[15]

The boycott ended with the Craig-Collins pact of January 1922. While it failed nationally, the Dáil's Belfast Boycott had a huge impact in Monaghan. The price was paid primarily by Protestant traders, whose domination of business life in the town was eroded from that point. That fuelled fears of what rule by Dublin would mean, and prompted many Protestants to migrate northwards. It also rendered Monaghan an 'economic cul-de-sac'. Consumers had to contend with higher prices because of the trade diversion it enforced; the *Northern Standard* noted that a Monaghan working man's cost of living was raised by 5 shillings more per week because of the Belfast Boycott.[16] Yet the final cost was the psychological separation of Monaghan from its traditional and natural centre, even before customs tariffs were imposed. The foreboding of Ernest Blythe was borne out in a century of separation that began with a boycott that had little if any impact on other parts of Ireland, and none whatsoever on the sporadic purges and pogroms in Belfast that had prompted it.

Christopher Fitz-Simon witnessed the end of the Second World War from the vantage of Aviemore, a large and elegant Georgian house that presides over the centre of the town from the top of Mill Street. It had been a townhouse of the Hamiltons of Cornacassa Demesne, and subsequently a private school for young ladies, before being acquired by Christopher's Aunt Mat and her husband Dr Killen. Christopher boarded there while attending a private school in the town, where his teacher Mrs Bradley marked the progress of the Allied troops 'up the leg of Italy on a wall map', and said it would 'not be long before the Allies invaded France or the Netherlands'.[17] Noting that the number of American soldiers on weekend leave to 'enjoy the bright lights of Monaghan had dwindled to nothing', he sensed they were 'massing at this very moment on the coast of southern England'. After rumours and speculation of false starts, D-Day happened and soon Cherbourg, Bayeux and Caen were taken by the Allies, with Mrs Bradley announcing that 'once Berlin was captured the war would be over'.[18] It was already almost over in Monaghan, with the relaxation of border controls: 'Identification cards ceased to be needed for cross-border visits, and the only border officials left were the Customs men' to search baggage on the GNR in order to 'stop people from Northern Ireland coming to places like Monaghan to buy our cheaper goods'.[19] His aunt's own aunt Zoë from Aughnacloy was one such Northerner. On one occasion she bought a woolly cardigan and four pairs of combinations, which she donned at Aviemore to go home on the bus 'looking considerable larger than she had been that morning'. Perhaps more memorable for most was the Customs officer who inadvertently opened a carriage door when Duffy's Circus was passing through town, and a lion stepped onto the platform. The *Northern Standard* reported that when the officer smacked the animal on his face with his cap, the 'King of Beasts' returned meekly to its wagon. With the end of rationing and the wind-up of cross-border rail, Monaghan town was reduced from a destination to a crossroads on the way to Dublin from Derry and from Belfast to Galway, where the 'coming and going of travellers gave a swirl to the edges of it'.[20]

There was no swirl for another writer removed from cosmopolitan Dublin, 'up on the border in our Irish-speaking convent' among 'imperfect adults, and living somewhere between twenty and two hundred years in the past'.[21] Even the teenage Nuala O'Faolain sensed that she was somewhere out of kilter with the rest of the world when she:

> smoked perched in the window embrasure of a lavatory high up in the attics, listening at the cold glass to the noises of the town, like the great roars from the rallies for the IRA men – one of them was a local – who were killed on the border in 1956.[22]

The local IRA man was 20-year-old Feargal O'Hanlon, who grew up just across Park Street from the convent. On the evening of Friday, 27 December 1956, the young Monaghan County Council clerk donned IRA battledress and – after they had a meal in his home – set off for the border in a minibus with the rest of the Pearse flying column.[23] He was the only Monaghan volunteer in the fourteen-member active-service unit led by Dubliner Sean Garland, and including four others from that city, two each from Galway and Fermanagh, individuals from Cork, Armagh and Wexford, and Limerick's Sean South. For three days, they lived rough along the border, moving by night as they tried to identify accessible targets while security forces roamed the roads. 'Cold, hungry, wet and alone in a barren and unknown terrain', they were anxious to engage the enemy. Finally, they settled on the RUC barracks at Brookeborough, a 'solid unionist citadel'.[24]

Around 5:30 p.m. on New Year's Day, armed masked men knocked on Leo Martin's front door in Lisnaskea and forced him to drive his lorry towards Brookeborough, where he was bound, gagged and left at the side of the road. Vincent Conlon then drove it with the others in full combat uniform up to the barracks, where two bags of gelignite were placed at the door. Daithí Ó Conaill fired into them, but the gelignite failed to explode. RUC Sergeant Kenneth Cordner opened fire from an upstairs window with a Sten gun and the attack party fired at will. Hampered by the lorry's proximity to the building, South could not get elevation with his Bren gun. He was shot and slumped over the machine gun. After grenades failed to breach the barracks, the IRA unit began to withdraw, as Cordner emptied his magazine, wounding four of the other men in the retreating lorry.[25] These included O'Hanlon, who had two bullet wounds to his legs, one of which had severed an artery and smashed his femur.[26] He was bleeding profusely as the lorry set off for the 10-mile journey across Sliabh Beagh to the Monaghan border at Roslea. As the old lorry ground its way through Moan's Cross and on to Altawark at the crossroads of the Clones-to-Fivemiletown road, it became obvious that South was dead and O'Hanlon dying. With the military and police encircling, the two men were left in a cowshed and the others made off through the hills of Eshywulligan towards the border with the aid of an outdated map and a compass, while flares lit up the night sky. After five hours in atrocious weather, they made it across the border and were arrested in Clones.

Almost immediately after their departure, the police arrived at the cowshed and found the two men inside. South was already dead, and O'Hanlon was 'gasping for air, moaning his last as his life ebbed away'; he died five minutes later. In Monaghan town, his sister Pádraigín Ó Mhurchada was with her family gathered around the radio when news came through of two killed in Brookeborough: 'My mother sensed immediately that Feargal had been killed.'[27] That was confirmed the following day when her father Eugene identified the corpse in Enniskillen. At the inquest he attended along with two of Sean South's brothers from Limerick, he heard Enniskillen Hospital surgeon J. W. Wilson suggesting that if his son had received 'timely medical attention' for his 'superficial' wound, his life would have been saved from death due to 'shock and haemorrhage due to a gunshot wound and fracture of the left thigh'.[28] A statement issued by the IRA on the same day said that he 'died after being captured by the enemy', leaving open the possibility that he had been summarily executed, but this was discounted by the inquest.[29]

While the IRA attack at Brookeborough was a bloody shambles in military terms, it became a huge symbolic victory for armed republicanism. The bodies of O'Hanlon and South were released to the families immediately after the inquests and were brought home in two hearses from Enniskillen to Clones and on to Monaghan town for O'Hanlon and on to Limerick via Dublin for South. Huge crowds lined the route once the cortège crossed the border at Clones, where a guard of honour composed of members of the local GAA club shouldered O'Hanlon's coffin through the town. At Monaghan, the hearses stopped once more, and the GAA was joined by 'civic dignitaries' in carrying the remains through the town centre to St Macartan's cathedral where the tricolour-draped coffins remained under IRA guard of honour through the night.[30] After Requiem Mass the next day, Feargal O'Hanlon was taken for burial at nearby Latlurcan cemetery, while gardaí saluted his cortège. His IRA comrade Noel Kavanagh, just released from detention in Dublin that morning, gave a graveside oration: 'To do justice to the volunteer who has been killed, one must understand why he has died ... If they wish to erect a monument to him, then it should be the monument of the 32-county Irish republic.'[31] As O'Hanlon was added to the roll of Ireland's 'patriot dead', his funeral was 'eclipsed utterly' by the huge public wave of sympathy that swept Sean South's coffin to a hero's funeral in Limerick.

Later that week, Dublin City Council voted sympathy for the two families, but a proposal to include the name of RUC Constable Scally caused a scathing rebuttal.[32] Sympathy was also voted by other councils in the far south of the country. And within months, possibly the ultimate accolade for the two 'martyrs to the cause' came in the form of rebel songs in their names, 'Sean South of Garryowen' and 'The Patriot Game'. The latter, written by Dominic Behan, introduces the singer: 'My name is O'Hanlon, I've just gone sixteen; My home is in Monaghan, that's where I was weaned.' Poetic licence from the lyricist, perhaps, since Feargal was 20 at the time when he lay there his 'body all holes'. It is also notable for its trenchant barbs about De Valera and his 'traitors'; and for the fact that it shares a tune with the loyalist song 'Third Battalion', and with Bob Dylan's anti-war song, 'With God on our Side'! In the Irish general election on 5 March 1957, Sinn Féin presented nineteen candidates around the country and had four elected. One of them was Feargal's brother, Eighneachán Ó hAnnluain, who secured the third seat in Monaghan as an abstentionist candidate for a single term.[33]

The wave of popular support was short-lived, however, as the might of the state and the Catholic Church turned on the rebels. Although O'Hanlon had lain in state at Monaghan's cathedral with a full IRA colour party, and been laid to rest after a concelebrated Requiem Mass, local Bishop Eugene O'Callaghan was among the first to move. At the Roslea funeral of Fr Daniel Gormley on 7 January, he declared it a mortal sin to 'take part in any of the occurrences that had taken place recently'. He warned his flock against the 'evil men going about trying to take advantages of the disturbances in the county', and added that communists in the IRA were trying to 'destroy us' by 'going around in sheep's clothing but inwardly are ravenous wolves'.[34] Then arrests on both sides of the border, IRA mishaps, some leading to self-inflicted deaths, and internment put paid to the IRA's Operation Harvest border campaign. Among those arrested was chief of staff Seán Cronin, and follow-up searches of his home uncovered detailed documents on the campaign, with many names.

In 1988, I spent an engrossing Saint Patrick's Day evening in Toronto with Seán Cronin, then nearing the end of his career as the *Irish Times* correspondent in Washington, DC.[35] We discussed many issues, including his 1950s strategy of deploying flying columns in the North. He said his arrest in Belturbet just a few days after the Brookeborough raid and subsequent court evidence – including from Detective Garda Pascal McArdle[36] – meant that the thrust was lost and never recovered. In the surge of support flowing from the funeral of Feargal O'Hanlon, he said, Monaghan could have been the launching pad for a fresh wave of attacks into Tyrone, Armagh and Fermanagh. While the flying columns were still central to his military thinking, as outlined in his border strategy, *General Directive for Guerrilla Campaign*, lack of on-the-ground logistical support across the border left them vulnerable. The plan would have been to resort to sorties from Monaghan against specific targets. I referred him to the Loughgall ambush the previous year when an IRA column based in Monaghan was wiped out. Somebody's been reading your mail, I observed!

Given its pivotal location and size, Monaghan was destined to be enveloped in the Troubles from the very outset. With the eruption of widespread violence in August 1969, nationalists flocked across the border, some using the town as a refuge, others as a staging post or a temporary respite. While most were genuinely seeking sanctuary, others had a political agenda and were 'opportunistic and anxious to capitalise on a condition of instability. Monaghan became a centre of conspiracy and intrigue, often fuelled by late-night drinking'.[37] A branch of the Northern Ireland Civil Rights Association (NICRA) was established in the town, and an impromptu public rally was held outside the courthouse in Church Square on 19 August 1969. Among a range of speakers from both sides of the border was Fianna Fáil TD Padraig Mooney, who addressed the meeting, which was chaired by his party colleague Cllr

Lorcan Ronaghan. Mooney told the crowd that the Irish Army should be recalled from Cyprus and deployed as a peacekeeping force in the North. Speakers from Dungannon, Omagh and Newry contrasted the 'freedom' of Monaghan with the policing and Special Powers legislation across the border. Austin Currie, then the Nationalist MP for East Tyrone, warned against acts of intimidation aimed at Protestants in Monaghan, saying that if they really were members of the B Specials, the matter should be dealt with when they crossed into Northern Ireland.

There was a lot of talk about the Dublin government helping communities to defend themselves against the onslaught of those times. Currie, who had moved his family south because of death threats, was staying at the Westenra Hotel in Monaghan. He was awakened on the morning of 22 August 1969 by someone knocking on his hotel room door and shouting that there was a telephone call for him:

> It was Charles Haughey TD, minister for finance. He told me that the previous day the government had taken a decision to make money available for the relief of distress in the North. Did my area require assistance? ... I informed him of the situation in Dungannon, where people had fled the housing estates and some were already in Gormanston Camp. Would they qualify? He indicated that he thought they would. I then pushed him a bit further – what did he mean by 'distress'? The reply was, 'Anything you want it to mean, Austin.' There was something in the way he said it that made me cautious. I said I would get back to him. I never did, nor did I have anything to do with the fund. I had reason to be glad of that later when a Dáil committee was established to inquire into the handling of the fund monies, amid allegations that some of the money had been used to arm what would later become the Provisional IRA.[38]

Others were obviously less reticent about receiving 'distress' relief in the form of arms, including some of those who attended a meeting in a private room of the same hotel the following day, Saturday, 23 August 1969. Chaired by Nationalist Party Senator Gerry Lennon, an

Armagh solicitor, it was allegedly attended by members of civil rights groups, refugee committees and others who 'reflected the feelings of fear, confusion and militancy which were present to varying degrees in the Catholic community in Northern Ireland'.[39] After an emotional speech about Southern betrayal of their own people in the North, a young politician left the room to make a phone call, then returned to announce that 600 rifles had been secured and named where they would be available at three locations along the border. 'He warned that the guns were illegal and anyone caught with them would have to take the rap and remain silent.' It should be noted however, that this version is contradicted by others and by the Arms Trial itself, which dated the first state commitment to supply arms to the meeting between Captain James Kelly and various 'defence committee' representatives held in Bailieborough, County Cavan, on Saturday, 4 October 1969.[40]

After that initial rally in Church Square, the civil rights group established its 'headquarters' at the old tax office on Dublin Street, with John Donaghy, a member of the NICRA executive from Dungannon, as manager. Given the frenetic activity, and the divergence of different strands of agitators at the time, it soon became embroiled in rumour and controversy. Austin Currie said that the purpose of the office was to act as a 'contact point for those coming over the border and also as a centre for the collection and distribution of aid for refugees', but 'before long NICRA found it necessary to issue a public statement disassociating itself from this office'.[41] It seems that a split was underway, as explained in another statement published in the *Northern Standard* which said that 'many civil rights officials' decided to operate from Monaghan during the crucial week from 11 August 1969 because they were not safe at home. While some of these were republicans, most were not. The decision to set up the office was taken by branches of NICRA in Tyrone and Armagh. Its function was to rally Monaghan people for civil rights, act as a base for information on the North and provide a centre for activities. The statement concluded by saying that the office would be staffed by 'the committee who set it up'.[42]

By then, British troops were deployed north of the border and events moved ahead quickly, with the subsequent split in Sinn Féin at its

Dublin Ard Fhéis in January 1970 between factions favouring Marxist class struggle and those demanding immediate armed action on behalf of Catholic nationalists. In December, the IRA had also been riven with the emergence of two IRAs known as the Official IRA and the Provisional IRA pitted against the crown forces and occasionally against each other. Internment was introduced, and more people flocked across to the 'safe haven' of Monaghan, which was increasingly swept up in protests and plots linked to the Troubles.

In a particularly violent border incident near Clones in 1972 at the interface of Mullanahinch, County Fermanagh, with Aghafin, County Monaghan, British soldiers fired two live rounds, sixty rubber bullets and thirty canisters of CS gas at a crowd of over 800 that had assembled to reinstate the cratered road.[43] Several shots were also fired by a local IRA gunman who arrived on the scene. When three republicans were subsequently arrested and taken to Monaghan, the Garda station there was surrounded and attacked by a crowd demanding their release. The gardaí asked for military support. The minister for defence, Jerry Cronin, subsequently told the Dáil that when a military party was dispatched to the town, the crowd at the Garda station grew from about 300 to between 1,200 and 1,500 and an armoured car was attacked by about 200 people who tried to set it alight.[44] 'In the fracas … two soldiers got detached from the main body, were knocked to the ground and beaten and had their rifles wrested from them. The rifles had not been recovered.' Condemning the incident, in which every officer and man deployed had been 'struck by a missile of some description, the minister said 'those taking part in such demonstrations in future could expect a further reaction by the military'.

As the worst years of the Troubles played out across the border, and sometimes spilled over, Monaghan town became even more of a sanctuary and playground. Young people, who for years had crossed the border for rest and recreation not available in the North, where pubs and dancehalls were closed on Sundays, now began to flock to the South in even greater numbers. In quick succession, two new hotels were opened in Monaghan, with modern lounge bars and discos aimed at the surge in demand. The Hillgrove Hotel, featuring the plush Apollo Lounge nightclub, which had a lunar-landing theme, was built beside the cathedral on the Old Armagh Road by the Brady brothers, whose business was founded on livestock marts. Poised on the northern approaches into the town from Derry, Tyrone and Armagh was the Four Seasons Hotel. It was built at Coolshanagh by Alan Clancy, who had emigrated from the deep south of County Monaghan and acquired a number of pubs in New York City, notably the Bogside Bar in Manhattan. In 1985, long after he had sold off the hotel, Clancy re-emerged from the shadows when the Irish government led by Garret FitzGerald froze a bank account containing £1.75 million on the ground that the money belonged to the IRA.[45] Clancy and another man, Dave McCartney, who were living in the USA and Mexico, respectively, claimed that the account in Navan, County Meath, belonged to them. Their claim was dismissed by the High Court in 1988, and twenty years later, the funds were handed over to the state since both claimants were dead. The frozen IRA funds had accrued interest in the meantime, and yielded the state a windfall of almost €6 million.

Along with other nightlife venues in the town centre, the new hotels were packed at weekends and fleets of hired coaches and buses transported patrons home in the early hours. As with any venue attracting young clientele, occasionally there was trouble, and the growing Garda presence in the town was often stretched to the limits as local rivalries played out in the car parks. Order was maintained inside the venues by bouncers and, of these, 'Big' Henry Diamond was probably the most popular. A towering full-back on the Derry county football team that won the Ulster GAA Championship in 1970, it was generally known that he could only play 'away games' south of the border, because if he played in the North, he risked being detained at Her Majesty's pleasure. Other GAA players who made their home in Monaghan town shared the same handicap, although some managed to make their way to America and work in the Clancy bars. Yet in many respects, the natural affinity and social exchange of Monaghan with its cross-border neighbours was stretched to the maximum limits of local tolerance during a period when Monaghan began to acquire, with other border towns, a reputation of lawlessness.

British security chiefs began to quantify one aspect of that reputation in a dossier entitled 'Cross-border activities of IRA after Operation Motorman'.[46] It was prepared by army and RUC chiefs for Britain's first Northern Ireland Secretary of State, Willie Whitelaw, who in turn presented it to Prime Minister Edward Health and Taoiseach Jack Lynch in November 1972. Over a five-month period, it charged, there were 286 security incidents on or close to the border, carried out by IRA units operating in a cross-border role or by units in the North that relied for men and materiel on IRA groups in the Republic.[47] As the IRA had reduced its activities in former no-go areas of Belfast and Derry, the border had taken centre stage, with frequent visits by IRA Chief of Staff Seán Mac Stíofáin. The units were composed of a 'hard core' of fugitive 'on-the-runs', backed by others from the Republic. The incidents included 'bomb attacks, shootings, mining incidents and assassinations'. The dossier named five main centres – Dundalk, Monaghan, Bundoran, Lifford and Buncrana – with other 'isolated groups operating in border sectors between the main centres'.[48] The dossier gave estimates of the numbers involved, as well as the names and addresses of leading Provisional IRA men, including veterans Kevin Mallon from Coalisland and J.B. O'Hagan from Lurgan, both now based in Monaghan town. The dossier named O'Hagan as a member of the IRA Army Council and its director of operations, and Monaghan town as an 'extremely active centre', used as a base for at least three active-service units. O'Hagan led an ASU of twenty-five volunteers, while also supervising other ASUs in the district. These included a Fermanagh unit based in the Clones/Roslea area, according to the dossier, although details on that seem sparse by comparison. The Monaghan town Volunteers were on the run from north Armagh and east Tyrone, and continued to carry out operations in their home areas. With other details, the dossier is an insight into the level of intelligence being passed across the border at this time. It is also worth noting that when Mallon and O'Hagan were subsequently arrested and held in Dublin's Mountjoy Prison, along with Chief of Staff Seamus 'Thumper' Twomey, the IRA command structure was so 'seriously curbed' that the dramatic helicopter escape of October 1973 was aimed specifically at getting them back in action.[49]

While the 1973–7 coalition government is generally credited with stamping down on 'subversion' in the state, the backlash began in earnest much earlier. The Offences Against the State (Amendment) Act passed at the end of 1972 was the last of a series of moves during the final year of Jack Lynch's Fianna Fáil government. Justice Minister Dessie O'Malley 'favoured a tougher line on subversion within the state, including selective internment'.[50] So in May 1972, he invoked the Special Criminal Court, with three judges and no jury, for terrorist offences. In October, Section 31 of the Broadcasting Act was introduced to censor journalists working for the national broadcaster, RTÉ, on matters related to the Troubles. The same month, Sinn Féin's office in Kevin Street in Dublin was closed down. The following month, IRA Chief of Staff Seán MacStíofáin was jailed. By December, the amendment to legislation meant suspected IRA members could be jailed on the word of a senior Garda officer. From the huge wave of popular sympathy in the South following Derry's Bloody Sunday at the start of the year, the tide was turning decisively against the Republican Movement and Northern nationalists in general.

Some people in Southern border towns and counties blamed Northerners in general for violence spilling over the border, and for the increasingly repressive laws. Republican fugitives or 'on-the-runs' became 'more feared, resented, socially excluded and defined as "bad people" than welcomed'.[51] The start of 1973 was heralded by more bombs in border towns and villages – Clones, Pettigo and Belturbet, where two teenagers were killed.[52] After an election in February, the new coalition government 'felt free to act and to talk tough in ways Lynch could never have done'.[53] Justice Minister Patrick Cooney instructed senior gardaí in border areas that they were to co-operate with their counterparts in the North. By June, a report for Northern Ireland Office Director of Intelligence Alan Rowley stated that Armagh RUC 'Chief Superintendent McCullough speaks to Chief Superintendent McMahon in Monaghan and is arranging to meet him locally'.[54] While the coalition held out against British demands for military liaison on the basis that it would not be appropriate given the different role of the Irish Army, the traffic of intelligence appears to have been a one-way street heading north, especially when it came to collusion between forces of the state and those intent on wreaking havoc and death.

The Monaghan bombing on 17 May 1974 was not totally unexpected. There had been bombs already in Clones and Castleblayney, and the county town was within easy striking distance of the sinister forces that lurked beyond. Yet what seems most hurtful in retrospect is that the blast has been remembered almost as an afterthought to the bombs that exploded in Dublin that same day.[55] The final toll in Monaghan was seven: Archie Harper, George Williamson, Thomas Campbell, Patrick Askin, Peggy White, Jack Travers and Thomas Croarkin. The combined incident, which involved four bombs and claimed thirty-three lives, is invariably referred to as the 'Dublin-Monaghan bombings', as if the terrorists had one left over on their way home from tearing the heart out of the capital city with three devastating blasts.

In his official report of 2003, Judge Henry Barron criticised the Gardaí for stopping their investigations prematurely, and the coalition government led by Liam Cosgrave for its inaction and lack of interest.[56] The report of a subsequent Irish parliamentary hearing on the Barron Report in 2003 added criticism of Prime Minister Tony Blair's British government for refusing to release key documents relating to the atrocities.[57] In the absence of vital evidence, the theory persists that the blast in Monaghan, an hour and a half after the last of the three bombs in Dublin exploded, was timed to draw security forces away from border checkpoints to allow the bombers to cross back to the North unimpeded.[58] Whatever the sequence or its purpose, the targeting of Monaghan town centre was an atrocity. If rendered in impact per capita, it was the equivalent of more than four times the dreadful fatalities that befell Dublin on that day.

The inquests held in June 1974 were told that in practically every case, death was the result of blast-wave damage to lungs and brains from the 150-pound bomb, although flying missiles and glass also caused extensive injuries. Scores of others were injured by the bomb placed in a 1966 Hillman Minx car stolen in Portadown several hours earlier.[59] It was parked just five minutes before it detonated outside Greacen's pub, opposite a Bank of Ireland branch.[60] That was where people usually awaited buses, including the express services to and from Dublin and Derry. As a university student in Dublin at that time, I frequently boarded and alighted from buses at that precise spot. The 7 p.m. timing on a Friday evening could have had even more devastating effect if one of those packed buses had arrived on the often-erratic schedule.

Monaghan was back in the eye of the storm with the Republican hunger strikes of 1980 and 1981 in the H-Blocks of the Maze Prison. Republican prisoners there had already endured years of protest demanding restoration of political prisoner status which had been removed in 1976. First refusing to wear prison uniforms, they escalated their action to a 'dirty protest' by smearing excrement on the cell walls when refused permission to wrap themselves in blankets to 'slop out' their latrine buckets. Feelings were already running high from the initial hunger protest, which ended in broken British government promises as Sean McKenna and Tommy McKearney, both former residents of Monaghan town, were on the brink of death. IRA leader Brendan Hughes took the decision to save McKenna's life when he was slipping in and out of a death coma.[61] Ending the hunger strike also saved McKearney when he had only hours to live.[62] So as hopes were dashed at the start of 1981, there was little doubt of the grim determination that would be brought to the new hunger protest for the prisoners' five demands: no prison uniforms; no prison work; free association and right to organise social activities and education; right to one visit, one letter and one parcel each week; and full restoration of lost remission. That determination was shared among the supporters of the H-Block committee based in McMeel's shop in Dublin Street, Monaghan. It was grimly borne out in the successive deaths of the initial volunteer prisoners, Bobby Sands, Francis Hughes, Raymond McCreesh and Patsy O'Hara.

By then, 25-year-old IRA hunger striker Kieran Doherty from Belfast had been adopted as the H-Block Dáil candidate in the Cavan-Monaghan constituency. His campaign was energetic and well-managed by his director of elections, Caoimhghín Ó Caoláin, a former senior bank official from Monaghan town, and many campaigners had already tasted bitter electoral success in neighbouring Fermanagh-South Tyrone when Bobby Sands swept to electoral victory before he died on the world stage. They were determined to tap the same global outrage with another elected representative. Doherty was duly declared elected on 11 June, having notched up 9,121 first-preference votes,[63] mostly from the Monaghan end of the constituency. He remained a member of the Dáil for almost two months, during which time two of his fellow hunger strikers, Joe McDonnell and Martin Hurson, perished.

As Doherty neared death, Monaghan was in a state of turmoil. This spilled south on 18 July with the Ballsbridge Riot in Dublin, when a determined protest march tried to force their way through a Garda blockade to reach the British embassy. It has been described as a 'watershed in Irish history',[64] and many of those on the front line were from Monaghan. This was followed by weekend rioting in Monaghan town and Castleblayney.[65] In 'Blayney, the rioting was in the centre of the town, whereas in Monaghan, it was confined to the Hillgrove Hotel area on the Old Armagh Road, where gardaí in riot gear charged the crowd to disperse stone-throwers. Extra gardaí were deployed in the town and the local H-Block committee condemned the rioting.

The committee also condemned other acts of vandalism, such as the daubing of slogans on the courthouse, in Old Cross Square and at Patton's Yard. Castleblayney council chairman Peter Lynch accused 'Northern hooligans' of causing the trouble, and this accusation was taken up by many Dublin-based commentators. A week later, when it was confirmed that those involved were local people, Lynch apologised;[66] the Dublin-based commentators did not. Angry tension was so pronounced in Monaghan as Doherty neared death, that it is probably worth noting the contrast in the demeanour of Down and Armagh football fans who attended the Ulster Final in Clones that weekend, and who were publicly complimented on their 'exemplary behaviour' by Garda Sergeant Jackie O'Connor in a *Northern Standard* report.

Kieran Doherty died on Sunday, 2 August 1981, a day after fellow republican hunger striker Kevin Lynch. Doherty had survived for seventy-three days without sustenance, the longest hunger strike of the H-Block protest, and just a day shorter than that of former Lord Mayor of Cork Terence MacSwiney, who starved himself to death in a 1920 protest at Brixton Prison in England. Word of his death reached McMeel's shop and was relayed to those gathering in Castleblayney for a major rally.[67] They rushed home to bang dustbin lids and blow whistles to notify others of the TD's death. A march was quickly organised in Monaghan town centre; some participants stoned the gardaí and there was the by-now-obligatory baton charge. A young woman was injured slightly, windows were broken and a council hut at the rear of the courthouse was set alight. Sporadic acts of vandalism occurred throughout the county, as the local H-Block committee appealed for a calm and dignified shutdown on the day of Doherty's funeral. As mourners on their way to the Belfast funeral on Tuesday, 4 August passed by the bombed-out shell of the Tyholland frontier customs post, reports of other incidents were coming in. These included a third attempt to blow up the radio transmitter mast at Tirkeenan used for Garda communications. Extra uniformed gardaí and armed members of the new Special Task Force were deployed to concentrate their efforts in the border district.

A huge demonstration, with a defiant show of IRA paramilitary force involving an estimated forty-five uniformed and about 1,300 other participants, took place in Monaghan town centre on the day of Doherty's funeral.[68] All the businesses closed down for two hours from 1 p.m. as the Belfast funeral was taking place, and the pubs only reopened at 10 p.m. Volleys of shots were fired over a symbolic coffin at the Fergal O'Hanlon Memorial on the Clones Road, and a large force of gardaí in riot gear kept watch as black crosses were placed against the door of their station. Speakers at the demonstration included Sinn Féin President Ruairi Ó Bradaigh, as well as Bernadette McAlliskey of the H-Block/Armagh Committee who warned Taoiseach Garret FitzGerald that 'if I have to go through hell for the [prisoners'] five demands, he'll go with me'.

The public outpourings continued, with three full broadsheet pages of sympathy messages in the *Northern Standard*. The following week's paper had more messages of sympathy, and among the letters to the editor was one from Vincent Conlon, veteran of the 1957 Brookeborough barracks raid, and another from Desmond Leslie of Glaslough Castle. Leslie was 'moved to tears at the sight of young men dying protracted and horribly painful deaths in prison', he wrote, and he bristled at being told he 'must not show sympathy for the "wrong people",' but he was outraged by the 'cliché slogans' attached to his name in the previously published expressions of sympathy.[69] The Ballybay home of Fine Gael

TD John Conlan was picketed by people demanding the recall of Dáil Éireann to acknowledge what Doherty had died for, and a series of rallies and other events was announced for Monaghan town. Supporters of the H-Block campaign organised a plebiscite in the Mullaghmatt district, which produced a large majority in favour of renaming the council housing estate there as Kieran Doherty Park.[70]

As the hunger strikes in the H-Block petered out to an inconclusive finale, the row over the renaming of the estate persisted into the new year and far beyond, perpetuated by those who wanted to reinforce the town's claim to republican credentials.[71] However, Desmond Leslie's heartfelt but qualified sympathy had undoubtedly reflected a view that was much more pervasive among Monaghan people. They were frightened and appalled in equal measure by the heartless response to the hunger strikes of Margaret Thatcher's Westminster government, and the prospect of being further embroiled in the violence espoused by the hunger strikers and the hard core of those who supported them. Undoubtedly, some residents even blamed the civil unrest in support of the hunger strikers for the tightening British border security, which effectively laid siege to Clones.[72] Even though Monaghan County Council had adopted a motion, supported by all the parties, expressing sympathy to the family of Kieran Doherty TD, the county town and the county at large were deeply divided, and there was a substantial and growing lobby that totally rejected the H-Block campaign and all who supported it.

The new year dawned with news of the violent death of Gabriel Murphy, a young Emyvale man who was shot four times in the legs in front of his wife in the early hours of New Year's Eve. He had just come home from his part-time job as a steward or 'bouncer' at the Hillgrove Hotel disco.[73] Rumours circulated that the pretext for the shooting, which led to the victim's death in hospital, was that he had challenged Jim Lynagh, a well-known IRA man from the Tully estate in the town. The IRA man's brother Colm was later convicted of the killing.[74] He served his prison sentence in the republican landings of Portlaoise Prison.

The Lynagh family would pay a heavy price for Jim's commitment to armed republicanism. After Jim was released in 1979 from a five-year sentence for possession of explosives in Long Kesh's Maze Prison, and then elected as a Sinn Féin councillor in Monaghan,[75] gardaí began to harass his family. On Friday, 10 September 1983, a young man hanged himself in his cell at Mountjoy Prison in Dublin. His name was given as 'Michael Ferguson', and he had been referred for psychiatric assessment the following day. His real name, however, was Michael Lynagh. At the subsequent inquest in the Dublin Coroner's Court, details emerged of the years of persecution by gardaí of Michael and the entire family of twelve siblings in Monaghan town.[76]

According to a detailed investigative article by Vincent Browne and Gene Kerrigan in *Magill* magazine (30 October 1982), Michael had begun to suffer from anxiety and depression under the pressure of the harassment. He was treated by his family doctor and two psychiatrists, one of them in Dublin. He had also been confined at St Davnet's psychiatric hospital in Monaghan on a few occasions. The Garda attention continued. After his brothers Jim and Colm were jailed in 1982, the latter for the Murphy shooting in Emyvale, Michael was advised by his Monaghan psychiatrist that he had better move down to Dublin. He did so, taking a flat with Finbar. There was no let-up, the coroner's court heard. Garda Special Branch frequently stopped and questioned the two brothers in Dublin, and arrested them under Section 30 of the Offences Against the State Act in March and again in April of 1983.

After the first arrest, the intimidation was stepped up: the brothers were followed to work; their neighbours were questioned; friends were followed and questioned; employers and workmates were approached. The brothers were asked to vacate their flat. Michael became more reclusive and was drinking heavily. Eventually he was arrested on a public street when adjudged to be a danger to himself or others, and he was incarcerated. He gave a false name to evade Special Branch attention, but had agreed to amend that and undergo psychiatric assessment before he killed himself. Nobody from An Garda Síochána went to the family home in Monaghan. His mother Carmel and his younger siblings learned of his death in a radio broadcast. Sometime later, they moved out of Monaghan town to live in Clones.[77]

These and other implications of the Troubles preyed on the minds of Monaghan electors in 1982. Buoyed by the success of hunger striker

Kieran Doherty's election, the H-Block lobby had decided to present a candidate in the next election, but they were overtaken by Sinn Féin's decision to put forward its own candidate. At the general election of 18 February 1982, that candidate, IRA prisoner Seamus McElwain, received 3,974 first preferences and was eliminated on the fifth count.[78] That was less than half of Doherty's tally, but it reflected the hard-core republican vote that would continue to gain seats at urban and county council level, and prime the constituency for a parliamentary breakthrough, with Caoimhghín Ó Caoláin almost trebling his first preferences to top the poll and capture a seat in 1997, after the IRA ceasefire. In that victory, the Monaghan man became the first Sinn Féin elected representative to sit in the Dáil since the Civil War.[79]

In the interim, Monaghan town passed through many dark days as the cockpit and launching pad for many of the atrocities and heartaches suffered by those who lived on both sides of the border that surrounded it on three sides. However, its strategic location would also ensure that it remained a hugely popular resort for those seeking respite from the conflict on their doorsteps in Armagh, Fermanagh and Tyrone. Industry also prospered through the enterprise and initiative of local business people involved in ventures from poultry to mushrooms, engineering, furniture and timber-frame home construction. The expanding economy drew many jobseekers from across the border, a process of evolution that ensured that the town mirrored in so many ways the character of other Ulster county towns, rather than the Southern experience.

In its religious composition too, Monaghan is decidedly Ulster, with two Presbyterian congregations, the Church of Ireland in Church Square, a Methodist church, a Gospel Hall and a variety of Pentecostal gatherings, as well as its Catholic cathedral of Saint Macartan and Saint Joseph's chapel of ease in Park Street. Of the evangelistic places of worship, the Elim Pentecostal Church has pride of place, with its large modern building. For it was here in Monaghan town on 7 January 1915 that the Elim Pentecostal mission was launched. On that date, evangelical minister George Jeffries met with seven young men in Knox's Temperance Hall on the Diamond to form the Elim Evangelistic Band, choosing the name for the biblical reference to the desert oasis of Elim, where the chosen people were refreshed.[80] In a short documentary film, Elim Pentecostal Church historian Maldwyn Jones visited Monaghan on the centenary and remarked that from its 'inauspicious beginning' here in the town, the Elim Pentecostal Church has grown to more than 600 individual ministries, with approximately 60,000 regular worshippers in Britain and Ireland.[81]

Resuming my path along the Ulster Canal just across the road from the Louis Convent entrance in Monaghan town, I set off for Old Cross Square and what lies beyond. In the absence now of a central canal basin or harbour, there is no indication of where the 'first-class steamer *Countess of Caledon*' would have tied up with its cargo of 'merchandise, cattle, pigs, grain and butter, all at very competitive rates'.[82] Yet that was promised in the advertisement that appeared in the *Northern Whig* newspaper on 1 October 1839 from the Ulster Canal Steam Carrying Company proclaiming the navigation was now open from Belfast to Monaghan, using the Lagan Canal and Lough Neagh. The service would operate every Monday and Thursday from Belfast, and rates were available from agent Robert Henderson on Belfast's Donegall Quay. The all-purpose steamer was owned initially by William Dargan and Lord Caledon, but Dargan subsequently bought all the shares. Built in Ireland of riveted iron, with a thirty-horsepower engine to turn the paddle wheel, the *Countess* was the first steamer to carry passengers on Lough Neagh, where it operated from 1838 until 1860.[83] In 1840, the Ulster Canal Steam Carrying Company had a fleet of fifteen boats capable of carrying 20 tons each on the canal. Two of these were plying the route between Monaghan and the Moy.[†]

From Old Cross Square, the towpath greenway soon opens up into the broad expanse of Saint Davnet's Hospital, now known as St Davnet's Campus, with a variety of health services, along with a traditional psychiatric hospital unit in Blackwater House. Formerly, it was known

---

† Although officially named Moy, local usage is 'the Moy' from the Gaelic '*an maigh*', meaning 'the plain'.

as Monaghan Lunatic Asylum, and that is what it was called when it was drawn to the attention of the new chief secretary for Ireland in the House of Commons at Westminster on 20 February 1919.[84] He may have been born and raised in Cork, but John Pretyman Newman was as British as Finchley, which constituency he represented as a Conservative MP from 1918 until 1923, whereupon he was knighted.[85] Newman wanted to know if Chief Secretary Ian Macpherson was aware that the 'medical officer and the staff of Monaghan Lunatic Asylum, with the aid of the inmates', had 'seized the asylum buildings and established a local soviet ... consisting of staff and inmates, to run the asylum'. He almost had it right; the medical officer was not part of the soviet, having been ousted by his 'subordinate staff'. The governor installed in his stead was Peadar O'Donnell, the revolutionary republican socialist from Donegal, who had just begun his new job as organiser for the Irish Transport and General Workers' Union (ITGWU), and was based in Monaghan town.[86] My friend and fellow journalist Anton McCabe has meticulously researched this extraordinary episode of industrial history, and the role of the man known in the *Voice of Labour* during this time as 'Monaghan Peter'.[87] Little wonder his work was noticed for, as he told a meeting in Clones, he had been involved in 'forty-eight wage movements and three strikes in four months'.[88]

O'Donnell's role in the asylum dispute was extracurricular, since the staff were members of the Irish Asylum Workers' Union (IAWU), which had settled a strike the previous year, gaining 4 shillings a week, union recognition and the reversal of an order sacking them all. Their conditions remained harsh however; not least the ninety-three-hour week they had to work. That was acceptable in the opinion of Medical Superintendent Dr Thomas P. Conlon, who pointed out that they 'work twelve hours a day for seven days, but they get off every thirteenth day, and every fourth Sunday from ten o'clock'.[89] He didn't mention that all attendants had to remain in the hospital after their shift. So, in the absence of an IAWU official in Monaghan, they called in O'Donnell, whose negotiations broke down on management's refusal of an equal pay raise for female staff.

The strike began on Thursday, 23 January 1919, and rumours soon began that the military or police were coming in. O'Donnell was then installed as governor, and the matron and deputy medical superintendent were allowed to continue their duties under supervision by the strikers, who armed themselves with farm implements, barricaded every door, and raised the red flag over the main buildings.[90] O'Donnell introduced a forty-eight-hour week, sacked the matron for insubordination, fined an attendant for wasting gas, and had a man 'spreading defeatism' locked in a padded cell for a brief spell. O'Donnell later told the *Derry Journal*, 'We did set up a soviet committee there; we hoisted the red flag; we controlled the service and no community interest suffered.'[91] It was also notable that clergy from all the local denominations ministered to their flock among the strikers and patients, 'their mixed religions a triumph of solidarity'.[92] Crowds soon gathered outside, shouting, 'Up the strikers!' and there was talk of a general strike in the town to support the soviet asylum. Eventually, the authorities caved in, granting a fifty-six-hour work week, permission for married attendants to go home after their shifts, an equal pay rise for the women and a commitment to press for a national pay-and-conditions scale in asylums. As McCabe notes, the victory dance was another resounding success: 'Police, strikers, some inmates, and outsiders, including Sinn Féiners, nationalists and unionists, all were gathered together.'[93] No wonder Belfast Nationalist MP Joe Devlin could remark when the episode was raised in the Commons, 'Is the right honourable gentleman aware that the only successfully conducted institutions in Ireland are the lunatic asylums?'

The Ulster Canal greenway snakes through the outskirts of the town and emerges at the Coolshannagh roundabout and the start of the Armagh Road. On the hill straight ahead looms a big grey, Victorian-style building that many have mistaken for the psychiatric hospital in the past. The confusion is understandable, for this rather forbidding institution is Saint Macartan's College, a Catholic school still known as 'the Sem' from its role as the junior seminary for the Catholic diocese of Clogher. Its primary role then was to promote vocations to the priesthood among the sons of farmers, minor officials and shopkeepers, who boarded there under rules and procedures adopted from the English public school system. Having endured some of my own teenage years there as a boarder, when it had a somewhat more secular mission (to educate us for 'church or state'), I scurry to the far side of the road, seeking asylum in the café at Maurice Graham's store.

6. Oriel Affairs

Monaghan to Middletown – 12 km

Monaghan and Armagh are tucked together like foetal twins in the map of Ireland. In the shifting sands of political hegemony and clan dominance, their identity was meshed from the earliest times, when they were carved out of Ulster to form the ancient province of Oriel. Along with Tyrone's Clogher Valley and contiguous parts of east Fermanagh and Cavan, their drumlin landscapes are virtually indistinguishable in the topography south of Lough Neagh. The linen industry thrived here during the eighteenth century and, today, they share a common tradition of rural enterprise in agribusiness and light engineering. They also share a passion for motorsports, football in all its codes, and even for road bowls in some neighbouring parishes. Their social fabric encompasses both 'traditions', and local accents differ on a north-south axis, rather than the east-west of the frontier that at this juncture divides them. For the past century, they have been split by a lengthy chunk of the border, a virtually undetectable line criss-crossed by small roads and lanes. As they might say hereabouts, the border imposed on them is 'hardly worth ignoring'.

When the Ulster Canal and the Great Northern Railway were built, the integrity of Armagh and Monaghan as a corridor of communication was beyond question. It was through here that great ideas moved in an eighteenth-century tidal wave of enlightenment. It was through here that sectarian prejudice later took root. As elsewhere, social ties of both traditions – Orange and Green – reach across the border, despite a century of partition. Yet with public attention focused on glaring differences elsewhere in the arena of conflict, the persistent similarities of the Monaghan-Armagh border slide under the radar.

When the Troubles erupted in earnest with Derry's Battle of the Bogside in August 1969, the Dublin authorities were caught short, and by a considerable distance. The nearest regular armed forces to Derry were in Longford town, 170 kilometres from the centre of conflict. Over the course of the following decade, the army's new role as an aid to the civil power meant an intense redeployment. It began with the immediate dispatch of troops to oversee the establishment of field hospitals and refugee camps on the border during the night of 13–14 August. Two of the camps were in Donegal, at Fort Dunree near Buncrana and at Rockhill, Letterkenny. Others were in Cavan town, Castleblayney and Dundalk.[1] Each field hospital had one medical unit consisting of two doctors, five nurses, five medical orderlies, around twenty military police and two ambulances. On the morning of 14 August, the Irish Government Information Bureau (GIB) issued a statement: 'Mobile patrols, consisting of medical transport and medical security personnel are operating on border roads and are intended to provide transport to the hospitals for those running it …'

Soon there were other posts, including one at Tanagh near Rockcorry, County Monaghan, to cover the frontier with Fermanagh, Tyrone and Armagh. Eventually, three new infantry battalions and a cavalry squadron were recruited and deployed in permanent barracks on the border. In all, ten military posts were established over the following years in border areas, including Monaghan town.[2] Yet the 27th Infantry Battalion was not exactly welcomed with open arms as it took up its post on Knockaconny (Hill of the Rabbits) on the Armagh Road at the edge of the Monghan town in December 1976.[3] Retired Sergeant Major Tommy Daly recalled, 'The locals resented us being there and we had a lot of hassle in the town. We couldn't socialise for a long time, but from 1978 onwards, things began to settle down.'

Because Monaghan town had for a long time been the entertainment centre for neighbouring counties, the soldier boys stood out with their southern accents and short hairstyles. They were resented as interlopers sent to quell the natives, as illustrated in the 1972 riot at the Garda station, when shots were fired and guns wrested from soldiers. The initial alienation was illustrated starkly as only one local candidate came forward when the first platoon was recruited in Monaghan. Just months after the post's establishment, moreover, republican claims about its future role seemed to be confirmed when a British Army helicopter landed there. Said Sgt Maj. Daly: 'We didn't want them to land, but they were out of fuel, so we had to let them … There were two guys in it. They were very embarrassed. They didn't know where to put their heads.'

The lack of a military presence on the border had been noted in late 1971 by reporter Joe MacAnthony of the *Sunday Independent*, who had observed that 'Only three hundred troops are posted to the border, while the two strongest units in the defence forces, 12th and 14th Battalions, are kept in Southern Command – the furthest military zone from the border. A small number of regular patrols are carried out each day by units based in Dundalk, Finner and Castleblayney, but the timings are so regular and routes so predictable that the IRA have no difficulties in avoiding them.'[4]

The late Billy Fox had raised the absence of military protection repeatedly in Dáil Éireann, and urged garrisons to protect and reassure people in Monaghan. Indeed, the location of an army barracks on the Monaghan border had been on the cards since 1973. Then there were efforts to place a garrison in Clones, considered more 'vulnerable to car bombers' because of its immediate proximity to the border.[5] Another security plan was the creation of vigilante-type recruits who would carry out 'rostered patrolling' and report to the local gardaí. That was promised by Taoiseach Liam Cosgrave after the 1974 bombings of Dublin and Monaghan. According to then *Irish Times* political correspondent Dick Walsh, the gardaí were strongly opposed to the idea.[6] Justice Minister Patrick Cooney told the 1976 Fine Gael Ard Fhéis that 'preliminary talks on the formation of the force had taken place with communities along the border, but the groups envisaged would operate purely as patrollers and observers in the case of bombings'. The Cosgrave coalition lost power to Fianna Fáil the following year, and the tentative plan for civilian patrols was shelved.

Reticence to commit resources to border security was understandable in light of Dublin's cautious approach to the frontier from the beginning. Having expanded the army rapidly for the Civil War, W.T. Cosgrave's

Dublin government then had to shed at least 35,000 of its 55,000 personnel.[7] A sizeable group of officers led by General Liam Tóbin, former assistant to Michael Collins, believed they had been 'gradually excluded from key positions' and would be first for demobilisation. A common link among them was that they had worked in Oriel House, the Free State intelligence centre, during the Civil War. They formed an organisation that became known as the 'Old IRA' to 'get control of vital sections of the army' and weed out 'undesirable personnel' who backed the government's unduly pro-British policy.[8] They were supported by Industry Minister Joseph McGrath, who organised a meeting in mid-1923 with Defence Minister Richard Mulcahy and Cosgrave at which the dissident officers were 'aggressive and discourteous' over 'abandonment of the republican ideal of national independence and unity'.[9] They were avidly loyal to Collins's insistence that the Treaty was a 'stepping-stone to the Republic'. Based on their strong intelligence, they believed the fault lay with the Army Council, an IRB-controlled directorate under Mulcahy with a mission to prevent the army 'falling into republican anti-Treaty hands'.[10]

On 6 March 1924, the Old IRA issued a written ultimatum demanding the removal of the Army Council and suspension of demobilisation. It charged that the government 'had betrayed the ideal of eventual unity' and declared 'we can no longer be party to the treachery that threatens to destroy the aspiration of the nation'.[11] About fifty officers resigned their commissions and some absconded with weapons. When their leaders were arrested, McGrath quit the government and Cosgrave went absent on health grounds. That left the debacle to his hard-line vice president, Kevin O'Higgins, and the saga took a bizarre twist. O'Higgins didn't trust Mulcahy, so he contacted his old pal Colonel Jephson O'Connell, who was among the mutineers, and learned of the IRB intrigue in the officer corps. O'Higgins then appointed Garda Commissioner Eoin O'Duffy to a new post of general officer commanding and inspector-general of the defence forces, which superceded Mulcahy. A deal was struck with the mutineers, who pledged their loyalty to the government and returned the weapons. O'Higgins informed the Dáil that the mutiny was 'nothing more than a series of innocent misunderstandings amongst patriotic men'.[12] In the process,

O'Higgins left his old adversary Mulcahy 'humiliated and abandoned by the executive council'.[13]

A consequence of the mutiny and the republican dissension that led to it, was the creation of a new army intelligence unit to monitor the ranks. The Second Bureau operated from Army HQ and at battalion level. It also operated within the Military Customs Brigade, set up to enforce customs and tariffs along the new land frontier, and part of its brief was to monitor economic affairs. It had agents in the North supplying information on the security forces there, as well as on republican, nationalist and unionist organisations. Among its customers was the North-Eastern Boundary Bureau, set up to prepare the Free State's case for a redrawing of the border.[14] Another role of the Second Bureau was to watch 'suspected agents of British and Northern Irish authorities, Boy Scout organisations, Orange Lodges, trade unionists, communists, and other bodies and individuals thought to pose a potential threat, however slight'.[15] Co-operation between army intelligence and the Gardaí ended when Eoin O'Duffy stepped down from his special commander post in mid-1925 and reassumed control of the Garda, which now involved an amalgamation with the Dublin Metropolitan Police and the creation of a new Special Branch.[16]

By the final months of 1925, while it was wrestling with the fall-out of the Boundary Commission debacle, the Dublin government made its checkmate move. Egged on by Justice Minister O'Higgins, who was 'still distrustful of the army in general and of intelligence in particular', Defence Minister Peter Hughes gave 'verbal instructions' that all Second Bureau files and control of all agents and informers should be handed over to Garda Special Branch. In February 1926, the transfer of between 23,000 and 24,000 personal files had begun, and by the end of that year, only two 'paid agents' of army intelligence remained, one of them in Northern Ireland.[17]

By then also, the entire structure of the IRA's Fifth Northern Division and the National Army that succeeded it had been dismantled in Monaghan and the entire garrison that had been headquartered in Clones was moved back to Dundalk, former headquarters of the Fourth Northern, which took the anti-Treaty side in the Civil War. From then until the recent Troubles were well underway, the National Army had no permanent garrison in the three Ulster counties of the Free State/Republic.

Even during the Second World War/Emergency from 1939 to 1945, Local Defence Force (LDF) units throughout Monaghan were the first line of defence, supplemented with regular troops from Dundalk and other points to the south. As for intelligence, the Garda Special Branch 'defined their task almost exclusively in terms of protecting the state against the IRA' and, to this end, they 'investigated and harried republicans with some enthusiasm' but showed 'no interest in continuing the political intelligence activities' of the military, which was now prohibited from collecting intelligence on Northern Ireland affairs.[18] So after 1925, the issue of the border is 'conspicuous by its absence' from intelligence records.[19]

When the North erupted, therefore, the Dublin government was unable to do much more than 'stand idly by' as Taoiseach Jack Lynch has usually been misquoted as saying. While some urged immediate deployment of troops to nationalist areas just across the frontier, Trinity College Dublin's Professor Eunan O'Halpin points out that 'the army was utterly unprepared for such a role, having neither the men, the equipment, the information, nor the places necessary to mount such operations'.[20] As Foreign Minister Paddy Hillery was dispatched to the United Nations to request international peacekeeping intervention, the government agreed to an initial sum of £100,000 for relief of distress in the North to be controlled by Finance Minister Charlie Haughey, who was appointed to a sub-committee comprising three other ministers, with the aim that he would 'counteract the supposed border hotheads'.[21] Meanwhile, to make up for the deficit in knowledge, 'a number of army officers were dispatched north under cover to collect intelligence and to assess political feeling. In furtherance of the possibility of intervening, the army also embarked on a series of "purely military" studies of Northern Ireland, something which it had not done systematically since 1925'.[22] One of those army officers dispatched to find out what was going on in the North was Captain James Kelly, a native of Bailieborough, County Cavan. His entanglement – along with his superior officer, Director of Military Intelligence Colonel Michael Hefferon – in the web of conspiracy, perjury and concealment that became the 1970 Arms Trial illustrates the paranoia that prevailed on all matters connected with the North and the border that contained it.[23] The vilification of Kelly and the ostracising of Hefferon contributed in no small measure to distrust of the armed forces in border areas during the early years of the Troubles.

Over time, however, the Army barracks was accepted and became an integral part of Monaghan town. Recruits joined, many crossing the border to report for duty in their national armed forces. They provided permanent guards on vital installations; served as armed escort parties for cash shipments, explosives and prisoners; and they were present at blasting sites. Special duties also involved bomb disposal, searches and security details for high-profile visitors. Off duty, they mingled freely, settled down and raised families. However, due to the arrival of peace in the North, and other demands, the Defence Forces undertook another major restructuring from the late 1990s, which involved the disestablishment of garrison units, the closure of barracks, and the development of a three-brigade structure. Monaghan and other border barracks were deemed surplus and closed, and the troops moved back to Dundalk once more. After thirty-two years, the Army No. 1 Band played 'Fáinne Geal an Lae' as Lieutenant John Byrne lowered the flag and Private Michael Molloy bolted the gates. Among those forming ranks for the occasion was Private Robert Speers, who remarked that the transfer to Dundalk would bring him closer to his County Down home, but that he would take fond memories with him: 'It was a good wee barracks and a friendly town.'[24]

The former army barracks – with its billets, parade ground and helipad – has been transformed into a modern educational campus housing the Monaghan Institute of Further Education (MIFE); an Irish-language-medium school for primary pupils (Gaelscoil Ultain); another for secondary pupils (Coláiste Oiriall); and the local theatre, which relocated from the grounds of the former St Davnet's Lunatic Asylum. Still called The Garage in homage to Patrick McCabe's *The Butcher Boy* and his play, *Frank Pig Says Hello*, the theatre gained a wonderful performance space but lost the irony of its name, which is derived from central character, Francie Brady's, speculation on where his mother was taken after her 'breakdown'. I pass the main gates, where a plaque says that the campus was officially opened by An Taoiseach Enda Kenny TD on Friday, 6 February 2015. I pause to briefly watch a Gaelic football match in which Coláiste Oiriall is trouncing the other team on the scoreboard.

Beyond the main gate, the footpath ends abruptly on this busy road, and, as cars and delivery vehicles of all sizes whiz by, my attention is caught by a roadside memorial stone dedicated to 'Treasured Memories of Marty Treanor', who was killed here on 14 August 2004. With that cautionary reminder, I set off gingerly on a parallel course to the Ulster Canal. It is tantalisingly close now, having swept around the back of Knockaconny hill, but totally inaccessible because of towpath overgrowth. Then, as if to mock my thoughts on this, a roadside sign for Willow Bridge in Bessmont Hollow has a vivid colour photograph of an arched bridge over a placid, clear canal with an idyllic towpath running alongside it. I hurry down the lane and find a totally overgrown canal once more, the banks on both sides of the bridge obscured by a profusion of branches and thickets enclosing a clogged channel. A sign just ahead notifies me: 'All properties covered by 24-hour CCTV.' As I retreat, I note that my eager arrival has probably been recorded on a pole-mounted camera about ten metres from the bridge.

A short distance away, I find one of the best-kept road junctions I have encountered. Well-trimmed lawn encloses the entire junction of the N54 to Armagh and the R185 for Glaslough, where a decorative rowing boat filled with flowers still in full bloom bids passersby 'Welcome to Silverstream'. A woman in wellington boots is busy with her domestic lawnmower, giving an end-of season cut to the finely manicured sward. I compliment her on her work and the splendor of her junction, saying it seems more like a park. 'It *is* a park,' she replies. We lapse into a conversation about the terrain and the route and, of course, the canal. She explains that her family farm straddles the channel in these parts, and that she and her neighbours have been restoring what they can of the towpath. She directs me just a short distance up the Glaslough road, past a second Silverstream welcoming boat and a wonderful rockery garden. Just beyond, the canal features a well-tended towpath surrounded by beautifully maintained grounds and a decorative water channel offering a glimpse of what might be once more. All this has been achieved by a woman with a busy family farm, an enthusiasm for garden landscaping, a strong commitment to community endeavor, and a drive to win her category of the national Tidy Towns competition. I compliment her again on the work. 'You should have been here when the begonias were in bloom,' she replies.

Just beyond the Glaslough road junction, the lawnmower woman told me, another canal bridge leading to her daughter's house is scheduled for restoration. I cross an adjacent car park to have a look where stones from the bridge have fallen into the channel. On the way back, I'm greeted by another gardener, who is placing a barrow-load of sods from the Tyholland GAA grounds opposite into a rutted section of the grass verge. Further along, a beautiful stone canal bridge straddles the channel a short distance ahead with a finger-post pointed to Skinnagin. From the summit of the humpbacked bridge, the squared steeple of Tyholland parish church peeps above a canopy of autumnal leaves. I guess that the former Hand and Pen Orange Hall once nestled there. Now it sits proudly in the Ulster Folk and Transport Museum at Cultra, County Down, where visitors are informed: 'This hall was built at Silverstream, in the heart of the Monaghan countryside, in 1884, although the associated Orange Lodge, Hand and Pen LOL 597, had been in existence from at least 1843. The reason for its curious name remains a mystery, but it is thought to have originated from a local shop that had an illustrated sign featuring a hand writing in a ledger.'

Perhaps the writing hand was that of one of the Leslies of Glaslough, a prolific lot whose family seat dominates this district, with all roads to the left heading that way. The great satirist Dean Jonathan Swift (1669–1745) once visited and wrote:

> Here I am in Castle Leslie
> With rows and rows of books upon the shelves
> Written by the Leslies,
> All about themselves.[25]

Sammy (Samantha) Leslie, current incumbent of the estate, remarks that there have been more than 200 books produced by family members since then. But then the Leslies were never noted for hiding their light under a bushel, revelling in their own history, which romps along to modern times when the family estate stands out as an aspirational retreat, even in the shadows of the border and all its dark legacies. Family lore has it that during the 1921 Treaty negotiations, Winston Churchill asked

Michael Collins to make sure no harm came to his cousins. Churchill and Sir Shane Leslie were first cousins through their mothers, the Jerome sisters, Jenny and Leonie, but they were on opposite sides now; John Herbert Leslie had converted to Roman Catholicism while at Cambridge University, changed his name to Shane to render it more Gaelic, and espoused Irish nationalism. In 1910, he contested the Londonderry city seat for the Irish Parliamentary Party, losing by a mere 105 votes to the unionist party's marquis of Hamilton.[26]

Shane Leslie's conversion to Romanism and Gaelic nationalism was quite a turnabout for a family descended from the 'Fighting Bishop' John Leslie, who came over from Scotland to the diocese of Raphoe in Donegal, then acquired Clogher Diocese because it was much more convenient to Dublin and the 'centre of political life in Ireland'. He bought the estate on land confiscated from the McKennas and given to Thomas Ridgeway, England's treasurer at arms in Ireland, who relocated to nearby Favour Royal and later became the first Lord Londonderry.[27]

The family were deeply involved in politics after Charles Powell Leslie became an MP for Monaghan in 1783. Bitterly opposed to the Act of Union, he spoke at the 1782 Dungannon Convention and voted against it when it first came before the Dublin parliament. He also opposed the United Irish Society, even though Glaslough district 'boasted a full regiment of the United Irishmen', many of whom were hanged on 16 October 1797.[28] He commanded the Monaghan militia on the loyalist side at the battles of Antrim and Ballynahinch in 1798, yet he died before the union on 1 January 1801. The following year, the seat passed to his son, also Charles Powell Leslie, who opposed Catholic emancipation from the penal laws, the issue which dominated British politics in the 1820s. That cost him his seat in the 1826 election, which was won by near neighbour Henry Westenra of Rossmore Castle, who had sided with Daniel O'Connell on the repeal issue. The Catholic and Presbyterian forty-shilling freeholders marched into Monaghan town to vote in 1826, a political watershed that provided an example for the rest of Ireland.

Almost a century later, Sir John Leslie was a staunch Ulster loyalist in the 1st Monaghan UVF Battalion. Based in Monaghan town in 1912, the battalion was commanded by Major E. J. Richardson of Poplar Vale, and by August 1913 it mustered 747 men, which rose to 1,037 a year later, and was drawn from Clontibret, Glaslough, Ballinode, Monaghan, Smithborough and Shanroe. The Glaslough company provided ten units with 257 men from the village itself, as well as Emyvale and Silverstream. In April 1914, a shooting competition was held at Glaslough for all the UVF of the Glaslough, Hand and Pen, Mullapike, Shanco, Emyvale and Corragh half companies. The trophy for second place was won by John 'Jock' Hazlett of Kilnadrain, whose steady aim in 1921 accounted for one dead and several wounded when he opened fire on an IRA unit raiding his house for arms.[29] Hazlett was shot in the neck by the raiders but survived.[30]

Glaslough was the venue for a full parade of the Monaghan UVF Regiment in 1914, with two special trains bringing volunteers to march behind the brass-and-reed bands of Clones and Monaghan and a part flute band from Ballinode. Both battalions received regimental and king's colours, and a telegram from Edward Carson was read out, saying, 'I know you will all keep your colours unsullied, and win for them honour and respect.' The Leslie family history records that as Sir John Leslie was reviewing the UVF parade, his son Shane 'was slipping out the back gate to drill with the nationalist Volunteers committed to winning home rule'. Meanwhile, Shane's youngest brother, Lionel, was one of the youngest members of the Ulster Volunteer Force, at the tender age of 14.[31]

With his nationalist ambitions set aside for the duration of the Great War, Shane Leslie was busy in New York thwarting efforts to keep America out of the war. He is also reputed in the family history to have saved Eamon de Valera's life by pointing out to superiors in the British diplomatic service that de Valera was American, so executing him with other leaders of the 1916 Rising could harm British efforts to woo America into the war. With the British departure from the Free State, the Leslies lapsed into genteel poverty. Sir Shane had been disinherited by his father for 'prolific anti-unionist writing'.[32] He took up the pen again, churning out a formidable array of books, including *The Irish Tangle for English Readers* and his memoir *Long Shadows*.[33] In the former, he sets out to explain why and how the Free State chose neutrality during the Second World War, as well as Irish attitudes to the Third Reich. He also illustrates the confusion of Irish attitudes with a true story from the 'remote Ulster borders' after the first month of the war:

> I found myself in an old man's lonely cottage without wireless or newspaper. He had seen the young men slipping over the border to join the British Army. Even the girls were going to work or nurse. In his loneliness, he turned to me and this dialogue followed:
> 'This war is terror, sir.'
> 'It is indeed – total terror.'
> (Whispered) 'Can ye tell me: has England declared war yet?'
> 'She has indeed.'
> 'Thank God' – (after a pause) – 'for our boys will not be alone!'

Shane Leslie also adds that the German maps for invasion of Ireland were hopelessly inadequate, and included using the Clogher Valley Railway to cut off Belfast. Sir Shane pointed out that the light railway was 'rooted up early in the war', and that the trains the Nazi invaders proposed to use were 'obsolete'.

During the Second World War, Sir Shane was in London serving in the Home Guard and occasionally using his time to salvage rare books from bomb-devastated libraries. Yet in his home locality around Monaghan and Armagh, he was best known as a chronicler of Irish ghost stories.[34] During my time at St Macartan's College, I recall seeing the octogenarian Sir Shane walking past the school, up the back road through Kilnadrain to Glaslough, dressed in a heavy tweed kilt, in keeping with his insistence that trousers were an English invention. The Leslie family predilection to kick at the traces of aristocratic behavior survived the doughty Sir Shane, who died in 1971 at the age of 89. His older son, Sir John but known as Jack, garnered international fame for spilling the beans on the 2002 Castle Leslie wedding of Paul McCartney and Heather Mills. Forever after, until his 2016 death just shy of his centenary, he was also known for his love of 'boom-boom music' disco dancing, frequenting local nightclubs regularly, and even venturing to Ibiza on his eighty-fifth birthday. His family described him as an 'art connoisseur, water colourist, ecologist, disco dancer and restorer of historic buildings'.[35]

Jack, who had been captured at Dunkirk and lived mainly in Rome after his release from a prisoner-of-war camp, didn't indulge the family publishing urge until his memoir, *Never a Dull Moment*, from the Castle Leslie imprint in 2006. It squeezed onto the shelves between tomes produced by his sister Anita Leslie (aka Anita Theodosia Moira Rodzianko King) and younger brother Desmond, who wrote dozens of books, including *Edwardians in Love* and *Flying Saucers Have Landed*. The disco mania that Jack caught had been pioneered by Desmond, who hosted a discotheque in the castle as early as the mid-1960s, and who even featured in an episode of the RTÉ TV series *Discovery* called 'Cutting a Rug at the Castle Leslie' in 1966, as the impresario in white dinner jacket and as occasional disc jockey.[36] Yet Desmond was once best known for having gatecrashed the hugely popular British TV show *That Was the Week That Was* to punch renowned critic Bernard Levin in front of 11 million viewers. Leslie had taken umbrage at a Levin review of a cabaret performance by his then wife Agnes Bernelle.[37] Another publication to which Leslie took grave exception described the Leslies as a 'mildly eccentric' family. 'Mildly eccentric?' he fulminated. 'We are very eccentric.' He had demonstrated this as an RAF fighter pilot during the Second World War, going about his daily business in pyjamas, according to his son Mark.[38] When pulled up by superior officers, he explained he would stand a much better chance wearing pyjamas if shot down over France than if he was wearing his RAF uniform.

Desmond Leslie boasted of his encounter with Bernard Levin when I interviewed him for a 1982 newspaper article. He didn't recall that we had met very briefly when I gatecrashed his son Mark's twenty-first birthday in 1973. The castle at that time was rather the worse for wear, but so were most of the invited guests, who included Mick Jagger and other Rolling Stones. I encountered the *pater familias* in the conservatory, where cases of champagne were stored. After a cursory enquiry as to who I was, he poured me a glass. That bacchanalian event left a lasting impression on my ideas of what the gentry did when we weren't looking. Indeed, the Leslies tended to do it when we *were* looking, as

I have since discovered during several overnight stays and many more dining experiences since Castle Leslie has risen from near ruins under the management of Desmond's daughter Sammy, to become possibly Ireland's most charming retreat.

I resist the urge to head there now from the thoroughfare on which I compete with speeding traffic while, immediately to my left, the Ulster Canal towpath remains inaccessible. A short distance further on, a huge lorry turns into the Monaghan Mushrooms plant. The road runs over the canal channel. A traditional canal bridge and lock are intact nearby and the canal banks are landscaped for factory frontage. This rural agribusiness founded by former Monaghan Collegiate School geography teacher Ronnie Wilson in the early 1980s has been plunged into 'turmoil' by the prospect of Brexit.[39] Using satellite growers on local small farms, it had developed into the largest mushroom producer in the world.[40] Now fluctuations in the currency market after the Brexit vote threaten the annual sale of about 55,000 tonnes of Irish mushrooms on the British market for a farm-gate return of €120 million representing 80 per cent of sales, while cheaper Polish competition muscles in on continental sales.[41] Uncertainty over post-Brexit border protocols is a significant worry even if market share can be held. Like other fresh food companies, Monaghan Mushrooms has expanded by creating and acquiring a network of outlets to serve a growing customer base in the European Union. Monaghan Mushrooms now provides 3,500 jobs here and at subsidiaries in Scotland and England, as well as facilities at Benburb just across the border, according to the company website.[42] All operate within the EU under the same directives and regulations, so the prospect of UK departure seriously undermines cohesion and future planning.

It is a similar scenario for other businesses that are heavily dependent on ease of movement for perishable goods. Town of Monaghan Co-operative (TMC) operates the Lacpatrick dairy conglomerate, while Lakeland Dairies has its base in Monaghan and Cavan. Having been hemmed into a geographical corner, both have expanded rapidly in Northern Ireland since the 1990s. Apart from its Coolshannagh facilities outside Monaghan town, Lackpatrick now has processing plants in west Tyrone and north Antrim, a workforce of 300 and 1,000 farmer suppliers on both sides of the border. Lakelands has 700 employees and 2,200 supplier-shareholders spread throughout sixteen counties in the northern half of the island. Since the single market and the open border, these vibrant and vital businesses have acquired a hinterland taken for granted in places removed from the frontier.

Such indigenous businesses are vital in the local economy because inwards investment and state support has been relatively low. Luckily, however, Monaghan has a 'particularly entrepreneurial population with a tradition of self-employment and a high level of new business start-ups'.[43]

On past the decaying front of Gilmours' shop and post office, on my left, a farmer has used the sturdy stone walls of a canal lock for an access bridge to his land. The more traditional and quaintly named Pipers Bridge is a short distance ahead, providing another road to Glaslough. The bridge is featured in the National Inventory of Architectural Heritage, which notes its 'elliptical arch with ashlar voussoirs', elements that probably escaped the canal builders who constructed it between 1825 and 1841. The architectural heritage website adds that Pipers Bridge 'represents an important part of Ireland's infrastructural history, and is an interesting and attractive landmark in the Monaghan countryside. The bridge exhibits good-quality stone masonry and fine, crisp joints and stands as a tribute to the skill and engineering employed in canal bridge construction.'[44]

There is a more practical approach in the transport infrastructure of the twenty-first century, as illustrated by the major road junction just ahead and to the right, where the N12 meets the R213. I recall a small creamery here from childhood road trips. It has been swept away to provide a road fit for bulk milk tankers and other logistical needs. Almost a century ago, this road to Castleshane that is now the R213 was taken by the IRA Volunteers who sprang Matt Fitzpatrick from hospital captivity in Monaghan town after he was wounded in the Roslea raids of 1921. More than a dozen were involved in the rescue party that infiltrated the Monaghan Infirmary, and many others were involved in blocking roads.[45] There had been a setback when Paddy McCarron from Monaghan town was wounded in a guardroom confrontation with soldiers from the King's Own Rifles before they gained access to the republican commander. John McKenna from Newbliss drove Fitzpatrick to freedom.[46] With two other commandeered cars, he drove along back roads to Tyholland, then turned for Castleshane. Fitzpatrick was handed over to the Clontibret company, who took him to Derrynoose, just over the Armagh county line, the first of many transfers while he was tended by volunteer doctors. Meanwhile, almost the entire battalion was mobilised to block the roads, leaving the road north through Tydavnet to the Clogher Valley only lightly impeded so that the police and military search party spent the following week raiding the mountain districts around Bragan. The crown forces also mounted searches around Rockcorry, where one of the cars, in which the wounded McCarron was taken, had been found with bloodstains.

The labyrinthine structure of the IRA during the War of Independence was impressive, as was the network of support from across the community, including medical doctors. However, cracks soon appeared after the Treaty. At Castleblayney, a split in the local IRA resulting from disciplinary action prompted some anti-Treatyites to take over the Hope Arms Hotel. On 19 March 1922, a squadron from Clones marched on the Hope Arms group and arrested thirty-three men. Divisional Commandant Dan Hogan released all but six ringleaders.[47] Through all the arrests and confusion, meanwhile, Ulster Council plans for an all-out IRA attack on Northern Ireland continued. The rising was set for 19 May 1922, but Fourth Northern Division commander Frank Aiken countermanded the order on the eve.[48] While IRA units mobilised in some parts of the North, action nearer the border was quelled by Special Constabulary raids and arrests. Many who evaded capture in the North moved into Monaghan, where they convened at Castleshane three kilometres from the border. Since February, the Lucas family estate there had been commandeered by the IRA's Fourth Northern Division, Third Brigade companies from Armagh city, Blackwatertown and Lurgan. Although the mansion, a 'neo-Elizabethan extravaganza' built by the Lucas family in 1836 to replace their sixteenth-century castle, had been burnt out by accident in 1920,[49] there was ample accommodation in the farmyard, lofts and riding school to provide 'all the comforts and facilities for training necessary in the soldiering life'.[50] And it was a 'convenient locality for those men to set up an armed camp as it was within easy distance from their home areas'.[51]

James Short of Armagh company was one of the volunteers at Castleshane. He had already attended intensive training at Killeavy on the slopes of Slieve Gullion and at Derrynoose for the big May offensive supported by 'both sections of the IRA in Southern Ireland, who had split on the question of the acceptance or otherwise of the Treaty'.[52] However, Short noted that as time progressed, the officers and men of Dan Hogan's Fifth Northern Division looked on those 'six-county IRA men with suspicion and their presence in Castleshane with resentment'.[53] By May, the Castleshane garrison was openly regarded as an 'anti-Treaty ASU', and estate steward George Morgan reported that it was 'impossible to get work done' and the yard offices occupied by IRA officers were in 'a disgraceful condition'.[54]

Then in mid-July, Hogan led a large body of Free State troops from Clones into Dundalk, where they captured the military HQ and two police barracks. Aiken's men put up little resistance because, as Charlie McGleenan of the Blackwatertown company noted, at that time 'men were changing their opinions and allegiance daily'. A short time later, Dundalk was recaptured by Aiken's Fourth Northern Division. The following day, a consignment of sixty rifles and ammunition arrived at Castleshane from Dundalk, with almost simultaneous orders from Aiken to dump arms and take no part in fighting 'the men on the pro-Treaty side who should be our comrades'.[55] Unwanted, unarmed, with no money for food supplies, Castleshane was 'getting bad for us', according to McGleenan. 'Wild talks and rumours of all kinds were going around. One morning we awoke to find our billets surrounded by Free State troops ... equipped with turreted armoured cars and machine-guns.' The September 1922 raid on Castleshane was hailed by the unionist-leaning *Northern Standard*: 'The cleaning up of this nest of rebels has caused a deep feeling of relief among the inhabitants of the district.'[56]

The demoralising impact of the Civil War in the South on the IRA in the six counties allowed the unionist government to add pressure in raids and arrests. James Short of Armagh noted, 'The B and C Specials took complete control and instituted a reign of terror for republicans, to which we had no answer.'[57] The terror persisted and lapped to and fro across the border, as with the abduction and murder of Ross Hearst of Middletown in 1980.[58] The 52-year-old father of five was taken at gunpoint outside a friend's house in Tullylush, back near where the Monaghan Mushrooms plant stands today. His corpse with four bullet wounds was dumped at Wards Cross, a short distance away on the border. Hearst was a member of Glaslough Orange Lodge, and he was known to attend a religious service with his friend each Wednesday evening and stop at the same pub on their way back. On 4 September 1980, the IRA was waiting for him and said in a statement later that he had admitted 'under interrogation' to supplying information to the British security forces. Seamus Soroghan of Monaghan town was later convicted of the murder. Yet no sentence could allay the trauma of the Hearst family, which at the time of the father's death was still mourning the 1977 killing of his daughter Margaret Ann Hearst, a 24-year-old single mother of a 3-year-old child, and a part-time soldier in the UDR.[59]

The impact of this doubly traumatic bereavement on the Hearst family became the focus of post-ceasefire allegations of 'ethnic cleansing' on the border by author Sam McAughtry, who noted that the family farm had been sold to another Protestant, who later sold it to a Catholic.[60] That angle is followed by the observation that 'Middletown, which had been 40 per cent Protestant in the 1960s, had only three Protestant families left.' McAughtry summed up a pervasive view:

> On the way from Armagh city to the border I travelled past fields and loanings and modest farm buildings and yards where Protestants have been slaughtered like turkeys by the IRA over the years since 1971. There seems almost a Vietnamese dimension to the slaughtering. The tiny fields carry such starved pasture; the ground is often stony and rushy. Yet the IRA want this land for their own – there is an undeniable pattern of attacks on unmarried Protestants, whose relatives will let the land go when the killing has been carried out.[61]

The situation did not look better to him on the other side of the border. He wrote that, 'The history of Monaghan is a dark, violent, murderous one. The tumbled, hilly countryside still has the whisper of it. It has a Balkan look about it, the feel of border country.'[62]

Yet the bloodshed was far from one-sided in this district. More than a year before Margaret Ann Hearst was gunned down, a car bomb was placed by the loyalist Glenanne Gang outside the Step Inn in Keady just 13 kilometres south-east of Middletown in Armagh. The explosion killed two Catholic civilians: the pub owner's wife, Betty McDonald; and a young man standing down the street outside his home, Gerard McGleenan.[63] Twenty-two others were injured when the car exploded without warning. It had been hijacked in Belfast's Shankill Road a week earlier, and the bomb had been intended for Renaghan's pub just across the border in Clontibret, County Monaghan.[64] Gang member John Weir, a serving RUC police officer, had selected the target in Clontibret, a place he knew well having grown up in Castleblayney.[65] Weir scouted the route, and when he reported unusually heavy security around Clontibret, the target was shifted to the Keady pub instead.

Shortly after joining the RUC, Weir had been recruited to the Special Patrol Group (SPG), a police anti-terrorist unit. He learned that John Francis Green, a senior IRA man from Lurgan, was staying at a house in Mullyash, a remote district of Monaghan just across the border between Keady and Castleblayney.[66] Green was shot dead there on 10 January 1975 during the IRA ceasefire. In the labyrinthine world of collusion and homicidal provocation between UVF loyalist killers, police, army and other state forces, there is strong evidence linking the enigmatic and 'disappeared' British Army hero, Captain Robert Nairac, to Green's murder.[67] Along with Constable William McCaughey, Sergeant Weir was subsequently convicted of murdering William Strathearn, a Catholic pharmacist in Ahoghill, County Antrim.[68]

Using reports on investigations by the Historical Enquiries Team set up as a unit of the Police Service of Northern Ireland (PSNI), Ann Cadwallader of the Pat Finucane Centre for Human Rights and Social Change has drawn on forensic and other evidence to connect the Glenanne Gang to a series of atrocities including sectarian murders of civilians in Armagh and Tyrone and the Dublin and Monaghan bombings of 1974. Inquests for many of these now historic murders, including those of Betty McDonald and Gerard McGleenan, have still not been held because documentary evidence is withheld by the state authorities on the pretext of 'national security'. Yet in a sense, the activities of the Glenanne Gang and the composition of its members illustrate the porosity of a border that has never been sealed against those who are determined to ignore it, or those who wished to expose it.

One such exposé was organised by Northern Ireland's former first minister, Peter Robinson, who was at that time deputy leader of the DUP, in what was one of the most bizarre and inept episodes of the Troubles. Named the 'Invasion of Clontibret', it involved a large crowd of 500 loyalists crossing the border on 7 August 1986 and marching through the tiny village of Clontibret (population 300).[69] The 'invaders' also daubed 'Ulster Has Awakened' on the wall of the vacant Garda station and the walls of a local Protestant school. They were dispersed by armed gardaí firing shots in the air, undermining their stated purpose of highlighting a lack of border security on the southern side. Furthermore, the 'invaders' also had been protesting the Anglo-Irish agreement that had been signed the previous year, but the incident actually served to strengthen Anglo-Irish relations, according to a senior official in the Northern Ireland Office in a letter to the then British ambassador to Dublin. Mark Elliott told Sir Alan Goodison that the Dublin authorities 'warmly appreciated' that the RUC had tipped off the Garda about 'the incursion by Peter Robinson and his loyalist thugs'.[70]

The *News Letter* in Belfast reproduced an official summary of the incident from a 'near-contemporaneous' report:

> In the small hours of August 7, a crowd of around one hundred and fifty loyalists, some wearing paramilitary uniforms and carrying cudgels, accompanied by (or, according to some reports, led by) Peter Robinson, crossed the border near Keady and marched through the County Monaghan village of Clontibret … Robinson, who appears to have lingered behind deliberately, was arrested and held in custody for thirty-six hours (during which

he refused all sustenance provided by the Garda, preferring the wholesome Ulster food brought to him by his wife) before being charged with four offences, including assaulting Garda officers and causing wilful damage. He was granted bail and is to appear in court in Dundalk, County Louth, on August 14.[71]

On that appearance, Robinson was further remanded on bail and then, after a week-long trial in January 1987, he pleaded guilty to unlawful assembly and was freed on paying fines of £17,500 and compensation.[72]

Robinson entered the guilty plea because a near-certain conviction on more serious charges would have meant a prison sentence and loss of his Westminster seat. Although he avoided that, the incident still had repercussions for him down the line, when his predecessor as First Minister, Ian Paisley, claimed that Robinson had drummed up the Clontibret event in a premature bid for leadership of the DUP. Others in the DUP disputed this, backing Robinson's assertion that Paisley himself was involved in planning the event and would have attended but for a funeral in America.[73]

I walk down a narrowing thoroughfare between leafy trees to a bridge and service station at Foyduff. Motorists are alerted that their speed will now be gauged in miles per hour. Another road sign welcomes them to Ireland, the word 'Northern' having been obliterated. Looking back, a road sign just on the other side of the bridge welcomes those crossing in that direction to County Monaghan. Resting momentarily on a wall of the bridge, I ponder on the confluence of channels as the River Cor flowing below marks the border. A short distance to the north where Armagh meets Monaghan, it will merge with another river and then, further along, between Tynan and Caledon, with yet another. Both those rivers are called the Blackwater, one rising on Sliabh Beagh on the southern side of the Clogher Valley and flowing through Monaghan's Tydavnet, Monaghan and Donagh parishes, the other rising on Murley Mountain and flowing through the Clogher Valley and marking the boundary between Tyrone and Monaghan. Two rivers with the same name is surely a prime example of the duplication brought about from partition of the island.

Opposite Hughes's service station at Foyduff stands the canopied skeleton of a former customs post, a gutted-out reminder of former times. Indeed, it is one of the few surviving examples of the built heritage of partition. Elsewhere since the creation of the European single market and onset of peace, customs posts and huge security checkpoints that once dominated cross-border routes have been obliterated from the landscape and often from contemporary memory. This one survives as a makeshift bus shelter with an Ulsterbus sign almost hidden high up on a steel girder set on a concrete post at its former entrance. Yet apart from a metal roof and walls on two sides, it remains largely open to the elements. In times past, buses from Belfast and Armagh stopped here and passengers going on to Monaghan had to disembark, walk across the bridge and board another bus.

There was a cold reception here back in 1921 when Michael Collins crossed the new frontier to address a big meeting in Armagh. Orangemen gathered nearby to greet him with a stoning, according to his biographer, Frank O'Connor. While the gunner in Collins's car 'looked longingly' at his machine gun, Collins laughed, 'Thompson guns aren't fair against stones.'[74] There is nobody waiting to ambush me now as I walk off from Foyduff along a stretch of road strikingly similar to the last bit of Monaghan I came through. The road, the drumlin terrain and its winding ways, trees, bushes and vegetation are indistinguishable. Difference is reduced to the shape and colour of road signage and the switch from yellow to white roadside lines. Even the custom of public shrines to those who had been killed on the roads is evident in the headstone surrounded by floral tributes for Gary Brennan of Cordevlish, Braddox in County Monaghan, erected on the side of this road into Middletown, County Armagh.

A little further on, a branch road to the left is marked by a sculpture of two imposing arches made from steel girders and embellished by tentacles that stretch across the entire width and beyond. On closer inspection, the tentacles are representations of the flight paths of giant stainless-steel honey bees. Created by Alan Cargo and Eleanor Wheeler, the inspiration is drawn from the bee house that sits in a little corner at the centre of Middletown. It fits with the ornate bridge over the River

Cor here in the townland of Shantally, an elaborate portal to the wooded road that stretches ahead to Glaslough, still only 3 miles away.

Around a final corner, past the Elizabethan House (built 1834), modern brick homes now sit on the site of what was once an ominous entrance to County Armagh, a fortress army checkpoint. The small development is named Canal Court, and a tourist-information noticeboard here says the original police barracks closed in 1965, becoming a security checkpoint during the Troubles, and a large police station after the Good Friday Agreement, before it was closed in September 2004 and the site was acquired by the Ulidia Housing Association.

Not everyone was pleased with the scaling-down of the police presence and other changes to peacetime policing to garner support from nationalists. Among these was Hilda Jardine, whose husband was shot dead by the IRA near Middletown while checking cattle being moved across the border on 8 March 1972.[75] The shooting led to temporary closure of customs clearance for cattle at Aughnacloy, Culmore (Derry) and here at Middletown, which had been handling traffic diverted from Killeen, already shut because of an attack there.[76] As well as a Ministry of Agriculture inspector, Joe Jardine was a lance corporal in the UDR and had also served in the B Specials. His widow was incensed about the name change of the Royal Ulster Constabulary to the Police Service of Northern Ireland in 2001 in a series of reforms recommended by the Patten Commission on Policing established under the Good Friday Agreement, saying it was an insult to her husband's memory: 'My husband spent sixteen years serving his country. It was the RUC to him and it will always be the RUC to me,' she told the BBC.[77]

Others were happy to see it go, including those who suspected that these front-line military bases spread 'dirty tricks' far and wide. For instance, while Britain was still denying that it had deployed the SAS in Northern Ireland, an army captain was killed when his jeep struck a pole near Trillick in County Tyrone on 4 April 1975, far from his assigned base at Middletown. Neither his name nor his role were ever revealed, and the incident was not reported by the RUC. Army HQ in Lisburn only confirmed the following day that he had died, and that he was 'non-operational' at the time. However, SDLP Councillor Tom Daly, brother of the former bishop of Derry, said this response only fuelled local suspicions about 'sinister events' in the area.[78]

Indeed, it was a sinister time in the conflict, when lines were blurred and atrocities on both sides were unattributed. It was a time of collusion and confusion, of abductions and assassinations, a time when sinister intelligence forces were vying for the upper hand. One of those most deeply involved was British Military Intelligence (MI6) officer Captain Fred Holroyd, who ran a Monaghan Garda informer codenamed 'the Badger', since identified as Special Branch Sergeant John McCoy.[79] In a 1987 interview with Brendan O'Brien, the then unidentified 'Badger' admitted he met a British military intelligence officer, Staff Sergeant Bernard 'Bunny' Dearsley on a number of occasions in the Garda station and in his own home.[80] He also recalled meeting Captain Holroyd in a darkened car between Middletown and Tynan, when he gave detailed information on IRA and INLA members, including how to get to their houses. Captain Holroyd, who claims he 'ran the Badger' with Bunny for two and a half years, and on his own for a further nine months, says he met him often and even ran two other Garda informants through him. The information garnered was used in cross-border abductions of fugitive republicans, when 'the Badger' had roads 'frozen' to allow easy passage.[81]

The notice board where the border police/military barracks once stood is a mine of handy information about Middletown, including that its development was associated with former bishop of Clogher, Dr John Stearne, who owned seven townlands here as well as land in Monaghan's Donagh parish. The village became Middletown because of 'its central position between Armagh, Monaghan, Keady, Caledon and Glaslough'. The board names and describes important buildings, including a distillery founded in 1831 by Matthew Johnson that produced 80,000 gallons of whiskey a year, and the market house, where grain sales were mostly for that useful purpose. I head for the market house, passing a house with vivid representations of the Madonna and Child, commemorating the fiftieth anniversary of 'Last Apparition at Garabandal'. Since the reported apparitions in northern Spain are not approved by the Roman Catholic Church, I conclude they certainly would not have been tolerated in his village by the Reverend Dr Stearne, a colleague of Dean Swift and often mentioned in his letters.[82]

At the handsomely restored market house, another information board, for the Blackwater Heritage Trail, lists 'hidden gems along the border in counties Armagh, Monaghan and Tyrone'. Amongst them is the Ulster Canal, and the short blurb mentions the 'recent reopening of the Ballyshannon canal', apparently a mistaken reference to the Ballyconnell-Ballinamore canal. To avoid further confusion, I hurry across to the aforementioned beehive and a big monument dedicated to Dr David Smith, local medical superintendent from his arrival fresh from Glasgow University in 1839 to his premature death in 1847. That was the Great Hunger, of course, but I could find no reference to this in the rather verbose tribute to his ministrations.

Nor was there a mention on either of the village noticeboards of one of the most fascinating Irish historical characters of the twentieth century. Eamon Donnelly was born here in 1877 and he became a thorn in the side of those politicians who would sooner forget the border. He was even arrested and imprisoned twice for the simple act of 'going home', living openly in defiance of an exclusion order issued by Home Affairs Minister Dawson Bates in October 1924. It didn't stop Donnelly winning an Armagh seat as an independent republican in the Northern Ireland parliamentary election of April 1925.[83] The only other republican elected that time was Eamon de Valera for South Down.

Son of Francis, a stone mason, and Catherine (née Haggin), whose father was an active Fenian, Eamon Donnelly was one of the first Irish Volunteers in Armagh. He mobilised with others in Coalisland, County Tyrone, on Easter Sunday 1916, and was arrested and jailed briefly in England.[84] On his release he was the central player in reorganising the Volunteers in Armagh City Hall in August 1916, recruiting local IRB members and others.[85] His organisational ability was such that he was appointed national director of elections for Sinn Féin, masterminding the party's 1918 landslide.[86] The following year, he was imprisoned for three months for soliciting contributions to the Dáil Éireann loan outside Saint Joseph's Church in Tynan.[87] Then in 1921, he was election agent for Michael Collins, who won a seat in Armagh, one of the few Sinn Féin victories in the newly designated Northern Ireland, where unionists captured forty-two of the fifty-five seats, despite huge republican effort and expenditure. Donnelly criticised the party's tactics in a letter to Patrick O'Keefe: 'The only effect that all our literature and leaflets etc. will have upon them (unionists) is to bring them out to vote against us in greater numbers.'[88] The Collins victory was followed by a huge rally organised by Donnelly, with trains to Armagh from Clones, Newry, Omagh and Belfast bringing in 20,000 people.[89] Collins was impressed, later inviting the Middletown man to join the Irish delegation to the 1921 peace talks in London as an adviser on the Northern question. Donnelly declined because his wife Marianne was ill.[90]

In 1922, after the May offensive against the Northern state was dropped because of rising tensions in Dublin, Donnelly sided with the anti-Treaty forces. After the Civil War, he was interned by the Free State military authorities and only released from Mountjoy in August 1923, when his daughter Nellie brought a writ of *habeas corpus* and the Free State couldn't prove a 'state of war' still existed. Appointed director of elections for the anti-Treaty wing of Sinn Féin in a surprisingly successful election campaign to the Dáil, he was quickly rearrested by the Northern authorities under new legislation and endured a forty-one-day hunger strike to secure his liberty.[91] On his release, Donnelly resumed as Sinn Féin's chief organiser, and also contested Armagh in the 1925 Northern Ireland election, securing the seat as an abstentionist MP. He was a founder member of Fianna Fáil in 1926, and served as liaison officer between the new party and Sinn Féin.[92] In 1927, he lost out narrowly to party colleague Dr Conn Ward for the third seat in Monaghan. In 1933, however, he won a Dáil seat for Leix-Offaly, when he was registered in the members' directory as a 'clerk, Armagh Prison'.[93] He was then in jail after his arrest under the exclusion order, while running the South Down election campaign for Eamon de Valera. While he spent a month in jail, his son Seán took over as election agent, and Dev retained his South Down seat with a bigger vote.[94]

In the Dáil, Donnelly's overriding concern was partition, which he stated was 'the predominant national issue. Nothing else counts. Nothing else matters.'[95] He pressed Fianna Fáil to run abstentionist candidates in the North, allowing those elected to sit in the Dáil. Dev rejected this, so Donnelly heckled him at the 1937 Fianna Fáil Ard Fhéis. He also tried to block the 1937 constitution, Bunreacht na h-Éireann, moving an amendment for deferral until partition ended. He recognised that while De Valera was preoccupied with the 'national question', he failed utterly to understand its origins, blaming the 'political greed' of Ulster unionists for appropriating 'significant areas with nationalist majorities which were contiguous to the border'.[96] Time and again, Dev called unionists a 'foreign garrison' and 'not Irish people', saying 'they would have to go under' if they 'stood in our way to freedom', and adding, 'we will clear you out of it'.[97] In a favourite comparison, Dev said unionists were like a 'robber coming into a man's house and claiming a room as his own'.[98] He rejected Ulster Protestant fears, insisting that they must succumb to the majority will on the island and stop serving 'English interests'.[99] He said he was even prepared for a 'forty-year wait' for them to come on side.[100] Donnelly wasn't prepared to wait. In a letter to his friend, Donegal-born Fermanagh MP Cahir Healy, he wrote:

> Partition is now in operation fifteen years and we are worse today than when it began. If the present position lasts for another ten years we may chuck in. No one will remember us except as a lot of weaklings who saw what to do and didn't do it.[101]

Donnelly didn't re-contest his Dáil seat in the 1937 election, although he was director of elections for another sweeping Fianna Fáil victory. He was already drifting back to his roots and devoting his efforts to creating an anti-partition front, the Northern Council for Unity.[102] When he was arrested the following year under the 1924 exclusion order while returning home from a meeting in Lurgan, even the Dominions Office acknowledged that to even suggest 'partition should be ended is a crime' in the eyes of Stormont.[103] Donnelly conducted his own defence, declaring:

I was born and raised in Ulster. My home is here, my wife and family reside here and I have a residence outside Newry. The time is approaching that some action must be taken to prevent my slinking into my house like a criminal.[104]

He was released from prison, fined £25 and never arrested again. While still jailed, he stood for the Seanad election and was shunned by erstwhile Fianna Fáil colleagues, getting only a single first-preference vote.[105] However, he was appointed by the party national executive to its anti-partition subcommittee, a face-saving ploy by Dev on the border question. When the Second World War broke out, Donnelly declared that if Fianna Fáil did not use that opportunity to reunite the country 'they could whistle for it afterwards'.[106] He fought vigorously against conscription in the North, organising a mass rally at Belfast's Corrigan Park in May 1941 where 10,000 young men pledged to 'resist conscription by the most effective means at our disposal consonant with the law of God'.[107] The final chapter in the Middletown man's pivotal career was played out in Belfast, where he stood as an independent republican and won the Falls seat in 1942, the first ever republican seat in Belfast.

In his nomination address for the Belfast Falls election, Donnelly had insisted he 'always held, and still hold, that it is possible to re-unite our country by constitutional means'.[108] To that end, he attended the Fianna Fáil Ard Fhéis in 1944, appealing for a fresh drive to remove the border by making it 'the burning question it used to be years ago before it became submerged in matters not so important'.[109] Two months later, Eamon Donnelly died in Dublin on 29 December 1944. The *Newry Reporter* said that while he had devoted his entire life to nationalist policy, he had 'set himself in recent years to follow the destinies of Sinn Féin, it being as he believed, the more virile movement, the best through which he would serve the Irish nation'.[110] Notwithstanding that shift in allegiance, Dev and his government ministers, along with politicians from North and South were present at his funeral.

Donnelly is often credited as a driving force and inspiration behind the Irish Anti-Partition League, which campaigned for Irish unity in the post-war years. It was the successor of several other alliances of Northern nationalists, such as Joe Devlin MP's National League of the North, founded in May 1928; the Irish Union Association, founded in 1936; and De Valera's Anti-Partition League, which was active briefly from 1938 until the start of the Second World War.[111] Each failed to attract all the nationalist politicians to a common platform, and the last was scuppered by the IRA bombing campaign in England in the late 1930s, which hardened English attitudes. The new organisation was launched by newly elected MPs including Eddie McAteer of Derry and Malachy Conlon of South Armagh in 1945.[112] However, Donnelly's successor in Belfast Falls, Socialist Republican Harry Diamond, refused to attend the inaugural convention in Dungannon on 14 November 1945 because the Socialist Republican Party and the Ulster Union Club, both with 'substantial Protestant membership' had not been invited.[113] The Dungannon convention of 480 delegates confirmed Diamond's denouncement of a 'sectarian manoeuvre' in the attendance of many priests with messages of support from Catholic bishops.

The organisation soon lapsed into factional infighting, and by the time of the first annual convention in April 1947, again in Dungannon. Attendance was down to 146 delegates from sixty-three branches. Differences continued over secretary Malachy Conlon's trenchant Catholic nationalism, counterposed against British Labour MPs, who had formed the Friends of Ireland support group. Prominent among the Friends were Geoffrey Bing, Ulster Protestant-born Labour MP for Hornchurch, and Communist MPs Willie Gallacher and Phil Piratin from West Fife and London Stepney.[114] The Irish Anti-Partition League was a 'rural, clergy-dominated organisation which, while verbally militant about partition was intensively conservative about social issues'.[115] Its chairman James McSparran even declared that his party's 'concept of education has been expressed by the Pope in an encyclical'.[116] In the 1949 Stormont election, known as the 'Chapel Gates election' because of the collections at churches in the south that were used to finance anti-partition candidates, the unionists rallied on the threat of Rome, and the Anti-Partition League made no headway.[117]

This election threw up another glaring fault-line of partition, since the Dublin Mansion House conference on 27 January 1949 that had initiated the collection had been organised by the Southern political parties, with no Northern consultation. That conference created another Anti-Partition League, with no North-South co-ordination and no agreed objectives. It founded the Irish News Agency, a propaganda unit of the Department of External Affairs, which produced some hard-hitting pamphlets on the evils of partition, much of the content of which was written by a young public servant, Conor Cruise O'Brien.[118] He re-emerged as a virulent anti-republican minister in the 1973–7 government, and even later as a member of the United Kingdom Unionist Party. Concern for Northern nationalists did not sway the Dublin government to accede to a petition of four Anti-Partition League MPs, including the newly elected Charlie McGleenan for South Armagh, and two senators to sit in the Oireachtas. As Michael Farrell commented, 'anti-partitionism didn't extend so far as giving a vote in their parliament to an unpredictable group of Northerners'.[119]

Thereafter, the League descended again into faction-fighting, mainly over the issue of refusing to take Stormont seats. When the abstentionists left, the league reorganised, with Eddie McAteer taking over as chairman from McSparran, who became president. Paddy McGill, my own illustrious predecessor as *Ulster Herald* editor, became secretary. The League was wound up in a few years having made no headway against the resurgent republicanism of the border campaign. But, like a pike hidden in the thatch, the League's extensive body of research on partition was retrieved and supplemented by civil rights activists such as Dungannon medical doctor Conn McCluskey and his wife Patricia during the resurgence of non-violent opposition to Stormont in the late 1960s.

7. Dark Edges

Middletown to Caledon – 5 km

A framed poster hanging in the Hunting Lodge at Castle Leslie advertises *Middletown*, a movie released in 2007 with a dramatic script from Armagh-born writer Daragh Carville. Set in the 1960s, it is about the return of Gabriel (Matthew MacFadyen) as an evangelical pastor to his home village, and it captures the strict no-holds-barred tradition of Ulster religious fundamentalism then typified in the ministry of Armagh-born Reverend Ian Paisley. Pastor Gabriel rails against his father's sideline business in smuggled diesel, against the villagers' involvement in cockfighting, against his sister-in-law's pub, where sabbatarian licensing laws are set aside for a few quiet pints behind closed doors during Sunday vespers. While it doesn't mention the imminent Troubles, or indeed the border's proximity, it evokes all the pent-up frustrations and inhibitions that bubble beneath the façade of the unionist state in Northern Ireland, especially on its rebellious frontier. As tensions build in the village, so does the prospect of an apocalyptic ending. So while the framed poster in Conor's Bar in the Hunting Lodge may be explained by the proximity of Middletown, it is hardly an enticement for guests to check out the neighbouring village.

I recall scenes from the film as I set off from the real Middletown, resuming my hike along the course of the Ulster Canal that shadows the border along a minor route called – somewhat ominously – Coolkill Road. Named for a townland through which it doesn't actually pass, it veers off the main A2 road to Armagh city and winds its way for the next 5 or 6 kilometres at a distance of 1 kilometer from the borderline. Immediately on leaving the village, a signpost points to the local Gaelic Athletic Association grounds. Through the decades of partition, and most especially in modern times, the GAA has been the popular vehicle of Irish nationalism in Northern Ireland. As religious fervour in the Catholic Church has declined dramatically, passionate adherence to GAA has risen to unprecedented levels. Through the Troubles, GAA clubs provided sanctuary when it was often dangerous to venture outside the tried and trusted for entertainment. For rural Catholics, community pride revolved around the GAA club, and so club premises and club members were targeted. The most extreme cases, such as the 1975 murder of Colm McCartney and Seán Farmer just after they crossed the border from Monaghan into Armagh or the 1997 murder of Seán Brown, shook the nationalist community to the very core – because almost everyone identifies with the GAA.[1] For that reason, success in Gaelic games resonates deeply North of the border, and that is reflected in the dogged pursuit of honours by teams since the bloody conflict gave way to peace and the Good Friday Agreement.

As the armed conflict gave way to the cultural wars that have been waged since, the GAA has been winning hands-down for the cause of Irish nationalism on the front line. Here in County Armagh, the offensive was launched in spectacular fashion by Crossmaglen Rangers, who won the senior All-Ireland club football title no fewer than six times between 1997 and 2012, and also dominated the county and Ulster provincial championships. Largely on the back of that club's success, Armagh won the Sam Maguire Cup, the all-Ireland inter-county football trophy in 2002 and vied successfully for Ulster dominance several times subsequently against an equally resurgent neighbour from Tyrone. Most communities in Ulster, as elsewhere, have to be content with more modest pickings in Gaelic games. For the nationalist side, however, community is encapsulated in the local GAA club regardless of success. Local parish identity, national culture and community pride are all invested in the club *gansaí* (jersey), which has become the favoured street fashion of rural Catholic youth.

Here in Middletown, the GAA club provides a fulcrum for community life, a fact that was forcefully conveyed by former club secretary Aidan Mallon:

A policeman once said that Middletown must be the most boring place in the world, because everyone he stopped was

199

either going to the GAA pitch or coming from it, and that they must have no time to do anything else. That's how it has always been, and continues to be.[2]

While Middletown is no different in this from most nationalist communities, it has a unique status in Ulster because it strongly promotes both football and hurling and gives equal billing to both in terms of club resources. Not that it has an overabundance of resources, as can be gauged from its membership of roughly 250. Yet from those numbers it fields no fewer than fifteen teams at all skill levels and ages, from both genders, in football, hurling and camogie. The only difference is that the footballers compete as Eoghan Rua (Owen Roe), while the hurling team lines out as Na Fianna, and the camogie (women's hurling) team competes as St John's.

These multiple personalities have not impeded the club's playing prowess, however, as the honours keep piling up across the various codes. Most recently, Na Fianna won the Armagh senior hurling league and championships in 2011; the senior hurling championship again in 2012, when they went on to become runners-up in the all-Ireland Intermediate hurling championship; and they recaptured the Armagh senior hurling championship in back-to-back wins for 2015 and 2016. Meanwhile, the camógs of St John's brought home the Armagh intermediate championship trophy in 2014. While the club has been less successful at football, that is a reflection of the predominance of that game and the very high standard of competition in County Armagh. Back at P.J. O'Neill Park, named for a former club stalwart and Armagh county board chairman in the 1940s, the GAA club's facilities have undergone a huge transformation in recent times. So also has the breadth of involvement in activities such as the Scór cultural contests.

As a result, Middletown Gaels are immersed in Irish cultural life from the earliest age. Their sense of national, community and cultural identity is suffused in their affiliation to this enveloping and consuming passion for Gaelic games and all they represent in Middletown. It is an affinity that directs personal and community allegiance not eastward to Belfast and other regions of the United Kingdom, but across the border. For it is the

Irish national flag that flies proudly over P.J. O'Neill Park and it is 'Amhrán na bhFiann' ('Soldier's Song') that is played as the national anthem before major matches. As religious identity and practice have waned over the past century, the GAA has grown in stature and importance. It has taken the place once occupied by the Catholic Church and all its lay manifestations – the Ancient Order of Hibernians, confraternities, sodalities and Knights of Columbanus. While unionists and political commentators were worrying about the prospect of 'Rome rule', nationalists in Northern Ireland were staking their allegiance to Croke Park.

So in Catholic parish communities, the GAA has provided the social capital for wider empowerment and economic development, often in lockstep with community-based credit unions with which it usually shares much of its officer board. The GAA has also been the launch pad for aspiring politicians. Meanwhile, the credit union has been a source of capital for business start-ups, home ownership and general improvements in living standards. The twin impact of these bodies on the fabric of communities on both sides of the frontier cannot be overestimated. It is certainly manifest here in the comfortable homes and parish pride of Middletown.

Over the next few kilometres, the Coolkill Road lollops through the drumlin border countryside, mirroring the twists and turns of the Cor River and the Ulster Canal, which follow more faithfully the line of the border hereabouts. The number of houses diminishes and there is a sharp fall-off in road traffic. As the land to the left relaxes into lush green parkland, the land on the right takes on a scorched-earth look where diggers are improving drainage. Watching this work momentarily, I am reminded of a story in Brian Cassells's book about the building of the Ulster Canal and the minor industrial dispute that happened hereabouts.

William Dargan's company was paying above-average wages of 9 shillings a week, which 'was double that which could be earned anywhere else in County Armagh at that time'.[3] It wasn't enough for the navvies of Tynan parish however. They destroyed ten wheelbarrows – 'the dumper trucks of the day' – on the evening of 4 November 1835 after a meeting near Caledon demanded higher wages. There was speculation that the dispute arose from local resentment that people from outside the immediate area were being employed; or that it arose from punitive conditions that meant a worker leaving employment without due notice could be transported to a penal colony for up to seven years. In any case, a notice in the English vernacular of the district was pinned to the door of Middletown's market house. Presumably referring to Dargan, it threatened to 'pay Him a visit'. The dispute obviously ran out of steam because the channel was completed in this district and the navvies moved on towards Monaghan.

The Coolkill Road turns a sharp right and left in front of a huge pair of wooden doors with heavy metal hinges, set into a twin-turreted cut-stone entrance. This is the impressive portal of Tynan Abbey, with an ornamented parapet on which marksmen might emerge from the large turret on the left and the smaller to the right to repel invaders. This is all that now remains of the neo-Gothic mansion in which one of the most memorable atrocities of the Troubles occurred.

Retired unionist MP and speaker of the Stormont parliament Sir Norman Strong of Tynan Abbey was shot dead by IRA raiders on 21 January 1981. He was 86 years of age. His 48-year-old son James Stronge – a former Grenadier Guards officer, Stormont assembly member, merchant banker and reserve constable in the RUC – was also gunned down in the cold-blooded attack. Both father and son had ignored repeated advice to relocate from the mansion, which sat in an 800-acre demesne right on the border where the counties of Armagh, Monaghan and Tyrone converge.[4] On that wintry night, a large group of men in army fatigues emerged from the dark edges of the border, forced their way into the abbey, sought out the victims and shot them dead. They then placed incendiary bombs and set the mansion alight, destroying it completely. As the dozen armed raiders, allegedly led by Jim Lynagh of Monaghan, left the scene, they encountered an armoured police car with several RUC officers sent from Middletown to head them off here at the gates of the demesne. The IRA riddled the car with automatic fire, pinning down the police and making good their escape.[5]

An IRA statement said the Stronges had been singled out as 'the symbols of hated unionism' in a 'direct reprisal for a whole series of loyalist assassinations and murder attacks on nationalist people and nationalist activists'.[6] This has been interpreted as a reference to the recent murders of four prominent republicans and an even more recent attempt on the lives of former MP Bernadette McAliskey (née Devlin), who had been very prominent in the H-Block/Armagh prison campaign, and her husband Michael.[7] That certainly provided an immediate pretext for the atrocity, but the scale of the operation, the intense brutality of the act of killing an old man, the destruction of an historic mansion, and the status of the victims as scions of the local ascendancy, suggest elaborate planning, cold-blooded deliberation and sanction at the highest level in the IRA.

The victims ticked many boxes for inclusion on the hit list. Sir Norman was a justice of the peace and high sheriff. Both father and son were also members of the local Derryhaw Boyne Defenders Loyal Orange Lodge, and Sir Norman had been installed as sovereign grand master of the Royal Black Institution. The uncle from whom he had inherited his estate, Sir James Stronge, had been grand master of the Armagh Orange Lodge and a vigorous champion during the partition period of his fellow Ulster unionists in 'the three counties', who had 'been thrown to the wolves with very little compunction'.[8] On succession, Sir Norman had also sat as a prominent unionist member in the old Stormont parliament for a record thirty-one years, and he was speaker of the house from 1945 until he retired in 1969. His son then took his seat, until Stormont was prorogued.

At the funeral service in St Vidic's Parish Church in Tynan, the pallbearers were from the 5th Battalion Royal Irish Fusiliers, and Queen Elizabeth II sent her condolences, saying she was 'deeply shocked'. The SDLP's Austin Currie remarked that 'even at 86 years of age … [Sir Norman was] still incomparably more of a man than the cowardly dregs of humanity who ended his life in this barbaric way'. Other reactions to the murders were less caring. According to several accounts, Gerry Adams is said to have stated that 'the only complaint I have heard from nationalists or anti-unionists is that he was not shot forty years ago'.[9]

Just weeks after the horrific double murder, on 12 February 1981, Rev. Ian Paisley stated in the House of Commons that the army patrol assigned to protect Tynan Abbey was being 'wined and dined in a well-known republican house in the area', and the helicopter sent to support the RUC 'ran out of fuel and had to return to base'.[10] According to official files released in 2012, the DUP leader's remarks were noted by a Northern Ireland Office (NIO) official, C. Davenport, who linked them to a letter from Armagh unionist MP Harold McCusker to Secretary of State Humphrey Atkins naming Hughes's Hotel in Middletown as the place where the soldiers were allegedly drinking. The NIO official said this allegation was investigated by the army, which 'flatly denied it'.[11]

Other rumours and allegations swirled around an attack that was clearly carried out to shake the unionist world to its foundations and mark a watershed in the conflict that had been notable in this district for the series of tit-for-tat killings that earned it a reputation as the 'Murder Triangle'. The Glennane Gang, with its cohort of members from the police, UDR and military intelligence, was a pivotal player in this lengthy bloodbath. So was the IRA's East Tyrone Brigade and its core group of Volunteers based in Monaghan, drawn mostly from the areas of mid-Ulster south of Lough Neagh and neatly bisected by the route of the Ulster Canal.

Local people had already been deeply shocked by the brutal murder of a young single mother, Margaret Ann Hearst, in front of her toddler child on 8 October 1977. The IRA had invaded her parents' home at Doogarry, just outside Middletown, and held her grandmother and younger brothers at gunpoint. When 24-year-old Margaret Ann returned from work as a civilian clerk at the UDR headquarters in Armagh city, her assassin burst into her mobile home in the garden and shot her dead in a hail of bullets. One bullet went through an internal wall into the room where her daughter was playing and passed through a toy frog the child was cuddling. The young mother had also been a part-time member of the UDR for four years.[12]

One vivid account names Margaret Ann's killer as Dessie O'Hare from Keady, County Armagh, also known as the Border Fox.[13] However, on 16 May 1979, a Middletown teenager was sentence to be detained indefinitely when he admitted in court that he fired the fatal shots.[14] He was only 16 years old at the time of the murder. In a BBC broadcast in August 1994, *The Dead*, one of the younger brothers held hostage said that when the killer saw the light come on and his sister's shadow, he left the house by the window and next thing there was a burst of ten or eleven shots. Amid the clamour of condemnation of the killing were statements from the Northern Ireland Civil Rights Association and the Roman Catholic primate Cardinal Tomás Ó Fiaich. Just three years later, on 4 September 1980, Margaret Ann's father, Ross Hearst, was abducted from a friend's house at Tullylush in County Monaghan, murdered and his body dumped close to the Armagh border.

The implication of Dessie O'Hare is hardly surprising. By the late 1970s, he was a hardened republican activist who had already acquired a notorious reputation in both jurisdictions. He was also high on the hit list of loyalist killers. When the Rock Bar was attacked at Granemore, near Keady, in June 1976, Constable Billy McCaughey, a member of the notorious Glennane Gang of UVF and security forces members, told interrogators that O'Hare was the intended target. Two months later, the same gang bombed Keady's Step Inn killing two people. McCaughey said he and his fellow RUC officer in the gang, Castleblayney native Sergeant John Weir, 'got away with things. We just had that kind of courage that was really recklessness.' He had learned from RUC Special Branch that O'Hare would be in the bar. Also involved in that attack, which involved spraying it with gunfire and detonating a 10lb bomb, were three other members of the RUC Special Patrol Group, Constables Laurence McClure, Ian Mitchell and David Wilson.[15]

From a strong republican background, Dessie O'Hare had been 'disciplined' as an IRA volunteer and then switched to the more cavalier republican paramilitary group, the INLA. He is said to have acquired his nickname because he used the border to evade arrests in several dramatic car chases. In 1979, he was shot twice in a car chase through County Monaghan, crashing his getaway car into a herd of cattle, then into another car before plunging into a field. His companion died and O'Hare broke both ankles. At a subsequent trial, he was sentenced to nine years in jail for possession of firearms, serving six before his release just as the INLA was immersed in a bloody feud between rival factions.

When several leaders of his chosen faction were gunned down, O'Hare identified Tony McCluskey as the informant. McCluskey was originally from D'Alton Park in Armagh and had been arrested as a 16-year-old in the police swoops after the 1972 assassination attempt on Stormont junior minister John Taylor; he was cleared of any involvement in that attack but served with detention orders and held on the Maidstone Prison Ship.[16] As McCluskey lay with his wife in bed at their Mullaghmatt home in Monaghan town in early February 1987, a gang burst in and took him away in his own car.[17] His mutilated body was subsequently found at Knockbane, near Middletown, just across the border from where Ross Hearst's body had been dumped in 1980. A pathologist's report on McCluskey revealed that his killers had severed his right index finger. In a subsequent interview published in the *Sunday Tribune*, O'Hare denied that McCluskey was tortured, saying, 'I had a deep hatred for McCluskey and all those guys. I did not want him to die lightly.'

Later that same year, O'Hare kidnapped Dublin dentist John O'Grady, cut off the tips of his fingers and included them with the ransom demand. After a number of bungled chases by Gardaí and other escapades, O'Hare was finally arrested when he crashed through a Garda roadblock and was caught in a shootout in which his driver Martin Bryan was killed. O'Hare was shot eight times, but survived to be tried in Dublin's Special Criminal Court, where he was given a forty-year sentence. However, he was released under the terms of the Good Friday Agreement in 2006 and subsequently moved back home, emerging from time to time in sensational headline-grabbing news. Most recently, in November 2016, he was granted bail when arrested at home in County Armagh on foot of an extradition application from the Republic for alleged involvement in offences including 'false imprisonment, threats to kill and violent disorder'.[18] The court had been told earlier that O'Hare posed 'no flight risk as he was married with children and grandchildren. He had a home that was worth between £200,000 and £300,000 in County Armagh and a handyman business. He also had a number of agricultural interests including a mushroom factory that he needed to tend.'[19]

From the gates of Tynan Abbey, Chapel Hill Road is a narrow diversion off the B210/Coolkill Road leading past the braeside church of St Joseph's. It is one of the two Roman Catholic places of worship in the parish, along with Middletown's St John's; they were built thirteen years apart, in 1813 and 1826. From the chapel, the road ascends to Tynan village itself, past the local pharmacy/post office and a derelict shop opposite. The fading name 'E. Graham' is above the door where the post office once resided. Although it is at the centre of a district accommodating no fewer than five almost equidistant villages, Tynan seems to have been bypassed long ago. It consists of small streets of mainly terraced stone buildings. The streets have evocative names such as Abbey Road and College Hall Lane. They are clustered around a high stone wall enclosing St Vidic's parish church and its ancient graveyard.

At a junction of two roads leading back down to Coolkill Road stands a tenth-century Celtic High Cross. One of three such crosses in the vicinity, this one formerly stood in the church grounds, where it was damaged. Subsequently it was relocated here and reconstituted with parts of other crosses. Without a modern focal point, Tynan village seems to languish in virtual silence, apart from the sixty-one souls calling it home, as recorded in the 2011 census. Lewis's *Topographical Dictionary* of Ireland noted that Tynan had a population of 243 for the village, out of more than 11,500 inhabitants of the wider parish bearing its name.

Lewis also noted that the village, which occupies an 'eminence', was once a place of 'great extent and importance', having been 'noticed in Pope Nicholas's Taxation in 1291 as belonging to the Culdees of Armagh'. Several streets in nearby Armagh city are called after the Culdees (derived from the Gaelic '*céile Dé*', meaning 'companions of God'), who were monastic communities of lay people attached to cathedrals in medieval Ireland and Scotland. As noted by Reverend William Reeves, an antiquarian and the rector of Tynan during the 1860s, the Culdees of Armagh survived the Reformation purge by a full century before they were dissolved and their property forfeited to the 'vicars choral' of the Protestant cathedral in 1627.[20] Ten townlands of this parish then became the property of the provost and fellows of Trinity College Dublin.[21] Similar property holdings that provided income for Trinity include the Collegelands district of County Armagh, outside Charlemont, and part of Slieve Beagh north of Roslea village.

Tynan now feels like it stands in the middle of nowhere, but it was once a bustling centre of communication. A fingerpost at the junction of

Abbey Road places Tynan at the centre of a cluster of nearby towns and villages. Omitted from the information is the distance from Glaslough, which is about 2.5 miles (4k) along the Cortynan Road, which crosses the Ulster Canal, the Cor River and the border. At one time, it would also have crossed the Clogher Valley Railway, the eastern terminus of which was at Tynan railway station, which occupied the bottom of the Abbey Road brae. The narrow-gauge system opened in 1887 and took off from Tynan for Calendon on a semi-circular route around the tip of County Monaghan to Maguiresbridge in Fermanagh. It was a tram service running alongside the road and up and down the main street of Caledon and Fivemiletown, but it also traversed the open countryside at times like a normal railway.[22] It relied heavily on fair days and Orange parades for traffic, and the same wagons were used to transport cattle and Orangemen after a 'quick scrub down' for the latter. When heavily laden, the trams/ trains threw out sparks with the engine exhaust and regularly set fire to nearby houses and cottages, which cost heavily in compensation claims. Already running at a loss, the line's catchment area was almost cut in two by the border right beside its route around north Monaghan. A new board of management was appointed in 1928 and its innovations included long-opposed Sunday services.[23] Even that wasn't enough to save the Clogher Valley Railway, which was further hit by the Economic War's impact on cross-border cattle trade and the Road Transport Act of 1932. The latter introduced stringent regulations for southern bus operations compared with their northern counterparts. On the northern side, that created competition between highly regulated railways and virtually unregulated road transport.[24] The Clogher Valley Railway closed down finally on New Year's Day 1942, before – as Sir Shane Leslie noted – it was included in Hitler's invasion plan.

Tynan's once bustling railway station was shared with the Great Northern Railway, which swept west from here towards Glaslough, Monaghan and Clones. Train arrivals on the light rail were timed to coincide with the schedules of trains running from Belfast to Clones. At the western terminus in Maguiresbridge, the Clogher Valley services were also timed to coincide with trains from Clones for Enniskillen and points beyond. Tynan village was also the location where the British customs checks were carried out, elevating it to an important cross-border location for passengers and goods. Christopher Fitz-Simon remembers it lovingly; he bid farewell to school and 'Belfast's fog-swathed streets' heading home by train past the 'glittering granite spires of Armagh Cathedral', and feeling comforted by the:

> return of the familiar landscape. Killylea. Tynan. Glaslough. Monaghan. Lakes with moorhens. Hawthorn brakes. Apple trees. McEntees' farm. And all of a sudden, round the grassy hill, the two-storeyed thatched farmhouse would come into view, great-aunt Zane leaning on the stile waving to us as the train slowed down … everything bright and familiar and welcoming.[25]

Like the Ulster Canal before it, the railway is gone and where its traces remain, 'the track is overgrown with blackberries and hazels and the yellow-brick station is no more'. At the intersection of Abbey Road with the Coolkill Road and Cortynan Road, only an old broken railway bridge bears testimony to Tynan's busy past as a railway junction. A short distance up the Cortynan Road, the Ulster Canal is dry, yet clearly discernible below the road, where it is enfolded in rich woodland. A hundred metres further on, the Cor River flows towards its merger with the Blackwater. This is a small forgotten pocket, where the ruined walls of Tynan Abbey meet the gapped walls of Castle Leslie on a contested border, and the uniform wall around Caledon Estate keeps its distance across the narrow road. It is where Armagh nestles into Monaghan to the west and Tyrone to the north. It is a no man's land of tranquillity on a fraught border, where lush drumlin countryside enshrouds history and division in the confluence of rivers, trees and walls.

The three estate families – Leslies, Stronges and Alexanders – were close friends once. In the closing years of the nineteenth century, Sir Shane Leslie and his brother Norman would join the four Alexander brothers at Tynan station for the train to Belfast, and thence journey across the Irish Sea to school at Eton. On Sunday evenings, family members walked between the great houses for afternoon tea visits, swapping gossip of life in their three respective estate villages as well as stories of high society doings.

Shortly after the millennium dawn of peaceful co-existence, Turtle Bunbury, a relative of the Stronges, set off 'hemisphered beneath a cloudless sky and surrounded by glorious autumnal sunshine' with Sir Jack Leslie to visit Caledon and Tynan, remarking on how 'exceptionally well-built' is the Caledon Estate wall, which 'extends for five miles'.[26] While Tynan Abbey and Castle Leslie show signs of wear, the Caledon Estate wall is as pristine as when it was it was built. Little wonder since the latter-day earls of Caledon married well and often, the sixth and seventh earls accumulating three wives each, from families including the Von Siemens of electronics fame, and a daughter of Greek shipping magnate Spiro Nicholas Coumantaros. Among the six wives over two generations was also, notably, Ghislaine Dresselhuys, wealthy heiress and noted TV panellist on the BBC version of *What's My Line?* hosted by Dubliner Eamonn Andrews.[27] Not to be outdone by the males of the family, Ghislaine also acquired a total of three spouses of her own during a life of celebrity on both sides of the Atlantic.

Meanwhile, Sir Jack Leslie recalled how his father Sir Shane had regularly visited one of those childhood friends, Harold Alexander. The Caledon boy had become the Second World War Field Marshal Alexander, then Lord Alexander of Tunis, and from 1946 to 1952 governor general of Canada, the last British aristocrat to hold that office. It was a pivotal time in world history, with the emergence of former colonies, including both Canada and Ireland, from the shadow of England. Lord Alexander, unwittingly perhaps, played a significant role in both. The Fine Gael-led coalition government of Taoiseach John A. Costello withdrew the Free State from the Commonwealth and formally declared a republic on Easter Monday 1949, with the repeal of the External Relations Act.[28] In retaliation, Westminster, in the Ireland Act 1949, pledged to maintain Northern Ireland as part of the United Kingdom so long as the Stormont parliament wished it, a guarantee thereafter regarded by unionists as their 'constitution'.

The background of the double hissy fit was that when Costello had visited Ottawa the previous year, he had dined at the governor general's residence after assurances that the formal toast to the king would be followed by a toast to the president of Ireland, recognising that Ireland now had its own head of state. But the governor general omitted the latter toast, which Costello regarded as a direct snub. Alexander also placed a table centrepiece facing his Irish guest: a replica of 'Roaring Meg', the iconic cannon that had defended Derry's walls during the 1689 siege. Costello fulminated about this to Canadian Prime Minister William Lyon Mackenzie King. At a subsequent Ottawa press conference, Costello confirmed the Free State's exit from the Commonwealth, an 'announcement' that surprised both the British and Irish governments.[29]

Not far the former Tynan station is the village of Killylea. That's where, on the dark evening of Tuesday, 17 March 2009, I attended my first parade of Ulster loyalist Blood and Thunder bands. It was a revelation I describe in my 2010 book, *Blood & Thunder*.[30] Essentially, I discovered that loyalist band parading is probably the closest cultural equivalent of the GAA in Ulster Protestantism. It is how young Protestant men and women in their teenage years and early adulthood discover their sense of ethnic identity in a peer group that inculcates pride in cultural belonging, and a huge attachment to their own community and its history. It is how they acquire skills of marching and music-making, skills in which they compete against similar communities.

Their pride of place is evident in the very names of the bands. Some forty marching bands took part in the Killylea St Patrick's Day parade, which was organised by the local Cormeen Rising Sons of William flute band. There was immediate local support from the Killylea Silver Band and the Enagh Accordion Band from Tynan. But the event was dominated overwhelmingly by Blood and Thunder flute bands, many proclaiming their borderland roots, as in the Drumhillery Pride of the Frontier from the Keady area, the Newtownbutler Border Defenders and the Castlederg Young Loyalist Flute Band from west Tyrone, with their banner proclaiming they had been 'Marching along the border for thirty years'. While there was strong representation from all the neighbouring counties, the Killylea event had the look and feel of a borderline celebration of Britishness. However, it also evoked the loyalist sense of

Irishness, not least in the indigenous music of jigs, reels and martial airs such as 'Killaloo' that wafted around the village on a dark and dank evening of St Patrick's Day.

That relatively huge village parade in Killylea was ignored by the mass media, including local newspapers, which I found surprising. So also was another parade organised by the Ulster Protestant Boys Flute Band in Coleraine. These two events are hugely important, not only in kick-starting the popular season of marching-band parades that runs through to October in villages, towns and cities throughout Northern Ireland, but also as an acknowledgment that Protestant Ulster is entitled to share the legacy of Saint Patrick. Yet Ulster loyalism was slow to wrest back a claim of Irish identity, and the Killylea parade was first organised in 2004. That was a time when Ulster loyalist confidence was at an all-time low in the wake of the Good Friday Agreement and a resurgence of Irish nationalist identity throughout Northern Ireland. Protestants, for their part, felt disenfranchised and threatened as their hegemony was dismantled to make way for the new shared future. This was most apparent in the loss of their virtual monopoly of policing and other security services, and the imposition of restrictions on public celebrations, under the Parades Commission. As the Orange Order floundered, the marching bands became the most popular and active manifestation of loyalism. At the same time, the bands also began to emerge from the shadows of loyalist paramilitary organisations, which dominated their working-class Protestant communities.

As the term 'cultural wars' was coined to describe the new internecine struggle, the loyalist bands became more assertive. Indeed, they were primarily responsible for promoting history and culture in their communities. So against strong disagreement, not least from others in their own communities, bands such as the Cormeen Rising Sons of William laid claim to a share of Saint Patrick's Day by hosting its annual parade on 17 March. When I first met him while researching *Blood & Thunder*, loyalist historian and band activist Quincey Dougan said loyalists were 'absolutely itching to get out and do something' on Saint Patrick's Day, and this gave them the opportunity. Noting that Cormeen's annual parade was outgrowing Killylea village, he predicted that it would soon have to move to nearby Armagh city.[31] That happened in 2012, despite dire warnings of mayhem from nationalist and republican political representatives. Almost unnoticed or unacknowledged in the furore was that the loyalist bands worked with the Parades Commission, still anathema to the Orange Order, and invited opponents to meet and discuss concerns. It also undertook to abide by any restrictions imposed on the parade in terms of flags, emblems, uniforms and choice of music.

I attended that initial Armagh city parade in 2012, which passed off peacefully and efficiently. The musical fare was refreshingly Irish and upbeat. It has continued to be a feature of the national holiday since then, the largest musical parade held on that day in the primal See of St Patrick's city of Armagh. Yet it is still completely ignored by the mass media in favour of fancy dress and samba band turnouts elsewhere.

Back on the trail, the bridge crossing the River Blackwater at the entrance to Caledon village is the county line between Armagh and Tyrone. Slightly to the east, a humpback bridge is half buried in a field. Landlocked, with no apparent purpose, it appears to be all that remains of the Ulster Canal hereabouts. The man-made navigation once mirrored the river's course from this point, before merging with it at Charlemont for the final stretch into Lough Neagh. The entire course of the canal is absorbed into the lush farmland that bounds the Blackwater.

Gone too are the industrial mills that once dotted this countryside, harnessing the power of the Blackwater and its tributaries to drive an industrial revolution based on locally grown flax. The linen produced from that crop transformed Ulster from the poorest province in Ireland to the richest by the dawn of the twentieth century.[32] Prosperity was built on the back of hard labour, especially during the early part of that transformation. The mostly agrarian process of growing, pulling, retting, drying, scutching and hackling the crop required many hands and huge effort, and all that preceded the industrial stages, when the flax was spun into linen yarn for tackling, weaving, bleaching, beetling and finishing into the linen cloth.

The drumlin topography of north Armagh, Monaghan and south Tyrone was particularly suited to the cultivation of flax and the subsequent watermill stages of processing it for the manufacture of linen. Mechanisation was slow at first. One of the earliest innovations was the introduction of the Dutch treadle-operated spinning wheel for making yarn. At the end of the seventeenth century, the Irish Linen Board gave them out free of charge to anyone who sowed good flaxseed between 10 March and 1 June 1796, an initiative that resulted in no fewer than 312 spinning wheels being distributed in the Monaghan parish of Clontibret.[33] The heartland of the industry that developed over the following century became the 'Linen Triangle' between Dungannon, Lurgan and Armagh city. Around this, the economy was hugely reliant on flax production and processing in small mills, such as the one that gave its name to Mullen (*muileann* or mill), a 'model' village in Monaghan just north-west of Caledon on the Blackwater. It gave rise to the highest density of cottiers in Ireland, complementing subsistence farming with cottage-based industry.

The burgeoning economy of the Linen Triangle and its peripheral overflow was a key element of the rural industry that the Ulster Canal would link to Belfast and the world beyond. In 1825, a private company was set up, backed by the marquis of Donegall, the marquis of Downshire, Lord Rossmore, Sir James Stronge and Sir Arthur Chichester.[34] It applied for a government loan of £100,000 for the project and engaged Thomas Telford, the Scottish civil engineer who had designed the Caledonian Canal among many spectacular projects, to review the plan. It was the redesign Telford requested that reduced the size of the locks and contributed to the canal's failure. Yet failure was never considered in 1834 when, after flags were hoisted, batteries were fired and bonfires lit, the:

> gentlemen connected with the Ulster Canal and also a good many others, comprising a number of the inhabitants of Caledon, dined together at the Caledon Hotel, in commemoration of the opening of the works. No pains were spared by Mr Taylor in furnishing the entertainment, and affording every accommodation to the company. Among the toasts were 'The King', 'The Queen, and the rest of the Royal Family', 'The Army and Navy', 'Prosperity to the Ulster Canal, and Lord and Lady Caledon', 'Sir A. Chichester, one of the earliest friends to the

undertaking'. The evening passed off in the greatest harmony, all present being highly delighted with the prospect of the blessings likely to result from the completion of the Ulster Canal.[35]

A decade earlier, work had begun at the corn mill built by James Du Pre Alexander, third earl of Caledon. It reopened in 1882 as a woollen mill with forty looms and a thousand employees on six floors and continued in business until 1930.[36] Caledon Mill was the scene of Peadar O'Donnell's next big industrial confrontation. In January 1919, around the time of his resounding victory at the Monaghan Lunatic Asylum, the ITGWU organiser called a night-time meeting under the 'big tree' in Caledon, where he signed up 107 millworkers, who were paid 18 shillings a week, with one shilling and sixpence bonus.[37] The union won better pay and conditions, until the mill owners struck back, using the Orange Order to pressurise union members. On 21 February, a strike began after the Goan brothers, ex-servicemen and ITGWU activists, were sacked. Most of the 220 strikers were women. The militant mood spread through Caledon, O'Donnell telling the *Derry Journal*:

> In South Tyrone, in a town where the majority of workers are Protestant, we have a nightly Red Flag procession – 'No Surrender' emblazoned on one side of the flag, 'Up the Irish Transport' on the other. The flag that can thus unite our Irish workers is the flag we want.[38]

A band was set up with Orange and Catholic members, and at nightly meetings around the 'big tree', a 'citizen police force' was established.[39] Yet there was constant fighting at the mill, and it spread back to the railway station, preventing non-striking workers getting through to the mill. 'There were frequent police baton charges, and O'Donnell was twice badly beaten, once by police and once by scabs,' according to McCabe's account based on local interviews. Meanwhile, striking Orangemen were deprived of even minor privileges in their lodge; strike-breakers were housed in huts and 'chosen for their loyalism rather than their skill', as the mill became 'a loyalist fortress with Union Jacks hung from the windows'.

There was a slow drift back to work, and the strike was broken in ten weeks; most of those who were still out by then were Catholic. While the local parish priest is said to have tried to negotiate a return to work, they voted to stay out and marched to Tynan station as a body, heading for England while singing 'The Red Flag'. Their families were subsequently evicted. Among them was James McMenamy, the local ITGWU secretary and a Protestant ex-serviceman who stayed out to the end. He had 'won the Military Medal; and because he objected to work for 6 shillings a week he is evicted, together with his mother'.[40] In Orange circles, the defeat of the Caledon strikers was heralded as part of a double celebration for the 'overthrow of the Hun and Irish Bolshevists'.[41] On the Twelfth of July, Caledon was hailed as 'the loyal village' that 'just signally defeated Sinn Féin's first attempt to cause strife in the unionist ranks through the Labour class'.[42]

If the threat of millworkers' unity in the face of rapacious capitalism was greeted as a rearguard republican threat, the early years of partition placed Caledon and its environs firmly on the front line. While two IRA divisions were ensconced entirely within the frontiers of the new Northern Ireland, the operational area of three others straddled the border, ignoring 'an artificial boundary created by an act of the British Parliament'. This meant: 'Some eight thousand IRA Volunteers lived and worked in the six counties area and, in the border counties especially, the truncation of the north-east was a more excoriating issue than that of the Oath [of Allegiance to the British crown] which had split the IRA in most of the 26 counties.'[43]

The porosity of the new border and the unity of the IRA divisions which straddled it became glaringly obvious on the night of 8 February 1922 when columns of the Fifth Northern Division crossed into Tyrone and Fermanagh and kidnapped prominent and well-to-do unionists. They were held as hostages for the release of the armed IRA men posing as the 'Monaghan footballers' arrested in Dromore when on their way to organise a jail break in Derry. The abducted unionists included William Allen of Ballagh, near Caledon, and 80-year-old Anketell Moutray of Favour Royal, deputy lieutenant for Tyrone. The latter 'greatly disturbed and embarrassed his captors by singing "God Save the King" and several penitential psalms in their ears until their eardrums seemed about to split and he would not desist despite appeals, commands and even threats of death'.[44] On a more serious note, the northern IRA columns underwent intensive training and weapons were shipped north as the sides – the IRA/Free State army and the Northern Ireland Special Constabulary – faced each other across the Blackwater. Five additional A Special mobile platoons were deployed in the Clogher Valley to reinforce the one already at Aughnacloy, and these were stationed between Clogher and Caledon. B Specials were also deployed and augmented all along the border, where main crossing points had permanent checkpoints and other bridges were blown and roads trenched.[45]

After the Clones Affray shoot-out between the Free State forces and the armed Special Constabulary passing through the railway station, the northern government demanded extra security and two extra British Army battalions were sent in March to strengthen the existing deployment of eleven battalions organised in three brigades, with five battalions in Belfast, three in south Down and three in the west.[46] The build-up of forces was mirrored on the other side of the new border, with the *Northern Standard* reporting that 500 IRA Volunteers were deployed between Caledon and Aughnacloy, a distance of only 7.5 miles. Mullan mill, Glaslough Orange Hall, next door to the RIC barracks, and three Protestants farmhouses in the district had been commandeered as billets. Some Glaslough families fled across the border and Catholics in Caledon were warned to clear out, until the Tyrone commandant of the Specials, Colonel McClintock intervened and halted any reprisal expulsions. Meanwhile, all roads in the area were blocked by A Specials on the northern side and the only way through was by fields and laneways.[47]

There were many reports in the *Northern Standard* of gunfire and battles. On 17 March, members of Caledon's A Specials platoon inspecting Burns's Bridge were fired upon from a house commandeered by the IRA just on the southern side. The following day, Colonel McClintock, Aughnacloy Platoon Captain Baker, Capt. Walter A. Montgomery of Blessingbourne, Fivemiletown, and Mr Ravensdale, an illustrator from a London magazine, were fired on as they inspected Ballagh Bridge between Aughnacloy and Caledon. Specials reinforcements under Captain Boyd commandeered the station store on Emyvale Road on 19 March, but he and three of his men were pinned down when over a hundred shots were fired at them.

On 21 March, there was a major gun battle at Aughnacloy and heavy sniper fire stopped a force of about 400 Caledon Specials from destroying Burns's Bridge, until that crossing point was visited by the joint Border Commission set up between the Dublin and Belfast authorities, which ordered that it be kept intact. On 26 March, 65-year-old farmer Robert Scott was killed as he foddered cattle at Kilsampson, outside Caledon. The fatal shot was fired by a sniper on Curley Hill near Glaslough. And when the Border Commission returned to Burns's Bridge, they were fired on, as were the Specials in a Crossley Tender at Comber, who had to dive for cover when they came under fire from hillsides in Monaghan, according to the *Northern Standard* report.

Border farmers moved out, including former kidnap victim William Allen, who abandoned his home and put it on the market. The conflict continued even after the Craig-Collins pact of 30 March 1922 for a cessation of IRA action in Northern Ireland in exchange for guarantees of fair treatment of nationalists. After a lull, there was an all-out attack on the Specials' stronghold at the Emyvale Road station, in which hundreds of rounds were fired. At Crilly nearer Aughnacloy, the home of Vaughan Montgomery JP came under heavy machine-gun fire from across the border as a Lancia armoured car containing a Specials platoon sent to relieve the garrison at Emyvale Road station was ambushed. The sniping continued, with the Northern authorities reporting that the front line extended from Caledon to Favour Royal. Farming in the Clogher Valley was totally disrupted by then, and 'starving poultry were fed under fire by the Special Constabulary'.[48]

The political and military ground shifted with the IRA convention split on 12 March and the impetus of the Ulster Council's military offensive flagged. On 6 June 1922, Special Constable Thomas Sheridan was shot dead with a single bullet by an IRA sniper when he reported for duty at Annaghroe, on the border between Caledon and Glaslough. He had joined the force eight weeks before and, after training at Newtownards, he arrived by bicycle to his assigned vehicle checkpoint about fifty yards from the frontier, where he was greeted by the local head constable. According to modern accounts, Sheridan was a 35-year-old single Catholic from County Cavan, and his family were 'unable to take his remains home … for burial', so instead, he was 'buried with full police honours' at St John's Church in Caledon. In 2016, the Ulster Special Constabulary Association (USCA) held a special ceremony and installed a headstone with First Minister Arlene Foster in attendance. USCA spokesman David Scott said he did not know why someone from the Free State would have joined the Special Constabulary: 'Maybe it's because in 1922 it was quite hard to get work – but as far as we're concerned he was an honourable man.'[49] There were many recruits to the Specials from the abandoned Ulster counties. Just the previous month, armed men at Arva Road Station in County Cavan arrested two Special Constables from Killeshandra who were home on holidays and about to return to the six counties. They were taken to an unknown destination and an unrecorded fate. [50]

Yet despite reports of imminent invasion of Northern Ireland by the IRA, relative peace descended on the border by early summer. That allowed the Northern regime to tighten its security net with widespread swoops, arrests and detentions. Those IRA activists who evaded arrest fled across the border, and many gathered at Castleshane, outside Monaghan. The attention of IRA volunteers shifted south, where the 'irregular' forces of the anti-Treatyites had moved into the Four Courts on 14 April 1922. Declarations of allegiance were coming from all over the country, but of the entire Ulster command structure, only the Fourth Northern Division covering Armagh and north Louth under Frank Aiken joined the anti-Treaty side, and then only after considerable prevarication through late spring and early summer, culminating in the Fifth Northern Division's August attack on Aiken's Dundalk barracks headquarters. The confusion of allegiances was shared by the overwhelming majority of northern volunteers, who opposed partition rather than the Treaty.[51] Since the anti-Treaty opposition led by De Valera had adopted the Treaty's Article 12 provision for a Boundary Commission in Document Number 2, there was little point for northern republicans to favour that side.[52] Many IRA volunteers who evaded arrest in the north drifted southwards to join the two sides in the burgeoning Civil War. Outside of a firm commitment to Michael Collins by all those who accepted his 'stepping-stone' strategy, allegiances were confused and shifting. When Collins was killed and the Civil War intensified, the IRA was left defeated and demoralised on both sides of the border.

What hope remained after hostilities ended in 1923 was now invested in the Boundary Commission which, after lengthy legal and procedural wrangling was set up in 1924 and convened in 1925. Evidence for the border around the north Monaghan salient was heard from witnesses at three different venues – Armagh, Omagh and Enniskillen. Yet because the Free State was focused on wholesale transfers of Tyrone and Fermanagh to make the North unsustainable, it was disengaged from the main considerations of the commissioners about smaller areas such as Clogher, Augher, Aughnacloy and Caledon, all contiguous with County Monaghan. Aughnacloy nationalists, backed by a petition of thirty-eight traders, pressed for transfer of their district to the Free State.[53] However, local unionists represented by Aughnacloy town commissioners wanted large areas of north Monaghan ceded to Northern Ireland.[54] Here as elsewhere along the border, local government had been suspended when nationalists boycotted the 1923 elections because the new Northern Ireland government scrapped its requirement to conduct polling through proportional representation.[55] Many councils with nationalist majorities had pledged allegiance to Dáil Éireann and a new law passed in 1922 scrapped proportional representation and enforced an oath of loyalty to the crown. Where unionist control could not be guaranteed, town commissions were appointed in place of elected councils. Meanwhile, nationalists of Clogher Rural District Council wanted the Clogher Valley moved to the Free State, while the unionists of Clogher Urban District Council supported the case for part of Monaghan to be transferred north.[56]

Nationalists pointed out that Aughnacloy was only '15 perches' from the border and the town served a market area extending 7 miles into Monaghan. This meant a 75 per cent business slump since the Free State set up its customs. There were arguments to and fro about population statistics and the impact of border security on voting registers. Town commission chairman Richard Vance said Aughnacloy was a 'decaying town', and asserted that while Monaghan people still came to sell livestock and produce, they didn't buy in Aughnacloy because of the customs checks, choosing instead to shop in Emyvale, which he described as 'a small place of little consequence'. Vance ended his submission:

> The Irish people … are a very conservative people and like to deal in the markets they have been accustomed to deal in and which their forefathers dealt in … From an economic and geographic point of view, the County Monaghan salient running into County Tyrone should be transferred to Northern Ireland in order to ensure the economic conditions of Aughnacloy and to shorten and make a straight boundary between Northern Ireland and the rest of Ireland.

Major General H. Montgomery for Clogher UDC also proposed a frontier running from the point where Fermanagh, Tyrone and Monaghan meet to Middletown, County Armagh, as a 'breathing space for Aughnacloy', and a shorter and more compact frontier. That proposed line ran just north of Monaghan town. It was also in line with a petition by some residents of Glaslough for transfer into Northern Ireland. This move came as a huge surprise to many Monaghan county councillors, who obviously saw any boundary changes as a one-way street, from north to south. Combined with moves to have the Drummully area of Clones and the Mullyash district of Castleblayney transferred to the north, it led to a heated debate in the county council chamber. Unionist Councillor Samuel Nixon of Clones said that 'there should be no boundary and that it should be swept aside by mutual understanding between the people on both sides of the border'.[57] The contrary view was expounded by unionist MP James Cooper, who told a rally in Aughnacloy that while local people might not like the border to remain as it was, it was best for 'the whole of Ulster if the boundary was left as it is at present'. However, he added his belief that the customs barriers would very soon disappear.[58]

With passions rising on both sides as the Boundary Commission deliberated its options during the long summer of 1925, the Orange brethren were told by platform speaker Arthur H. Coote at the Clogher

Valley Twelfth that 'we have still to stand together and hold the glorious place in the empire. The danger is not past until every foot of Ulster soil is free from the envious eyes of troublemakers across the border.' Coote might well have been thinking of a recent case that had come before the Monaghan Circuit Court, when Patrick McNeel of Altadaven, County Tyrone, sued Toal 'Francis' McKenna of Greagh, County Monaghan, for £10 damages for trespass on his land. McKenna allegedly removed soil and built a ditch with it. State Solicitor J.J. Keenan remarked, 'In this particular case, the defendant had gone further with regard to the boundary problem than a good many people, for he had actually transferred some of the soil of Northern Ireland into County Monaghan.' Because of its cross-jurisdictional nature and the difficulty of processing any judgment, the case was struck out.[59]

The final report of the Boundary Commission was also struck out, of course, when the *Morning Post* newspaper disclosed its findings and caused a political uproar in the Free State. Since the report had been shelved, it was not confirmed for another half century that the commission had recommended no changes in the border along north Monaghan's interface with Tyrone, although further south on the Armagh boundary, the Mullyash transfer was included and offset against the proposed transfer to the Free State of huge tracts of south Armagh in the Crossmaglen and Forkhill districts. Having returned from London, where he met Prime Minister Stanley Baldwin, Free State leader W.T. Cosgrave rushed 'uninvited and unexpected' to Emyvale, where he addressed a public meeting in late November 1925. 'This lamentable result can only be explained by the persistent and unscrupulous use of threats of violence and political pressure' from the North, he declared, calling for 'restraint and dignity … particularly by those most closely and most directly affected. A new and grave situation has undoubtedly arisen, but good citizenship dictates that no heated words or foolish acts should render our task more difficult.'[60]

Perhaps Edward Kelly of Clones, chairman of the Monaghan County Health Board, didn't hear that part. He told the Emyvale meeting that, while he had never fired a shot at any time in the Trouble, he 'promised he would fire a shot in this case'. Senator Thomas Toal said the Truagh area of north

Monaghan would never be 'thrown to the mercy of Craig and his followers', and he 'thought it was a terrible state of affairs if this boundary farce should be the means of smashing up the peaceable relations that existed between the inhabitants, both Protestant and Catholic, of this county'. After the public meeting, Cosgrave then met a deputation from Keady, but there is no record of what he told them. Yet, as historian A.T.Q. Stewart noted:

> it is beyond doubt that the tripartite agreement (secured by Cosgrave's "damn good bargain") was a bitter disappointment, especially to Catholics in the border areas who had regarded the transfer of their areas as inevitable. They now felt that they had been let down by the Free State government and were trapped in a unionist state which would always regard them as second-class citizens. More and more of them turned from moderate forms of nationalism to the uncompromising absolute of republicanism, and this further hardened unionist attitudes.[61]

Among those who certainly turned to uncompromising republicanism was Aughnacloy-born Sean McCaughey, who took over as IRA chief of staff when he oversaw the court martial of his predecessor, confessed Special Branch informer Stephen Hayes.[62] Jailed for his part in the abduction and murder of Hayes, McCaughey went on a hunger and thirst strike and died on the twenty-third day in Portlaoise Prison on 11 May 1946. His death acted as a catalyst for a regrouping of the IRA, and the launch of its border campaign when constitutional politics failed again in the 1950s. The outcome of that dismal episode seemed to have put paid to any prospect of renewed insurrection against the northern state. Within a few short years, however, a catalyst for renewed insurrection emerged here in the village of Caledon.

Originally called Kinnaird, a stronghold of the O'Neills, the present village of cut-stone houses and public buildings grew up around Caledon House, which was built in 1799 by James Alexander, subsequently Viscount Caledon. The old place name was resurrected in the late 1960s when a small scheme of council houses was built in a cul-de-sac off Mill Street. Kinnaird Park included ten two-storey houses, two bungalows and three smaller homes for older people.[63] As the construction neared completion, the houses were allocated to tenants at a meeting of Dungannon Rural Council on 9 October 1967. Sean Hughes, a reporter for the *Tyrone Democrat* newspaper who attended the meeting, reported that there was no discussion about the tenancies or the 'relative merits of different applicants', and only local unionist Councillor W.R. Scott seemed to know the names that were on a list he 'handed in', saying he would 'need another twelve houses'.[64] A request by the reporter to see the list of names was declined, and he was informed that this was the standard method of allocation and the local councillor's 'word is final'. It turned out that only one of the fifteen houses had been allocated to a Catholic, a woman whose former home had been condemned as 'unfit for human habitation' and whose case had been brought to Stormont Minister for Home Affairs William Fitzsimons after Councillor Scott had told her, 'You will never sit your backside in a house in Caledon.'[65] However, almost immediately after the council-meeting allocations, two of the houses were occupied by squatters: number 9 by Brian McKenna and his wife and child, and number 11 by Francis Goodfellow with his wife and their two children.

Under intense pressure from political wrangling and mass publicity, the families sat it out in Kinnaird Park, even after their water supply was cut off. Eviction was delayed for six months by court order. Finally, the McKennas succumbed and vacated number 9, which was then reallocated because the original 'tenant' was no longer interested because of the publicity. In an unbelievable snub to fairness, however, every needy Catholic family living in atrocious conditions was passed over in favour of a 19-year-old unmarried woman, Emily Beattie, who took up residence on 13 June 1968.[66]

Five days later, police officers smashed their way into number 11. Mary Theresa Goodfellow was sitting on the floor with her mother Ann, sister-in-law Geraldine Gildernew and their four children. 'When I told them I was pregnant, it put them off for a while, but eventually they just dragged us out of the house by our feet,' recalled Mrs Goodfelllow.[67]

East Tyrone nationalist MP Austin Currie raised the Caledon housing issue in the adjournment debate of 19 June 1968, pointing out that the young, single woman to whom the house had been given was a secretary of Armagh solicitor Brian McRoberts, the prospective Westminster election candidate for the Unionist Party in West Belfast, and a former unsuccessful candidate in South Armagh.[68] In reply, unionist MP for South Tyrone John Taylor insisted that the house had been allocated to four 'grown-ups' who were in occupation when he visited the previous night. When Currie accused Taylor of telling a 'damned lie', he was ejected from the Stormont chamber shouting, 'All hell will break loose, and by God I will lead it.'[69] The following day, in the company of local men Joe Campbell and Phelim Gildernew, a brother of Mrs Goodfellow, Currie broke into number 9 and barricaded the doors with Emily Beattie's furniture.[70] As press and TV reporters arrived, local RUC Sergeant Ivan Duncan came by and Currie informed him that this was a 'non-violent protest against the system of house allocation'. Other police arrived, including senior officers, and a crowd gathered. Then after about two and a half hours, a man with a 'good-looking young girl' approached the house and he demanded Currie and the others leave. They were Emily Beattie and her brother, a police officer in Armagh who was out of uniform. When Currie refused to vacate, the man forced his way in with a sledgehammer. He approached the MP threateningly, so Currie and the others walked out into the media throng.[71]

From there, Currie went to the new Northern Ireland Civil Rights Association. The body had been set up in January 1967 at a Belfast meeting, a low-key event evocatively portrayed in Glenn Patterson's novel *The International*.[72] The young MP convinced NICRA to sponsor a march from Coalisland to Dungannon on 24 August 1968 to highlight the housing issue.[73] 'We were disappointed with the publicity it received … but then of course the week it happened the USSR invaded Prague. So the media went to Prague instead of Coalisland,' he recalled.[74] Yet the Caledon incident reverberated, and there were other civil rights marches, notably in Derry city on 5 October 1968, when the media did show up.

Currie would become minister for housing in the short-lived power-sharing executive set up under the 1974 Sunningdale Agreement. Later, he moved south and was elected as a Fine Gael TD for Dublin West, and then served as a minister of state in the Irish government (1994–7). His fellow Caledon squatter Phelim Gildernew, whose pregnant wife Geraldine was dragged out of number 11 with her sister-in-law and mother-in-law, was subsequently elected as a Sinn Féin councillor and in 2012 became mayor of Dungannon Borough Council. His daughter Michelle is Westminster MP for Fermanagh-South Tyrone and has held the seat since 2001 for all but two years. And what of Emily Beattie? At a subsequent criminal trial of Austin Currie in Caledon's courthouse, her RUC constable brother testified that the house in Kinnaird Park had been allocated to the Beattie family. That was proved false, and it was pointed out that he would have been an 'illegal sub-tenant' had he taken up residence. The case was dismissed, but on appeal was sent back by the High Court 'for conviction' and the magistrate imposed a derisory fine of £5. Currie declared that that was 'the best fiver's worth I ever got'.[75]

It has since been widely noted that houses were not allocated to Catholics in places such as Caledon because residency would have entitled them to a vote in local elections. As for Emily Beattie, the 1969 Cameron Report into disturbances in Northern Ireland noted:

> She was 19 years old, a Protestant, and secretary to the local councillor's solicitor, who was also a unionist parliamentary candidate living in Armagh. The councillor's explanation for giving her the house was that in effect he was rehousing her family, who lived in very poor conditions; also he had expected her to be married before she took possession of the house. In fact she did marry soon afterwards.[76]

Lord Cameron's report, however, did not reveal that Emily's groom was from neighbouring County Monaghan, and thereby did not qualify for tenancy in public housing.[77] According to Michael Cunningham, 'This explains the reason for an unmarried girl being awarded the house and, once in occupation, she could marry and retain tenancy. Had she married first, the husband would have been deemed tenant.'[78]

8. A Maimed Capital: Armagh

The friendly man at the Armagh County Museum lists all the other attractions of the city, one of Ireland's historic and scenic gems. Yet he can't resist a barb about the lack of status accorded to his home town: 'My mother used to always say that Armagh was a city when Belfast was a swamp.' Certainly, the wee Cathedral City set in the heart of the Orchard County has a fabled past. Although somewhat smaller in scale than Rome, Armagh also was built on seven hills and it was a founding centre of the Christian faith. Even before Saint Patrick chose it as his primatial see, Armagh was also a centre of power founded on a myth of twins. While Rome's Romulus and Remus were suckled by a wolf in the cave of Lupercal, Eamhain Macha's twins were suckled at the bosom of the goddess Macha, who gave birth immediately after winning a running race against the chariot of Conchobar Mac Nessa, king of Ulster.[1]

A centre of pagan worship and learning before Patrick, Eamhain Macha gazed at the heavens as a 'hairy star' (comet) passed above in AD 443, heralding what historian Colin Johnston Robb hailed as 'the coming of our Patron Saint', followed by an eclipse of the sun about a year after his arrival.[2] For centuries a monastic city and episcopal see, the ancient astronomical and mathematical methods were preserved here through Europe's Dark Ages. Today, it is home to the Armagh Observatory and Planetarium on College Hill. BBC celebrity stargazer Patrick Moore was the planetarium's director until 1968, when he wrote a history of the observatory, which had been founded in 1790 by Archbishop Richard Robinson, apparently as an impetus for a university in Ulster.[3]

Armagh's astronomical importance had already been greatly enhanced in the early eighteenth century by the small observatory built on the Castledillon estate of Samuel Molyneux. He was chief engineer of Ireland, and a founder also of the King's Observatory at Kew House, which he acquired through marriage to Lady Elisabeth Capel, daughter of the earl of Essex. Molyneux was a member of the Westminster parliament between 1715 and 1728, and he was elected for Dublin University (Trinity) to the Irish House of Commons in 1727. The following year, he had a fit and was treated at home by court physician Nathaniel St André, but died in April. On the very night he succumbed, the royal surgeon eloped with his wife Lady Elisabeth, and they married in 1730. Samuel 'Premium' Madden of Hilton Park, Clones, later claimed St André poisoned his first cousin Molyneux.[4] St André sued for defamation and won, but never again secured regular work. One wonders if that defamation ruling was related to the contemporaneous destruction by Madden of his 1733 work of science fiction, *Memoirs of the Twentieth Century*.[5]

Today, the Georgian streetscapes of Armagh, its notable buildings and especially the elegant charm of its impressive Mall testify to a glorious past. On the east side of the Mall, the Armagh County Museum provides fascinating glimpses into the ancient and recent past. When I visited, an extensive exhibition entitled 'Mad or Bad' (5 October 2016 to 18 February 2017) delved into crime, gender and mental health in Victorian Ireland. The location is appropriate since the Cathedral City was deeply immersed in these fields. Armagh Jail was built just off the southern corner of the Mall in the 1780s, in time to accommodate the miscreants of agrarian and sectarian unrest that engulfed the district, and later, to accommodate the United Irishmen. During the more recent conflict, it housed female prisoners from 1973 to 1986. The district 'lunatic asylum' was established in 1825, the very first of the district asylums established around Ireland. Armagh Asylum also served Tyrone, Donegal, Fermanagh and Monaghan, taking inmates based on population. So Armagh, with a population of 196,577 in the 1822 census, was allocated 20 places for patients; Monaghan, with 178,183, got 18; Tyrone, with 259,691, got 27; Donegal, with 249,483, got 26; and Fermanagh, with 130,399, got 13.[6]

What was most striking about the 'Mad or Bad' exhibition, however, was the similarity of reconstructed conditions in the prison and the asylum. A wonderful 24-page brochure was also replete with fascinating photos, tables and other details – not least the prisoner mugshots, including 10-year-old Joe McKernan, jailed for stealing 14 shillings, and one of nineteen boys under age 12 incarcerated that year.[7] I searched in vain for anything related to the infamous case of murder for which Joseph Fee was the last man to be hanged in Armagh Jail, but that didn't occur until 1903.[8] Fee's victim, John Flanagan, a Belfast merchant who came to Clones for eggs, went missing for nine months along with the £80 cash he was carrying. He was found in a 'dung heap' in Fee's slaughter yard when it was dug up following nuisance complaints. The story lived on, and partly inspired Patrick McCabe's superb 1993 novel *The Butcher Boy*. It also inspired a ballad that was hugely popular in the first decades of the twentieth century. The final verse describes Fee's last moment on the Armagh gallows:

Saying fare ye well to Clones town where I spent many's the year and day,
Likewise unto that slaughterhouse from you I now must go away.
Good Christians all, both great and small I hope you pray for me.
The bolt was drew, and Fee soon flew on to Eternity.[9]

While many towns and cities had slaughter yards that disappeared as regulations governing abattoirs came into force, the Shambles in Armagh is preserved as an open-air market with a fine streetscape on Dawson Street, which forms its perimeter with Edward Street and Cathedral Road. That places it right between the two St Patrick's Cathedrals for the two faith groups. It is also the important boundary line, used by Armachians to denote whether they come from the 'top end' or the 'low end' of the town.[10] I pass the Shambles on my way to 4 Vicars, the restaurant recommended by the museum receptionist for its superb lunchtime soup. He wasn't wrong. It set me up between visits to Armagh's cathedrals.

My earliest memory of the Catholic cathedral was the lying in state of Cardinal John D'Alton, the primate who died in 1963. I recall a long line of mourners moving in a shuffle through the cavernous interior, where the ceremonial mitres of previous primates were suspended overhead. I returned to see them several times when visiting my Magee cousins from Fermanagh, who were boarders at the adjacent St Patrick's College, a place recalled with a nod to the nearby jail by poet John Montague in his 1993 collection *Time in Armagh*, a catalogue of wanton cruelty, deprivation and humiliation familiar to those who spent time in a Catholic boarding school when corporal punishment and bullying were not only tolerated but encouraged:

> Our stiff upper lip was an Ulster clamp.
> No whingeing. No quarter for the crybaby.[11]

I did not visit the Church of Ireland Cathedral of St Patrick until 17 March 1998, although I was aware that the great hero of medieval Irish history, High King of Ireland Brian Boru, was buried in its lee. On that occasion, just before the Good Friday Agreement when reconciliation between the two traditions in Northern Ireland was needed for political impetus, I became aware of the cathedral's other historical treasures. At one point, seeking to query something about the many regimental flags of the Royal Irish Fusiliers, I encountered from behind a cassocked figure who turned out to be none other than the genial Archbishop Robin Eames. He appreciated my interest and spent some time showing me around. Among topics we covered in our conversation was the current Orange Order protest centred on the small shared churchyard cemetery of the Church of Ireland parish church at Drumcree, where some of my family are buried. Following protests by nationalist residents of the Garvaghy Road in Portadown, the Orangemen were forcibly prohibited from marching along their 'traditional route' of return through the Catholic district and kept up a vigil of several years centred on that small rural place of worship. I felt the Church of Ireland primate's dilemma over the association of his church with the protest, and subsequently learned that he had called it his 'personal Calvary'.[12]

The path of the Ulster Canal does not pass through Armagh city. However, the original 1814 plans drawn up by John Killaly for a canal of 35 miles with twenty-two locks costing £223,000 did include a branch to Armagh.[13] It was reckoned that the branch navigation would be about 5.5 miles in length and cost up to £20,000. The Directors General of Inland Navigation thought at the time that the inclusion of Armagh would 'further enhance trade in the north', since it 'was seen as a leading market for brown linen' and its 'huge hinterland' extended 'even as far as Monaghan'.[14] That plan was shelved. Then when the proposal resurfaced a decade later, with Thomas Telford in charge, for a canal linking two great Ulster waterways, the proposed cost and the number of locks was cut back and the branch to Armagh was quietly dropped.

Fast forward a century or so to the imminent prospect of partition, and nationalist Ulster was lobbying to proclaim Armagh city as an alternative capital for the island of Ireland. Nor was it only the representatives of councils controlled by nationalists who gathered in convocation under Derry Mayor H.C. O'Doherty at Omagh's St Patrick's Hall on 19 November 1920 who favoured unity under an Armagh parliament over partition.[15] Thomas Shiffington, president of the Portadown Chamber of Commerce, told that body that a 'big parliament in Armagh' with an administration based in Dublin might 'reconcile the difference in opinion'.[16] An Armagh parliament would have a 'strong Ulster influence around it', while the Dublin administration 'might satisfy the rest of Ireland'.

By opting for the Cathedral City, which was the primal see of both main Christians faiths in Ireland, it was argued, unity could be built on trust and understanding between the Orange and Green traditions. Already, provision had been made for a Council of Ireland to act as the constitutional bridge between the two parliaments envisaged in the Government of Ireland Act of 1920. This was reiterated in the Anglo-Irish Treaty of 1921. Sitting in Armagh, it was intended to become the gel to bind together the island.

As if affronted by the upstart notion, however, both Belfast and Dublin stuck to their guns, both resisting the notion of an Armagh parliament. In the debacle of the Boundary Commission, the Council of Ireland was abolished. Armagh was bypassed again. A further century on, the Council of Ireland was resurrected under the Good Friday Agreement 1998 as the bridge between the two political traditions and their governments in Belfast and Dublin. And it is based in a building on English Street, Armagh. Not that one might notice, for the council is reduced to an occasional ministerial talking shop. There is no grand council chamber to match the little city's other architectural gems, nor does the council itself engage even mild interest from most people.

In the time of the Troubles that preceded partition in 1922, the Armagh IRA actions like those in neighbouring Monaghan, were largely concentrated on raiding for arms, tree-felling and other road blockades to hamper the crown forces. As partition took hold, the Armagh IRA had to contend with the newly emerging Special Constabulary. Arms raids were invariably carried out on Protestant homes, invariably referred to as 'unionist'. They were of limited value and only succeeded in accentuating the sectarian nature of the war in Ulster. One huge operation involving several Armagh companies, as well as others from Tyrone and east Down, was an arms raid on the home of a family called Copes, which netted 'only one old shotgun', according to John McAnerney, a former neighbour of ours on the Diamond in Clones, where he set up his soft drinks company, Erne Mineral Waters. He saw action in both Armagh city and during a brief work-transfer to Clones, where he remarked on how the IRA patrolled the streets at night.[17] In both places he was involved in the kidnapping of railway workers who defied IRA orders on not moving British military ordnance and personnel. In Clones, a railwayman called Wallace was wounded, while in Armagh, a man called Stutt was tarred and feathered, which 'caused a bit of a sensation in the town'.

The crudity of the IRA campaign can be gauged from Frank Donnelly's description of a bomb attack on the police barracks on Upper Irish Street late in 1919.[18] The explosives were packed into the metal axle box from a horse cart, clamped with iron plates, and a fuse fitted with a detonator attached. This was taken to the barracks, where a sledgehammer was used to break one of the ventilator covers on the front wall. The mine was put in and the fuse lit, with the armed attackers taking up positions on the far side of the street. When the bomb exploded, it showered them in glass from the windows opposite the barracks, which was virtually unscathed. Donnelly adds that there was an 'amusing sequel' when RIC Sergeant Collins from the barracks went to the home of 'one of the oldest Sinn Féiners in the town' and charged him with 'attempting to blow up his wife and children'. Not so amusing for the old man, I suspect.

In his submission to the Bureau of Military History, McAnerney described a major confrontation in April or May 1921, after the homes of two nationalist families were attacked by B Specials, who wounded one man and set fire to his house. In a reprisal, attacks were ordered on the homes of Specials at Todds' Corner, about 4 miles from Armagh city.[19] About 60 men mobilised for the dawn raid. Their first target was to be the home of a family named Georges:

> It proved most unfortunate for us that all the B Specials from all the other houses to be raided were assembled in Georges' house for the purpose of getting refreshments after coming off patrol. As soon as we came quite close to the house a heavy fire was opened on us from the house and we were forced to take cover. One of our men named Gerry Hughes got wounded in both his legs. It appeared that a B Special was on a hill some distance from us and he started to snipe our position and shot Hughes. The bullets which caused the wound was a dum-dum and inflicted horrible wounds on both legs.

With the wounded man taken away, the attack on the Georges' home was resumed: 'The house was burned down but we got no arms from the defenders who succeeded in holding us off until we had to retreat from the vicinity when the danger of reinforcements of military coming from Armagh became urgent.'

Another raid for arms, in the summer of 1921, brought James Short and three others to the home of a Major Boyle, where they found no guns but came away with a couple of pairs of binoculars, a Sam Brown belt and some ammunition for a large rifle 'suitable for elephant shooting'.[20] The concentration on raiding for arms seems strange given that the Armagh IRA had a steady supply of weapons from rebels among the Royal Irish Fusiliers, or from soldiers who sold them from the Gough Barracks armoury. In one case, a deserter traded his uniform and rifle for a change of civilian clothing![21]

Probably the biggest operation carried out by the IRA in Armagh city during the period was the 'official visit' of Commander in Chief Michael Collins on 4 September 1921.[22] The *Ulster Gazette* noted that, while ostensibly there to address his constituents, who had elected him as their abstentionist Sinn Féin representative to the Northern parliament in May, his real purpose was 'an elaborate demonstration of Sinn Féin in Mid-Ulster'. The *Belfast Newsletter* reported that 'The IRA took control of a large portion of the city, and its "police" regulated the traffic and picqueted [*sic*] the entrances to the unionist quarters. Very few of the Royal Irish Constabulary were noticed on duty.' Special trains were laid on from Warrenpoint and Newry, Clones and Monaghan, Omagh and Dungannon and Belfast. The *Armagh Guardian* totted up the numbers: 500 on the Keady train; 600 from Newry; and Clones and Monaghan exceeding 1,000. Others arrived by charabancs, cars, bicycles and on foot.

IRA units met the Collins party and escorted them to the Charlemont Arms Hotel, right beside the city hall, which the *Ulster Gazette* noted, had 'rarely … been so densely packed'. After formal proceedings, the procession formed up in Greenpark, with ranks from the 4th, 5th, 2nd and 3rd divisions; Sinn Féin clubs from Armagh, Lurgan and Clones districts; and marching bands from Armagh, Aughagallon, Lurgan, Monaghan and Darkley. One account says Collins 'was escorted by over 1,500 Volunteers and auxiliaries, 1,100 Irish National Foresters, 100 bandsmen, 450 cyclists, [and] republican police armed with hurleys …' Yet the *Ulster Gazette* made sure to point out that numbers were grossly exaggerated, with most coming from Monaghan and Tyrone, and 'a few stragglers from Belfast and other Northern centres'. The *Gazette* also disputed estimates of the crowd at the College Grounds, which ranged as high as 30,000, saying the gathering was no larger than the 20,000 Ulster Volunteers under Colonel Blacker who had turned out for Carson's visit in 1913.

Expectations that Collins would use the public meeting – which was chaired by Seamus O'Reilly, chairman of Armagh Urban Council – to rally the rebels with sabre-rattling threats proved false. One description notes that his speech combined 'a markedly conciliatory tone towards the Ulster unionist with a firm stand on Irish unity'.[23] According to the *Armagh Guardian*, that disappointed the 'extreme section' and 'enthusiasm died away'. That section will not have been disappointed by the other main speaker, Eoin O'Duffy, chief liaison officer for Ulster and an 'influential voice' on the military triumvirate with Collins and his fellow Munsterman Richard Mulcahy, then IRA chief of staff. O'Duffy was proving intemperate, and when queried about the upsurge in loyalist violence, he had told a journalist, 'We'll give them the lead.'[24] He repeated the phrase in Armagh in a clear bid to raise the passions, saying that he had just come from Belfast, where he had 'escaped the bombs and bullets of Sandy Row', and if it 'might be necessary to cut off Belfast from the rest of Ireland … Belfast would be a deserted city in three months'. If Belfast stood against 'Ireland and their fellow countrymen', the IRA would have to take 'suitable action … [I]f necessary they would have to use the lead against them.'[25]

O'Duffy later claimed he was dismissed as the Dublin government's liaison officer for Ulster because of his Armagh speech.[26] However, he continued in that role as recorded in several meetings with senior British officials in the following months. It certainly earned him the nickname 'Give 'em the lead' among local unionists, and it resulted in a ballad entitled, 'The Defence of Scotch Street Bridge':

> First came the guard of honour, a sorry looking crew,
> With woebegone expressions, and full of mountain dew;
> There were scavengers from the Shambles, and loafers from the Rocks,
> Who stepped in front of Mickey, like a bunch of banty cocks.
>
> Now Owen Duffy made a speech, 'twas marvellous it was said,
> For him to tell the Rebels the way to use the lead,
> Against the loyal Ulstermen, who won't acknowledge Rome,
> And who only want the privilege of supporting Britain's Throne.[27]

The title of the song refers to an incident later in the day, after Middletown's Eamonn Donnelly, the final speaker, urged the crowd to disperse and go home quickly to avoid a Royal Black Preceptory event on the Mall. Small boys threw apples at a couple of cars. A man in one of the cars drew a revolver and fired, hitting nobody. The shot was immediately returned by men firing from the crowd, and one of the motorists, Edward Hanna of Newry, was shot in the abdomen and rushed by his companions to Newry Union Infirmary. He was later awarded £700 on his claim for £6,000 at Armagh Assizes in January 1922. The second victim, a farm labourer called Quigley, was brought home dead in the car, but no information was given to police, who were told the 'matter was in the hands of the IRA'. Back in Armagh, meanwhile, pedestrians were attacked – including three young men and a young woman who intervened, all of whom were 'savagely beaten', and a 'Catholic' who was treated for injuries at the infirmary.[28]

After the Treaty, many of the arms acquired by the Armagh IRA company ended up in Castleshane when the Fourth Northern Division mustered and trained for the post-Treaty assault across the border. McAnerney, Donnelly and Short all ended up there too, having evaded the big swoop in Armagh when the authorities got wind of the Ulster Council's military plan. The arms were dumped after General Dan Hogan's forces captured Dundalk and arrested Frank Aiken. John McAnerney had been sent from Castleshane down to Dundalk just before the attack. With others, he was presented with the choice of joining the National Army with the same rank as he had in the IRA, or being imprisoned in Mountjoy.[29] He refused to join and was released the next day, returning to Castleshane to await invasion orders that never came, and ending up in the internment camp in Kildare, where he joined the general hunger strike before his release in October 1923.

Almost three decades later, James Short summed up the aftermath of those tumultuous times for Armagh's soldiers of destiny:

> The outbreak of the Civil War had a most demoralising effect on
> the outlook of the IRA in the six counties area. The Northern
> government were not slow to realise the weakening effect the

Civil War had on the position of the IRA within their area and they applied the pressure; raids and arrests were the order of the day. In areas where there were unionist majorities, the 'B' and 'C' Specials took complete control and instituted a reign of terror for republicans, to which we had no answer.[30]

Increasingly, the unionist regime closed off expressions of nationalist identity in their new northern state. One of its first acts was to scrap the proportional-representation system introduced by the British for local elections in Ireland. In the 'first serious challenge to unionist hegemony', the 1920 local elections, Sinn Féin and the United Irish League (Nationalist) had won control over Fermanagh and Tyrone county councils, as well as Derry city and ten other urban councils, including Armagh city, Omagh, Enniskillen, Newry and Strabane, and thirteen rural district councils.[31] Not for long though, as those councils were dissolved in April 1922 and replaced with commissioners. In the case of Armagh and neighbouring Keady, the commissioner appointed by Craig's government was Colonel Waring, later county commandant of Armagh's B Specials.[32]

The *Handbook of the Ulster Question*, published in 1923 by the Stationery Office in Dublin, is the most highly prized book on my shelves. It is a 164-page hardback with a beautiful Celtic-motif cover designed by Theodora Harrison, featuring the Red Hand of Ulster and the Celtic Harp. Inside are colour-coded maps and graphic illustrations, and page after page of data, statistics, tables and background information of population breakdowns, trade and communications. Whole sections are devoted to the historical and political implications of partition; the wishes of the inhabitants; economic and geographic conditions; and analogous problems in other countries. It is exhaustive, painstakingly put together in a relatively short time by the North-Eastern Boundary Bureau (NEBB), a high-powered body set up by the Free State government with the most talented experts available.

The bureau came together under the meticulous Omagh-born solicitor Kevin O'Shiel, who had been appointed in September 1922 after apprising Cosgrave of the northern policy of the recently assassinated Michael Collins.[33] Collins's plans had included the publication of this book, for which a publisher had been arranged in advance. Priced at 2 shillings and 6 pence, the *Handbook of the Ulster Question* could be purchased from practically any bookseller in the Free State and nationalist areas of the North from its publication in 1923.

In essence, the *Handbook of the Ulster Question* sets out in minute detail all the arguments that would be presented to the Boundary Commission for the transfer from the North to the Free State of Derry city, all of counties Tyrone and Fermanagh, and portions of counties Armagh and Down. Right down to the final map of Ulster in a special inside-cover pocket with its little rectangles showing population breakdowns in orange and green, it omits nothing of what the Dublin government fully expected would sway the commissioners to render Northern Ireland truncated and unviable. It was also aimed at swaying the opinion-forming sector in Britain, and the *Economist* of 19 December 1923 noted that it was having this effect.[34] The underlying motivation of the NEBB was to achieve Collins's objective of furthering 'national union'.

The *Handbook* is a statistical snapshot of Ulster at the time of partition, and even the most illiterate could read, for instance, that while Armagh urban district had a majority of 53.9 per cent of the population who wanted to join the Free State, it was in Northern Ireland's mid-Armagh parliamentary constituency, which had a majority of 22,558 against an all-Ireland parliament, compared to 16,937 for it. On the map of colour-coded rectangles, Armagh city electoral district is swamped by the surrounding orange boxes of Richhill, Hamiltonsbawn, Killeen, Ballyards, Brootally, Tynan and Glenaul. In another map, outlining what the Free State could expect as a maximum outcome, Armagh is encircled in a line embracing it into the 'south', while in the minimum outcome, it is ensnared in the North with the loss of its western and southern hinterland.

The Boundary Commission arrived on Tuesday, 3 March 1925, in Armagh city, one of five locations where it would hear submissions.[35] The following day, it started with the nationalists of Middletown, then the unionists of Glaslough, following by Aughnacloy Town Council,

Keady Urban District Council, the Armagh Urban Council and 'parish head'. It took a break on Sunday, and then resumed with the unionists of Mullyash on the Monday, 9 March. E.M. Stephens of the Boundary Bureau was at hand, assisting groups that were for the Free State, and keeping Dublin informed of events.

Stephens had already visited the venues in advance to meet with the network of eight Northern solicitors retained by the North Eastern Boundary Bureau, including Patrick Lavery in Armagh. In his report from there, dated 18 December 1924, Stephens had written:

> Travelled to Armagh and stayed with Lavery. Eight o'clock meeting at Senate House to consider written case for Commission. Meeting was 'not very well attended, but all those present seemed quite unanimous in their desire to be included in the Free State'. Found general impression in Armagh 'nervous of any boundary', and were for this reason probably more interested in the idea of ultimate union than the people of towns lying near the border which could conveniently be included in the Free State with their entire hinterlands.[36]

According to one interpretation, they feared that 'even though they had a small majority in the urban area – that they would be cut off from south Armagh', which they thought was certain of transfer under the minimum scenario.[37]

On the other side of the boundary equation, Craig's unionist government adopted a policy of truculence and non-participation, declining even to appoint a member of the Boundary Commission. Into the vacuum, Westminster appointed Joseph R. Fischer, former editor of the *Northern Whig* and a staunch unionist with many inner-circle contacts. Sitting on the opposite side of the South African chairman Mr Justice Richard Feetham was Antrim-born Eoin MacNeill, the Free State Education Minister. His ongoing ministerial duties meant MacNeill was absent from lengthy periods of deliberation. That allowed Fisher to jostle Feetham further into his preference for minor rectifications rather than the wholesale transfers of large tracts. Apart from that, the Belfast authorities did little or nothing. However, shortly after the Boundary Commission had moved on from Armagh, Craig arrived on his extensive tour of the border.[38]

If there was any rallying of troops to what Prince William of Orange is reputed to have first called the 'last ditch', then it was done by the Orange Order.[39] That year, the Armagh County Grand Lodge celebrations of the Twelfth were in Richhill, where Sir William Allen was deputising for the ailing County Grand Master Sir James Stronge of Tynan Abbey. Sir William declared that no matter what the Boundary Commission decided, 'they would show a firm and united front against disrupting this little area of ours'. On the same Richhill platform, Attorney General for Northern Ireland Richard Best said, 'I prefer the out-and-out Republican who wants to swallow me whole at once to the man [Cosgrave] who tries to bite in and in, and who would leave me bleeding and suffering so that I would have to go to Dublin and sue for peace.' Best, who was appointed that same year as lord justice of the Supreme Court of Northern Ireland, reminded his audience that Premier Craig had promised to place himself at the head of the Specials if the Boundary Commission report was 'unfavourable'.

Embarassingly, in hindsight at least, Deputy Grand Master Sir William Allen made an allusion that day that might have resonated with Eoin O'Duffy, subsequently founder and leader of the Blueshirts, although the Armagh MP was certainly not thinking of a common cause. Referring to the IRA, he said:

> Italy has had to deal with a similar antagonist a short time ago, and in that country a body of men sprang up and followed in large measure the principles of the Orange Order – they support everything constitutional and stand by the Constitution. They have the Fascisti in London also, but the only Fascisti we want in Northern Ireland is the Orange Institution.[40]

As elsewhere in the North, the war years (1939–45) are remembered fondly as a time of excitement, a time when vistas opened beyond the humdrum life of poverty that was the common lot. Armagh had long been a garrison town, centred on Gough Barracks and the Royal Irish Fusiliers, which recruited throughout the south Ulster counties of Armagh, Monaghan and Cavan. Added to this, for a brief period, were the American GIs. In an article for *History Armagh*, the journal of the local historical group, Kevin Quinn provided a wonderful glimpse into those war years through the memories of Maureen Hennessy, who lived at Mill Row, built originally for workers at the adjacent Drumcairn spinning mill on the edge of the town.[41]

Hennessy recalls that the first troops to be billeted in the mill were British, and that they put on dances, concerts and Christmas parties for the residents. This made up for air-raid warnings, when residents were 'evacuated to the Stony Loning, spending the night on the banks of the Callan River'. Then came the Yanks with parties and concerts and 'a lot more luxuries to hand out such as chocolate'. At Christmas 1943, the Americans laid on Christmas dinner, and Maureen recalls the main course and dessert being 'served together on a sectional tray'. These American GIs, who wore a shoulder-sleeve insignia of a Native American Indian chief, were the 2nd Infantry Division, which was stationed in Northern Ireland from October 1943 to June 1944. On the day the GIs left the mill, heading off for Normandy's Omaha Beach, the Mill Row residents walked with them 'cheering and clapping all the way' to the train station.[42]

The GIs made their train in any case, for it would be another decade and more before the Belfast Government forced the Great Northern Railway to close its rail lines to Armagh and beyond across the border to Monaghan and Clones.[43] That occurred on 1 October 1957, although the rail services had been winding down steadily since partition and only got that reprieve and a welcome boost from the war. Yet already the elaborate latticework portrayed in one of the maps inserted in the *Handbook of the Ulster Question* was frayed and torn. That map showed that Ulster had by far the most intensive network of railway lines in Ireland, criss-crossing the entire province, and so far barely impeded by the intrusion of the new border. The lines included the service from Portadown through Armagh and on through Tynan to the border, as well as the Castleblayney, Keady, Armagh rail line that once serviced a series of mills and their workers. That link to Castleblayney closed down in 1923, just thirteen years after its completion. Nine years later, the link to Keady followed into the shunting yard, and a year on, the Newry services to Armagh terminated at Markethill. A once-bustling rail junction limped along for a couple of decades, but it was doomed by partition.

The permanent exhibition at the Armagh County Museum on the Mall features artefacts and memorabilia of the railway. For many Armagh city residents, the railway's legacy is firmly rooted in remembrance of the disaster that claimed a total of eighty-nine lives in 1889, making it Ireland's biggest-ever rail disaster.[44] The Wednesday outing by the Armagh Methodist Church Sunday School was to Warrenpoint, and included people of all ages and faiths – Catholic, Church of Ireland, Methodist and Presbyterian – who had set off for the station behind the band of the Royal Irish Fusiliers for the train which departed the platform at 10:15 a.m. Just a few miles out of the city, the train struggled to get up a slope, held back by the weight on board. It was decided to uncouple the first carriages, move them to Hamiltonsbawn and then return for the others. However, when decoupled, the back carriages rolled over the stones placed beneath their wheels, gathered pace and crashed into another train. 'Many a bitter battlefield did not display such carnage,' observed Surgeon Major Lynn, one of the excursion's organisers.

Interestingly, recent moves to commemorate properly those killed on that dreadful day nearly 130 years ago have prompted calls for the reinstatement of a 10-mile-long commuter-rail link between Armagh and Portadown.[45] The Portadown and Armagh Railway Society (PARS) has presented a petition of 10,000 names to the Stormont authorities demanding Armagh services as part of new expansions of the rail network.[46]

Yet the demise of the rail service was not even the most significant news story from Armagh in the mid-1950s. On 12 June 1954, in broad daylight, the historic headquarters of the Royal Irish Fusiliers was raided, disarmed and humiliated by a small party of IRA activists. The Gough Barracks raid was the prelude to the 1950s IRA border campaign, Operation Harvest. The

IRA success inspired many young Irishmen to join the republican armed struggle and take part in military actions that would in turn leave the IRA vanquished and humiliated for the following decade. Barry Flynn's book, Soldiers of Folly, shows that humiliation began with the IRA's decision to simply replicate the Armagh operation a few months later at St Lucia Barracks, HQ of the Royal Inniskillings in Omagh.[47]

The Gough Barracks operation had begun with the infiltration of 20-year-old Dubliner Seán Garland, who enlisted in Armagh to find out where the guns were kept. He proved a good soldier and was soon promoted to colour sergeant, and at one stage he was posted at Hillsborough as a sentry at the official Northern Ireland residence of Queen Elizabeth II.[48] All the while, he was passing vital information to the IRA. Two trusted senior IRA Volunteers, Charlie Murphy and Éamonn Boyce, were dispatched from Dublin. Garland signed them in to Gough Barracks for the weekly dance, and gave them an extensive tour. On a Saturday afternoon in broad mid-summer daylight, when all the weaponry would be in the armoury for a planned inventory, a cattle lorry drove up to the main barracks gates in Armagh city centre at about 3 p.m. Paddy Ford got out and engaged the sentry in chat about enlisting, and another soldier was called into the conversation. Ford then produced a handgun, whereupon some other volunteers jumped out, disarmed the guards and ordered them inside as one of the raiders took up guard duty at the gate, in the full regimental dress of the Royal Irish Fusiliers. The cattle lorry then proceeded inside, drove up to the armoury and the IRA raiders began to load up rifles, Sten and Bren machine guns, and revolvers.

With senior officers in Portadown that afternoon at a reception for the new governor of Northern Ireland, Lord Wakehurst, the atmosphere around the barracks was relaxed. Soldiers came and went, greeted and saluted by the IRA sentry on the gate. But Mary Elliott, a young woman working in her mother's wee shop opposite the front gate, noticed something amiss in the sentry, who was 'wearing the wrong cross-belt and saluting officers incorrectly'.[49] She pointed this out to an officer who came into the shop, who ran to the gate and was taken prisoner at gunpoint. Elliott saw this, rushed upstairs, saw from a window the arms being loaded into the cattle lorry, and called the police. The loading ended and the cattle truck departed, travelling at speed down Thomas

Street, where it was waved through by a policeman on traffic duty, and drove off for the border, arriving in Dundalk before 5 p.m., when the general alarm was raised.

Ten minutes after its departure and Elliott's phone call, an RUC officer had arrived at the barracks on his bicycle to see what was going on. Much too late, a massive manhunt was mounted, with thousands of RUC officers and B Specials mobilised. The Special Powers Act was invoked in the North, allowing draconian police powers of arrest and detention. Homes and farms near the border were searched and extra guards were placed on all military installations. When it became obvious that it had been an inside job, an internal investigation was begun in Gough Barracks. Among those questioned was Seán Garland, who 'of course, knew nothing and had seen nothing'.[50]

In the following months, as tensions rose, the B Specials were 'given carte blanche to patrol the border'. Amid rumours of another armed raid on Gough Barracks, the border was sealed off on 12 March 1955.[51] That evening, 18-year-old Arthur Leonard was driving his two sisters home from Keady to Darkley when they saw that the main road was blocked by a car. Assuming there had been an accident, Arthur began to reverse. Immediately, the B Specials with the car blocking the road opened fire, killing Arthur and wounding his sisters. The B Specials later claimed Arthur had ignored a warning to stop. This claim rang hollow when, on the following night, another innocent young man, Arthur Stinson, 23, was shot and seriously wounded by B Specials as he performed a U-turn on the road between Augher and Aughnacloy, close to the border with Monaghan – but not at it, as claimed by a subsequent account supporting the B Specials' account.[52] These shootings sparked a torrent of outrage. Nationalist MP Eddie McAteer said, 'Something must be done to protect the public from these over-armed, overbearing, over-excitable and under-intelligent commandos,' and the *Irish Press* in Dublin described the Specials as a 'menace to the people'. Two politicians from the Dáil managed to have themselves ejected from Stormont's parliamentary chamber when they entered via the public gallery and shouted at Northern Ireland Home Affairs Minister G.B. Hanna about his 'crossroads murder gangs'.[53]

With the weapons and the huge publicity boost from the Armagh raid, the IRA simply adapted the same plan for Omagh. In the early morning of 16 October 1954, three raiders scaled the wall of St Lucia barracks but when they attempted to knock a sentry unconscious, he managed to fire a shot at them alerting his four fellow guards. The main IRA part responded with machine-gun shots wounding five soldiers, three of them from south of the border. In the panic, the escape vehicles made off, abandoning the raiders. As army, police and B Specials scoured the countryside, one raider trying to get across the border into Monaghan was captured in the Clogher Valley by a farmer and his five sons, all in the B Specials. The tally of arrests soon rose to eight IRA raiders with nothing to show for their efforts.[54]

In fact, another raid *was* planned on Gough Barracks, and Seán Garland was back in Armagh city on 12 December 1956, the night the border campaign began, as co-commander with Dáithí O'Connell of an IRA column of fifteen men. Their objective was to seize arms and head back through Monaghan for Fermanagh, where they would join others. That plan broke down, however, when Constables Malcolm McKeown and Stanley Morrow intercepted two raiders planting a bomb at the telephone exchange in English Street.[55] As they approached, the IRA men opened fire, and McKeown was wounded as the van sped off for the border. At Milford, there was a gun battle when B Specials stopped the IRA vehicle and arrested Séamus Heuston from Keady and James Smith from Bessbrook. Meanwhile, back at the military garrison on Armagh's Barrack Hill, the attack began just after 1:30 a.m. with a burst of fire aimed at the metal doors and four petrol bombs thrown over the walls. A sentry opened fire with his machine-gun and the two IRA volunteers responded as a large bomb was placed at the wall. It failed to explode. Maroon flares suddenly illuminated the streets, alarm bells went off and the raiders made a run for the border, effectively taking Operation Harvest with them.

The 1960s proved no better for Armagh city, jostled into a naughty corner by a state that was suspicious and distrusting of its border fringes. When a decision was taken to drive a new motorway to the west, rather than south towards Dublin, it hurtled past Lurgan and Portadown, not to the capital of the Orchard County, but to Dungannon and east Tyrone. An earlier scheme coinciding with plans to shut down rail lines west of the River Bann had included an upgrade of the A3, or the T3 trunk road as it was then known. That went by the board when Northern Ireland's Home Affairs Minister William Craig unveiled his M1 plans in February 1964. To avoid Armagh city, perhaps, a section of the motorway hugged the southern shore of Lough Neagh from Portadown to Tamnamore and was constructed across a peat bog. That required removing almost 3.5 million cubic metres (4.5 million cubic yards) of turf.[56]

Then the idea arose for a new city, a planned conurbation of suburban homes, with integrated work, shopping and leisure facilities. Rather than choose the titular city of Armagh, Stormont again opted for its nearest rivals to enclose the hub. The new city of Craigavon, named after the first prime minister of Northern Ireland, would include the existing towns of Portadown and Lurgan. A subsequent attempt to relocate the administrative centre for the county to the new city was strongly resisted by Armagh City Council, despite the insistence of Stormont premier Brian Faulkner.[57] The impasse ended in 1973 with the reorganisation of local government following direct rule. That split the county between three councils, leaving Armagh city with only a rump area comprising Armagh city, Cusher, Crossmore and the Orchard, stretching from Loughgall to Darkley. Efforts to maintain the county town's status as Armagh City and Borough Council were blocked; instead, it became the Armagh City and District.[58]

The pervasive sense of official neglect west of the Bann was felt particularly by nationalists. The strategy of the Belfast government of concentrating development in constituencies with unionist majorities, came to a head with the choice of Coleraine over Derry city for the campus and administrative centre of the new University of Ulster founded in 1968.[59] The civil rights movement was inspired and grew from such grievances.[60]

The reorganisation of local government in 1972 followed almost immediately on from the creation of the Northern Ireland Housing Executive after the civil-rights protests fuelled by the Caledon housing protest of 1968 and the ensuing Cameron Report. One of the problems the new body had to cope with was the segregation of housing along sectarian lines.[61] This served a dual purpose, maintaining the political status quo by concentrating voters in wards according to sectarian/ political loyalty, and also providing security in areas wracked by rioting in the past. That held true in Armagh as in other urban areas. Sprawling housing estates replaced higgledy-piggledy tiny terraced houses, but led to large concentrations of high unemployment and social deprivation on the edges of the urban centres. In Armagh city, one such estate was Drumarg, built in the late 1960s in an area west of the centre around the GAA playing grounds. Any chronology of republican unrest, arrests and deaths in Armagh city is laced with the name of Drumarg.

It was where the Northern Ireland Civil Rights Association chose as its starting point for an Armagh march on Saturday, 30 November 1968 after the 5 October march in Derry city garnered such huge publicity that Home Affairs Minister Bill Craig banned all demonstrations there. The choice of Armagh was apt, not least in terms of the demand for 'one man, one vote', since a *Belfast Telegraph* investigation in 1969 determined that Armagh city was the only council area in which a shift of power would occur in the event of franchise reform, all other unionist councils having an insurmountable majority.[62] Under existing local government franchise, votes were linked to property and thus favoured the unionist establishment whose Protestant electors included many business and multiple property owners. Furthermore, the system of representation meant that the nationalist majority was corralled into heavily populated wards designed to maintain a unionist majority on the council drawn from more sparsely populated wards.

Sean O'Hagan, now a leading journalist and critic for the *Guardian/ Observer* newspaper group in London, was a teenage marcher from Drumarg in 1968. He recalled:

I can remember the excitement and trepidation as the marchers set off from the Killylea Road towards the town centre, their ranks swelled by coachloads of protesters from across the province. The source of that trepidation was one man, the Rev Ian Paisley, a Free Presbyterian firebrand, who, having been born in Armagh in 1926, had returned with a vengeance to haunt the city. Convinced that the Northern Irish Civil Rights Association was 'a front movement for the IRA', he had called for 'every loyalist in Ulster' to assemble in Armagh that same day and 'take control of the city'. This they duly did, though only in their hundreds, assembling in the town centre, where, according to the rumours that spread through the marchers, they had armed themselves with crowbars and cudgels, and, according to local sources, with pick-axe handles provided free by a Protestant-owned hardware shop.[63]

Chilling images of loyalist protesters in Armagh brandishing those cudgels with nails driven through them were captured by *Irish Press* news photographer Colman Doyle.[64]

In any event, the civil-rights protesters didn't get to see them, as they were turned away from the town centre by the RUC. Paisley and his eccentric lieutenant, Major Ronald Bunting, were convicted of unlawful assembly and sentenced to three months' imprisonment. Yet resistance to civil rights was not confined to the outer fringes of loyalism. Home Affairs Minister Bill Craig was clear about who he blamed: 'One of these days one of these marches is going to get a massive reaction from the population. Ordinary decent people have been at boiling point for some time. It is not just Mr Paisley.'[65]

When he was ambushed in Armagh's Russell Street in February 1972, John Taylor MP had succeeded Craig in the Stormont Ministry for Home Affairs. Taylor's car was riddled with fifteen bullets in the Official IRA attack, six hitting him in the neck, chest and jaw. He 'slumped over the steering wheel, bleeding profusely from the wounds'.[66] The attackers escaped in a car parked around the corner on the Mall, before the police and regular troops, backed up by reservists and UDR, 'sealed off the city and all roads leading to the border'. The following day, police arrested seven men in Armagh city, five of whom were quickly released. The other two were cleared within two days of the attack, but held under detention orders and named as James Sheridan, 24, of Drumarg Park, and Anthony ('Tony') McCloskey, 16, from the adjoining D'Alton Estate.[67]

Meanwhile, 200 loyalists had gathered in the Mall, where Alastair Black of the Vanguard wing of the Unionist party urged them to close ranks and attend a monster rally in Portadown, while the Armagh Young Unionists called for the dismissal of the Catholic local police commander, RUC Chief Supt James O'Hara. In the following weeks, summonses were issued to participants in an anti-internment march from Drumarg;[68] there was outrage at the possibility of a People's Democracy May Day parade;[69] but there were no repercussions for '10,000 loyalists who brought Portadown business centre to a standstill', with local Westminster MP Jack Magennis, and Stormont MPs Herbert Whitten, Robert Mitchell and James Stronge under the Vanguard Unionist banner.[70]

There were gatherings also at the Tunnel in Armagh, the pedestrian underpass that connects Drumarg to the town centre. It became a major point of confrontation during the Troubles. In an evocative piece about an innocent victim caught in a riot, Sean O'Hagan recalls his Catholic youth as one of those 'addicted to danger' who took part in these almost ritual confrontations, 'throwing stones and bottles at the RUC and British Army patrols that regularly skirted the housing estates, playing cat-and-mouse with the snatch squads who hit the ground running from the backs of Saracens and Land Rovers'.[71] Thirty years later, he recalled the Protestant woman into whose lap a burning Molotov cocktail landed through a shattered window on her bus when thrown at the army by a rioter. Although rushed to hospital, she died from her serious burns and:

> Ruby Johnston slipped almost unnoticed, save by friends and family, into history: the second person to die in the tribal violence that would claim another 508 lives in County Armagh before the Troubles ended; the 323rd victim in a war of attrition that would last 30 years, and eventually claim more than 3,600 lives.

Meanwhile, the very heart was being bombed out of the Cathedral City, along with every other town in Northern Ireland. Armagh's rich architectural heritage was no deterrent to the bombers, who insisted that their attacks were aimed at 'military and commercial targets'. In Armagh city centre, their targets included a terrace of seven Georgian homes in English Street Lower, known as the Seven Sisters.[72] Designed by George Ensor of Dublin and built between 1768 and 1770, they were erected by Dean Averell, rector of Tynan for his seven sisters. Describing it as a 'noble terrace', former Housing Executive chairman Charles Brett was proud of his success in having it restored 'at considerable cost' for office accommodation, 'only to be quickly bombed and judged beyond restoration'.[73]

Yet individual tragedies, even singular atrocities, do not convey the dark times thrust on Armagh during those painful decades of conflict. The Cathedral City was key in three dominant episodes – alleged mistreatment of detainees during interrogation; the prison crisis leading to the 1981 hunger strikes; and alleged shoot-to-kill operations that grew from collusion with loyalists. The interrogation suite at Gough Barracks opened as a self-contained unit in November 1977 at a cost of £247,000, to cover the North's southern security region's 'worst trouble spots' and the nearby 'border with County Monaghan'.[74] The barracks, built in 1773, had been the HQ of the Royal Irish Fusiliers until 1960 and then of 2nd Battalion UDR until it moved to Drumadd in 1975. Although the new Gough Interrogation Centre was run by the RUC, it was under the direct control of Castlereagh RUC interrogation centre in Belfast, where police physician Dr Bertie Irwin had raised concerns about injuries inflicted on detainees being questioned by police about terrorist offices.[75] According to a Northern Ireland Office memo dated 21 October 1977, the issue of brutal RUC interrogations had already united the SDLP, Sinn Féin, the Civil Rights Association and loyalist organisations.[76] Filed with that memo was a report dated 28 October 1977 from Gerry Fitt MP on the case of Tony Crozier from Keady, alleging that police interrogators beat him on the knuckles and legs with an iron pipe during his Armagh detention, and he was forced to do press-ups to exhaustion, threatened with electric shocks, and had a gun put to his head while being told he would be killed and dumped on a border road.

Two senior medical officers were appointed for the Armagh interrogation centre at Gough barracks. One of the appointees, Dr Denis

Elliott at Gough, was an experienced police surgeon, prison doctor and coroner, as well as a unionist councillor and justice of the peace. At the time of Elliott's appointment, Amnesty International was investigating Dr Irwin's complaint. Amnesty didn't find anything particularly untoward at Gough until January 1978, when three complaints of assault were made by detainees, one of these from a Monaghan man arrested for allegedly having suspicious documents in his possession when crossing the border.[77] Peadar Mohan from Clontibret was examined shortly after being brought to Gough at 5 a.m. on 28 January and found to be in good health and with no obvious injuries. At his subsequent trial for IRA membership, it was stated that Mohan made no complaint until the third morning of his detention, when he said in the presence of Dr Elliott and the duty inspector that he had been beaten on the head and face while bent over a table in a crab-like position. Dr Elliott found 'two abrasions on his lower back, swelling and tenderness around the spine and a reddening and swelling area on his scalp, around his ear', all of recent origin. This diagnosis was confirmed when Mohan's family doctor came from Monaghan to examine him. Dr Elliott testified that Mohan suffered 'some physical abuse during interrogation'. Nonetheless, Mohan was convicted and sentenced to five years.

Dr Elliott's misgivings were confirmed a month after Mohan's case, when he found detainee Hugh Canavan with a black eye, bruising to his nose and both ears, an eardrum slightly inflamed and bleeding, abrasions on a shoulder, and tiny patches of his scalp bleeding – all inflicted by police officers during interrogation in 'a case of serious assault'.[78] On foot of Dr Elliott's diagnosis, the Director of Public Prosecutions withdrew charges of explosives possession, and Canavan was released. As complaints mounted at Armagh and Castlereagh, the doctors threatened to bring the matter to the British Medical Association. At a Police Authority committee meeting in March 1978, Dr Elliott described in 'some graphic detail' what he could hear from his office during interrogations; when he complained, it was suggested he could be moved to a 'more suitable area'.[79]

The following month, the police inspector in charge of the Gough centre was transferred at his own request and replaced with two others, including one from Castlereagh; complaints were halved at Castlereagh, while they doubled in Armagh.[80] Then, over the Easter weekend, Elliott found progressive injuries on Daniel Hamill, a skinny teenage detainee from Portadown, and reported to the Police Authority his conclusion of 'considerable physical abuse'.[81] Hamill was charged with attempted murder, but was suddenly released before trial; and Elliott subsequently learned his report never made it to the Police Authority.

The pattern of interrogation, medical examination, complaint and charges dropped was repeated, even with Robert Benedict Livingstone, accused of murdering a 14-year-old Portadown schoolboy, Thomas Gerald Rafferty, with an INLA booby-trap bomb set for the security forces.[82] After the same happened with Stephen Gilpin, a loyalist detainee accused of a sectarian murder, the dam burst and the Police Authority received letters putting on record that four local GPs working for Dr Elliott did not condone ongoing ill-treatment at Gough Barracks; from Dr Elliott requesting his transfer because he did not wish to be party to ill-treatment of prisoners; and from the Association of Police Surgeons requesting the Police Authority to notify Amnesty International, then completing its report in London, of the doctors' concerns.[83]

Following submission of the Amnesty report to the British government on 2 May 1978, measures that had been put in place to protect detainees during the investigation were suspended again. The Gough Centre was temporarily shut down, and interrogations were moved to the 'ancient police station at Dungannon'. Although deeply concerned that these interrogations were unmonitored, Dr Elliott was transferred to the Maze prison.[84] For breaking ranks in a conspiracy of abuse, he and Dr Irwin were subjected to 'appalling treatment' from the establishment.[85] Secretary of State Roy Mason appointed a commission of inquiry under Judge Bennett to 'examine police procedures and practice' in interrogation, but with no reference to the reports of Dr Elliott and the others.[86] Dr Elliott submitted testimony to the inquiry, with a cover letter dated 14 August 1978, stipulating;

My sympathies lie with the law-abiding population and particularly with the RUC whose members are at considerably greater risk than any other group ... Any degree of rancour which may be apparent in the statement comes only from a strong feeling that the activities of a few have caused the majority of the present difficulties.[87]

Just around the corner from Gough Barracks, meanwhile, tensions were rising to boiling point in the building that straddles the southern end of the Mall. Originally built in the 1780s, and reconstructed during the 1840s in the architectural style of London's Pentonville Prison – but in the characteristic local pink limestone – this was Armagh Gaol. It was used to house male prisoners until they were transferred to the new Long Kesh prison camp in August 1972. Among those held was Armagh man Niall Vallely, chairman of the Civil Rights Association, who was incarcerated in 1969 for defying the ban on assemblies. In a recent film recording for Queen's University Belfast, he names others detained at Armagh during his time, a list of 'dentists, solicitors, teachers. None of us expected to find ourselves in jail, but the circumstances were such that you did something'.[88]

Armagh then became the women's prison on New Year's Day 1973, when 19-year-old Elizabeth McKee was the first female arrested under the Detention of Terrorists (Northern Ireland) Order.[89] She was soon joined by others as the number of female detainees rose to a high of 31 before internment without trial was ended in 1975 and Special Category status as political prisoners was phased out for those convicted of political or terrorist crimes committed after 1 September 1976.[90] In a contemporaneous 'Catholic Prison Chaplain note' for 1973, published in his subsequent book about the women's prison, the late Raymond Murray recorded that the recent detention in Armagh of a dozen women had accentuated the 'sense of injustice' for the Catholic community, when set against the total of ten loyalist internees (all male) in Long Kesh, despite the sectarian killings of 137 Catholics.[91] During the initial injustice of internment in the spartan conditions of Armagh prison, however, the mood was almost akin to a girls' boarding school. Aged between their mid-teens and mid-twenties, these young women could wear their own clothes, associate freely, and avail of educational facilities that perhaps were not available to them outside, in a world described by Monsignor Murray as 'one of poverty, deprivation, mass unemployment, internment, harassment by police and soldiers, repeated arrests and long detentions incommunicado'.[92]

By 1976, the prison population in Armagh had risen to a hundred, and Britain's Labour government introduced its 'The Way Forward' policy, which had three strands – 'Ulsterisation, normalisation and criminalisation' – aimed at confining the conflict to Northern Ireland and modelled on the disastrous US policy of 'Vietnamisation' during the final stages of the Vietnam War.[93] That meant the phasing out of Special Category status, and a rise in prison protests. In 1977, the women in Armagh joined the struggle of the men in the H-Blocks against the removal of political status. That meant loss of many privileges and rights They were locked up for most of the day as punishment for refusing to do prison work. Denied fresh air, greenery and exercise, many prisoners became ill, and seven suffered from anorexia nervosa.[94] The situation deteriorated further with the murder of prison officer Jean Wallace on 19 April 1979.[95]

The 40-year-old mother of six was just emerging from the main gates, heading to a nearby café for lunch with three colleagues from her new prison job, when a grenade was thrown from a nearby car and gunmen raked them, killing Jean Wallace and wounding her colleagues. Her funeral took place in the church where her daughter had been married just two weeks before. The Catholic chaplain at Armagh Gaol attended, noting that Wallace was the eighteenth prison officer murdered since Special Category was removed.[96] In 1980, a young Keady man was acquitted of killing Wallace, but jailed for the killing of John Anderson of nearby Barrack Street, in 1977.[97] Anderson, a 61-year-old father of two, was a former police reservist and a taxi driver, who was lured to his death at Girvan's Bridge, just outside Armagh city. There were unconfirmed reports that Dessie O'Hare, the Border Fox, was involved.

The prison protest in Armagh was stepped up in 1980 after an incident on 7 February when the women claimed they were 'beaten by male officers'. This prompted the republican women to begin their own 'no wash' or 'dirty' protest in line with their male colleagues in the H-Blocks.[98] This meant lock-up for twenty-three hours a day in cells that were left dirty for six months. An angry Nell McCafferty, a Derry-born feminist journalist, described in sickening detail the scene as 'upwards of thirty Republican women were using their prison cells as toilets, each constructing from their own bodily waste a silent smelly cave'.[99] Of most concern was the fact that in addition to the filth and festering corruption experienced in the H-Blocks, the women in Armagh had to contend with menstrual discharges and much higher risks of serious infection. This added urgency to the efforts of those seeking some satisfactory way out of the prison impasse.

The way out seemed ominously extreme when the dirty protest was suspended on 1 December 1980 and the prison hunger strike began. Three women in their early twenties – Mairéad Nugent, Mary Doyle and Mairéad Farrell – began their fast-to-the-death, and they lost weight more rapidly than the men who had begun their fast in the H-Blocks on 27 October. Other women prisoners lined up to take their place. On 17 December, Cardinal Tómas Ó Fiaich, the Catholic primate living at Ara Coeli, just a short distance from the prison, called for British Prime Minister Margaret Thatcher to intervene personally, and also appealed to the hunger strikers to end their protest 'in the name of God'.[100] The following day, the H-Blocks prisoners ended their hunger strike, on the assurance of concessions from Northern Ireland Secretary Humphrey Atkins. The day after that, on confirmation of the deal from a republican source and before the women learned that Atkins had reneged, they ended their fast after nineteen days.

The Armagh women were not involved in the subsequent hunger strikes which began in pursuit of the same concessions that Atkins had promised. This time, ten protesting prisoners starved themselves to death in the H-Blocks, and the Armagh chaplain railed about the punitive penal system that prevailed, insisting that 'prisoners have suffered enough'.[101] With fewer prisoners in Armagh, he urged that the imminent move to a new prison at Maghaberry be accompanied by releases, remissions and concessions. Among those eventually released as Armagh shut down was

Mairéad Farrell, who enrolled as a university student, but dropped out and was shot dead in an SAS ambush in Gibralter in March 1988.[102]

Tensions remained high in the interim, as those republican prisoners who remained in Armagh insisted on segregation from non-political prisoners and loyalists. That would allow them to regulate their own daily routines through a military command structure in terms of discipline, education and recreation as had applied before the 1976 criminalisation policy. Into that volatile mix stepped Jacqui Upton, a young loyalist prisoner who entered the prison in 1983 and soon found herself as the only Protestant woman on a wing full of Catholic, mostly republican, prisoners during 'a delicate time'.[103] Such was the constant intimidation, that eventually Upton refused to leave her cell until she was transferred to a wing with other Protestants. The authorities had refused to move her because that would have meant de facto segregation, she said.

Meanwhile, Raymond Murray noted the steady decline in numbers with only twenty political prisoners remaining in Armagh when he completed his term as chaplain. They were transferred in March 1986 to a much smaller prison at Maghaberry, where they were broken into smaller groups and mixed with other inmates. Yet the punitive, aggressive regime of strip-searching and punishments continued there until 1992, despite Murray's final Armagh Prison admonition that 'generosity and compassion always pay off'.[104]

The criminal justice system and policing in Armagh already had a dubious reputation before the first allegations of a concerted shoot-to-kill strategy in 1982. Maverick RUC Sergeant John Weir and Constable William McCaughey were attached to the RUC's Special Patrol Group in the city while engaged in terrorist crimes for the Glennane-based UVF gang, which ended in their 1977 conviction for the sectarian murder of Catholic pharmacist William Strathern. Weir's affidavit implicated other serving members of the RUC, the SPG and the UDR in terrorist-type crimes.[105] Then the disclosures of two British officers at the centre of military espionage, Colin Wallace and Fred Holroyd, began to cast light on the group or unit composed of former or seconded members of the SAS.[106] Variously known as the Military Reaction Force, 4 Int, Field Survey Troop, the Northern Ireland Training and Advisory Team and the Special Reconnaissance Unit, it was based at Castledillon, the former grand home of the Molyneaux family, previously an open prison. Commanded by Captain Julian A. Ball, the second officer in command was Captain Robert Nairac, who was abducted and believed murdered in April 1977 in south Armagh.[107] Though based in Castledillon, Nairac was more frequently found at the military base in Bessbrook. It was this Castledillon group that worked with, or 'controlled', the operations of the Glennane Gang. Derek McFarland, a member of the gang, was convicted and jailed for the attempted murder of 19-year-old Marian Rafferty and her boyfriend Thomas Mitchell, 20, in November 1974. McFarland had been an RUC constable from May 1969 to October 1970, a Ministry of Defence police constable at Castledillon from 9 July 1972 to 24 October 1975, and a member of the UDR from 1975 to 1977, when he was dismissed 'for reasons unknown'.[108]

The final phase of the Troubles, between the end of the 1981 hunger strikes and the onset of ceasefires, was dominated by the security forces' adoption of a ruthless shoot-to-kill policy. One Armagh city family found itself in the firing line. In 1982, Seamus Grew was shot dead by an RUC Headquarters Mobile Support Unit; at the end of 1990, his brother Dessie Grew was shot dead by the SAS just outside Loughgall. Both were seasoned veterans of terrorism: Seamus was 30 years old, and his brother was 37. The killings appear to have been carefully planned executions of the brothers, who were high on the British wanted list, and their younger accomplices – 21-year-old Roddy Carroll from Armagh, and 23-year-old Sinn Féin councillor Martin Gerard McCaughey from Galbally, County Tyrone.

The circumstances of the first killings, in 1982, have been extensively documented, but never formally established in the absence of an inquest. They were at the core of a special inquiry led by English Chief Constable John Stalker, which became embroiled in chicanery, obfuscation and downright sabotage emanating from the senior ranks of the RUC. INLA members Seamus Grew, from Armagh's Mullacreevie Park, and Roddy Carroll, from nearby Cambridge Park, had been tailed by an RUC inspector earlier on the day of their deaths when meeting INLA leader Dominic McGlinchy in Monaghan, where he was then living.[109] They had crossed the border, heading back home, when they were forced to halt as they turned off the Killylea Road. A car immediately pulled up behind them, from which Constable John Robinson of the RUC Headquarters Mobile Support Unit (HMSU) emerged. Robinson walked up to the passenger window and shot Carroll.[110] He then walked around to the other side, where Grew was scrambling to escape, and shot him four times. Both victims died at the scene. The police initially claimed they had crashed through a roadblock at Paper Mill Bridge on the road from Keady.

The executions on Killylea Road followed a recent and local pattern of summary execution. On 11 November 1982, the HMSU killed Sean Burns of Armagh, and Eugene Toman and Gervaise McKerry of Lurgan, all wanted IRA suspects, after they 'crashed through a roadblock'.[111] All three victims were unarmed, two had multiple wounds from the 109 bullets the HMSU had fired, and Toman was 'shot through the heart, evidently after he had left or was leaving the stationary car'. Despite the best efforts of the Stalker inquiry and five abandoned inquests by five different coroners, the truth of this incident has never been established, because 'national security and public interest immunity' were granted to the law officers involved.

Thirteen days later, on 24 November 1982, 17-year-old Michael Tighe was shot dead by police officers of the HMSU, who were staking out a shed near the boy's home at Ballyneery, Craigavon, which they believed was an arms dump. Martin McCauley, 19, was seriously wounded in the same incident. Following his investigation, John Stalker emphasised that Michael Tighe was not a terrorist, 'had no security record or criminal convictions' and was a 'good and simple son who lived at home quietly' before dying in a 'hail of police bullets'.[112] The surviving victim was subsequently prosecuted for possession of old rifles found in the shed. The police were then proven to have concocted an initial cover story at a Gough Barracks debriefing. However, despite Lord Justice Kelly having 'reservations about the credibility and accuracy' of the revised police evidence given under oath, he noted that McCauley showed a 'marked unease of his demeanour during cross-examination', so he concluded the victim was lying and sentenced him to a two-year suspended sentence.[113]

Attempts to arraign the police involved in the other two incidents were thwarted at every stage, including by RUC Chief Constable Jack Hermon, who threatened to resign if charges went ahead (he didn't).[114] Those involved in the first killings were found innocent by Lord Justice Gibson, who commended them for 'bringing the three deceased men to justice, in this case, the final court of justice'. Then when Constable John Robinson was tried in 1984 for the summary killings of Seamus Grew and Roddy Carroll, he revealed that he had been ordered to 'give a false version' of events by Special Branch officers at Gough Barracks.[115] The target of the cross-border operation had been Dominic McGlinchey, who was supposed to have been coming into Armagh in the car with Grew.[116] The incorrect intelligence about the INLA leader's movements had come, apparently, from an informer in Monaghan who was associated with the IRA, 'but not an activist'.[117]

The subsequent furore in the Republic over this cold-blooded killing revolved entirely around the disclosure that an RUC Special Branch officer had been operating in the southern jurisdiction, as if that was something out of the ordinary at the time. Taoiseach Garret FitzGerald summoned the British ambassador and formally protested over this violation. The more serious outcome was that before the disclosure at trial of a paid RUC Special Branch informer in Monaghan town, the INLA had incorrectly identified a 45-year-old married father of five as the source of the intelligence. Eric Dale was abducted from his home at Inniskeen, County Monaghan, reportedly tortured, then murdered and dumped at Clontygora, on the Armagh border.[118]

While the Grews and the other families involved in the shoot-to-kill allegations were waiting for inquests, eight years later in October 1990, Dessie Grew and Martin McCaughey were killed in a hail of 'over 200' bullets as they approached a mushroom tunnel at Lislasley, near Loughgall. The families disputed the evidence that they had Kalashnikov AK-47s, insisting they were unarmed at the time of their deaths.[119] Within hours, the RUC had released details of the alleged crimes of Dessie Grew, who had switched from the INLA to the IRA. Amid reports that the scene of the shooting had been staked out for some time, the incident sparked fresh allegations of a shoot-to-kill operation.

Over a lunchtime sandwich with former Dublin-newspapers colleague Andy Pollak some years back, we discussed why the Cathedral City had not leapt ahead after peace came to it. At that time, Andy was director of the Centre for Cross-Border Studies, one of the institutions housed in the former Armagh City Hospital, a formidable buff-pink sandstone building on Abbey Street just behind the central Church of Ireland Cathedral of St Patrick where it also had a commanding view of the Roman Catholic Cathedral of St Patrick on another of the small city's seven hills. His sense was that other 'county towns' of comparable size – Omagh, Enniskillen, Monaghan – had fared much better, even with smaller injections of funded projects. Standing in front of the Protestant Cathedral and looking down on the finely groomed Market Square, with its modern theatre, paved streets and coffee shops, I have the feeling that Armagh, for all its charm, has still to get over the wilful neglect of partition. So as poet John Montague put it 'doomed as any Armada, the lost city of Ard Macha coiled in upon itself, whorl upon whorl, a broken aconite …' and 'even the elegance of the Mall was of no avail against simpleminded sectarianism; Armagh, a maimed capital, a damaged pearl'.[120] Like other border towns, Armagh was shorn of its natural hinterland and lapsed into the shadows of commercial rivals further back from the frontier.

Even as the North's other border towns – Newry, Enniskillen, Strabane and Derry – were drawing in hordes of cross-border shoppers, Armagh city missed its share of the bonanza. Its once-vaunted department store, A. Lennox and Sons of Market Street, opened in 1887 and closed its doors for good in 1998, just as the possibilities of cross-border trade were reawakened.[121] It then fell into dereliction and was demolished in 2004 (and replaced by a nondescript commercial building). A favourite haunt of my draper dad, we had occasionally visited its Wheel and Lantern Coffee Lounge between forays through the twenty or so departments that made the store one of the North's leading retail outlets. Today, it barely lingers in the memory as Armagh is bypassed once more for rival shopping centres and outlet malls.

As a spur to the peace process, and a catalyst to cross-border engagement in peace-building through education after the 1994 ceasefires, Queen's University Belfast established an Armagh campus, also situated in the former city hospital. The Queen's University at Armagh opened in 1996 with the aim of providing a thousand places for part-time students. Within a decade, it shut down, when Queen's decided not to renew its lease, which expired in 2005.[122] At that point, it had fewer than 100 registered students taking degree courses in general studies, but Dominic Bradley, a local SDLP member of the Northern Ireland Assembly, said it was providing a 'valuable service for the border counties'.

As upstart towns to its east prospered and grew, Armagh relaxed into the glories of its past and hoped in vain for a future. It has been so through a century of partition.

9. O'Neill Country

Caledon to Benburb – 13.5 km via Dyan

From Caledon, the Ulster Canal veers off from Monaghan and the border to follow the somewhat less contentious county line between Tyrone and Armagh. In the absence of a towpath, I follow the north-west shore of the Blackwater, heading up Church Hill Road, where St John's parish church commands the village heights. St John's was built in 1767 by the prolific Primate Robinson, and the spire was added later by one of the Lord Caledons. In Lewis's *Topographical Dictionary*, St John's is described as 'a large and handsome edifice, in the later English style of architecture, comprising a nave, chancel, and south transept'.[1] I enter the quiet churchyard and search for the grave of Brian McCoy, a victim of one of the worst atrocities of the Troubles, a dark, dastardly and bloody episode that summed up the depravity of those times.

McCoy was gunned down in cold blood in the early hours of 31 July 1975, nine dum-dum bullets tearing through his body as he lay in a field. A Protestant from Caledon, he was murdered with Fran O'Toole and Tony Geraghty, both also members of the Dublin-based band The Miami.[2] Two others were killed in the mayhem of that night on the road between Banbridge and Newry. Harris Boyle and Wesley Sommerville, well-known members of the UVF, were torn to shreds by the premature explosion of the bomb they were planting on board the band's minibus. The two have been linked, notably in Anne Cadwallader's book, *Lethal Allies*, to numerous terrorist crimes committed by the loyalist Glennane Gang.[3] Northern Ireland Secretary of State Merlyn Rees told the House of Commons that little more than a human arm with the letters 'UVF' tattooed on it was recovered from the scene. Immediately after the blast, the surviving ambushers opened fire on the band members. One of the guns they used was linked directly to the 1974 murder in Mullyash, County Monaghan, of John Francis Green.[4]

Remembered as the 'Miami Showband Massacre', this episode stands out in the catalogue of atrocities because it was aimed at a group of young performers from mixed North-South backgrounds who brought light entertainment into lives overshadowed by the Troubles. McCoy had joined the line-up under Dickie Rock and manager Tom Doherty when the original showband split in 1967 and was deeply involved as The Miami was transformed into a new mainstream pop group.[5] He had been the trumpeter with a well-established Belfast band called The Secrets, but his stage presence and vocal talents moved him into a more central role. With Des McAlea from Belfast, McCoy was recalled as one of the 'old guard' by Stephen Travers, who had recently joined the band and was wounded in the atrocity:

> Brian was a real gentleman. He was a father figure to the newer guys. He came across as much older than the others even though he was only thirty-two. He was the sensible one. Soft-spoken and dignified, he had a lovely dignified way about him.

A third Northerner, Ray Miller from Antrim, was seen by Travers as the link between the old guard and the new pop line-up.

Perhaps it was down to his Northern Protestant background that Brian McCoy was so relaxed when flagged onto the side of the road by men in UDR uniforms, one waving a red lamp, as he was driving the band's minibus back to Dublin from Banbridge.[6] The 'checkpoint' was bogus, manned by active members of the notorious UVF gang. However, the band members did not know this, and, urged on by band leader Fran O'Toole, McCoy edged the vehicle closer to the side of the road to avoid a possible collision. The uniformed men lined up the five band members on the side of the road above a ditch. They exchanged some banter as the van was ostensibly searched, which is when Sommerville and Harris loaded a bomb on board. According to Travers, the atmosphere changed when a car pulled up and a man emerged dressed in a different coloured military beret, smart combat trousers and a combat smock. Speaking with 'an educated, curt military voice' and an English accent, he took charge and McCoy assured Travers, 'It's OK, Stephen, this is British Army.'[7]

It has since been accepted that the pretext for the ambush was to create the impression, once the bomb exploded after crossing the border, that the band was carrying explosives for the IRA.[8] That doesn't stack up, however, since the band was travelling south, home from Banbridge. Whatever the motive, it was abandoned with the premature explosion, in a hail of bullets after the blast hurled the band members from the roadside into a field.[9]

Back at their home in Dublin, Helen McCoy had got a phone call from Brian's brother-in-law to alert her about a radio report of a band being ambushed. She tuned in to the news that her husband was among the dead. They had met when they were both 16, at dances in the parochial hall and the Orange Hall, gone out for eight years, and then been married for eight years. In the immediate aftermath of his murder she was sedated heavily, and missed seeing her husband for a final time because the coffin was closed. Helen was also unable to attend the funeral in Caledon, where arrangements were handled by the local undertakers, where Brian's cousin Trevor McCoy worked part-time.[10] She felt she was not given the opportunity to grieve properly by those who wished to protect her. She decided not to return north, but to stay in the home she and Brian had shared in Dublin. Tragedy struck again when Brian McCoy's brother-in-law Eric Smyth was shot dead by the IRA outside his home in Salter's Grange Road, just north of Armagh city in April 1994.[11] He had been a member of the UDR, medically discharged in 1990 after eighteen years.

Such tales of murder and mayhem abound in the placid country that spills out from the high ground where St John's church stands opposite Churchill primary school. In the valley below and to the right, the Blackwater marks the county boundary with Armagh. To the left, Tyrone's Clogher Valley snakes along the eastern shore of the Blackwater to nestle below the northern side of Sliabh Beagh. This is one of the very few districts on the border with a clear majority of Protestants, and geographically it is the most extensive, stretching from Caledon to the

Fermanagh county line at Fivemiletown, about 25 miles (40 kilometres) distant. It also seems to have fewer border crossings than elsewhere along the frontier with Monaghan. That could be a consequence of geography, with the Blackwater River, or of history, with a clear demarcation of political hegemony dating back to the time when this was O'Neill country and across the river were the McKennas, a division reinforced by subsequent patterns of enforced settlement when Monaghan was not included in the Plantation of Ulster but was settled before and since. For whatever reason, the large-scale withdrawal of unionists from front-line border communities seems not to have happened here. Their history has been as marked by sectarian tensions, killings and standoffs.

From the establishment of Northern Ireland, the Protestants of the Clogher Valley rallied to the cause and to the security forces, both full-time and part-time. It was a lucrative devotion to the cause, described in Susan McKay's book on Northern Protestants as 'virtually a type of farm diversification'.[12] Sons followed fathers into the security forces; brothers and cousins joined up in succession; firm friendships were forged in the camaraderie of nights spent on patrol before relaxing in the social facilities of district and regional barracks. In areas of relative social isolation all along the border, joining the B Specials, then the UDR, RIR and police reserve became a rite of passage for Protestant men, and for many young women who enlisted as UDR Greenfinches. Across the sectarian divide, the protestations that those who joined the UDR and the RUC Reserve did so for altruistic reasons of 'protecting the community' never rang true against those obvious social and financial motivations. Those who joined soon found themselves on the front line of Ulsterisation, and in the crosshairs of republican gunmen. Reflecting the views of many in his community, however, former Ulster unionist MP Ken Magennis was in no doubt that when the IRA shot farmers, teachers, businessmen and others who were members of the UDR, it was an attempt at 'ethnic cleansing', and that this was 'an area under siege'.[13]

Church Hill Road is a quiet access route with so little traffic that a flock of pheasants can graze nonchalantly in a field nearby. Eventually, the road veers to the left and I rejoin the main route to Dungannon just beyond Enagh Lough. Even then there is little to disturb my ramble along the hedgerows and a stretch of white fenceposts encircling a stud farm on a small hill. Eventually, the road narrows for a short stretch before entering the hamlet of Dyan, with an impressive mill to the left. It is in superb structural order, with green doors, a beautiful spoked iron gate and a relatively small sign advertising Old Mill Pine. Across the road, there is an equally impressive Orange Hall, built in 1878. This is the home of Dyan No. 1 Loyal Orange Lodge, the first to receive its warrant from the formidable brotherhood of Protestant loyalists. And though that designation has long been a contention with the brethren at Loughgall, where the Battle of the Diamond took place, there is evidence that the Dyan lodge's ancestors played an equally prominent role in that foundational event.

In 1792, a Protestant Orange Boys' Club was started here by James Wilson.[14] Three years later, on 21 September 1795, Wilson led his Orange Boys to the Diamond in the Loughgall townland of Grange Lower, where they formed ranks with other Protestants, including the Peep o' Day Boys, against their common Catholic rivals the Defenders, massed on Faughart Hill opposite. In the sectarian war between these oath-bound secret agrarian societies for cottage tenancies and a greater share in the flax/linen industry, battle was enjoined and the Defenders were defeated with a reported death toll ranging from sixteen to sixty.[15] Protestant injuries amounted to only a single window pane at the cottage of Dan Winter, a cousin of Wilson. In the aftermath of battle, Wilson, Winter and James Sloan, former schoolmaster and Loughgall innkeeper, set about founding the organisation that would become the Loyal Orange Institution of Ireland.

According to Hilda Winter, curator, guardian and guide at the small museum now housed in 'Diamond Dan' Winter's cottage, 'Those from the Dyan Club who fought at the Diamond always said they went into battle as Orange Boys and came out as Orangemen.'[16] So when Orange Lodge warrants were issued by James Sloan, recognised as the leader, Wilson secured the first for Dyan. By the time the Loughgall men got over their sulking and sought a warrant for their lodge, the numbers had moved up considerably. Loughgall became Loyal Orange Lodge No. 118. Although they missed out on the top spot numerically, Loughgall has captured the imagination as the birthplace of Orangeism, and that brings a lot of visitors to the door of Dan Winter's cottage.

The present Orange Hall in Dyan, which is locked up and quiet and does not feature a museum, is a sturdy building in beautiful cut stone, its arched windows picked out in bright red. It was built in 1878. That was during the second great wave of Orangeism, as the threat of home rule loomed in the late-nineteenth-century ascendancy of William Gladstone's Liberals, and the emergence of the Irish Parliamentary Party at Westminster. Espoused and led by now by big-house unionists – including families such as the Alexanders, Stronges, Leslies, Rossmores and Maddens – the Orange Institution became the rallying movement for Protestants of all denominations.

Its origins, however, had been very much rooted in the Church of Ireland population of mid-Ulster, where rapid expansion of the rural population had led to sectarian outrages, including murders, largely attributable to economic competition for cottage tenancies and linen work. On the Protestant side, the atrocities were carried out by groups known as the Peep o' Day Boys for their dawn raids, but also as Orangemen and Wreckers. The latter name came from their destruction of weaving looms in homes belonging to Catholics, as well as Presbyterians (Dissenters) and Quakers.[17] The problem, as they saw it was the relaxation of the penal laws, which had been drawn up in the wake of the Glorious Revolution to ensure the supremacy of the established church through the alienation and suppression of Catholicism and non-conformist Protestantism.[18] Many of these Peep o' Day Boys became adherents of the Orange cause, although the authorities that became the Grand Lodge discouraged their recruitment.

The superb condition of the Orange Hall in Dyan is explained in reports of a reprehensible act by those that today's Orangemen would describe as 'wreckers'. In January 2008, the building was attacked by vandals, who smashed fourteen windows, destroyed the window blinds and damaged other exterior fittings.[19] This was condemned by local DUP politician Lord Maurice Morrow, who said it was part of recent vandalism in the Caledon area. The Orange Hall incident, which occurred on a Monday night, followed a weekend attack on a GAA club premises near the Moy. Such reciprocal attacks are not as rare as one might hope in our post-conflict society. Even a cursory examination of media reports finds references to attacks on Orange Halls and GAA clubs with tiresome regularity. Nor are attacks on Orange Halls confined to a particular district; they happen across Northern Ireland and the neighbouring border counties. The Peep o' Day Boys and the Defenders may have disappeared, folded into their modern successor societies, but their spirit of vindictive and wanton sectarian raids at dawn continues in the recesses of the Clogher Valley and beyond.

The drumlin district that comprises the most southerly stretch of the Clogher Valley forms an inverted triangle on the map. Almost exactly in the middle of this triangle is Minterburn, its name derived from the people who inhabited the area before it became a firm stronghold of the O'Neills. Today, Minterburn is a tiny hamlet dominated by its Presbyterian church, church hall, manse, school and graveyard. A previous generation of children from the congregation here received glowing praise in a report to the Hibernian Sunday School Society dated 26 May 1814. It noted that the school proved hugely popular with 'upwards of two hundred regularly attending children'. Nor were they there just to fill seats:

> The progress of the children … was amazing; many who scarcely knew the letters when coming to us, are now able to spell distinctly, and others, who could spell words of three or four syllables imperfectly, can now read pretty accurately in the New Testament. The eagerness for instruction on the part of the youth was greater than anything I ever witnessed. When the days were short we were obliged to commence very early, and the poor little children would have their breakfast taken by daylight, and be standing about the Meeting-House at sunrise.[20]

Protestants in this part of the Clogher Valley are not usually so eager for new ways of doing things. They take immense pride in old-fashioned unionism, a style they see as reminiscent of the days before the Troubles. They bask in eulogistic accounts of their way of life, their history and their values. They see themselves as a pioneering people living on the frontiers of civilisation, wrestling pastoral order from the chaos of what was before and may come again. In her 'intimate' portrayal, *The Faithful Tribe*, Ruth Dudley Edwards played to their gallery: 'Clogher Valley Protestants are hard-working, God-fearing, sober, frugal but warm people with a fierce pride in the land which many generations of their forefathers made so prosperous.'[21] They are also proud of living in districts abutting the border, yet they choose resolutely not to see beyond the Blackwater River, which forms the physical frontier of their world. Especially since the Second World War, the adjacent world of Monaghan is 'foreign and exotic or foreign and hostile, but always foreign'.[22] Their history is fragmentary, almost scriptural, always framed in current contexts that place a family living 'south of the border in County Monaghan from King William's time until, in the 1860s, as a result of some skulduggery by the landlord and his steward … they had to move' to the Clogher Valley.[23] As another observer remarks, for them, 'Partition has been a complete success. Or at least it has been complete.'[24]

Within their bastion, they have retained the practice of holding their own annual Twelfth parade, with few or none of the urban affectations of bigger centres. While lodges from adjacent parts of Monaghan take part, they are 'greeted in much the same way as the lodges from Ghana or the Mohawk Lodge' from the Bay of Quinte, Ontario.[25] Yet while these Clogher Valley brethren see themselves as integral, they themselves are seen elsewhere in Protestant Ulster as 'distant kin, rather than neighbours and siblings'.[26] That doesn't affect their faith in their place within the unionist fold. Local unionist councillor Robert Mulligan sums up its values as reflected on the Twelfth: 'It's the kind of Twelfth you would think about from your childhood. It never changes, maybe it has in other areas, but with us it has remained as I remember it all my life.'[27]

So the security of their world is threatened by those who would place it into a wider vista. Harking after the past, they bristle at any encroachment of modernity, even in the form of improved infrastructure. Councillor Mulligan of the UUP and Councillor Sammy Brush of the DUP have vigorously opposed the upgrading to a dual carriageway of the N2/A5 North Western Transport route that crosses the border at Aughnacloy and links up with the A4 dual carriageway and M1 to Belfast, before proceeding through Tyrone to Derry city and northern Donegal. They viewed the proposal, which was to receive a huge injection of financial support from

Dublin, and the European Union, as 'a serious waste of public funds'. Councillor Brush argued that improving the present A5 'would service local residents much better and cause less upheaval'.[28] Such a refusal to see the road as anything other than a local thoroughfare portrays the world they prefer to inhabit. It is a world where everyone moves at the pace of the slowest vehicle – usually a farmer's tractor; where inter-city traffic must halt for a 'Give Way' sign on entering Aughanacloy; where thousands of vehicles must negotiate through the higgledy-piggledy parking on the town's Moore Street; and where all the other impediments to traffic movement, commerce, communication and industrial development are encountered in that first mile across the border.

Yet one native son of Aughnacloy saw the wider vistas, and he was instrumental in opening up the closed world of Northern Ireland to other possibilities. James Young Malley was the 'right-hand man' of Northern Ireland Premier Terence O'Neill in the 1960s.[29] A decorated war hero who flew more than a 130 RAF missions over mainland Europe, Jim Malley returned to the Stormont civil service and was posted to serve in finance under then Minister O'Neill, who soon appointed the Aughnacloy man as his private secretary. They moved together to the prime minister's office in 1963, and O'Neill began to act on a plan they had often discussed but only in private, fearing it would cause a revolt in the Unionist Party. Malley was dispatched to arrange a summit with Taoiseach Seán Lemass, liaising with his opposite number in Dublin, T.K. Whitaker, a native of Rostrevor in County Down. It was Malley who personally conveyed the invitation for Lemass to visit Belfast in January 1965 at a private meeting in Dublin. Unbeknownst to most of O'Neill's cabinet, Malley also met Lemass at the border and escorted him to the summit. Such rapprochement came to naught with the unionist roadblock even of O'Neill's modest reforms, and he was gone in 1969. Malley became registrar general of Northern Ireland until retirement, while also serving in the Scotch-Irish Trust of Ulster, which was the prime mover behind the Ulster-American Folk Park outside Omagh.

Aughnacloy reverted to a border outpost, with more than its share of tit-for-tat killings in those early years. Franklin Caddoo of Rehaghy was a 24-year-old married father of a 1-year-old daughter, with a pregnant wife. A farmer and part-time UDR soldier, he was leaving out milk churns for collection on 10 May 1973 and police say he jumped from his tractor and tried to run but was shot twice in the head at close range.[30] Next up was Francie McCaughey, 36, a Catholic farmer from the neighbouring townland of Glasdrummond, who was killed at early morning milking when a UVF bomb went off in the byre on 28 October 1973. A prominent member of the local GAA, McCaughey had recently helped to buy land near the police station for new club grounds, and a loyalist statement said he was targeted in reprisal for Franklin Caddoo.[31] Then McCaughey's 41-year-old brother-in-law Owen Boyle was standing at the kitchen window of a new bungalow home in Glencull when he was shot dead as he helped his wife Winnie with the dishes in April 1975. A father of eight children, Boyle was the nineteenth Catholic to be killed in the 'murder triangle' bounded by Moy, Aughnacloy and Coalisland, according to local SDLP politician Austin Currie.[32]

Of course, the death blows were felt on both sides of the community and both sides of the border, and often in the cruelest manner. Cormac McCabe, a 43-year-old father of two, was the first headmaster of Aughnacloy secondary school.[33] On 20 January 1974, he left his Clogher home with his wife Eleanor and two daughters, one of them physically handicapped. They went to Monaghan town, where they called in to the Four Seasons Hotel for a meal. Returning from the toilet at one point, he said he had seen somebody he knew. His wife later told the inquest that two men later came in and 'appeared to be staring at us'. Her husband excused himself, went out and never came back. When she later asked the receptionist if she had seen him, she was told that 'there was a scuffle at the door by some drunks'. The following morning, Cormac McCabe was found blindfolded and shot dead just across the border at Altadaven, near the Favour Royal estate in the Clogher Valley.

His abductors and killers knew that Cormac McCabe, a Protestant, was the commander of the Aughnacloy Company of the UDR.[34] According to his friend and UDR colleague, former MP Ken Magennis, Cormac McCabe was 'the kingpin of this little community' who was 'targeted' and 'carefully selected': 'You destroy the talent. Dishearten the community. It is a takeover.'[35] McCabe had joined up as a part-time member of the UDR in 1971 and was commissioned to the rank of captain. The IRA was already moving its gunsights to the UDR, especially in border areas, and not only because they were 'easy targets', as claimed then and since. Tommy McKearney, who was active in the local company of the IRA at that time, observed that:

> Both the UDR and RUC Reserve were recruited locally and had, therefore, a comprehensive and detailed knowledge of their areas. In closely mixed rural areas they were intimately familiar with the rhythm and pattern of life in their district and could recognise instantly if something was out of place ... on or off-duty these men acted as the eyes and ears of the regular army... employed as school bus drivers, postmen, refuse collectors, they had a perfect 'cover' for travelling through Republican districts.[36]

The esteem in which the UDR is now held by the border Protestant community of the Clogher Valley was not apparent in the early days. The regiment, set up in 1970 after the Hunt Report into the conduct of the Special Constabulary, was seen as a sop to Catholic nationalists, and a betrayal of those who had served in the B Specials. Vanguard Unionist hardliner Bill Craig even set up a Third Force to 'liquidate the enemy' because of misgivings about the UDR's commitment to protecting Protestants.[37] Individual members of the regiment seemed determined to prove otherwise, and there were repeated instances of lawlessness, including violence and murder in the force. When Brigadier Harry Baxter, commander of the UDR, remarked in late 1976 that the regiment had attracted a 'few bad apples', I documented dozens of crimes carried out by soldiers under his command in an article published in *Hibernia*.[38] In less than four years, UDR men were convicted of eighty crimes, including murder and attempted murder, causing explosions, illegal possession of arms, ammunition and explosives, and armed robbery and assault. In defending the integrity of his force and the experience of its 1,600 ex-B Specials, the monocled brigadier also confirmed that 120 members had been dismissed on 'security' grounds. My research on the UDR also revealed a disturbing traffic in firearms from the regiment to loyalist paramilitary organisations, and noted that UDR part-timers in the Dungannon-based 8th Battalion in the 'murder triangle' were 'allowed to take their weapons home for security reasons, and quite a few of these were "taken" from the homes of members'.

Even as British security policy projected the UDR into the primary role, the demands for disbandment had become a clamour among nationalists. SDLP politicians Ivan Cooper and Seamus Mallon highlighted numerous breaches of the law by UDR soldiers and Cooper, a former Young Unionist who became involved in the Civil Rights movement, referred to the UDR as the 'armed wing of unionism'.[39] Local SDLP politician Austin Currie, who had initially encouraged Catholics to join the UDR despite the imposition of an oath of allegiance, spent the remainder of his political career in the North facing accusation that he was the 'UDR recruiting sergeant', and worrying that Catholic recruits who were targeted might have joined on his advice.[40] Perhaps among those was 29-year-old Daniel McCormick, who had joined but left the UDR before he was shot with his UDR mate Kenneth Smyth in west Tyrone in December 1971, among the earliest victims of the IRA campaign targeting off-duty members of the regiment.[41] By 1974, the abduction and murder of Cormac McCabe followed an established pattern. Only a couple of nights before, another UDR part-timer, Robert Noel Jameson, had been shot dead when he stepped off a bus near Trillick as he was returning from his regular job at the bus depot in Omagh.[42] Yet McCabe, who according to his deputy headmaster was outgoing and known throughout the Aughnacloy community, felt drawn to continue frequenting the hotel in Monaghan that had become 'a favourite haunt' for his family.

Delays on the N2/A5 Western Corridor are not as bad as they once were at Aughnacloy, of course. For decades, the name of the small Tyrone border town was synonymous with its notorious checkpoint. The British army built the deeply entrenched military checkpoint of sangers and steel walls just north of the Blackwater River on the main road from Dublin through Monaghan and Tyrone to Derry city and Donegal. Here motorists, lorry drivers and bus passengers had to endure up to two hours of delays at a time, which accumulated over the years into resentment, anger and frustration. Usually the excessive delays were attributed to security alerts and reports of shots being fired. However, the truth may have been more mundane than that. Irish government files released at the end of 2009 disclosed a 'confidential note' sent in 1976 from the Department of Foreign Affairs in Dublin to the Irish Embassy in London saying that only two out of thirty shootings reported by British security forces at the Aughnacloy checkpoint could be verified.[43] The aim of the delays, it speculated, was keeping traffic to and from Donegal out of Northern Ireland:

> There are good grounds for believing that searches of vehicles at the checkpoint have been made not only for security purposes but to delay traffic deliberately with the ultimate objective of forcing Donegal-bound traffic to avoid Northern Ireland entirely and take the longer route, via Sligo and Ballyshannon.

Long delays for traffic at Aughnacloy were nothing new, of course. They had been a part of life ever since the border was set up and the Free State government imposed a customs frontier. With alternative routes blocked or destroyed, it was also an opportunity to discourage traffic on the primary route connecting the south to nationalist Derry city through the most nationalist county in Northern Ireland. Perhaps that was also the reason why the crossing from Monaghan into Tyrone at Moybridge was served by a temporary military-style bridge for so many years. The bridge had been blasted during the IRA's border campaign and the Bailey bridge installed there carried the traffic for more than a decade on the road between Ireland's biggest city (Dublin) and its fourth largest city (Derry).

Yet the Aughnacloy checkpoint that grew up on the Monaghan Road beside Coronation Park and Lettice Street seemed a permanent and ever-growing feature of the town. Staffed by both regular Army and UDR, it seemed an alien presence on a country road, where military personnel sought relief from boredom in taunting passers-by and occasionally in much worse.

Aidan McAnespie had been to a family funeral at Carrickroe, just over the border in north Monaghan on 21 February 1988. He returned home and was making his way back to the GAA grounds of the Aghaloo O'Neills, which was hugged into the cusp of County Tyrone by a loop in the Blackwater just beyond the checkpoint. After he walked through, a soldier from the Grenadier Guards discharged three bullets, killing the 24-year-old local man.[44] Later the soldier would claim his wet finger slipped on the trigger of his heavy machine-gun. He was charged with manslaughter, but never convicted. Those charges were dropped in 1990, and he was fined for negligent discharge of a weapon and given a medical discharge. Meanwhile, the McAnespie family protested that Aidan's death was preceded by years of intimidation and open threats at the checkpoint. Their sense of injustice was exacerbated when he was omitted initially from an RUC list of victims of the Troubles.[45]

For a Tyrone family whose sense of place and identity is entwined with neighbouring Monaghan, the devastation and denial of justice has never eased. I've known members of the McAnespie family for decades, including Aidan's sister Eilish McCabe, a press photographer and co-founder of the group Relatives for Justice. She campaigned vigorously for Aidan before her own untimely death from cancer in 2008. I interviewed Aidan's brother, Vincent, for a 2015 book, *To Tell You the Truth*, which contained the stories of people who survived the loss of loved ones during the years of conflict.[46] He told of how he, his girlfriend Brenda, and Aidan had arranged to go to a Wolfe Tones concert at the Four Seasons Hotel in Monaghan town that night. Aidan was to pick them up at Brenda's family home in Scotstown. Then he related how the family had been alerted to the shooting while at the wake house in Carrickroe; how the parents had been driven past the Gardaí at Moybridge and found Aidan lying dead in the road, surrounded by his Gaelic football teammates; how the Aughnacloy funeral Mass was concelebrated by Cardinal Tomás Ó Fiaich, who described Aidan's death as 'murder'; then the burial in Clara graveyard, back across the border in Monaghan.

Vincent also told of all the painful years when family members could barely talk about what had happened to Aidan, about the drip-feed of discovery and the frustration of cover-up during successive investigations, an exhumation and legal wrangling between North and

South. He talked about moments that shone light into the darkness: the time Tyrone won its second All-Ireland Football Championship in 2005, when the team bus stopped at the place where Aidan had fallen and team manager Mickey Harte, with star players Brian Dooher and Peter Canavan, stood with the family to pay their respects. Most of all, he talked about the deep comfort and support of the GAA and others who rallied around when Aidan's name came up.

Vincent and most of his siblings chose to live in Monaghan during all those years of darkness, seldom venturing near the checkpoint, which remained in place throughout the closing years of the twentieth century. He returned home to Aughnacloy in 2003, living next door to his sister Eilish and just across the road from the family home. With family, social and sporting ties to Emyvale and other places in Monaghan, his sense of community straddles the border, which is now virtually invisible – the checkpoint is gone and only the road signs about speed limits disclose the fact that the bridge over the Blackwater is the border. Thirty years after that fatal shooting at the Aughnacloy checkpoint, Vincent and others in the family still have faith that the truth will come out:

> My late sister Eilish fought a hard campaign to get justice for Aidan and, just before her death in 2008, the HET (Historical Enquiries Team) released a statement stating that the British Army version of events surrounding Aidan's death was 'the least likely version'.

In 2016, Director of Public Prosecutions Barra McGrory ordered a review of why the manslaughter charges were dropped against the soldier responsible for the death. Welcoming that decision, another brother, Seán, said, 'We knew the original decision was wrong … The family would like to make a point to the British Army that no one is above the law.'[47]

The locality played a pivotal role in military offensives against the border, and in its defence. Several platoons of the A Specials were stationed here during the early years of partition. Once the customs frontier was put in place, its customs posts were bombed, replaced and bombed again. It spawned a succession of IRA activists, including Sean McCaughey, whose death in Portlaoise prison in May 1947 inspired a new generation of young men to take up arms.[48] The adjutant-general and Northern commander of the IRA, McCaughey was arrested in Dublin for overseeing the 'court martial' of former IRA Chief of Staff Stephen Hayes, who admitted being a Special Branch informer. McCaughey was tried at a military court and sentenced to death by firing squad in 1941. With his sentence commuted to life imprisonment, he spent five years naked and in solitary confinement for his refusal to wear a prison uniform and be treated as a 'common criminal'. Finally, he embarked on a hunger strike demanding political status, which was then raised to a hunger and thirst strike after ten days. He died on the twenty-third day of his protest, his tongue 'shrunk to the size of a threepenny bit', in the words of prominent republican Paddy McLogan.[49]

Among those he inspired was Kevin McKenna, born just the year before McCaughey's funeral, which brought a huge surge in support for republican politics and prisoners, and led to Clann na Poblachta winning ten Dáil seats, which toppled De Valera from power. Growing up, McKenna's interest would lie more in the martial than the political wings of republicanism. He joined the IRA in the mid-1960s before emigrating to Canada, returning after several years when internment was introduced. He helped form a local company of the Provisional IRA in the south Tyrone area, referred to by its members as the 'Brantry Brigade' and celebrated in Monaghan pub singalongs to the chorus of the more widely known song, Belfast Brigade, 'No surrender is the war cry of the Brantry Brigade'.

The Provisional IRA's Tyrone commander in the period following the 1969 split at the IRA convention between the Provos and Officials (Stickies) was Kevin Mallon from Brackaville, Coalisland. In a series of photographs published by the American photojournalist Michael O'Sullivan, there are several depicting Mallon armed with a sub-machine gun while handling a bomb in a wooden crate.[50] He is accompanied by Brendan Hughes, who succeeded him as Tyrone IRA commander, but who disappeared from the IRA in 1972. McKenna took over at that point, but was soon arrested and interned for eighteen months.[51] When he was released in 1975, McKenna resumed command of the brigade, which was by now firmly ensconced in its Monaghan town base. There McKenna rose to Northern commander of the IRA, the army council and eventually to IRA chief of staff, in which role 'the fighting men had time for him; he was always there for them'.[52]

During his extended period in command at the local and national levels, there were many serious setbacks for the IRA in Tyrone, but it was one of the most consistently active and successful units in the organisation. An early incident was the death of two IRA bombers, 16-year-old Patsy Quinn from Dungannon, and 27-year-old Dan McAnallen, a plumber from the Brantry area living in Monaghan. They were killed when the home-made mortar bomb they were firing at the police station in Pomeroy backfired.[53] McAnallen was described in death notices as an 'adjutant' in the IRA. Only five days before that double fatality, two other IRA bombers, Seamus Harvey and Gerard McGlynn, had been killed when the bomb they were transporting across the border exploded near the Kilclean customs post, just outside Castlederg, at the far side of county Tyrone.[54]

The cessation of hostilities along the border meant merely an uneasy coexistence and the resumption of a cultural stand-off as the faltering peace process got underway. Yet even those tentative early steps to create a shared society were frustrated by another native of Aughnacloy and former resident of Monaghan town. Vincent McKenna boasted of his family relationship to the late Sean McKenna, one of the IRA hunger strikers in 1980, and his paramilitary partnership with Jim Lynagh, the Monaghan-born leader of the east Tyrone IRA. In the guise of a reformed terrorist, McKenna almost succeeded in sabotaging the entire peace process through false claims and concocted 'statistics', as well as outrageous challenges to British Northern Ireland Secretary Mo Mowlam. McKenna insinuated himself into the role of spokesman for Families Against Intimidation and Terror (FAIT), which was funded through the Northern Ireland Office. His bizarre claims, self-contrived 'attempts on his life', outlandish press statements and other antics eventually caused FAIT to cease operations. McKenna then set up his one-man Northern Ireland Human Rights Bureau, and continued undermining the peace.

Nothing succeeds like excess, of course, and this maverick mayhem-maker became the darling of those not enamoured of a peace involving former combatants. With prominent politicians from the British Tory party and anti-agreement unionists, as well as enthusiastic media sponsors including Charles Moore of London's *Daily Telegraph* and David Burnside, he became a hero. In 1999, he was the star speaker for a 'Save the RUC' rally, sharing the Ulster Hall stage with former Chief Constable Sir Jack Hermon and an array of prominent politicians who opposed policing reform. He featured in glowing newspaper profiles, was sought out by visiting TV crews and even starred as a 'human rights activist' in the influential *60 Minutes* TV show in America.

I entered stage left, curious about a character who had appeared from nowhere, with a past that seemed highly dubious and a present bearing no relation to informed observation. As other media lapped up his nonsense, I sought the truth from those who knew Vincent McKenna – his sisters, former in-laws, neighbours, acquaintances and those who had welcomed him into FAIT. I also spoke to the police in Monaghan town, where he had lived since he was a teenager and had a family, and where he said he was active in the IRA. I uncovered a young man with a troubled past who had built an alternative reality for himself. He wasn't a former IRA member, although he had spent time in prison for a bizarre sectarian arson attack in Aughnacloy when he was infatuated by illusions of IRA heroes. He had abandoned his family, undergone a 'conversion' to evangelical Protestantism, and completed a university course. Just as the peace was gaining true momentum, Vincent McKenna began issuing false statements, even abusing his former university with a fabricated opinion poll that resulted in Queen's University Belfast publicly disassociating itself from him.[55] I discovered that he had sabotaged FAIT from the inside even as the RUC issued cautions and contradictions to his claims. However, the most startling thing I unearthed about Vincent McKenna was that he faced criminal charges 'of a serious, sexual nature', which was confirmed by Garda Inspector Joseph Sullivan, the senior investigating officer, who was fully satisfied a conviction would be secured.

When I brought the story to Irish newspapers, they would not publish it without couching it incorrectly as 'Sinn Féin allegations'. So

I contacted Niall O'Dowd, editor of the *Irish Voice* in New York, who shared my dismay at media complicity in McKenna's constant efforts to wreck the peace. My story led the *Irish Voice* on 8 September 1999.[56] Then silence, with no media follow-up until Beatrix 'Bea' Campbell, an investigative reporter from England, called me about a fortnight later. I introduced her to my sources. She spoke to them alone. Her story appeared in the *Independent on Sunday* on Sunday, 26 September 1999.[57] Next day, the *Irish News* in Belfast gave free rein to McKenna in its front-page lead story to deny that he had ever been questioned about child sex abuse.[58] His Belfast solicitor, Alan McAlister of J.C. Taylor and Company, threatened legal action against the *Independent on Sunday* in London, alleging that its article had put McKenna's life 'further at threat'.[59] McKenna followed up with a blitz of denials and claims that he was being targeted in a plot by the IRA and the Garda Special Branch.[60] Again, none of my press colleagues contacted me about my supposed collusion with the co-conspirators. I then worked with Kevin Magee and the BBC *Spotlight* team in Belfast on an investigation, which aired on 9 November 1999, exposing McKenna as a charlatan and a suspected child abuser. It won several awards and halted his gallop.[61]

Shortly thereafter, Vincent McKenna was found guilty of thirty-one counts of child sexual abuse against his daughter Sorcha when she was aged between 4 and 12. Sorcha waived anonymity to ensure nobody would believe her abusing father was a defender of human rights. In doing so, she faced down her abuser and his web of deceit. She became a remarkable champion of sexual abuse survivors. Newspapers that had provided a platform for his propaganda and lies published glowing testimonials and the truth about her abusive parent.[62] Vincent McKenna was sent to jail in manacles and his sentence was doubled to six years on appeal.[63] He refused treatment or therapy during his incarceration and was released in May 2005, discredited, but unbowed.[64] None of those who regurgitated his spurious propaganda aimed at scuppering the peace have bowed either.

Back from the border, my trek from Dyan takes me past a large factory with a 'for sale' sign, a poster invitation for 'special Gospel Meetings' at the Brantry Bard Cultural Centre and a small roadside paddock with a bright red circular notice attached securely to the farm-gate warning, '*Sortie*

Véhicules – Ne pas stationer, merci'. I suspect it was not erected by Dungannon Borough Council or its Mid-Ulster successor. Then as Knocknacloy Hill pushes the river around to the right, through a gap in the hedge to my left, I see a small roadside lake furnished with fishing stands and other rustic amenities, and just ahead of me down the road, I see a small car park with information boards. They tell me that Tullygivern Lough was a monastic site once upon a time; that the small lake had a *crannóg* dwelling; that the area is of special scientific interest for its variety of plants and grasses; and, most notably, that this is the site of a famous battle that took place during the seventeenth century War of the Three Kingdoms (England, Ireland and Scotland). I forge ahead into the battlefield across a beautiful old stone bridge spanning the River Oona, which rises in Brantry Lough and flows through Eglish village before joining the Blackwater.

Just a short distance away, the Battleford Bridge across the Blackwater roughly marks the spot where Eoghan Roe O'Neill inflicted a heavy defeat on Major General Robert Munro and his Scottish Covenanter army on 5 June 1646. It is also where the Blackwater River and its former shadow, the Ulster Canal, turn sharp right and away from the border. According to a lengthy description published in November 1922 in *An t-Óglách*, the journal of the Irish National Army, the battle was fought around the place then called Thistle Hill, named for a Scottish family who had settled there.[65] The accounts tell how Munro was advancing from the east through Armagh and his brother, Colonel George Munro, was marching his forces south from Coleraine along the western shores of Lough Neagh, while Robert Stewart was leading his Laggan Army from Derry in the north-west. The plan was to rendezvous at Clones and Glaslough and then hold a line at the Blackwater to prevent Eoghan Roe making his way north from Cavan.[66] However, O'Neill had already set off for Benburb and took up a strong position on the eve of battle. Munro's main force advanced, sacking Armagh city en route.

Arriving at the Blackwater, however, Munro found O'Neill protected on the left by bog and on the right by the junction of the Blackwater and the Oona River, while in front was rough, drumlin landscape covered with scrogs and bushes. After some skirmishing, Munro's men saw cavalrymen advancing from the north-west. Munro identified them as his brother's forces and urged his men on. They turned out to be Monaghan horsemen under

Colonel Bernard MacMahon and his brother-in law Colonel MacNeeny, who were coming to join O'Neill, having repulsed George Munro at Dungannon. They rode among the Scots Musketeers and drove them back across the stream by 'push of the pike'. O'Neill then ordered a full advance, holding back only the Fermanagh regiment under Rory Maguire.

A total rout ensued, with only forty horsemen of Munro's forces making it across the river. Most of his infantry was cut to pieces – 3,423 fell on the field; Munro's field pieces were seized; Lord Montgomery, 21 officers and 156 men were taken prisoner; and other Scots deserted to the Irish cause. O'Neill's casualties were light in comparison; he lost an estimated 300 men. It was a resounding victory in the first head-to-head battle against 'British' forces in the field and it was 'celebrated throughout Catholic Europe'. It was also the last field victory in a struggle that persisted in one form or another for more than 370 years. O'Neill was ordered by the Confederation of Kilkenny, the Irish Catholic parliament, to move his forces south, and Ulster was lost by neglect, even before the 'Curse of Cromwell' descended on Ireland in 1649.

There is no trace now of the two inns, Lockart's and Manair's, that once sustained travellers along these roads, so I push on for Benburb, with the map telling me that the battlefield site is now on Goak Hill. Given its former name, I scan the countryside for thistles but am surrounded by lush meadows and a farm to the right with a big expanse of newly planted tillage and big expansive farm buildings dominating the heights of a sweeping corner on the Drumflugh Road to Benburb village. There is no sign of the river, but I know it is just beyond my horizon. Past a side road signposted for Gortmerron Baptist Church, a small orchard on my right is spilling its autumnal harvest of apples onto a freshly mowed lawn and around several beehives placed between the trees. Then a corner on the road reveals signposts welcoming me to Benburb.

It is a lush entry to the village with the gorge on my right spilling down and then back up in a blanket of trees with leaves ranging from russet to dark green and yellow. Past a landscaped roadside park with information on the flora and fauna, the village opens up, dominated on one side by the priory and the remains of Benburb Castle, and on the other by a picturesque row of cottage-style houses. And nestling at the heart of the village is McAnallen's Spar shop, with the offices of the Cormac Trust above. It is a local Tyrone-based charity dedicated to providing defibrillators, especially to sports and youth clubs, and disseminating information about the risks of cardiac arrest among otherwise young and healthy people. It is a charity born out of a poignant tragedy that created an emotional surge through Tyrone and well beyond. That was the sudden death from heart failure in 2004 of Cormac McAnallen, the newly installed captain of Tyrone's senior Gaelic football team, at the age of 24, just months after he and his team had stormed to victory in their first-ever All-Ireland final.

To understand the full extent of that response, it helps to remember the pivotal role the GAA plays for nationalists in Northern Ireland in the expression of their identity. As seen earlier with the club in Middletown, the GAA is at the core of community life. Further south on Armagh's border with Monaghan, the Crossmaglen Rangers club became a national totem, cited repeatedly by GAA national congress delegates for the retention of a ban on members of the crown security forces, after the British Army occupied part of its grounds for a military heli-base. As peace descended after the ceasefires, Crossmaglen Rangers came into its own. In thirteen years between 1996 and 2013, it won seventeen Armagh senior football titles, ten Ulster provincial titles and six All-Ireland club football championships. When club team manager Joe Kernan moved up to county level, Armagh won its first ever All-Ireland Championship title in 2002, and seemed almost invincible as the Ulster Championship resumed the following year. However, the neighbours in Tyrone had been looking on across the Blackwater, and they wanted a piece of the action too. In 2003, a hard-fought final in Dublin's Croke Park was contested for the first and only time since by two teams from Ulster. Tyrone won, spreading the jubilation to that county in a triumphant homecoming.

As the editor of the newspapers most read by Tyrone nationalists, I was in the thick of the rapturous joy that descended on the community. In those years after the Good Friday Agreement and the horror of the Omagh bombing, the 2003 GAA victory lifted a pall of fear, trepidation, insecurity and mourning. The joy enveloped other sections of the community, and I was particularly struck at the time by the symbolism of the All-Ireland champions of 2002 and 2003. Armagh played in orange jerseys, a deliberate connection with the Orange tradition among their neighbours; Tyrone jerseys bore a crest of the Red Hand of Ulster, ancient symbol of the O'Neill dynasty and a shared symbol with Protestant Ulster. Much mileage was also made of the fact that the Sam Maguire Cup, the trophy that took up residence north of the border for two successive years, was named for a Protestant GAA stalwart from Cork. So while the new playing style of these champions was dismissed as 'puke football' by critics from down south, Ulster enthusiasts recognised that the heavy emphasis on defensive play reflected the history and character of the communities from which it sprang.

Cormac McAnallen's sudden death on 2 March 2004 was a body blow that knocked the wind out of the celebrations. A dedicated and resolute leader, he was an inspirational role model in Tyrone, where he grew up in the Brantry district, and also across the Blackwater in Armagh city, where he worked as a young teacher of history and politics at St Catherine's College and as a youth sport coordinator for the local council. The mourning was shared across the community and beyond the boundaries. I attended the funeral and wrote the following:[67]

> Like a tray of eggs, Brantry is the very heart of Tyrone's drumlin country where higgledy-piggledy roads rise and dip and veer around sharp bends, where every turn holds a promise or a shock. It is country that easily conceals large crowds, enveloping them in the tuck of its braes. It is country that demands singular focus on an event, for it provides few distractions in its narrowed vistas. Eoghan Roe O'Neill knew that. In the folds of the Brantry, he mustered his forces for the 1646 battle named for neighbouring Benburb, a singular victory. They know that still around the Brantry. To this day, they celebrate it in music and words at the Brantry Bard Cultural Centre, a few twists and turns from majestic Brantry Lough, a few more from the comfortable McAnallen home.
>
> Cormac McAnallen knew it well. It was imbued in the very fabric of his heart and soul throughout a too short life. It was there in the passion and dedication he learnt in a family environment

that treasured above all the spiritual and cultural, and the value of kith and kin. It was there in the passionate love and respect for cultural traditions, the language and the sense of place and belonging that the Brantry inspires. Cormac learned that at the knees of his parents, Brendan and Bridget, moving lights of Brantry's pride in its culture. They are meticulous students of its historical legacy, recorded each year in a highly regarded historical journal edited by Brendan and called appropriately *Dúiche Néill* (*O'Neill Country*). From his mother's side, Cormac McAnallen was Cinéal Uí Néill, from the bloodline of Tyrone's greatest family, a people too used to burying heroes cut down in the flush of young manhood or in their greatest hours. On Friday, he joined those heroes as he was laid to rest in a funeral ceremony worthy of the greatest of Cinéal Uí Neill, the Brantry's pride.

They came from the four corners, the great, the good and the humble, and they gathered in a place called simply An t-Eaglais, the Church. They surged around Teach an Phobail, the Mass House built in 1834, among the oldest in all of Tyrone.

It all began shortly after 10am at the McAnallen home, where crowds had come for days to pay homage to their fallen hero. The mortal remains of the pride of Brantry was borne along on the shoulders of his father Brendan, brothers Fergus and Donal, uncles and cousins. The cortège rounded the bend at the foot of the lane and bore along the dead hero between hedgerows poised to burst forth with spring's new life. Two television cameras recorded the passage and stewards held back a small gathering of friends and neighbours waiting to accompany the cortège down the main road between Eglish and Benburb. There was no sense of hierarchy among the mourners at this stage, clustered around the family and Cormac's grieving fiancée Ashlene. But there were familiar and prominent faces – among them Michele Gildernew, local SF MP.

This was an occasion of deep mourning for her, for Gildernews and McAnallens go way back. In 1967, the McAnallens set out to right an injustice that burned at the very heart of the Brantry.

Brothers Sean, Brendan and Dan McAnallen helped to occupy a council house in the nearby village of Caledon. When it was allocated to a young single Protestant woman, secretary to the local unionist MP, they moved in a Catholic family with children, Michelle Gildernew's family, who had been passed over repeatedly for housing. They were joined by the young nationalist MP Austin Currie, the TV cameras arrived and the rest, as they say, became history in the birth of the Civil Rights Association and the too-rapid spill to civil conflict from a vicious backlash. A few short years later, young Dan McAnallen was killed in action and buried in the Brantry with full republican honours.

Such thoughts lingered among the gathering as the cortège passed on the first leg of its procession. While the chief mourners moved off in one direction, others paid their respects in silence and then headed for their cars to negotiate their way into the village along the back roads down by the trout farm. There was a quiet, poignant dignity to it all from the start. Nobody was there simply to be seen. Veteran republican Gerry McGeogh, now farming in the locality, accompanied Geraldine McCabe of the National Graves Association among the neighbours at the head of the lane. He noted in passing how well such sad occasions are conducted: 'Unfortunately, we are probably too well practiced at burying young men about this country.'

In Eglish, the silent crowds waited. Some filtered through to the church grounds when vetted, while stewards urged others to move back to allow room for the hearse. The crowds complied without a murmur of disagreement, then drifted back with the will of the curious and the grieving. Moments later, they had to be reminded once more. Where the village roads meet, Eglish was a sea of silent mourning and, across from the chapel gates, press photographers and TV cameras clambered for height vantages around scaffolding and road signs. The moments ticked away and members of various guards of honour held position – among them schoolgirls of St Catherine's College, Armagh, where Cormac taught, and his club teammates from Eaglais Naomh Pádraig. The designated hour of 11am passed by and still no stir. The wait did not matter. They would do what was right.

Then, like the resumption of a championship final after the half-time break, the teams emerged from the tunnel of the crowd. The Tyrone senior squad, dressed in smart suits, shirts and ties, had come to bury their captain in his native heath. Their All-Ireland rivals, Armagh, also filtered through in a group. The dignity of their presence in mourning spoke volumes. Then the crowds fell silent as the hearse arrived, with only the whirr of digital cameras audible in the silent lull of mourning and respect as the young hero of Brantry was delivered up at last for the final public rites of his passing. There in the heart of his homeland, another hero of the Cinéal Uí Néill was being laid to rest. What preceded the public phase of the event had been carried out with familial caring and dignity. What came with the final obsequies of the Requiem Mass and the interment were fitting public farewells. For here was a hero honoured by fellow heroes, a champion of Cinéal Uí Néill laid to rest in the Brantry ... and an entire nation had come to mourn his passing.

10. Friend or Foe

Benburb to the Moy, via Charlemont – 7.5 km

My final leg of the Ulster Canal was actually its first, starting with the construction of four locks that carried the channel through the deep gorge of the Blackwater River below the walls of Benburb Castle in County Tyrone. On 23 May 1834, in the townland of Carrickaness, just across the river in County Armagh, blasting began in the quarry that would supply the material for construction.[1] According to Brian Cassells's book, *The Ulster Canal*:

> Notable local gentry were in attendance at the opening ceremony at Benburb, including Sir James Stronge from Tynan Abbey. Flags flew, the Royal Standard was hoisted from the old castle at Benburb, once home to the O'Neills of Tyrone. A salute of twenty-one guns rattled out to announce the commencement of work.

It adds that 'During intervals from blasting in the quarry, the local people were liberally supplied with ale'. Over the following years of construction, almost 2,000 navvies and others were employed, most of them local. They earned 9 shillings a week, well above the going rate and almost double the wages available elsewhere in Armagh.[2]

Today, the channel gouged from the gorge languishes in neglect, so stilly green beside the busy, babbling river and overshadowed by towering trees that crowd out the banks and cliff faces on both sides. On the Armagh side, the derelict industrial buildings of Milltown feature a towering chimney stack and disparate pieces of winding and grinding apparatus that are rusting in the sunshine behind 'keep out' notices. They stand opposite a row of terraced houses called Tyrone View. Across the way, a 'for sale' sign is posted in front of a typical Ulster Canal cottage of cut stone and curved frontage. It faces an unused arched bridge over a channel of the canal that is now disrupted by the driveway down to the mill. An 'eco-path' runs along the banks of the Blackwater to a small jetty where somebody has improvised a swing from one of the towering trees. It is a lagoon of peace and solitude, a recess developed for recreation in those heady first days of funding under the EU Programme for Peace and Reconciliation, amid high hopes for tourism. Now the information boards at its entrance are almost obscured by grime and the small sculpture of a face and hands in a 'peekaboo' moment is being blinded by the surrounding foliage. The expectation that day-trippers and tourists might come to walk and enjoy these paths, even in glorious weather, seems hopelessly naïve.

Yet it is by any standards one of the most scenic places in Ireland and, therefore, in the world – a wonderful retreat and place of reflection beneath a sturdy castle and also accessible by forest paths from the parkland surrounding the adjoining Benburb Servite Priory. That retreat and conference centre was built as a manor home by the Bruce family in the 1880s, and served as a British military and US Army hospital during the Second World War, before it was purchased by the Servite Order from Chicago in 1947. Apart from a quartet of young men frolicking about in a couple of canoes and another man walking his dog, Benburb Gorge is as deserted and abandoned as the Ulster Canal itself.

The end of the canal just beyond Charlemont Bridge, whence the Blackwater itself provides the navigation to Lough Neagh, is just a few miles further from the border. Yet is hard to fathom the depths of despair, desperation and the sense of isolation and vulnerability felt by nationalists in a region where bitter sectarian strife stretched back centuries, where the sides were starkly drawn between friend and foe. Abandoned by the Dublin government they supported, they retreated from civic life into an almost forlorn hope that they would eventually be delivered. Two testimonies in the Bureau of Military History archive in Dublin illustrate the plight of those who had taken up arms in the fight for Irish freedom in the immediate aftermath of partition. While the split IRA fought a bitter civil war down south in the aftermath of the Treaty and then got down to the business of building a state, on the other side of the border Jack Shields from Benburb and Charlie McGleenan from Blackwatertown found themselves hunted down by the Special Constabulary, betrayed by erstwhile comrades, shunned by neighbours and even worse.

Jack Shields commanded his Benburb IRA company in 'practical isolation' from battalion headquarters about 8 miles away in Dungannon through a district with a 'most hostile unionist population'.[3] Yet he had managed to establish lines of communication through which the guerrilla army passed on orders and ordnance through mid-Ulster and beyond. Arrested on 12 September 1919, he was taken to Benburb Barracks and on to Belfast in a car hired from James Trodden of Armagh city, a 'sincere Republican', who subsequently refused to hire out to the police.[4] He was sentenced to nine months hard labour by a court martial he refused to recognise, moved from Belfast to Derry, then released on 15 July 1920. Back as a volunteer, he took part in raids, including an attack on Benburb police barracks on the night of 5–6 July 1921, a diversionary manoeuvre to allow other units to hold up a mail train further down the line. The following day, he was arrested again when staying at a house owned by Catholic neighbours who were 'unfriendly to the Republican movement'.[5] This time he was taken to Derry, where prisoners were handcuffed in pairs each night making 'rest or sleep difficult'. He was then taken to the internment camp at Ballykinlar, County Down, a place that invoked 'no pleasant feelings', until the general release in December 1921.

Returning home, Jack Shields learned that Benburb had been transferred from Tyrone's 2nd Northern Division IRA to the 4th Northern (Armagh) Division and merged with the Blackwatertown company under Charlie McGleenan. Until the following May 1922, he was involved in training and arming 'for use if and when the truce ended'. The arsenal was boosted by rifles from divisional headquarters at Dundalk Barracks for a 'general attack on British forces then occupying northern Ireland, the six north-eastern counties'.[6] Meanwhile, his company commander was deploying arms, ammunition and explosives from a 'depot' at Allistragh between Blackwatertown, Moy and Armagh city. Mick Feighan's laundry van was used, and the IRA even had a reserve munitions dump 'for the big plans ahead of us'.[7] However, on 22 May 1922, there was a sudden swoop by British forces. They only got two IRA volunteers from Benburb district, including Jack Shields who was taken to the *Argenta* prison ship in Belfast Lough. The wooden-hull cargo steamship's under-deck had been converted into cages. Among an estimated 300 detainees, Shields was one of forty-five locked in cage P2. With no access to the crammed topside deck in bad weather, the locked-up prisoners were in constant danger of being sunk and drowned. The cages were congested, with no chairs, tables or lockers. Detainees slept in swing hammocks suspended above and below each other and sat on the floor while eating.[8] An open latrine at the end of the cages was a wooden trough washed by seawater. The smell got worse as faecal matter seeped into the bilge.

With his lifelong friend, Eamon Rice from Tyholland, later elected as a Fianna Fáil TD from Monaghan, Shields endured *Argenta* life between June 1922 and December 1923. It became more testing from April 1923, when new arrivals were men who had returned north from fighting on both sides in the Civil War. Factions pursued vendettas, rallying others and 'many miniature battles royal took place'. Finally, when scores of detainees embarked on a hunger strike during October and November 1923, they were removed to Crumlin Road Prison after four or five days fasting. The others on the *Argenta*, including Shields and Rice, were moved to Larne Workhouse. Throughout Northern Ireland, the IRA was deep underground, with no help from mutinous members of the Free State army in the south. But in December 1923, a secret Ulster Federal Army was formed, and it took limited action on 19 February 1924 against the B Specials. This organisation maintained some contact with De Valera and Austin Stack, but 'apparently faded away sometime in 1926'.[9]

In a top-floor Larne Workhouse room with broken windows, Shields, Rice and fifteen others lay on floor mattresses and once awoke covered in snow. Rice commented that his brother's cows were better looked-after.[10] Finally, Shields was released on 13 November 1924. Another Tyrone internee fared even worse because of constant harassment of his family during his detention. He told Shields the tormentors included unionists, who made up more than half the local population, and nationalists cowed by the Specials. Even a local Catholic priest treated the family like outcasts, so his wife went to Larne to see her husband. When telling Shields this, the man exclaimed, 'I have had to sign the form (promising good future behaviour) ... I have renounced all I have fought and suffered for: I have eaten dirt.'[11]

Meanwhile, as IRA forces mustered along the border for invasion in mid-1922, McGleenan travelled in Feighan's laundry van to the Keady IRA camp near Castleblayney before going on to Dundalk Barracks, the new HQ of the 4th Northern Division. From there, he was posted to a border camp at Dungooley, taking part in raids into south Armagh with Mullaghbawn Company. Finally, he moved on to Castleshane, where his own men had gathered with others from 3rd Brigade, 4th Northern Division. He was in charge there until the Free State raid, when most captives were taken to an internment camp at Ballybay. McGleenan and Frank Hannaway, as 'officers of the IRA', were taken to the Newbridge internment camp in Kildare.

Before long, McGleenan and others escaped by tunnel and made their getaway 'through a hail of bullets'. They were recaptured at Amiens Street railway station in Dublin, gave false names and were questioned at Wellington Barracks, where detainees were badly beaten in the 'knocking shop': 'I was told that some of the prisoners in Wellington had their heads nearly kicked off them in the "knocking shop", especially one fellow named Coyle from Derry City.'[12] Others fared even worse. Four Dublin 'boys' were taken out to face 'a firing party composed of former pals who sent them to eternity because they were loyal to the Republic', and to pave the way for the execution of Erskine Childers.[13] McGleenan observed, 'From the time I joined the Volunteers first, those executions were the hardest blow off all, as it showed the reality of the IRA split in all its grimness.'[14]

When McGleenan was moved to Harepark internment camp in the Curragh, the adjutant called McAllister from south Down related that customs huts were being erected. When McGleenan said this was 'recognising the border', McAllister replied that the Boundary Commission would soon bring in Tyrone, Fermanagh, south Armagh and south Down. McGleenan asked McAllister if he would resign his Free State army commission if south Down wasn't moved, and 'after some discussions in which he got a bit heated, he walked away' and 'never bothered about me again'.[15] On his release in May 1924, McGleenan was escorted from the camp by a Captain Hughes, who had grown up near Castleshane and who gave him 'wise advice' not to cross the border or he would be arrested. So he went back to County Monaghan, where he 'was welcomed in more houses than one'.[16] On GHQ orders, he set about reorganising the IRA's Monaghan Brigade from May 1924 until January 1926. At one point, when arrested in Roslea and taken to the barracks, which accommodated fifty-nine Special Constables, he gave his name as Pat McCabe of the Mall Road in Monaghan town. This was confirmed by the police 'intelligence officer'. However, that implicated him in the burning of Roslea barracks, which he admitted after some argument, and he was then released with an exclusion order.[17]

Returning home after the Free State formally recognised the border in December 1925, he was arrested again and taken to Crumlin Road Prison, where he was shown complaints from neighbours, 'who did not want me back near them'.[18] Finally, he was brought before the governor and 'a man from the Home Office who had … the usual order for me to clear out of the six counties except I was prepared to live in a prescribed place in County Antrim'. McGleenan said he would go home and would continue to do so even though they doubled his sentence each time. The governor then asked where he wanted his railway voucher for and he said Armagh. 'I can't do that,' said the governor. 'Well then, make it out for Monaghan and I'll leave the train at Armagh.' The voucher said Monaghan, McGleenan got off at Richhill and walked home from there to Ballytrodden and was informed later that he was free to live there. As for his neighbours:

> I must say that my unionist neighbours, to all outward appearances, were very nice to me and, in fact, some of them came to help me at threshing and such work without being

asked to do so by me. I settled down to my work as a farmer, but never forgetting that I was a soldier of the Irish Republic.

While the forces of Irish republicanism were otherwise engaged, of course, partition was consolidated. By the start of 1925, the 'provisional' border had grown more permanent when the Free State government deployed additional Civic Guards to twenty-three frontier towns to assist in collecting customs duties and preventing smuggling.[19] Northern Ireland voters went to the polls in April while the Boundary Commission was conducting hearings and Belfast nationalist leader Joe Devlin undertook to lead his MPs into the Northern Ireland parliament. Even though the *Irish News* said he could have had Dáil seats for the asking, Devlin said his 'first and highest allegiances were to his own persecuted, victimised people'.[20] Also in the North, Craig committed £2,250,000 to maintain his Special Constabulary until September 1926, even though London would finance only £500,000 of that.[21] Craig then told a meeting in Aughnacloy that the Specials would never be disbanded so long as he was in charge. The full-time Royal Ulster Constabulary had by then become a force of 2,990, of whom 541 were Catholic, many of those former RIC officers with strong unionist sympathies.[22] While the border itself had become an almost impregnable armed camp, the security net spread inland as the prospects of transfers of territory to the South became imminent. Unionist MP Major D.G. Shillington was able to inform parliament approvingly that when travelling between Armagh and Belfast on a 'miserably dirty night', he had been stopped by no fewer than fifteen different patrols of B Specials.[23]

Among many strongholds of Special Constabulary in Armagh was Todds Corner, a rural area between Benburb and Armagh city. According to Charlie McGleenan, commander of the IRA's Blackwatertown company, which now incorporated Benburb, 'In this unionist locality all the farmers or their sons were armed members of the B Specials.'[24] That didn't deter McGleenan and his men from pursuing two Specials they suspected of having shot and wounded local republican leader John Garvey. The IRA shot them both, wounding one and killing the other, 18-year-old Samuel Milligan, at his home.

In all, seventy-two of the total ninety-five members in the Special Constabulary Roll of Honour were slain during the war with the IRA along the border in those early years. Yet the Special Constabulary stood firm to maintain the border for half a century before its eventual disbandment following the Hunt Report in 1970. Nor were they just a rag-tag army of subsistence farmers, clerks and labourers, but a formidable body of trained military ex-servicemen commanded by commissioned officers who had been decorated for valour. Those officers were mostly 'big house' unionists with a considerable stake in maintaining the border at all costs.

Although born at Clayton in Contra Costa County, California on 3 August 1878, the son of a Wells Fargo Railway Company engineer, Charles Howard Ensor was comfortably at home in Ardress House. From the gable windows of the original plantation dwelling, which had been doubled and restyled into a Regency mansion by an architect ancestor, he had a panoramic view of his command as head of Armagh's Special Constabulary. From that elevated site, the county spills south towards Sliabh Gullion and the border with County Louth. To the west, the countryside envelops another border with Monaghan, while the housefront presents a secure eastward vista towards Portadown. Captain Ensor's northern flank, meanwhile, was set against Lough Neagh, providing him with a secure redoubt from which he commanded the Armagh platoons of the Special Constabulary from their formation until his retirement in 1952, aged 74.

Formally announced in late 1920, even before the border was established, the Special Constabulary incorporated informal vigilante groups largely composed of former members of the Ulster Volunteer Force. That meant an immediate supply of weapons from the UVF armoury, provided by former Quartermaster General Wilfrid Spender, who was appointed by Sir William Craig as head of the new force.[25] Captain Ensor had served as a UVF company commander for ten months prior to enlisting with the 9th Royal Irish Fusiliers, with a commission as Second Lieutenant on 15 September 1914. Wounded on the first day of the Battle of the Somme, he lay in a shell hole for four days, part of it while submerged up to his armpits, before he was rescued. His wounds precluded further front-line duty; he was eventually demobilised with the rank of captain in 1919. Shortly thereafter, he was appointed Armagh county commandant of the Special Constabulary.

At full establishment, the Special Constabulary consisted of three classes – 5,500 A Specials deployed mostly to border areas as full-time paid police officers backing up the RIC/RUC; almost 20,000 B Specials organised in local platoons of paid part-time members; and roughly 7,500 C Specials, an unpaid force of usually older reservists called up for static duties near their homes. In late 1921, a supplementary C1 class was added to the Special Constabulary as a non-active reserve for emergencies, made up of unionist militias, including the UVF.[26] So while the unionist government was precluded from raising military forces, it soon had a force of 50,000 regular and part-time policemen under its control, yet paid for by the Treasury in London; that is, one policeman for every six families, or one for every two Catholic families in the six counties.[27]

In those early years, the strategic alliance of unionist bourgeoisie and British ruling classes had created a state with a 'sectarian-populist flavour' and 'repressive' security.[28] At the height of the IRA's border offensive in April 1922, Major-General Sir Richard Solly-Flood was appointed as Military Adviser to the Northern Ireland government at the behest of 'ultra-imperialist and ultra-reactionary' Sir Henry Wilson, chief of the Imperial General Staff, who almost simultaneously resigned to become unionist MP for North Down. Wilson had already observed to Sir Neville Macready that the Special Constabulary would need strict outside discipline: 'To arm those "Black men" in the north without putting them under discipline is to invite trouble.'[29] In a diary observation, he noted that it would mean 'taking sides', with 'civil war and savage reprisals'.[30]

Solly-Flood took on his role with gusto, to the annoyance of local Special Constabulary commandants, three of whom resigned.[31] He described the B Specials as a 'sedentary force', whose 'ability is greatly impaired by their lack of commanders, discipline and training'. By the end of June, however, his position was weakened after Wilson's assassination in London. Two London-based IRA members shot the field marshal outside his home but were captured, convicted and hanged.[32] Unbeknownst to defence minister Richard Mulcahy, Collins is believed to have ordered the assassination because of ongoing assaults on nationalists in the north.[33] London Metropolitan police investigations centred on Collins's chief intelligence officer in London, Sam Maguire, the Cork Protestant honoured in the eponymous GAA trophy.[34] In September, the unionist leadership decided to centralise security under RUC Inspector-General Charles Wickham. Solly-Flood quit. However, he passed on his criticisms to the War Office, and his staff continued to leak evidence of serious wrongdoing in the police and Special Constabulary, including murders of Catholics and floggings of IRA suspects under the Civil Authorities (Special Powers) Act. That compendium of statutory powers had been enacted on 7 April 1922, allowing internment and summary jurisdiction with sentences of penal servitude and death.

Solly-Flood's reports had raised disquiet in London. From the War Office, Lord Derby dispatched General Sir Archibald Montgomery in early 1923 to enquire into Northern Ireland's security. The unionist reactionaries were appalled, and as late as 14 December 1925, this was seen as a major wrong. The commandant of the B Specials' Loughgall company wrote to Sir Wilfrid Spender:

> There was a flavour of the late Military Adviser's [Solly-Flood's] opinions in General Montgomery we did not like. Any voluntary force like the 'B' force is a delicate instrument needing to be played skilfully not banged on; and whatever their shortcomings, they don't like to be told they are no good and must either be swept away or completely reorganised, officers and all.[35]

By January 1925, the permanent British Army garrison in Northern Ireland had been reduced to one brigade of five battalions, with a battery of howitzers and an armoured car company, totalling about 3,000 men.[36] A second brigade of four battalions with artillery would be sent in if needed. Border security was firmly in the hands of the Special Constabulary, and since April 1924, the B Specials' strength had been established at a total of 19,950 men, heavily concentrated along the border. Of these, 3,630 were in Tyrone, 3,200 in Armagh, 2,700 in Fermanagh, 1,350 in Derry city, 2,150 in County Derry, and 2,750 in County Down. Rates of pay were fixed at £3 a year for reserves, £7 for 'half patrol' and £10 for 'full patrol', meaning one night in every twenty or ten, respectively.[37] Backed up by another 20,000 A and C Specials, the B men exerted a 'powerful influence' on the deliberations of the Boundary Commission, with Craig declaring that in the event of an 'unfavourable' report, he would resign as premier and 'take any necessary steps' to hold the border with this armed force.[38]

Yet it was the A section of that very force that posed the most imminent threat to the new northern state after the Boundary Commission was neutralised and shelved in late 1925. With the Free State's acceptance of the border, Craig informed Colonial Secretary Winston Churchill that he would start winding up the Special Constabulary.[39] The A Specials would go first, and Craig asked London for a final allocation of two-months' full pay for each of the 3,553 A Specials.[40] He also appealed to employers to give them jobs. Westminster had already picked up the tab of £700,000 for arms, ammunition and equipment. It now agreed to pay a further £1.2 million for disbandment. Indeed, the British government had already armed and paid for the Specials at a total cumulative cost of £6,780,000, meaning Craig's government had a paramilitary 'army' at its disposal for five years at a total cost of only £720,000 from its own coffers.[41]

The redundancy agreement did not sit well with some A Specials, who demanded three-months' pay. Some mutinied, placed their own officers under arrest and took control of their armouries and stores.[42] When their representatives met, they demanded a £200 tax-free bonus on disbandment, offering in return not to claim dole for a year. Finally, on 18 December 1925, Home Affairs Minister Lord Londonderry issued an ultimatum that further 'displays … of insubordination' would be met with immediate dismissal and loss of the proposed pay-off. The revolt by these 'unlikely rebels' collapsed the following day, and by Christmas Day 1925, the A Specials had been disbanded.[43]

The B Specials remained as a standing army of Protestants committed to defending the frontiers of Northern Ireland. Already, they were regarded by most Protestants as the 'men who saved Ulster', and their reputation flourished over succeeding decades. On the other side, so did their fearsome reputation as a body composed of suspicious, intimidating and dangerous neighbours. For although two initial efforts had been made at the behest of Westminster to recruit Catholics to the B Specials – at the inception in 1920 and again in 1922 – it remained a wholly Protestant force for the remainder of its history. No subsequent efforts were made, and unionist spokesmen are recorded proclaiming its Protestant loyalty at Orange gatherings, in the Stormont parliament and in London. In the first instance, Sir James Craig himself declared on the Twelfth in 1922, 'It is also from the ranks of the Loyal Orange Institution that our splendid Specials have come.'[44] Then William Grant MP confirmed in the Stormont chamber that the composition had not changed by 1936, when he said, 'There are no Roman Catholics among the Special Constabulary.'[45] Finally, in 1947, Edmond Warnock, Stormont's attorney general, qualified the Orange association when he told a London press conference that 'The B Specials were exclusively Protestant', but he denied they were recruited from Orange Lodges, although they all "belonged to his side of the House".'[46]

As with the RUC and UDR, some argue that this exclusively Protestant composition was a consequence of intimidation and unwillingness of Catholics to join, rather than fixed policy. Military historian Sir Arthur Hezlet points out, however, that while Catholics did not want to join, 'undoubtedly many Specials would rather not have had Roman Catholics for security reasons'.[47] The Hunt committee found that 'whilst there is no law or official rule that precludes any person, whatever his religion, from joining the USC, the fact remains that for a variety of reasons no Roman Catholic is a member'.[48]

While the Ulster Special Constabulary did not change in composition, they went through a radical remake during the Second World War, when they became the Ulster Home Guard. It was a straight swap, with the commandant of the Special Constabulary in Armagh, Captain Ensor, assuming the title of commandant of the county's four battalions of the Home Guard. However, unlike in Britain, where it was part of the military establishment as a rearguard defence force, the Home Guard in Northern Ireland was kept firmly under police rather than military control, thereby ensuring local unionist rather than London authority.[49] Then with the outbreak of the 1950s Troubles, beginning with Saor Uladh's attacks on six border customs posts, followed by the IRA's Operation Harvest with ten simultaneous attacks in border areas, the B Specials were mobilised once more. From December 1956 until February 1962, they kept up a constant schedule of patrols and checkpoints on border roads. Six regular members of the RUC were killed in that campaign, along with eight IRA volunteers and two members of Saor Uladh. There were no fatalities among the Specials, which were described by my former editor at the *Irish Press*, popular historian Tim Pat Coogan in a 2002 book, as 'the rock on which ... the IRA in the North has inevitably foundered'.[50]

The Hunt Report of October 1969 is the rock on which the B Specials foundered, shortly after the shooting death in Armagh of 30-year-old factory worker and father of three John Gallagher by a group of seventeen poorly trained and panicked B Specials from Tynan. They had been ordered to the scene of a riot on Cathedral Road, crashed through a makeshift barricade, and believed they were isolated. The B Specials let loose two 'ragged bursts' of gunfire, hitting Gallagher in the back and injuring two other men.[51] Twelve of the Specials testified before the Scarman Tribunal that they had 'fired into the air', while another had accidentally shot his machinegun 'into the ground'. Then they had gone to an RUC station, cleaned their weapons and deliberately failed to report the shooting by saying they were elsewhere. The Scarman Report largely exonerated them because they were an 'untrained but armed party ... drawn from a country area into an alarming town riot without briefing or leadership', and they succumbed to 'a state of panic' that was 'certainly consistent with a sense of guilt'. The state of panic spread from this atrocity, impinging on the early memory of journalist Sean O'Hagan, who recalls how 'unprecedented that first violent death in Armagh was' at the start of the modern conflict.[52] It was also recorded in the police records as the 'first official fatality of the Troubles', although it comes tenth in the detailed and exhaustive tome *Lost Lives*.

From Blackwatertown, the Ulster Canal's course ran through the townlands of Tullykeevan, Crocknamoyle, Shanamullagh, Corr and

Dunavally to Charlemont, passing under Tullykeevan Bridge and Miller's Bridge. Today, the B106 road closely follows that course until it merges with the main A29 Moy Road as the canal veers off across the B28 Collegelands Road to meet the Blackwater once more at the final Charlemont Lock. It passes within a very short distance of Aghanlig, where on the evening of 19 February 1974, Pat Molloy was enjoying a quiet drink in Traynors' Bar with his long-time friend Jack Wylie. Pat rose from the bench seat they were sharing in front of the bar and remarked to the owner: 'Some of your children must have put something on the fire, for I smell burning.'[53] The owner turned to investigate and was propelled forward and buried in the rubble of a blast that demolished the front of the building. The owner survived. Pat Molloy and Jack Wylie were found dead in the rubble. They made a gruesome even score of the bloodletting in a tally of just over a thousand fatalities by that time. Pat from Allistragh was a Catholic family man and an enthusiastic GAA supporter, while his close friend Jack, from Kilmore, was a member of the Diamond Memorial Orange Lodge in Loughgall District.[54]

The investigation into the bombing of Traynors' bar, which was incorrectly attributed to the UDA/UFF at the time, was called off in October 1974. Six years later, a neighbour of Jack Wylie, who was connected to the UVF-affiliated Glennane Gang, was arrested and taken to Gough Barracks, where he was interrogated over five days.[55] On 29 April 1980, Stuart Ashton admitted his involvement in the bar explosion, among other crimes. He had been working at a Loughgall quarry owned by William George 'Geordie' Elliott, and so he had access to explosives. Ashton assembled the bomb that killed Wylie and Molloy at the home of Edward Tate Sinclair, an Orangeman and former B Special. He named others as being involved in the attack, including members of the police and UDR. He said he had then driven the bomb the 4 kilometres to Traynors' in his own car, placed it outside the front door of the bar, which was attached to the Traynors' family home and a shop, with petrol pumps on the other side, lit the fuse and drove off. He even admitted hearing people talking inside as he delivered death to their door.[56] For his combined crimes, Ashton served fifteen years in jail, where he became an evangelical Christian and was freed in March 1993.

Sinclair, in whose home the bomb was assembled, was never convicted of the Traynors' bombing, but he had been jailed previously for other crimes, including possession of a gun used in the massacre of Brian McCoy and other members of The Miami band. He only served three years and he died of natural causes in 1985. Others affected by the bombing have served a life sentence, including Pat Molloy's then 19-year-old daughter Patricia, whose wedding day was imminent when her dad was killed. She married in private and still recalls how the photographer remarked that, while he understood the tragic circumstances, 'couldn't she just smile a bit?'[57]

Meanwhile Geordie Elliott, the Loughgall quarry owner who had employed Ashton, was shot dead on 30 June 1980 while examining some cattle he had bought at Ballybay Mart, across the border in County Monaghan.[58] A former member of the UDR, Elliott frequented Ballybay to buy cattle. He had been an executive member of the Official Unionist Party, and a former vice chairman of the Armagh Unionist Association. With Unionist Party backing, his family subsequently took an action against the Dublin government in the European Court of Human Rights for allegedly encouraging terrorism by its policies on extradition. The case was argued by the Unionist Party's young legal adviser Edgar Graham, who published a pamphlet called, *Ireland and Extradition: A Protection for Terrorists*. It declared:

> It is clear beyond any reasonable doubt that much of the violence in Northern Ireland emanates from the Irish Republic. In the period between January 1978 and June 1981, 35 per cent of the deaths resulting from terrorism in Northern Ireland occurred within a zone of twenty kilometres of the land frontier with the Irish Republic. County Monaghan, in particular, acts as a stockpile of IRA munitions and they strike out from it into Northern Ireland. The cases which have actually been dealt with under the Criminal Law (Jurisdiction) Act show the preponderance of terrorists who come from County Monaghan.[59]

Edgar Graham was shot dead by the IRA in December 1983 outside the library at Queen's University Belfast, where he was a law lecturer.[60]

Meanwhile, a 25-year-old man from County Armagh living in Monaghan was convicted in Dublin's Special Criminal Court for Geordie Elliott's murder and sentenced to life imprisonment. A second man had his life sentence quashed on appeal. However, according to Chief Superintendent Tom Connolly, one of the Garda team who investigated the Ballybay Mart shooting, the chief suspect was himself later 'shot dead during the course of an IRA attack on the RUC station in Loughgall' on 20 August 1988.[61]

The Ulster Canal comes to an end at Charlemont lock, where it eases its way at last into the River Blackwater for the final navigation to Lough Neagh. By 1840, company reports state that there were fifteen boats working the canal, each capable of carrying 20 tons and a further five boats were in various stages of commission and construction from the Moy boatyard.[62] Two of these boats were plying the canal from the Moy to Monaghan twice a week, while the formidable steamer *Countess of Caledon* was providing passenger services between Verners Bridge on the Blackwater and Portadown, connecting with morning train services to Belfast. As the railways forged west, however, the dream of a bustling Ulster Canal sank beneath the waves. By 1858, Moy was connected, albeit at a distance of 3 kilometres from the village, to the Portadown, Dungannon and the Omagh Junction Railway (PD&O), which eight years later was absorbed into the Great Northern Railway. Soon, the dry dock at the Moy boatyard became redundant, as over time did the lock-keeper's cottage at the Charlemont confluence.

The slipway beside Charlemont Bridge provides a riverside resting place for a lone angler on a warm summer bank holiday. Stretched out and reclined fully with his back on the dry concrete, his fishing rod and tackle box resting beside him, he stirs at my casual greeting and replies in a heavily accented Eastern European voice, 'Yes, it's a nice day, but no fish.' One of a huge population of migrant workers living in the east Tyrone/north Armagh region, this riverbank fisherman tells me he works for the huge local food-processor, Moy Park, and he comes from Lithuania. That puts him among the 6,500 Moy Park employees in Northern Ireland, overwhelmingly concentrated in the Dungannon-to-Portadown corridor, and heavily made up of people from other EU countries. Their industry and personal livelihoods have already been thrown into turmoil by Brexit. With the entire agribusiness sector, there are huge concerns about the future prospects for food exports on the UK's departure from the single market. Meanwhile, the value of earnings and the regular remittances to families back home have been falling as sterling weakens against the euro. Even if he can stay in the UK on Theresa May's guarantee of amnesty for three years' residence, his freedom to travel socially from his home in the Moy will be severely curtailed, possibly cutting off his regular contact with the Lithuanian community across the border in Monaghan. Throughout the food industry, meanwhile, there are also huge concerns for the seasonal migration that is the mainstay of harvesting produce such as soft fruits, which cannot attract enough indigenous workers with the skills and patience for the job. Resting in the sun on the bank of the Blackwater River, the lone angler shakes his head with worry as we discuss the immediate future of the food sector that provides so many mutual benefits in this rural economy. We speculate that Moy Park, one of Europe's leading food processors with an estimated 12,000 employees across the Continent is probably too big and too diversified to fail.

Within a couple of weeks from our brief conversation, however, news breaks that Moy Park is on the market again, just two years after it was bought by Brazil-based JBS for €1.5 billion (£945 million).[63] As the unions expressed fears for their members, leading local economist John Simpson called it a 'worrying development' because of the negative Brexit impact, not least on the trade in grains used for poultry and animal feeds. Even before the Brexit vote, however, there were loud and persistent warnings that Moy Park's future would be gravely jeopardised by leaving the European Union.[64] Chief Executive Janet McCollum said, 'The EU has imperfections but it is a massive market which offers export security and the UK needs to remain within it.' A year later, during a Westminster debate on the impact of Brexit on poultry producers, Ian Paisley MP quantified Moy Park's contribution to the economy, saying its staff bill is £226 million in a population of only 1.7 million.[65] The loss of those earnings would be devastating to local economies in the region.

It would not be the first devastation to visit the district. The twin villages straddled by Charlemont Bridge over the Blackwater stand in a spot where two civilisation clashed in a fight to the death. At the very start of the seventeenth century, Charles Blount built a fort here and named it in his own honour as Charlemont. It faced across the stream at the Gaelic kingdom of Tír Eoghain, home of the recalcitrant earl of Tyrone, Hugh, the Great O'Neill. From here, the invading forces of Blount, better known as Lord Mountjoy, watched flames lick the sky as O'Neill razed his stronghold at Dungannon, about half a dozen Irish miles distant, and repaired to the woods rather than see it fall into English hands.

Nowadays, the Moy is an attractive village ranged around its rectangular square, which once hosted a monthly horse fair that lasted a full week. Today, it is marred only by the constant stream of traffic on the main A29 road from Dungannon to Armagh city. Yet beneath the outer façade of attractive coffee shops, antique outlets and village stores, the Moy carries an unenviable legacy from the time when it was the very core of the 'Murder Triangle'. Many of the Moy murders were family-related, the assassination targets identified because of links, or assumed links, to republican activists. Many of them were innocent, peaceful, vulnerable couples gunned down in ruthless attacks.

The reign of terror began on 5 August 1973 when Francis and Bernadette Mullen were caught in a hail of gunfire at their farmhouse in Broughadowey, a townland just outside the Moy.[66] Their 2-year-old son was struck by four bullets in the leg as he stood between them, and was later found by his older sibling crying over their bodies. In their 1975 pamphlet *The Triangle of Death: Sectarian Assassinations in the Dungannon-Moy-Portadown Area*, Denis Faul and Raymond Murray wrote, 'This double assassination and the failure to arrest or intern a single suspect, made the Catholic people realise that the RUC and the British Army had no interest in stopping the sectarian assassinations, which were serving a useful purpose.'[67]

Two years later, a short distance from the Mullen farm in Listamlet, Peter and Jane McKearney were shot dead by a gunman with a Sterling machine gun.[68] The man convicted for these murders and other crimes was linked to the infamous Glennane Gang, with its police and military connections. In this instance, the killings were associated with the failed extradition from Dublin of an unrelated young Moy woman, Margaret McKearney, who was under threat that the UVF would 'eliminate' her. I knew Maggie when we were neighbours in a suburban district of Dublin in the early 1980s, and at no stage saw anything to justify Scotland Yard's description of her as 'possibly the most dangerous woman terrorist in Britain'.[69] On the contrary, I recall her as an exceptionally bright, friendly and hard-working young mother who wasn't even 'in Britain'.

The Glennane Gang was also behind two pub attacks on 15 May 1976 at Charlemont, which targeted Clancys' Bar with three fatalities, including the owner, widower Felix 'Vincy' Clancy, 54, and two customers, Robert McCullough, a single man of 41, and Sean O'Hagan, 22 years old from Loughgall, married and a keen Gaelic footballer.[70] As the UVF bombers drove off, they raked the adjacent Eagle Bar with gunfire and struck Frederick McLoughlin. The 48-year-old creamery manager, convert to Catholicism and father of four from Benburb, died from his wounds on 1 June 1976.[71] His son Jim described that lingering death as a 'nightmare'.[72] Two men, Garfield Gerard Beattie and David Henry Dalziel Kane, with links to the security forces, were convicted and given life sentences for Fred McLoughlin's murder. Neither was charged for the simultaneous attack on Clancys' Bar, even though they were directly implicated in the subsequent conviction of Joseph Norman Lutton, an RUC Reserve constable and former customer in Clancys'.[73]

The attack on the Charlemont pubs appears to have prompted a rapid sectarian response in the killing of Robert and Thomas Dobson, Protestant brothers and family men in their thirties at their egg-packing factory in the Moy.[74] They were targeted as they sat at their desks at 10 a.m. on 17 May 1976, and their deaths were described in the *Guardian* as 'cold-blooded sectarianism'. Then followed a lengthy lull in the bloodletting in this locality, until Christmas week of 1991, when 19-year-old student Robin Farmer, a Protestant, was shot dead while helping out in his father's field and fishing sports shop after coming home from Strathclyde University in Scotland.[75] The young man pushed aside his father, a reserve policeman, and was struck by the four bullets fired by an INLA gunman from Armagh city, who was then trapped by an electric lock and subdued by the shop manager with a legally held weapon while he reportedly 'screamed for mercy'. The gunman received a life sentence.

The following month, on 3 January 1992, the Moy bloodletting resumed in the fatal shooting of John and Kevin McKearney in their family butchers shop in the square. Kevin, 32 and married with four children died instantly.[76] His uncle John 'Jack' McKearney, 69, lingered until 4 April, when he died from wounds he received in the attack.[77] The targeting was deliberate, for they were the uncle and brother of Margaret McKearney; Sean McKearney who died when a bomb he was transporting exploded outside Dungannon in May 1974; 1980 IRA hunger striker Tommy McKearney; as well as Padraig McKearney, killed in the Loughgall ambush of May 1987.[78] In a concluding act of this macabre sequence for the tiny community of the Moy and Charlemont, Charlie Fox (63) and Tess Fox (53) were shot dead at their Listhamlet home on 6 September 1992.[79] Kevin McKearney was their son-in-law and their son Paddy Fox had just been sentenced to ten years for possession of a bomb in Dungannon. He blamed security forces' collusion for setting up his family for UVF assassination 'callously designed to instil fear in the nationalist community on the one hand, and to distract the IRA away from the war against the British establishment and into a sectarian war'. A senior UVF member was later convicted for the double murder. A final observation that knits up this tangled web of bloody terror is that Charlie and Tess Fox were among the first at the home of neighbours Peter and Jane McKearney when they were gunned down in 1975.

When the police Historical Enquiries Team (HET) report on the murders of Kevin McKearney and his uncle Jack was made public in 2012, Ulster unionist peer and former UDR officer Lord Ken Magennis slammed it as 'slovenly and speculative'.[80] He pointed to the victims' family connections with the IRA, saying they 'set the scene for much of the carnage that Moy village had to endure'. He then listed the Moy's Protestant victims – the two Dobson brothers; Robin Farmer; Geordie Elliott, killed in Ballybay; Cyril 'George' McCaul, killed in 1973 when his car crashed into an IRA roadblock; Fred Irwin, a part-time UDR soldier shot dead in Dungannon in 1979; Roy Leslie, a young

RUC constable shot dead in Strabane in 1971; and Jack Donnelly, a prominent Ulster unionist and a founding member of the UDR, who was shot dead by the INLA on 16 April 1981 while sitting in his local pub, Hughes' Bar in the Moy. At the time of Donnelly's death, Lord Magennis's colleague in the Ulster unionist peerage, Lord Kilclooney (aka John Taylor), remarked that loyalists in the Moy area 'lived amongst 30,000 potential accomplices of murder'.[81]

Loyalists had other concerns by the mid-1980s, as the Anglo-Irish Agreement was signed at Hillsborough, giving a consultative role in Northern Ireland affairs to the Dublin government. While Sinn Féin harnessed the bitter disappointment and political energy of the 1980/1981 hunger strikes into electoral gains that began to shift the balance of power in council chambers, the loyalist hegemony of civic space was broken at last during the era of direct rule.

Since the 1972 dissolution of the Stormont regime, unionism had fragmented into an assortment of internal factions and external challengers – Official Unionist, Vanguard Unionist, Democratic Unionist, Volunteer Unionist, Unionist Party of Northern Ireland, Ulster (Loyalist) Democratic Party, Popular Unionist Party, Progressive Unionist Party and United Ulster Unionist Party. By the mid-1980s, they had coalesced into two main competing groups, the Ulster Unionist Party under Jim Molyneaux and the Democratic Unionist Party led by Ian Paisley. These now came together in an apparently unassailable alliance of unionism around the 'Ulster Says No' campaign against the Hillsborough accord. That united front masked a decisive blow to the heart of loyalism delivered by none other than Margaret Thatcher's Conservative government. It was the Public Order (Northern Ireland) Order 1987, which removed the unqualified legal protection for the loyal orders under the Northern Ireland Public Order Act (1951) to parade wherever and whenever they wished.[82] The 1951 act had allowed the Orange, Black and Apprentice Boys to march along their chosen 'traditional routes' without any requirement of prior notification or any recognition of the local residents they might offend in doing so. These processional rights of loyal orders were withdrawn from that point in 1987, and a requirement that they notify police one week in advance was imposed. Moreover, the new public order gave the RUC similar powers to deal with unruly behaviour as police forces in Britain had already been given to deal with the miners' strikes there.

Through the concluding years of the conflict and well beyond, the issue of parading has dominated Northern Ireland politics. The epicentre of the storm is Portadown, self-styled Citadel of Orangeism, a title assumed because of its proximity to Loughgall and the site of the Battle of the Diamond. Yet the symbolic importance of Portadown in Ulster loyalism goes back centuries to the oft-exaggerated, but nonetheless atrocious, massacre of Protestants who were drowned in the River Bann during the Catholic uprising of 1641. Today, the market town straddles the Bann, its centre on the west bank and its population ratio – 32 per cent nationalist – roughly reflecting the historic demography of partition. Because of its location on the cusp of where the map and its political constituencies fade from bright orange to deep green, Portadown remains a contested frontier within the divided province of Ulster.

Down the decades since the Loyal Orange Lodge began its marching tradition in 1796, Portadown has been the scene of frequent disruptions, confrontations and riots, nowhere more frequently than at Obins Street, an area known as the Tunnel for the underpasses of the Northway Road and railway bridges in the town centre. It was this neighbourhood that my own grandparents forsook with their two eldest children when they moved to Clones just before partition. It was here that Catholic residents holding a sit-down protest on 7 July 1985 were forcefully removed by riot police when they tried to prevent an Orange parade following its traditional route through their area to Drumcree. A week later, when their Twelfth parade was blocked and diverted away from Obins Street, it was the Orangemen who clashed with police in riots lasting two days and resulting in multiple arrests and injuries. The following year, on 1 April, a huge crowd of loyalists forced their way past police and marched along Obins Street in the middle of the night. Police allowed a parade there on 3 July, then banned others on 12 and 13 July, leading to almost a week of continuing riots. The conflict between loyalist rights and public order, led Westminster to enact new rules of engagement with increased police power and authority in 1987.

However, the pattern of the imposition of police strictures followed by reversals in the face of mass loyalist action was repeated almost a decade later. In 1995, it played out again in Portadown in what became known as the 'Drumcree crisis'. Although these parades through nationalist districts were long-standing traditions providing 'an empowering sense of unity to diverse sections of unionism', they could not be sustained.[83] Yet it took global outrage to halt the mayhem. When the RUC banned the pre-Twelfth march to Drumcree parish church, returning along the Garvaghy Road, an overwhelmingly nationalist area leading into the Tunnel, the lines were drawn. Two thousand police officers met a barrage of bottles and stones from loyalist protesters, and replied with plastic bullets and tear gas. The police relented under Orange pressure, and unionist leaders David Trimble and Ian Paisley led the parade holding hands in what was seen as a triumphalist gesture, but which Trimble insisted signalled relief from the tension.[84] In 1996, there was another violent standoff between police and Orangemen, with about 10,000 of their loyalist supporters. As rioting spread, loyalists murdered Catholic taxi driver Michael McGoldrick.[85] Again the police reversed their prohibition on the parade proceeding down Garvaghy Road; again there was widespread rioting, this time from the nationalists, with the police accused of using 'excessive force' in quelling residents' opposition to the Orange parade past their homes.

In a prelude to the Drumcree parade in 1997, a Catholic man Robert Hamill was kicked to death by a loyalist gang in Portadown while police officers watched.[86] Then as the parade loomed, police and British soldiers swept into Garvaghy Road in the early hours of the morning. Among those injured by police forcibly dragging protesters off the road was human rights lawyer Rosemary Nelson, who was subsequently murdered by loyalists in a booby-trap bombing in March 1999.[87] As police barricades confined Catholic residents into their homes, the 1,200-strong Orange parade took place on Sunday, 6 July 1997. Rioting ensued for days throughout nationalist areas. That was the last time the Orange marched Garvaghy Road. As tensions rose again the following year amidst riots, protests and sectarian attacks, the UVF firebombed a home at Ballymoney in north Antrim and killed brothers, Richard, Mark and Jason Quinn, aged 10, 9 and 7.[88] Children of a mixed marriage, they were raised by their Catholic mother Chrissie as Protestants to 'avoid the hassle' in the overwhelmingly Protestant neighbourhood.[89] After several years of adverse publicity from growing international media attention, the death of the Quinn children unleased a global clamour of outrage over the Orange parades at Drumcree.[90] The British government was forced to take the situation in hand rather than leave it to the prevaricating decisions of local police commanders.

At the start of 1998, Westminster brought in the Public Processions (Northern Ireland) Act and the Parades Commission was established. Over the course of the following two decades, it has defused formerly explosive situations, not least by maintaining the ban on the Orange procession along the Garvaghy Road in Portadown. Elsewhere, on Belfast's Lower Ormeau Road; in Newtownbutler, County Fermanagh;[‡] Castlederg, County Tyrone; Rasharkin, County Antrim; and many other places, the Parades Commission has negotiated the narrow ground between loyalist demands to parade 'traditional routes' and the rights of residents to prevent them from doing so. A sign of its remarkable success is that more parades than ever now take place, but without any major disturbances. In 2016, there were 2,851 loyalist/unionist processions, and 219 nationalist/republican parades, many of the latter connected to commemoration of the 1916 Easter Rising in Dublin.[91] Less than a decade earlier, the Parades Commission annual report for 2007 recorded 2,755 unionist/loyalist parades, up 335 on the previous years, and 186 nationalist/republican parades.[92]

The IRA's violent onslaught on the state of Northern Ireland faltered during the 1980s following a huge reversal here within the Citadel of Orangeism. Eight highly experienced volunteers led by east Tyrone commander Patrick Kelly were caught in an ambush and shot dead when they drove into the village of Loughgall to destroy the local police station.[93]

---

‡   For twenty years, the annual parade of the Border Defenders Flute Band has drawn protests from nationalist residents of Newtownbutler. The band complies with restrictions: https://www.paradescommission.org/viewparade.aspx?id=63857

A civilian passer-by, 36-year-old Anthony Hughes from Caledon, was also killed in the hail of bullets during the 8 May 1987 ambush.[94] Loughgall was the latest IRA target in a 'scorched earth' campaign to wipe out the British security presence in small outlying centres of their area of operation. It was devised for and by the Monaghan-based active-service unit known within the IRA as the 'A team'.[95] The strategy was dubbed the 'Tet Offensive' – recalling the Viet Cong/North Vietnamese campaign of 1968 – and it is attributed to veterans Jim Lynagh from Monaghan town and Padraig McKearney from the Moy, both of whom were killed in Loughgall.[96] Apart from hitting operational centres of security control, the targets were deliberately chosen in places that had 'remained untouched' by the conflict, to demonstrate that there was 'no normalisation'.[97]

Both in their early thirties and active in the IRA since their teens, Lynagh and McKearney had already endured imprisonment and family deaths. Lynagh, whose extended family was centred in Clones, grew up in the Tully estate of Monaghan town. He was arrested when he narrowly survived the premature explosion of a bomb he was handling in the Moy in 1973, and served five years.[98] While incarcerated, he studied guerrilla warfare and devised a 'third phase' for the IRA's campaign. This followed the traditional military structure of the first phase, followed by the second phase of the 'cell' structure brought about by the attrition of post-1976 Ulsterisation and criminalisation.

The third phase aimed to create 'liberated zones' along the border, along the lines of south Armagh, where British forces had to operate from isolated fortresses with helicopter support. All support for the British security forces in these 'liberated zones' would be denied by repeated attacks on operational centres and on those engaged to repair the damage. It was a ruthless, meticulous and concerted strategy that has fuelled 'genocide' claims because it targeted part-time soldiers and police while they were doing civilian jobs, on the basis that they were still the 'eyes and ears' of the security forces.[99]

Among gardaí in Monaghan town, Lynagh was known as the 'Executioner'.[100] In the North, Special Branch regarded him and McKearney as 'irreconcilables', who had become 'intoxicated with republican myths and had lost touch with reality'.[101] Although he had been a Sinn Féin member of Monaghan Urban Council since 1979, Jim Lynagh never saw himself as a politician but as a soldier leading groups of heavily armed combatants on specific missions within his border zone. He was 'the leader of a guerrilla band, not a member of a terrorist cell', according to a British Army intelligence officer.[102]

McKearney was first arrested in 1972 for blowing up the Moy's post office, but released after six weeks for lack of evidence.[103] The following year, he got seven years for possession of a rifle and became close friends with Lynagh while they were political prisoners in Magilligan. During that time, Pádraig's brother Seán McKearney was killed with Eugene Martin during an IRA operation. Three years after his 1977 release, Pádraig was sentenced to fourteen years after he was arrested with a loaded Sten gun.[104] His brother Tommy was already serving life for the murder of UDR Lance Corporal Stanley Adams in October 1976, and subsequently went on the first IRA hunger strike.[105] In September 1983, Pádraig was one of thirty-eight prisoners who broke out of prison in a spectacular escape, teaming up with another close friend from Monaghan, Seamus McElwain, to make their way back across the border and report for duty.

After McElwain was killed near Roslea in April 1986, Lynagh took charge of the guard of honour for the huge funeral. Then, equipped with arms from the first of four huge arms shipments from Libya between 1985 and 1986, he and McKearney pushed ahead with the 'Tet Offensive' on the Tyrone-Armagh front. The operations were complex and ambitious, involving dozens of locally based IRA volunteers acting in support of a hardened corps or flying column based in Monaghan town. On 7 December 1985, they assaulted Ballygawley RUC station, gunning down RUC Constable George Gilland and Reserve Constable William Clements. The IRA ransacked the station, stealing weapons and documents, gutted the building with a flame thrower, and then exploded a 100lb beer-keg bomb that reduced it to smithereens.[106]

They tweaked their modus operandi for a similar attack in August 1986 on the RUC station at the tiny hamlet of the Birches, just north-west of Portadown. This time, about thirty-five volunteers were involved, including those involved in a diversion about 20 kilometres away at Pomeroy. The main group used a mechanical digger hijacked at Washing Bay, on Tyrone's Lough Neagh shore, loaded a bomb in the bucket, tore through the perimeter wire defences, and then detonated the device, destroying the building before escaping by boat across Lough Neagh.[107]

When contractor Harold Henry, who did building work for the police, was shot dead in April 1987 using a gun taken from the corpse of Constable Clements at Ballygawley, the RUC Special Branch came under 'pressure from the government to get results'.[108] Operation Judy was an intelligence and surveillance strategy based at Gough Barracks and involving SAS stake-outs. Among its intelligence sightings was a known IRA volunteer checking out heavy construction machinery in the Loughgall area. It 'became apparent' that 'Lynagh and other Tyrone OTR (on the run) terrorists were to execute a similar attack' using a hijacked digger.[109]

Five armed men then hijacked a digger at Peter Mackle's farm in Collegelands, and Declan Arthurs drove it by a circuitous route to Loughgall, picking up the 200lb bomb on the way.[110] He had already been spotted by a surveillance team, and a suspicious sighting of a van slowing down in front of the RUC station had also been reported back to Armagh.[111] When he arrived with the bomb, Arthurs drove the digger past the police station, turned back again through the 'deadly still' village, before turning once more and driving directly through the perimeter fence at 7:20 p.m. As he dismounted to set alight the fuse, others jumped from the van and opened fire on the police station.[112] From the control centre back in Gough Barracks, the words 'Go, go, go' boomed over the radio before the bomb exploded with a 'deafening roar'.[113]

In the ensuing barrage from six covert SAS units totalling twenty-four soldiers, the eight IRA men were gunned down in 'withering fire' that 'continued for five minutes', with 1,200 rounds fired. The bodies were riddled with 'multiple wounds', each having shots to the head, including wounds at the back of the ear, or straight down through the top of the head.[114] According to Raymond Murray's account, the SAS did not attend the subsequent inquest, and the families of the IRA men withdrew after one day. Controversy has since then raged over whether the deaths were permissible under the British Army's 'rules of engagement' in Northern Ireland, often referred to as its Yellow Card. Mark Urban's account of the event from the security forces' side quotes an explanation of the SAS commander's decision:

> The Yellow Card rules are officially seen to cover Loughgall, but of course they don't. You put your men in the station. That way they [the IRA] are threatening you without even knowing it. That's how you get around the Yellow Card.[115]

That SAS strategy to comply with the Yellow Card, including posting three men inside the otherwise deserted police station, may also explain the bizarre experience of two IRA Volunteers driving the getaway cars.[116] According to one of these men in an interview with *Irish News* reporter Connla Young on the thirtieth anniversary, they waited on the Armagh city side of Loughgall during the explosion and gunfire; then, realising something was wrong, drove down to see if they could find the others. They were stopped at the scene of carnage and an elderly couple pulled up behind. Two SAS soldiers leaned on the bonnets of the getaway cars, clearly aware that they were involved, and pointed their M16 carbines directly at the two IRA men. The interviewee claims the two soldiers who had them in their sights were perfectly calm while other SAS men were 'dancing' in a 'frenzy' and an 'odd isolated shot' rang out. When 'regular' soldiers arrived by helicopter, the SAS 'disappeared' and all the cars were ordered to turn around and leave. His escape was clearly linked, he now believes, to the elderly couple, who would have been eyewitnesses to a breach of Yellow Card rules in the shoot-to-kill operation. He also drove through an RUC checkpoint nearby before reaching safety, while the other scout picked up Liam Ryan, later killed in a UVF attack on his pub at Moortown on Tyrone's Lough Neagh shore.[117] After Loughgall, they made their way back to Monaghan, as did others with peripheral roles.

Clearly no prisoners were being taken in this ambush that passed into republican folklore as the 'Loughgall Massacre', yet is referred to by the RUC as the 'Loughgall Incident'. Former RUC Special Branch detective William Matchett writes that the cross-border offensive of the east Tyrone/Monaghan IRA had to be stopped through ruthless annihilation to prevent 'South Armagh's cancerous instability … from spreading'.[118] On the ground it would have made it 'extremely difficult' to maintain a 'permanent police presence in isolated rural areas'. Matchett also writes that the intelligence gathering leading up to Operation Judy relied largely on low-level breaks.

In the republican lexicon, the 'Loughgall martyrs' rank alongside the 1981 hunger strikers, and notable among them is Lynagh, who has been elevated by some to a latter-day Michael Collins as leader of a guerrilla army of freedom fighters on the border. The fervour and passion of his funeral reflected this. When the funeral cortege from Craigavon Hospital arrived in Emyvale, mourners blocked gardaí and formed a phalanx as the coffin was shouldered in relays of six through the village, flanked by a uniformed IRA guard of honour.[119] At the small bridge over the Mountain Water stream, three masked men in battledress emerged and fired single shots, then a volley over the coffin, before retreating through the cheering crowds. When two plain-clothes detectives were spotted blocking the gunmen's retreat, their car was heaved into the stream with one of the gardaí still inside. According to Justice Minister Gerry Collins, his colleague then fired six or seven bursts from his Uzi submachinegun to disperse the crowd, although filmed news reports clearly show that the garda shooting preceded that incident. The gunmen disappeared.

The next day, hundreds of gardaí in riot gear approached Lynagh's town centre flat in Monaghan, but were fended off by dozens of young male mourners linking arms. In an angry standoff, the coffin draped in a tricolour flag and IRA uniform emerged with a masked and uniformed IRA bodyguard of nine men and two women, who saluted their fallen leader, then retreated to cheers and applause from thousands of mourners thronging Old Cross Square. Again flanked by mourners linking arms, the coffin was carried to St Macartan's Cathedral, accompanied by mourners including Gerry Adams, Martin McGuinness and IRA veteran Joe Cahill. Requiem Mass was celebrated by Father John Nolan with no reference to what had happened at Loughgall, to the annoyance of Sinn Féin leader Gerry Adams, who said in his graveside oration, 'Loughgall will become a tombstone to British policy in Ireland.'[120]

There can be no doubt now that what happened in Loughgall on that sleepy Saturday evening of 7 May 1987 heralded a series of events that propelled the Republican movement towards peace. For not only did it signal the end of the 'Tet Offensive' cross-border strategy, according to Matchett, 'it also signalled the decline of the IRA terrorist campaign'.[121] He quotes a Special Branch colleague:

> They [the IRA] stood the entire [east Tyrone] brigade down after Loughgall. It totally wrecked them. The witch-hunt for a mole destroyed them mentally. They'd lost all confidence. Nobody was in a rush to join or at least nobody with any sense. After Loughgall they were never the same.[122]

Within a year, the IRA had suffered other major setbacks arising from public abhorrence of the Remembrance Day bombing in Enniskillen and the succession of horrors unleashed by the shooting in Gibraltar of three unarmed IRA volunteers. The war continued, but the IRA now operated in an atmosphere of paranoid suspicion about informers. This fuelled internal bloodletting, ironically spearheaded by its internal security unit chief Freddie Scappaticci, a key mole for the police and British intelligence.

The decisive shift from the Armalite to the ballot box in the wake of Loughgall was proving more fruitful on both sides of the border. Caomhghín Ó Caoláin, who managed the 1981 Dáil election of hunger striker Kieran Doherty, had been elected to Monaghan County Council in 1985. When Sinn Féin dropped its policy of abstaining from the Dáil, he contested national and European elections and eventually won a seat in the Dublin parliament, on a vote overwhelmingly concentrated in north Monaghan. He became the first Sinn Féin TD elected since 1957 and the first to take his seat since partition. By 2000, Monaghan County Council had its first Sinn Féin chairman, Brian McKenna of Emyvale, and since then Sinn Féin has been the largest party on the county council. In this, Monaghan mirrored the political metamorphosis of Fermanagh, Tyrone and Armagh, where Sinn Féin made exponential gains in elections and now holds all the Westminster constituencies along the entire border.

What happened in north Armagh after 1987 also had a huge impact on the future for loyalism, which had long exerted absolute hegemony in the Citadel of Orangeism and beyond. The consequences of the Public Order (Northern Ireland) Order meant that 'Ulster Says No' unionist intransigence would no longer succeed in blocking progress towards full representation and equal rights. Having been denied their traditional route through the Tunnel in Portadown, Orange parades were curtailed elsewhere, notably along the Garvaghy Road. While refusing to recognise or engage with the Parades Commission established under Acts of the UK Parliament, loyalism found itself on the wrong side of the law time and again. Subsequent adverse rulings and the prevailing sense in loyalism that the peace process not only favoured Catholic nationalism, but that nationalist communities, often because of the GAA, were better equipped to exploit such favours, was compounded with implementation of the Patten Commission's report on policing. The RUC was replaced by the Police Service of Northern Ireland (PSNI) and clear quotas were set for recruitment of Catholics. The arrangement whereby the police existed primarily to uphold the unionist state of Northern Ireland was broken. Indeed, the absolute security of the union was made conditional in the 1993 Downing Street Declaration, even as the apparatus of security was changed.

Peace talks between London and Dublin had begun in July 1992, just as the Ulster Defence Regiment was being wound up after two decades and amalgamated into the Royal Irish Regiment. Seven home service battalions of mostly part-time RIR soldiers built on the framework inherited from the B Specials through the UDR, became three battalions in 2003. When the Operation Banner military deployment in Northern Ireland ended, the home battalions were disbanded entirely in 2007. The fractured succession of the original Ulster Volunteer Force, the 36th (Ulster) Division of Kitchener's New Army, the Special Constabulary and RUC, with the UDR and RIR, was broken at last. There was a real sense in loyalism of the loss of a tradition stretching from the Muster Rolls of the Ulster Plantation, from Enniskillen, Derry and the victors at the Boyne, to militias, yeomanry and volunteer corps.[123] It was a loss of the masculinities built into modern Protestant Ulster's martial identity. Already, the B Specials had assumed a place of 'almost mythic proportions' within unionist folklore, notably in the formation of an Orange Lodge dedicated to their memory.[124]

So as loyalism scrambled for ammunition in the cultural wars that ensued, it adopted twin icons to revere. In the border loyalist communities of Armagh, Tyrone and Fermanagh, annual parades often feature participants dressed in B Special and UDR uniforms. They evoke cheers and tears for those who patrolled border roads, manned checkpoints, defended village police stations and fended off harm. They were fathers, brothers, cousins and close neighbours who risked death. On the other side of the community, the B Specials and UDR are recalled as armed agents of a repressive state, wearing ill-fitting uniforms and wielding guns, who pretend they don't know their near neighbours. Yet in the new popular loyalist imagination, they share a bloodline with those who rode the border marches of England and Scotland, with those who pushed west beyond the Ohio to forge America's manifest destiny. They are heroes of Ulster, God's frontiersmen.

11. The End Is Neagh

From Charlemont lock, the Blackwater glides north for the remainder of the navigation to Lough Neagh. It flows past the beautiful landscaped grounds of The Argory in County Tyrone, once home of the MacGeogh-Bond family. Their primary residence until 1917 had been at Drumsill House in County Armagh, just 7.5 miles away outside Armagh city. The previous year, The Argory's owner had died without heir. That was an ironic departure for Captain Ralph Shelton MacGeough Bond, who is credited with coining the phrase 'women and children first' during his evacuation of HMS *Birkenhead* off the South African coast in 1852, thereby establishing a chivalrous code of maritime practice.[1] Drumsill House was later converted into a hotel owned by Unionist politician John Taylor (Lord Kilclooney), who had vigorously opposed Austin Currie in the 1968 Caledon housing protest and who was seriously wounded when shot by the Official IRA in Armagh city in 1972. Drumsill House was badly damaged in an IRA bombing in June 1979, just after its owner had been elected to the European Parliament. That coincidence made international news in an era when the mayhem and murder of Northern Ireland, and especially of its border fringes, had been relegated to also-ran status in the media.[2] That same year, the sumptuous surroundings of The Argory were taken over by the National Trust, and in all their languid beauty, they seem far removed from the border and its bloody preoccupations.

The incumbents of The Argory certainly never spent nights wandering the maze of country roads in the cause of loyalty, much less subversion. Though intolerant of the damp cold in the Blackwater Valley, they lived in an idyllic world of Victorian wealth and privilege that still resonates through rooms and grounds that remain much as they were before partition. Yet like everywhere else in Northern Ireland, trouble arrived on the very doorstep of The Argory shortly after it was sold to the National Trust. As caretaker Frederick John Lutton, a married father of two, was locking the gates on 1 May 1979, two masked men fatally shot him at close range.[3] He had recently resigned from the police reserve.

A short distance further, the river passes under the M1 Motorway at Tamnamore and then meets the Coalisland Canal. Built as the Tyrone Navigation, that canal extends for only 4.5 miles (7 kilometres), yet it took fifty-four years to build, having been started in 1733 and officially opened in 1787.[4] Its purpose was to carry coal for the Dublin market, slowly proving the adage of the duke of Bridgewater, the 'greatest of canal builders', that every canal 'must have coals at the end of it'.[5] The Coalisland Canal closed to commercial traffic in 1954. Current efforts to restore it as a recreational resource are tied up with the campaign for the Ulster Canal. A regatta for small boats was staged on the fully intact channel in 2008.[6]

From here it is almost plain sailing for the short distance to Lough Neagh at the Maghery shore, where a group of Ribbonmen attacked an Orange parade in November 1830 and punctured some of their drums. The Orangemen retaliated by burning the Catholic village of Maghery to the ground.[7] Derrywarragh island sits not far from Maghery, near the mouth of the Blackwater River, surrounded by shallow waters and sand bars, so a special channel known as the 'Maghery Cut' had to be excavated in the early nineteenth century so that vessels coming down the river could safely gain access to the lough.

The largest body of fresh water in the United Kingdom and Ireland, Lough Neagh has also been the subject of a jurisdictional dispute between commercial eel fishermen and the Shaftsbury Estates, a company owned by the Chichester family, descendants of Lord Donegall, who was granted title to the entire lough by Charles II in 1661. The title was upheld in a landmark case before the House of Lords in 1911.[8] The waters contain the largest stocks of freshwater eels in Europe, and the fishermen's co-operative pay the estate an annual rent to harvest them. About ten years ago, it emerged that the beneficiary of this payment had been Lord Shaftesbury, Anthony Ashley-Cooper, who was murdered by his third wife, Jamila

M'Barak and her brother in 2004. They went to prison and the earldom passed to the earl's eldest son, also Anthony Ashley-Cooper, but a month later he died at the New York home of his younger brother Nicholas Ashley-Cooper, who then became the twelfth earl of Shaftesbury. In 2013, he began legal action to wrest the Lough Neagh title deeds from his imprisoned step-mother. However, the title deeds are also being contested by the Lough Neagh Eel Fishery Co-op, and that effort is championed by local MLA and former Agriculture Minister Michelle O'Neill, who is now leader of Sinn Féin in Northern Ireland.[9]

It was another O'Neill who in 1958 hatched a hare-brained plan to get rid of the lake altogether by draining it, thereby creating another county for Northern Ireland.[10] The future Northern Ireland premier Terence O'Neill said, 'County Neagh would have no mountains or bogs and might be quite fertile. It could be planted with trees and a new town could be built at its centre.' It would certainly have confounded nationalists, who invariably countered the unionist persistence in referring to their state as 'Ulster' by calling it the 'six counties' or even diminishing it further to the 'wee six'.

Here on the shores of Lough Neagh, the border seems remote, no longer accessible by a direct route. On pushing off from the Ulster Canal at Charlemont, we have slipped over the edge of borderland into Upper Bann, and beyond lies Lagan Valley, both parliamentary constituencies floating safely in a sea of Brexit-flavoured unionism. They look eastwards to Belfast and beyond, their vista untroubled by frontier incursions. Conflicts of identity become marginal, the preserve of the minority, and those who voted to remain. Here the tide flows for illusions of sovereignty and getting back control outside the European Union.

Back in Armagh city, borders and Brexit are hot topics at the 30th annual John Hewitt International Summer School (24–9 July 2017). There's a play about policing the border by former IRA hunger striker Lawrence McKeown; a lecture on Brexit by sociologist Katy Hayward from Queen's University Belfast; another on the 'garlic' border between Spain and Gibraltar; and readings from a new book on walks along the border. I attend a morning lecture, which promises a philosophical view of Brexit that will be 'calm and unflustered'. That is an attractive offer on a process that seems destined to follow a philosophy of chaos to an uncertain future driven by rampant nationalism. It is reinforced by a chart showing how our long fractious border has been transformed by the European Union as relations were depoliticised and normalised, by trade, common EU citizenship and closer union. To think all that is jeopardised, not by a resurrection of Irish nationalism but of English nationalism and its flag-waving acolytes in Ulster unionism!

While Lagan Valley MP Jeffrey Donaldson speculates on electronic border surveillance to create a 'frictionless' post-Brexit border to which 'no nationalist could object', the parallel worlds we inhabit on both sides of the border emerge in stark outline. They communicate in what Queen's University lecturer Katy Hayward named the 'negative silence' that pervades and that prevents wider discourse about the future in this corner of the world, even as we face into the real crisis of Brexit. That prompted the suggestion from a summer-school participant during the mid-morning coffee break that the lecture could have made reference to John Hewitt's quest for a common identity rooted in what he called Ulster regionalism.[11] Regionalism, said Hewitt, is 'based upon the conviction that, as man is a social being, he must, now that the nation has become an enormously complicated organisation, find some smaller unit to which to give his loyalty'. He outlined his regionalism in his poem, 'Freehold', first published in the Belfast literary magazine *Lagan* in 1948:[12]

> My region's Ulster. How can we afford
> To take the shouting politician's word,
> Map-makers' frenzy, who with crazy line,
> Cut off three counties history marked her own?
>
> Mine is historical Ulster, battlefield
> Of Gael and Planter, certified and sealed
> By blood, and what is stronger than the blood,
> By images and folkways understood
> But dimly by the wits, yet valid still.

Yet also in that poem, he illustrated plainly that his people did not encompass all the inhabitants of either the historic or the truncated Ulster:

Yet we shall ride the waters in their spite,
who thrash and wallow to the left and right,
drop gurgling down into the Romish pit,
or on a melting iceberg scold at it.

That final passage, according to University of Liverpool's Frank Shovlin, was the 'most striking example of Hewitt permitting the mask of regionalism to slip to reveal an unsettling ethnic exclusivism'.[13] Similarly, his much-vaunted poem 'Ulster Names', now etched for immortality in the atrium of the Public Records Office of Northern Ireland (PRONI) in Belfast's Titanic Quarter, stakes out his 'Ulster' by namechecking places it enfolds in his embrace. The list of place names spills out in verse after verse, without crossing the border once:

County by county you number them over;
Tyrone, Fermanagh … I stand by a lake,
And the bubbling curlew, the whistling plover
Call over the whins in the chill daybreak
As the hills and the waters the first light take.

Each of the half dozen counties in his Ulster is namechecked in a poem that ends,

So it's Ballinamallard, it's Crossmaglen,
it's Aughnacloy, it's Donaghadee,
it's Magherafelt breeds the best of men,
I'll not deny it. But look for me
On the moss between Orra and Slievenanee.

That final verse hops neatly from Fermanagh to Armagh, to Tyrone and back to Down, before touching Derry and then to Antrim. In terms of his Ulster regionalism, 'six counties were for the time being, it seemed, small enough for Hewitt', Shovlin writes.[14] Perhaps there's little wonder therefore at Hewitt's utter perplexity in 'Postscript, 1984', written for those thirty-year-old verses. Again his list of names resonates, but this time with memory of frontier conflicts and recent atrocities:

Banbridge, Ballykelly, Darkley, Crossmaglen,
Summoning pity, anger and despair,
By grief of kin, by hate of murderous men
Till the whole tarnished map is stained and torn,
Not to be read as pastoral again.[15]

The regionalist poetry of Hewitt, Belfast-born but insisting on Armagh roots in Kilmore, between Portadown and Tandragee, attempts to create an amorphous sense of place and identity based on a new post-partition 'Ulster'. It is a place that devolves from the border, but not beyond, except in nostalgic allusions to Donegal as a place apart, once connected in a romantic sense: 'I recall / the friendly doors and hearths of Donegal …'[16] It reflects a trend as one moves east beyond the borderland, to places where county designations are lost in new administrative geographies, such as 'Craigavon'; places where the tarnished map is reimagined into a fresh configuration and the edges are blurred and then abandoned as beyond the new Pale. The poetry of Paul Muldoon, on the other hand, is cosmic in its reach across and through the border on the fringes of his own native home in Collegelands, where the Ulster Canal discharges into the Blackwater. His vision encompasses the bloody story of the border right from its inception:

A year since they kidnapped Anketell Moutray from his home
at Favour Royal,
dragging him, blindfolded, the length of his own gravel path,
eighty years old, the Orange County grand master. Four A
Specials
shot on a train
in Clones. The Clogher valley
a blaze of flax mills and haysheds.[17]

The theme of transcending frontiers and boundaries is a constant through Muldoon's work. Sometimes allegorical, charting the dilemma of dislocated identities, of 'streams that had once flowed simply into the other, one taking the other's name'.[18] Other times it is starkly direct, as in 'Good Friday, 1971'. Driving west:

I gave a lift to the girl out of love
And crossed the last great frontier at Lifford.
Marooned by an iffing and butting herd
Of sheep, Letterkenny had just then laid
Open its heart and we passed as new blood
Back into the grey flesh of Donegal.[19]

From Muldoon, it can be a terse frontier allusion, just enough to pique speculation as in the tiny five-line poem 'Ireland':

The Volkswagen parked in the gap,
But gently ticking over.
You wonder if it's lovers
And not men hurrying back
Across two fields and a river.[20]

It can be casually personal, as in the troubled primary school classmate from Collegelands, whom he later meets as an IRA leader 'just over the Irish border' where those in his command answer in the schoolroom Irish roll-call response, 'Anseo'.[21] Or it can be formally indifferent, as in his rejection of regionalism founded in the:

fatal belief that fate
governs everything from the honey-rust of your father's terrier's
eyebrows to the horse that rusts and rears
in the furrow, of the furrows from which we no more deviate
than they can from themselves, no more than the map of Europe
can be redrawn, than the Hermes might make a harp from his
harpe
than that we must live in a vale
of tears on the banks of the Lagan or the Foyle …[22]

Throughout Muldoon's work, themes of fluid identity and maps that cannot curtail movement are flights of fancy from the vantage of an Armagh childhood entwined in a Tyrone village connected across a river that flows from Monaghan. It is that sensitivity that bristles and bridles at a fickle line on a map imposed on a virtual whim a century ago, and that is now claiming an integrity it never earned.

Muldoon's most apposite poem in this regard is 'Unapproved Road', a delightful frolic starting with a customs checkpoint encounter while doing some minor smuggling of whiskey, cigarettes and butter just after Sean South and Fergal O'Hanlon were killed in the Brookeborough raid.[23] The hostile customs man, wrapped in a scarf, transmogrifies into a Tuareg herdsman from the Sahara, who rests his coffee on a zarf in Rotterdam and cogitates about Scairbh na gCaorach, or Emyvale, and the link to his ancestors who 'drove their flocks from tier to tier through Algeria, Mali and Libya all the way up to Armagh, Monaghan and Louth with – you'll like this – a total disregard for any frontier'. That frontier-less frolic ends as the Tuareg sets off 'at a jog-trot down an unapproved road near Aughnacloy' and the 'Black Pig's Dyke fades into the piggy bank'.

The career-long poetic fixation on the border of the Pulitzer prize-winning Princeton professor continues in his 2015 collection, *One Thousand Things Worth Knowing*, the hardback edition of which has a dust jacket featuring Rita Duffy's painting, *Watchtower 2*. The painting illustrates an alien military sanger in an Irish border setting of seeming rural insignificance, a tower festooned with cameras and antennae focused on the 'olive drab the Brits throw over everything'.[24] The collection's final poem, 'Dirty Data', is a Frank Kitson-ian weave of low-intensity information-gathering that preoccupied military strategists using electronic surveillance on the border. It connects Armagh fuel smugglers through the Roman empire tale of Ben Hur/Massala to author Lew Wallace's US cavalry career among New Mexico Apaches and the Lincoln County War 'between Prods and Papes', as well as the civil-rights struggle in east Tyrone. By any stretch, it is a cosmic overview of the utter mess that constitutes the border, where:

> Disinformation about a
> dawn swoop,
> half-truths and old-style spelling errors
> only partly account for the imbroglio.[25]

The border has skewed our shared history, our shared geography and our shared language. It has created two main narratives from which flow all the misunderstandings we can pack into our own tailored versions. It has stunted conversation, reducing us to the 'negative silences' of mirror worlds. In the borderlands we communicate in coded asides, conveying just enough meaning for those who share our views, without letting down our guard against those who don't. For now, it's the telling look, the grunted aside, the raised eyebrow, the half-smile: that'll do rightly; say nothing till you hear more!

Within those silences, we harbour resentments, traditional and trivial. Unionists bristle and fulminate at nationalist references to 'the North of Ireland', insisting there is no such 'legal entity'.[26] Yet even in his oft-misquoted reference to a 'Protestant parliament and a Protestant State', Lord Craigavon referred to 'the North' as did many other unionists in unguarded utterances.[27] Irish nationalists and republicans on both sides of the border have also called it a 'statelet', a 'failed state', the 'Black North', and even the 'British-occupied six counties'. Unionists and loyalists call it 'Ulster', 'the province', and 'our wee country'. At best, we all lapse into the shared yet disparaging comic-talk of 'Norn Iron'. So also on the nationalist side with the 'south', the Republic, the twenty-six counties, the Free State, southern Ireland, Éire and simply Ireland.

Between them lies that amorphous borderland, a fluid frontier zone whose territorial limit 'depends on the geographic reach of the interaction with the "other side"', as Oscar Martinez put it.[28] Whatever those parameters, the districts that occupy south Ulster between Lough Erne and Lough Neagh are inextricably linked, just as they have always been. To all intents and purposes, they are virtually indistinguishable. They share the same drumlin topography of small hills and lakes; the same demographic mix of 'planters' and Gaels; the same languages; the multiplicity of similar accents; the same twisty wee roads; the same entrepreneurial drive; the same general political stances; the same conversational reticence; the same family lineages; and the same history and cultural traditions. They have been connected by natural lines of communication on roads, rail and a former canal. They work together, worship together and play together.

Their interaction is impeded only by a border that has intruded on their lives for the past century, creating new political and economic barriers, political estrangements, socio-economic divergences, disrupted passage and institutional duplication. Yet that is precisely what borders are meant to do. They are designed to keep people apart and to prevent, control or regulate interactions. They create frontiers far from the core of the state, zones of transition, places where people and institutions are shaped by forces 'not felt in the heartland'.[29] Yet on both sides of the border region our Ulster Canal path has traversed, people have endured together the horrific legacy of atrocities wrought on close-knit communities, fragmenting neighbourly relations, family networks and business alliances. They have passed through the valley of death and emerged into an uneasy peace growing in promise and prosperity under the protective umbrella of the European Union.

Brexit, opposed vigorously by strong, even overwhelming majorities in all of those border constituencies, now threatens to return it to the heart of darkness, to all the confusions, anomalies, and misplacements that were never resolved from the very start of a border that was imposed where none had ever existed before. That is a place where the border is a disembodied light swinging to and fro in the darkness; a makeshift customs post; chalk lines on a railway platform; barricade spikes and concrete bollards; neighbour watching neighbour in fear and suspicion; the low-gear growl of a lorry labouring up a smugglers' track; a signal to pull over and stop – friend or foe?; Brian McCoy's misplaced confidence that 'It's OK, this is the army'; a spot checkpoint around the next corner; the sudden and dreadful realisation of danger in friends returning from a football match; a corpse with a fertiliser bag over its head dumped on the roadside.

Endnotes

Introduction: Always on Edge

1. Tomás Mac Curtain (1884–1920), lord mayor of Cork city, was murdered by crown forces during the Irish War of Independence.
2. Gloria Anzaldúa, *Borderlands/La Frontera: The New Mestiza* (San Francisco: Aunt Lute Books, 2007), p. 25.
3. Damian McCarney, 'Greenway Mooted to Go along Ulster Canal from Castle Saunderson to Clones', *The Anglo-Celt*, 19 March 2015.
4. Tim Haughton, 'It's the Slogan Stupid: the Brexit referendum', *Perspectives*, University of Birmingham, https://www.birmingham.ac.uk/research/perspective/eu-ref-haughton.aspx, accessed 21 January 2018.
5. Claudio Magris, 'Who Is on the Other Side? Considerations about Frontiers' in *Leopard III: Frontiers* (London: Harvill, 1994), pp 8–25.
6. Joseph M. Curran, 'The Anglo-Irish Agreement of 1925: Hardly a "damn good bargain"', pp 36-52, *The Historian* 40:1 (1977), pp 48-50.
7. Maureen Wall, 'Partition: The Ulster Question' in T.D. Williams (ed), *The Irish Struggle, 1916–26* (London: Routledge Kegan Paul, 1966), pp 79–93 at p. 87.
8. Jonathan Bardon, *A History of Ulster* (Belfast: Blackstaff Press, 1992), p. 486.
9. Jenny Edkins, 'Introduction: Trauma, Violence and Political Community' in J. Edkins (ed.), *Trauma and the Memory of Politics* (Cambridge: Cambridge University Press, 2003), pp 1–19 at p. 4.
10. Catherine Nash, Bryonie Reid and Brian Graham, *Partitioned Lives: The Irish Borderlands* (Farnham, Surrey: Routledge, 2013) p. 64.

1. Border Hopscotch

1. Henry Saunderson, *The Saundersons of Castle Saunderson* (privately printed, 1936).
2. Saunderson, *The Saundersons*, p. 31. Bardon's *A History of Ulster*, p. 159, provides a somewhat more modest account of the Battle of Newtownbutler on 28 July 1689, estimating that Mountcashel's Jacobite force of 3,000 was

defeated by 2,000 Enniskilleners commanded by Gustavus Hamilton, who led the charge with cries of 'No popery!', driving 500 men to their doom at Wattlebridge, with only one escaping to the southern shore. Bardon adds that while 400 Jacobite officers were given quarter, almost 2,000 men at arms were put to the sword in a 'ruthless annihilation' that provided the greatest Williamite victory of the war so far.

3.   'Restoration of Ulster Canal Proves a Technical Challenge', *Afloat*, 3 April 2017, https://afloat.ie/inland/inland-waterways/item/35407-restoration-of-ulster-canal-proves-a-technical-challenge, accessed 19 Jan. 2018.

4.   Brian Cassells, *The Ulster Canal* (Donaghadee: Cottage Publications, 2015).

5.   Ibid., p. 43; Ruth Delaney, *Ireland's Inland Waterways* (Belfast: Appletree Press, 2004), p. 157.

6.   Bardon, *A History of Ulster*, p. 374.

7.   Ibid., p. 379.

8.   Ibid., p. 414.

9.   Saunderson, *The Saundersons*, pp 65–6.

10.   *Henry's Upper Lough Erne in 1739* (Whitegate, Co. Clare: Ballinkella Press, 1987), pp 26–7.

11.   David McKittrick, Seamus Kelters, Brian Feeney, Chris Thornton and David McVea, *Lost Lives: The Stories of the Men, Women and Children Who Died as a Result of the Northern Ireland Troubles* (Edinburgh and London: Mainstream, 2004), pp 196–7.

12.   Patrick Mulroe, *Bombs, Bullets and the Border – Policing Ireland's Frontier: Irish security policy, 1969-78* (Dublin: Irish Academic Press, 2017), pp 103-4.

13.   Liz Walsh, *The Final Beat: Gardaí killed in the line of duty* (Dublin: Gill and Macmillan, 2001), p.23.

14.   McKittrick et al., *Lost Lives*, p. 157.

15.   Ibid., p. 153.

16.   Shane Connaughton, *A Border Diary* (London: Faber & Faber, 1995).

17.   Paul Muldoon, 'Macha' in *Poems, 1968–1998* (London: Faber & Faber, 2001), p. 8.

18.   Shane Connaughton, *The Run of the Country* (London: Penguin, 1992), p. 4.

19.   Ibid., p. 80.

20.   '30 Year Papers Reveal Row over Aghalane Bridge', *Impartial Reporter*, 28 Dec. 2012.

21.   McKittrick et al., *Lost Lives*, p. 285.

22.   Ibid., pp 286–7.

23.   Brian MacDonald, *The 'Pitchfork' Murders: Uncovering the Cover-up* (Newtownbutler: privately published, 2013); Deaglan Ó Mochain (dir.), An Radharc na Súl/Out of Sight, Out of Mind, TG4, 25 October 2016, https://dearcanmedia.com/as-radharc-na-sul-out-of-sight-out-of-mind/, accessed 20 Jan. 2018.

24. McKittrick et al., *Lost Lives*, p. 284.

25. Henry Patterson, *Ireland's Violent Frontier: the Border and Anglo-Irish Relations during the Troubles* (Palgrave Macmillan, 2013), p. 144.

26. Ibid., p. 130.

27. Ibid., pp 134, 217n.

28. Patrick Nolan, 'End to Border Killings Urged', *Irish Times*, 19 June 1980.

29. 'Diary of Events', *Fortnight*, 178 (Oct.–Nov. 1980), p. 11.

30. Lt Col. Michael Dewar, *The British Army in Northern Ireland* (London: Arms & Armour Press, 1985), p. 124.

31. Peadar Livingstone, *The Fermanagh Story: a Documentary History of the County Fermanagh from the Earliest Times to the Present Day* (Enniskillen: Cumann Seanchais Chlochair, 1969), p. 287. In all, nine men from the Wattlebridge Company were involved in this operation, and four, including Matt Fitzpatrick, were arrested and sent to Crumlin Road Jail in Belfast, as 200 British soldiers were dispatched to Newtownbutler to occupy the barracks in case it was the next target.

32. Ernie O'Malley, *On Another Man's Wound* (Dublin: Anvil Books, 1979), pp 116–7.

33. Letter from H. Murphy & Son, solrs, Clones, to Ministry of Defence, Dublin, 27 September 1927, file W2D288MATTHEWFITZPATRICK.pdf in Military Service Pension Collection/Defence Forces Military Archive; http://mspcsearch.militaryarchives.ie/detail.aspx?parentpriref=, accessed 19 Jan. 2018.

34. Ibid., letter dated 26 Oct. 1927.

35. Connaughton, *A Border Diary*, p. 1.

36. 'Nine in Court Over Fake Goods at Clogher Market', BBC, 21 Mar 2012, http://www.bbc.co.uk/news/uk-northern-ireland-17460511.

37. 'Market Target of Fake Goods Swoop', BBC, 16 June 2007, http://news.bbc.co.uk/1/hi/northern_ireland/6760079.stm.

38. *Ordnance Survey Memoirs of Ireland*, iv: *Parishes of County Fermanagh I, 1834–5, Enniskillen and Upper Lough Erne*, ed. Angélique Day and Patrick McWilliams (Dublin: Institute of Irish Studies in Association with the Royal Irish Academy, 1990), pp 34–40.

39. Ibid. p. 36.

40. Aidan Walsh, 'Excavation at the Black Pig's Dyke', *Clogher Record*, 14:1 (1991), pp 9–26.

41. *Northern Standard*, 1 May 1925.

42. Sean O'Faolain, 'No Country for Old Men' in *I Remember! I Remember!* (Boston: Little, Brown, 1961), republished in *The Heat of the Sun* (London: Penguin, 1983), pp 241–59.

43. The Boundary Commission was established under Article 12 of the Anglo-Irish Treaty to determine the boundary between Northern Ireland and the Irish Free State.

44.   Class Cabinet 61.42, R.F. 40, Public Record Office (PRO), London.

45.   Class Cab. 61.56, R.F. 101, PRO, London.

46.   Class Cab. 61/56, p. 5; Peter Leary, *Unapproved Routes: Histories of the Irish border, 1922-1972* (Oxford: Oxford University Press, 2016), p. 31.

47.   Class Cab. 61/66, p. 183.

48.   Ibid., p. 31.

49.   Class Cab. 61.15, report of the Irish Boundary Commission, 1925, p. 110.

50.   E. Staunton, 'The Boundary Commission Debacle 1925: Aftermath & Implications', *History Ireland*, 4:2 (1996) pp 42–5.

51.   *Northern Standard*, 18 Sept. 1925.

52.   Cassells, *The Ulster Canal*, p. 90.

53.   May Blair, *Once Upon the Lagan: Story of the Lagan Canal* (Belfast: Blackstaff Press, 1981).

54.   Patterson, *Ireland's Violent Frontier*, p. 26; 'History of Partial Border Closures in 1970', annex to Northern Ireland Border Control Report by Headquarters Northern Ireland (HQNI), May 1971, National Archives, London (NA) CJ4//213.

55.   Patterson, *Ireland's Violent Frontier*, pp 27–8; Peck to Howard Smith, UK representative, Conway Hotel, Belfast, 22 Apr. 1971, NA, CJ4/213.

56.   Nash et al., *Partitioned Lives*, p. 101.

57.   Andrew Hamilton, 'Confrontation on the border', *Irish Times,* 27 Oct. 1971.

58.   Patterson, *Ireland's Violent Frontier*, p. 33.

59.   John Hughes, 'Frank Kitson in Northern Ireland and the "British way" of counterinsurgency', *History Ireland*, 22:1 (Jan./Feb. 2014).

60.   Caroline Elkins, *Britain's Gulag: the Brutal End of Empire in Kenya* (London: Jonathan Cape, 2005), p. 54.

61.   Peter Taylor, *Brits: the War Against the IRA* (London: Bloomsbury, 2001), pp 128–130.

62.   Edward Longwill, 'The Irish Army and State Security Policy, 1956–74' (PhD, UU, 2009), p. 210.

63.   Patterson, *Ireland's Violent Frontier*, p. 56.

64.   Ibid.; Sir Arthur Galsworthy to W.K.K. White, 25 May 1973, NA, FCO 87/245.

65.   Garret FitzGerald, *All in a Life: an Autobiography* (Dublin: Gill & Macmillan, 1991), pp 201–2.

66.   Galsworthy to White, 25 May 1973, NA, FCO 87/245.

67.   Patterson, *Ireland's Violent Frontier*, p. 58; Dáil Éireann, Debates, vol. 166, 13 June 1973; Donnacha Ó Beacháin, *Destiny of the Soldiers: Fianna Fáil, Irish Republicanism and the IRA, 1926–1973* (Dublin: Gill & Macmillan, 2010), pp 364–5.

68.   Fearghal McGarry, *Eoin O'Duffy: Self-Made Hero* (Oxford: Oxford University Press, 2007), p. 43.

69. Madden Papers, 1610–1935, PRONI D3465.

70. F.P. Shirley, *History of the County of Monaghan* (London: Chiswick Press, 1877), pp 190–2.

71. Letter dated 23 Apr. 1878, PRONI D1071/H/B/D/78/61.

72. PRONI D3531/B/4.

73. 'Selfless Hero with an "Irish Sixth Sense"', (obituary), *Daily Telegraph*, 24 April 1996.

74. 'Shorts', *NthWORD*, 9 June 2010.

75. Jodi Kantor and Megan Twohey, 'Harvey Weinstein Paid Off Sexual Harassment Accusers for Decades', New York Times, 5 October 2017; https://www.nytimes.com/2017/10/05/us/harvey-weinstein-harassment-allegations.html, accessed 19 January 2018; Former Irish Film Producer Wins Praise, Irish Independent, 15 October 2017, https://www.independent.ie/entertainment/movies/movie-news/former-irish-film-producer-wins-praise-for-helping-expose-decades-of-sexual-misconduct-by-harvey-weinstein-36228411.html, accessed 19 January 2018.

76. Nash et al., *Partitioned Lives*, p. 43.

77. 'Ireland's Greatest All-Round Sportsman', *Irish Identity*, n.d., http://www.irishidentity.com/extras/famousgaels/stories/parke.htm, accessed 16 Nov. 2017; Kate Newman, 'James Cecil Parke, 1881–1946, Tennis Player', *New Ulster Biography*, n.d., http://www.newulsterbiography.co.uk/index.php/home/viewPerson/1381, accessed 16 Nov. 2017.

2. Cheek by Jowl

1. Patrick Shea, *Voices and the Sound of Drums* (Belfast: Blackstaff, 1981), pp 58–9.

2. Statement of John McGonnell, Bureau of Military History (BMH), Witness Statement (WS) 574, file S1832.

3. *Northern Standard*, 3 Feb. 1922.

4. Shea, *Voices*, p. 76.

5. Robert Lynch, 'The Clones Affray, 1922 – Massacre or Invasion?', *History Ireland*, 12:3 (Autumn 2004).

6. Robert Lynch, *The Northern IRA and the Early Years of Partition, 1920–1922* (Dublin: Irish Academic Press, 2006), p. 97; Aiken interview with Ernie O'Malley, O'Malley Notebooks, UCDAD, P17b/193.

7. Shea, *Voices*, pp 74–5.

8. *Northern Standard*, 20 Jan. 1922; Arthur Hezlet, *The 'B' Specials: History of the Ulster Special Constabulary, 1914–2007* (London: Tom Stacy, 1972), p. 55; Michael Farrell, *Northern Ireland: the Orange State*, London: Pluto, 1980) p. 48.

9. *Northern Standard*, 10 Feb. 1922.

10. Ibid., 17 Feb. 1922.

11. Ibid.
12. Lynch, *The Northern IRA*, p. 111.
13. Ibid., pp 116-7
14. *Northern Standard*, 20 February 1922; Lynch, *The Northern IRA*, p. 115.
15. *Northern Standard*, 20 February 1922.
16. Ibid., p. 115.
17. *Northern Standard*, 20 Feb. 1922.
18. Hezlet, *The 'B' Specials*, pp 59–60; Farrell, *Northern Ireland*, p. 49.
19. Farrell, *Northern Ireland*, p. 49.
20. Report of Border Commission, 21 Feb. 1922.
21. *Northern Standard*, 27 Feb. 1922
22. *Northern Standard*, 10 Mar. 1922.
23. Farrell, *Northern Ireland*, p. 71.
24. Patrick Buckland, *Irish Unionism, 1885–1923* (London: HMSO, 1973), p. 154.
25. Paul Bew, Peter Gibbon and Henry Patterson, *The State in Northern Ireland: Political Forces and Social Classes* (Manchester: Manchester University Press, 1979), p. 65.
26. Farrell, *Northern Ireland*, p. 52; Bew et al., *The State*, p. 65.
27. Hezlet, *The 'B' Specials*, p. 68.
28. Farrell, *Northern Ireland*, pp 55–6.
29. *Northern Standard*, 30 Apr. 1922.
30. Farrell, *Northern Ireland*, pp 57–8.
31. Wall, 'Partition', p. 88; Farrell, *Northern Ireland*, p. 59.
32. Farrell, *Northern Ireland*, p. 61.
33. Farrell, *Northern Ireland*, p. 62.
34. Gilbert Denton and Tony Fahy, *The Northern Ireland Land Boundary, 1923–1992* (London: H.M. Customs & Excise, 1993), p. 20.
35. K.J. Rankin, 'The Role of the Irish Boundary Commission in the Entrenchment of the Irish Border: from tactical panacea to political liability', *Journal of Historical Geography*, 34 (2008), pp 422–47 at p. 434.
36. Donal Hall, 'Partition and County Louth,' *Journal of the County Louth Archaeological and Historical Society*, 27:2 (2010), pp 243–83 at p. 262.
37. *Northern Whig*, 3 Apr. 1923; David S. Johnson, 'Partition and Cross-Border Trade in the 1920s' in Peter Roebuck (ed.), *Plantation to Partition: Essays in Ulster History in Honour of J.L McCracken* (Belfast: Blackstaff, 1981), pp 229-246 at p. 232.
38. Catherine Nash, Dennis Lorainne, Graham Bryan, 'Putting the Border in Place: Customs Regulation in the Making of the Irish Border, 1921–1945', *Journal of Historical Geography*, 36 (2010), pp 421–31 at p. 424.
39. Fergus Mulligan, *One Hundred and Fifty Years of Irish Railways* (Belfast: Appletree Press, 1983), p. 101.

40. *Northern Standard*, 6 Apr. 1923.
41. Paddy Ryan, 'So Little Time and So Much to Do: the setting up of the Border from the Customs' Point of view' in Mary Harkin (ed.), *It's Us They're Talking About*, v: *Borders, Boundaries and Divisions: Proceedings from the McGlinchey Summer School 2002* (Clonmany: McGlinchey summer school committee , 2003), pp 39–44 at p. 40.
42. Johnson, 'Partition', p. 237.
43. *Northern Standard*, 4 May 1923.
44. Nash et al., 'Putting the Border in Place', p. 426.
45. *Frontier Sentinel*, 7 Apr. 1923.
46. Eunan O'Halpin, *Defending Ireland: the Irish State and Its Enemies Since 1922* (Oxford: Oxford University Press, 1999), p. 41.
47. Dáil Éireann, Debates, vol. 3, no. 2, 13 April 1923.
48. Johnson, 'Partition', pp 233–4.
49. Hall, 'Partition', p. 263.
50. *Northern Standard*, 4 Sept. 1925, speech in Clones.
51. Class Cab. 61.6–61.15.
52. Class Cab. 61.42, R.F. 40.
53. *Northern Standard*, 12 June 1925.
54. *Northern Standard*, 26 June 1925.
55. Interestingly, local house painter Robert Molloy, who chaired Clones UDC in the 1960s, proudly proclaimed himself an 'Ulster unionist'.
56. *Northern Standard*, 7 Aug. 1925.
57. *Northern Standard*, 23 Oct. 1925.
58. Farrell, *Northern Ireland,* p. 78.
59. *Daily Mail*, 16 Nov. 1925.
60. *Northern Standard*, 27 Nov. 1925.
61. Desmond Ryan, 'Sinn Féin Policy and Practice (1916–1926)' in Desmond Williams (ed.), *The Irish Struggle, 1916–1926* (London: Routledge & Kegan Paul, 1966), p. 37.
62. J. Bowyer Bell, *The Secret Army: a history of the I.R.A., 1916–1970,* (London: Sphere Books, 1972), p. 73.
63. Bardon, *A History of Ulster*, p. 509.
64. Ryan, 'Sinn Féin', p. 38.
65. Michael Laffan, *The Partition of Ireland, 1912–1925* (Dublin: Dublin Historical Association, 1983), p. 105.
66. *Northern Standard*, 4 Dec. 1925.
67. Nash, Lorainne and Bryan, 'Putting the Border in Place' p. 423.
68. Louise Fuller, *Irish Catholicism Since 1950: The Undoing of a Culture* (Dublin: Gill & Macmillan, 2002), pp 3–4.
69. Ibid., p. 5.
70. John Bowman, *De Valera and the Ulster Question, 1917–1973* (Oxford: Clarendon Press/Oxford University Press, 1982), pp 34–6.

71. Fuller, *Irish Catholicism*, p. 6; Ronan Fanning, *Independent Ireland* (Dublin: Helicon, 1983), p. 59.
72. Johnson, 'Partition', p. 246.
73. Joe Joyce, 'Pioneer Spirit Found along the Border', *Irish Times*, 14 May 2009.
74. *Northern Standard*, 2 Jan. 1925.
75. Interview with author on 21 June 2016.
76. Denton and Fahy, *The Northern Ireland Land Boundary*, pp 26–7.
77. TNA, CUST 49/875, cited in Nash et al., 'Putting the Border in Place', p. 426.
78. Hall, 2010:266.
79. Revenue Commissioners, *Instructions to Preventive Men Employed at Patrol Stations and Frontier Posts on the Customs Land Frontier* (1940), Appendix B. quoted in Hall, 'Partition and County Louth', p. 265.
80. Hall, 'Partition', pp 266–7.
81. Robin Morton (collated), *Come Day, Go Day, God Send Sunday: the Songs and Life Story, Told in His Own Words, of John Maguire, Traditional Singer and Farmer from Co. Fermanagh* (London: Routledge & Kegan Paul, 1973), pp 32–5.
82. Morton, *Come Day*, p. 33.
83. May Blair, *Hiring Fairs and Market Places* (Belfast: Appletree Press, 2007), p. 128.
84. Robert Harbinson, *Song of Erne* (Belfast: Blackstaff Press, 1987), pp 17–18.
85. Mary O'Brien, *Not a Leg to Stand On* (Cambridge: Vanguard Press, 2013), pp 39–40.
86. Ibid., p. 103.
87. Ibid., pp 103–4.
88. Ibid., pp 104.
89. Patrick McCabe, *Carn* (London: Picador, 1993), p. 11.
90. Liam Clarke, 'Arlene Foster Relives Horror of Father's Shooting by IRA and Tells How Bus Blast Could Have Killed Her', *Belfast Telegraph*, 18 Dec. 2015.
91. Barry Flynn, *Soldiers of Folly: the IRA Border Campaign, 1956–1962* (Cork: Collins Press, 2009), pp 49–54.
92. Ibid., pp 43–6.
93. Ibid., pp 136–7.
94. Ibid., pp 160–2.
95. Automobile Association (AA), *1962 Members' Handbook* (Dublin: AA, 1962), pp 25–30.
96. Maurice Leitch, *Poor Lazarus* (Belfast: Blackstaff, 1985), p. 53.
97. Ibid., p. 38.
98. Ibid., p. 31.
99. Ibid., p. 60.

100. Ibid., p. 188.
101. McKittrick et al., *Lost Lives*, p. 710.
102. Justin O'Brien, *The Arms Trial* (Dublin: Gill & Macmillan, 2000), pp 70–6.
103. James Kelly, *Orders for the Captain?* (Dublin: privately published, 1971), p. 18.
104. O'Brien, *The Arms Trial*, p. 71.
105. Ibid., p. 76.
106. Ibid., p. 78.
107. Patterson, *Ireland's Violent Frontier*, p. 31.
108. Joan McGuigan, *Incidents in Clones, 1950s–1970*, in Clones Community Forum, *A Clones Miscellany*, n.d.
109. McKittrick et al., *Lost Lives*, p. 722.
110. Alan Rogers, *Clones – A needs Survey* (Clones: Clones Study Group, 1985), p 36
111. Ibid, p. 36.
112. Sam McAughtry, *Down in the Free State* (Dublin: Gill & Macmillan, 1987), pp 67–71.
113. Colm Tóibín, *Bad Blood: a Walk along the Irish Border* (London: Picador, 2010), p. 121.
114. Ibid., p. 126.
115. *Impartial Reporter*, 1 May 1980.
116. *Impartial Reporter*, 5 Feb. 1981.
117. Eric Kaufman, *The Orange Order: a Contemporary Northern Irish History* (Oxford: Oxford University Press, 2007), p. 132.
118. 'Arlene Foster – Profile', BBC, 11 January 2010, http://news.bbc.co.uk/1/hi/northern_ireland/8452628.stm, accessed 15 Nov. 2017.
119. David McKittrick, 'Protestants in NI Town Want the Border Sealed', *Irish Times*, 23 June 1980.
120. Patterson *Ireland's Violent Frontier*, p. 193; under the sub-heading 'Ethnic Cleansing on the Border' he quotes Darting's lecture, which he got from Reverend Kille.
121. Ibid., p. 194.
122. Colin Randall, 'Anger over Memorial in Honour of IRA Killer', *Daily Telegraph*, 5 Oct. 1998; Graham Dawson, *Making Peace with the Past? Memories, Trauma and the Irish Troubles* (Manchester: Manchester University Press, 2007), p. 234.
123. Brian Harvey, Assumpta Kelly, Sean McGearty, Sonya Murray, *The Emerald Curtain: The social impact of the Irish Border* (Carrickmacross: Triskele, 2005), p. 89.
124. Donald Clarke, 'Time to Take off to Clones', *Irish Times*, 19 Oct. 2012.
125. Brendan Hughes, 'Casement Park Transport Plans "Unacceptable" say Stormont Officials', *Irish News*, 27 Sept. 2017.

3. Cloak and Dagger

1. 'Clones, Co. Monaghan', *The Workhouse: the Story of an Institution,* http://www.workhouses.org.uk/Clones, accessed 15 Nov. 2017.
2. Brian MacDonald, *A Time of Desolation: Clones Poor Law Union, 1845–50* (Enniskillen: Clogher Historical Society, 2001).
3. Catherine Wylie, 'Minister Denies Postponing Famine Event', *Irish Times,* 11 July 2011.
4. Lynch, 'The Clones Affray'.
5. Britishpathe.com, film ID 258.08, canister G 853, sort number G 0853.
6. Connaughton, *A Border Diary,* p. 147.
7. Ed Moloney and Bob Mitchell, 'The British Army's War with Garda Sgt McArdle: a Collusion Controversy from the 1970s', *The Broken Elbow,* 6 Feb. 2014, https://thebrokenelbow.com/2014/02/06/the-british-armys-war-with-garda-sgt-mcardle-a-collusion-controversy-from-the-1970s, accessed 15 Nov. 2017.
8. 'GAA Annual Awards', *Hoganstand.com,* 15 Dec. 2009, http://www.hoganstand.com/monaghan/ArticleForm.aspx?ID=121762, accessed 15 Nov. 2017.
9. Sean Slowey, 'Clones 1963', *The Clones Clarion,* Christmas 2003.
10. Pilip Ó Mórdha, *Cumann Peile Thiarnaigh Naofa Cluain Eois, 1886–1993* (Monaghan: R&S Printers, 1994), p. 83.
11. Patterson, *Ireland's Violent Frontier,* p. 59.
12. Ibid., p. 59; White to R.C. Cox, NIO, 25 June 1973, NA, FCO/248.
13. Longwill, 'The Irish Army', pp 214–5; cites Dáil Éireann, Adjournment Debate, 'Border Road Cratering', vol. 257, 1 Dec. 1971; vol. 257, 9 Dec. 1971.
14. Longwill, 'The Irish Army', p. 216.
15. Patterson, *Ireland's Violent Frontier,* p. 55.
16. Dail Éireann, Debates, vol. 166, 13 June 1973.
17. James FitzGerald, *What Disturbs Our Blood: a Son's Quest to Redeem the Past* (Toronto: Random House, 2010).
18. Ibid., pp 125–6.
19. Harry McGee, 'Arlene Foster Seeks Conciliation with Republic over Brexit', *Irish Times,* 13 Jan. 2017.
20. Turtle Bunbury, 'Bishopscourt, Clones, Co. Monaghan', http://www.turtle-bunbury.com/history/history_houses/hist_hse_bishopscourt.html, accessed 15 Nov. 2017.
21. 'Army May put Garrison in Clones', *Irish Times,* 3 Jan. 1973.
22. Brian MacDonald, 'South Ulster in the Age of the United Irishmen' in Thomas Bartlett, David Dickson, Daire Keogh and Kevin Whelan (eds), *1798: a Bicentenary Perspective* (Dublin: Four Courts Press, 2003), pp 226–42 at p. 227.

23.   Ibid., p. 231.
24.   Now the site of the Tyrone Guthrie Centre for artists and writers under the aegis of northern and southern arts councils.
25.   MacDonald 'South Ulster', p. 238.
26.   Bardon, *A History of Ulster*, p. 240.
27.   Ibid., p. 245.
28.   *Tyrone Constitution*, 13 Jan. 1912.
29.   *The Times*, 6 Aug. 1913.
30.   Quincey Dougan, 'Monaghan Unionists, a People Betrayed', *Bygone Days*, 13 June 2013, http://quincey.info/?p=154, accessed 15 Nov. 2017.
31.   'Fermanagh and Monaghan Volunteers: in Camp at Knockballymore: Prepared to Fight for Faith and Fatherland', *The Times*, 19 Jan. 1914; 'Ulster Police Visit the Orangeman's War Camp, Near Clones, and Ask Volunteers Drilling There for Their Gun Licences,' *Daily Sketch*, 24 Jan. 1914.
32.   Brian McConnell, 'Covenanting Families - The Clarkes, McConnells & Kings: Three County Monaghan Families who supported the Ulster Covenant', http://www.ulster-scots.com/uploads/14452046830796.PDF, accessed 19 Jan. 2018
33.   Hansard, House of Commons, vol. 127, 990–901.
34.   *Northern Standard*, 17 June 1921.
35.   David Fitzpatrick, 'The Orange Order and the Border', *Irish Historical Studies*, 33:129 (2002), p. 52.
36.   Brian Harvey, Assumpta Kelly, Sean McGearty, Sonya Murray, *The Emerald Curtain: the Social Impact of the Irish Border* (Carrickmacross: Triskele, 2005), p. 99.
37.   Terence Dooley, 'Protestant Migration from the Free State to Northern Ireland, 1920–25: a Private Census for Co. Fermanagh', *Clogher Record*, 15:3 (1996), pp 87–132.
38.   Class Cab. 61.39, R.F. 63.
39.   Class Cab. 61.45, R.F. 11, PRO, London.
40.   Fitzpatrick, 'The Orange Order' p. 57.
41.   McGarry, *Eoin O'Duffy*, p. 41.
42.   Dougan, 'Monaghan Unionists'.
43.   John McKenna, BMH, WS 552.
44.   McGarry, Eoin O'Duffy, pp 71–2.
45.   John Thomas Connolly, BMH, WS 598, pp 2-6; Hezlet, *The 'B' Specials*, p. 32.
46.   John McGonnell, BMH, WS 574, p.7.
47.   Morton, *Come Day*, p. 152.
48.   Connolly, BMH, WS 598, p. 5.
49.   George Lunt, 'Family Life on the Fermanagh-Monaghan Border', *Border Roads to Memories & Reconciliation*, Dec. 2015, http://www.

borderroadmemories.com/search-border-crossings/memories/family-life-on-the-fermanagh-monaghan-border, accessed 15 Nov. 2017; Lunt is grandson of William Gordon.

50.   Connolly, BMH, WS 574, p.6.

51.   Hezlet, *The 'B' Specials*, p. 36.

52.   John McGonnell, BMH, WS 0574, p. 8.

53.   Shea, *Voices*, p. 78.

54.   Fitzpatrick, 'The Orange Order', p. 62.

55.   *Northern Standard*, 14 July 1923.

56.   Assistant Commisioner Ó Cugáin to Ó Frighil, Secretary, Department of Home Affairs, 20 July 1923, NAI, Home Affairs Files, H 75/15, cited by Fitzpatrick, 'The Orange Order', p. 62.

57.   Susie Minto (ed.), *The Forgotten People of Ulster: Stories of Orangeism South of the Border* (Kesh: CADOLEMO, 2013), p. 6.

58.   *Northern Standard*, 3 July 1925.

59.   Fitzpatrick, 'The Orange Order', p. 64.

60.   Ibid., p. 66.

61.   Ibid., p. 67; a footnote cautions, however, that the ageing profile of southern Protestantism contributed to the decline in Orangeism.

62.   Minto, *The Forgotten People*, p. 40.

63.   Ibid., p. 32.

64.   Peter Woods and Sean Rocks, *Rumours from Monaghan* (Dublin: RTÉ Radio 1, 2009), http://www.rte.ie/radio1/doconone/2009/0609/646016-rumours, accessed 15 Nov. 2016; a documentary on Billy Fox.

65.   McKittrick et al., *Lost Lives*, pp 426-8.

66.   Ibid, p. 427.

67.   Ibid.

68.   *Northern Standard*, 15 March 1974.

69.   Joe Joyce, 'Gauntlets Go Down on Floor of the 19th Dáil', *Irish Times*, 4 Mar. 2010.

70.   Patterson, *Ireland's Violent Frontier*, p. 25.

71.   Woods & Rocks, *Rumours from Monaghan*.

72.   Longwill, 'The Irish Army', p. 215.

73.   *Irish Independent*, 10 Dec. 1971.

74.   Longwill, 'The Irish Army', p. 216–17; Patterson, *Ireland's Violent Frontier*, p. 30.

75.   Woods & Rocks, *Rumours from Monaghan*.

76.   'Monaghan: 1973 General Election', *ElectionsIreland.com*, http://electionsireland.com/election.php?elecid=12&electype=1&constitid=103, accessed 15 Nov. 2017.

77.   Ibid.

78.   Patterson, *Ireland's Violent Frontier*, p. 67.

79. Ibid., p. 62; White to J.T. Williams, NIO, 14 Nov. 1973, NA, FCO 87/248.
80. Patterson, *Ireland's Violent Frontier*, p. 62.
81. Ibid., p. 67.
82. Michael Cunningham, *Monaghan: County of Intrigue* (Tantallon, County Donegal: privately published, 1979), pp 49–50.
83. Ibid., p. 50.
84. Woods & Rocks, *Rumours from Monaghan*.
85. Minto, *The Forgotten People*, p. 32.
86. McKittrick et al., *Lost Lives,* p. 311.
87. *Northern Standard*, 1 Mar. 1974.
88. Gene Kerrigan, 'The Crime and Punishment of Michael Kinsella', *Magill*, 1 Oct. 1984.
89. *Northern Standard*, 1 and 8 Mar. 1974.
90. Cassels, *The Ulster Canal*, p. 32; attributed to Fergus Mulligan, *William Dargan: an Honourable Life, 1799–1867* (Dublin: Lilliput Press, 2013).

4. At the Summit

1.   Christopher Fitz-Simon, *Eleven Houses: a Memoir of Childhood* (London: Penguin, 2007), p. 3.
2.   Ibid., pp 5–22.
3.   Philip Marron, BMH, WS 657, pp 7–11.
4.   Patterson, *Ireland's Violent Frontier*, p. 43; 'IRA Adopt New Tactic of Pillaging and Burning Homes of Protestants Along the Border', *Impartial Reporter*, 27 July 1972.
5.   Nash et al., *Partitioned Lives*, p. 89.
6.   Ibid., p. 100.
7.   Thomas Hubert, '2 Sisters Owner to Buy Ireland's Largest Turkey Producer', *Farmers Journal*, 24 May 2016, http://www.farmersjournal.ie/2-sisters-owner-to-buy-irelands-largest-turkey-producer-206086, accessed 18 Nov. 2017.
8.   *Belfast Telegraph*, 13 Jan. 1982; also cited in Darach MacDonald, *The Chosen Fews: Exploding Myths in South Armagh* (Cork: Mercier, 2000), p. 29.
9.   Interviewed by James Leonard, Scoil Mhuire, Magherarney in Sarah Moloney (ed.), *Reminiscences: Clones Erne East Partnership Schools' Folklore Collection, 2006–2008* (Clones: Clones Erne East Partnership/Clogher Historical Society, 2008), p. 6.
10. Adrian Rutherford, 'Arlene Foster's Fury as SF MLA Hails "Man Who Shot Her Father"', *Belfast Telegraph*, 2 April 2016, http://www.belfasttelegraph. co.uk/news/northern-ireland/arlene-fosters-fury-as-sf-mla-hails-man-who-shot-her-father-34592138.html, accessed 18 Nov. 2017.

11. Tírghrá: *Ireland's Patriot Dead* (Dublin: National Commemoration Centre, 2002), p. 278.

12. Mark Urban, *Big Boys' Rules: the SAS and the Secret Struggle against the IRA* (London: Faber & Faber, 1992), pp140–1.

13. 'Seamus McElwaine', *Electionsireland.org*, n.d., http://electionsireland.org/candidate.cfm?ID=2713, accessed 18 Nov. 2017.

14. Alan O'Day, *Political Violence in Northern Ireland: Conflict and Conflict Resolution* (Westport, CT: Praeger, 1997), p. 88.

15. Raymond Murray, *The SAS in Ireland* (Cork: Mercier, 2004), p. 374.

16. Ed Moloney, *A Secret History of the IRA* (London: Penguin, 2002), p. 315.

17. Ibid., p. 529.

18. Murray, *The SAS*, pp 365–74.

19. Brian MacDomhnaill, 'Remembering McElwaine', *An Phoblacht*, 25 May 2006.

20. Murray, *The SAS*, pp 369–70.

21. Moloney, *A Secret History*, pp 18, 386.

22. Toby Harnden, *Bandit Country: the IRA and South Armagh* (London: Hodder & Stoughton, 1999), p. 245; McKittrick, *Lost Lives*, p. 354.

23. Moloney, *A Secret History*, p. 243.

24. Ibid., pp 313–4.

25. Flynn, *Soldiers of Folly*, p. 67.

26. Harnden, *Bandit Country*, p. 240.

27. Moloney, *A Secret History*, pp 312–3.

28. 'Micheál Martin, Gerry Adams and Martin McGuinness', *Broken Elbow*, 12 Feb. 2011, https://thebrokenelbow.com/category/kevin-mckenna, accessed 18 Nov. 2017.

29. Moloney, *A Secret History*, pp 445–7.

30. Ibid., p. 477.

31. Ibid., p. 478.

32. Bardon, *A History of Ulster*, p. 12.

33. Theo McMahon, 'The Tragic Deaths in 1871 in County Monaghan of Emily and Mary Wilde – Half-Sisters of Oscar Wilde', *Clogher Record*, 18:1 (2003), pp 129–45.

34. Ordnance maps spell the name as 'Drummaconor', but there is only one town-land of the name, and the spelling of Drumaconnor is interchangeable.

35. McMahon, 'The Tragic Deaths', p. 130, citing Heather White, *Wildfire: the Story of Oscar Wilde's Half-Sisters* (Drumskinny: Principia Press, 2002).

36. Brian de Breffny, 'The Paternal Ancestry of Oscar Wilde', *The Irish Ancestor*, 2 (1973), pp 96–99.

37. T.G. Wilson, *Victorian Doctor: Being the Life of Sir William Wilde* (Wakefield: EP Publishing, 1974).

38. Eamonn Mulligan and Fr Brian McCluskey (compiled), *The Replay: a Parish History* (Monaghan: privately published, 1984), pp 90–1.

39. Fitz-Simon, *Eleven Houses,* pp 227–8.
40. Armagh Meteorological Records for Oct. 1871 are available at http://climate.arm.ac.uk/scans/1871/10/INDEXA.html.
41. McMahon, 'The Tragic Deaths', p. 131.
42. Ibid., pp 142–3.
43. Ibid., p. 134, notes.
44. Mulligan and McCluskey 1984:90.
45. McMahon, 'The Tragic Deaths', p. 144; Hesketh Pearson, *The Life of Oscar Wilde* (Twickenham: Senate, 1998), p. 16, first published in 1946 as *Oscar Wilde: His Life and Wit.*
46. 'The Tragedy of Oscar Wilde's Sisters', *Irish Identity,* n.d., http://www.irishidentity.com/extras/gaels/stories/wilde.htm, accessed 18 Nov. 2017, gives the room's measurements as 14 feet by 12 feet.
47. Cassells, *The Ulster Canal,* p. 41.
48. Ibid., pp 42–3.
49. Ibid., p. 43.
50. Ibid., p. 45.
51. Tóibín, *Bad Blood,* p. 139.
52. Nash et al., *Partitioned Lives,* pp 49–50.
53. Nash et al., *Partitioned Lives,* p. 67.
54. Nash et al., *Partitioned Lives,* pp 61–2.
55. Tóibín, *Bad Blood,* pp 139–46.
56. '1820s – Cornacassa House, Monaghan, Co. Monaghan', Archiseek, n.d., http://archiseek.com/2016/cornacassa-house-monaghan-co-monaghan, accessed 18 Nov 2017.
57. Cassells, *The Ulster Canal,* p. 25.
58. Sean Farrell, *Rituals and Riots: Sectarian Violence and Political Culture in Ulster, 1784–1886* (Lexington, KY: University Press of Kentucky, 2015), p. 272.
59. James Loughlin, 'Parades and Politics: Liberal Governments and the Orange Order, 1880–86' in T.G. Fraser (ed.), *The Irish Parading Tradition: Following the Drum* (New York: Palgrave Macmillan, 2000), pp 25–43 at p. 36.
60. Hansard, Parliamentary Debates, vol. 284, 8 Feb. 1884.
61. J. Wallace Taylor, *The Rossmore Incident: an Account of the Various Nationalist or Counter-Nationalist Meetings Held in Ulster in the Autumn of 1883* (Dublin: Hodges & Company, 1884).
62. 'The Roslea Incident', *Ask About Ireland,* n.d., http://www.askaboutireland.ie/reading-room/history-heritage/big-houses-of-ireland/rossmore-castle/the-roslea-incident, accessed 18 Nov. 2017.
63. 'Monaghan United Exited the League of Ireland Four Years Ago Today', League of Ireland.ie, http://leagueofireland.ie/index.php/2016/06/18/monaghan-united-league-of-ireland, accessed 18 Nov. 2017.

64.   'Monaghan United Exited the League of Ireland four years ago today', LeagueofIreland.ie, 18 June 2016 http://leagueofireland.ie/index.php/2016/06/18/ monaghan-united-league-of-ireland/, accessed 19 Jan. 2018.

65.   'Stadium', *Monaghan United*, n.d., http://monaghanunited.tv/?page_ id=95, accessed 18 Nov. 2017.

66.   Richard Henshaw, *The Encyclopaedia of World Soccer* (Washington, DC: New Republic, 1979), p. 380.

67.   David Toms, 'Rule 27: When a Love for the 'Wrong' Kind of Football Would See You Ostracized', *Póg Mo Goal*, 25 (Apr. 2015), http://www. the42.ie/gaa-ending-of-ban-on-foreign-games-2096952-May2015, accessed 18 Nov 2017.

5. County Town

1.   McAughtry, *Down in the Free State*, p. 65.

2.   Ibid., p. 64.

3.   Terence Dooley, 'From the Belfast Boycott to the Boundary Commission: Fears and Hopes in County Monaghan, 1920–25', *Clogher Record*, 15:1 (1994), pp 90–106; *Miontuairisc an Chead Dála, 1919–1921: Minutes of the Proceedings of the First Parliament of the Republic of Ireland: Official Record* (Dublin: Stationery Office, 1994), pp 191–4.

4.   Ibid., p. 193.

5.   Ibid., p. 194; the only two deputies from the 'North of Ireland' recorded as speaking were MacEntee and Blythe, both Belfast-born.

6.   Dooley, 'From Belfast', p. 91, cites County Inspector's Confidential Monthly Report, Apr. 1921 (PRO, CO, 904, pt III).

7.   Dooley, 'From Belfast', p. 92.

8.   *Northern Standard*, 24 Sept. 1920.

9.   Dooley, 'From Belfast', p. 92; article entitled 'Sinn Féin Courts', dated 20 Oct. 1921 (PRO 904, pt 6).

10.   Dooley, 'From Belfast', p. 93; report of Monaghan Brigade IRA to GHQ, Apr. 1921 in UCD Archives, Collins Papers, P7/A/39.

11.   Ex-Commandant John McGonnell, BMH, WS 574, p. 5.

12.   Dooley, 'From Belfast', p. 93; report of Monaghan Brigade, IRAQ to GHQ Apr. 1921.

13.   McGonnell, BMH, WS 574, p. 6.

14.   Philip Marron, BMH, WS 657, p. 7.

15.   Ibid., p.7.

16.   *Northern Standard*, 27 Jan. 1922.

17.   Fitz-Simon, *Eleven Houses*, pp 232–3.

18. Ibid., p. 234.
19. Ibid.
20. McAughtry, *Down in the Free State,* p. 65.
21. Nuala O'Faolain, *Are You Somebody?* (Dublin: New Island, 1996), p. 38.
22. Ibid., p. 42.
23. Flynn, *Soldiers of Folly*, p. 100.
24. Ibid., p. 104.
25. Ibid., p. 106.
26. Ibid., p. 107.
27. Ibid., p. 110., cites *Sunday Tribune*, 24 Dec. 2006.
28. Flynn, *Soliders of Folly*, p. 111.
29. Ibid., p. 119.
30. Ibid., p. 120–1.
31. Ibid., p. 122.
32. Ibid., p. 128.
33. 'Mr. Eighnaechán Ó hAnnluain', *Dáil Éireann Members' Directory*, n.d., http://www.oireachtas.ie/members-hist/default.asp?housetype=0&HouseNum=16&MemberID=2101&ConstID=152, accessed 18 Nov. 2017.
34. Flynn, *Soldiers of Folly*, pp 126–7.
35. I was a staff journalist in Canada and part-time *Irish Times* correspondent.
36. Flynn, *Soldiers of Folly*, p. 137.
37. Austin Currie, *All Hell Will Break Loose* (Dublin: O'Brien, 2004), p. 142.
38. Currie, *All Hell*, p. 143.
39. Cunningham, *Monaghan*, p. 14.
40. Justin O'Brien, *The Arms Trial* (Dublin: Gill Books, 2000), pp 70-71.
41. Currie, *All Hell*, p. 142.
42. *Northern Standard*, 29 Aug. 1969.
43. Patterson, *Ireland's Violent Frontier*, p. 32.
44. 'Protest Lodged with Britain over Border Incident', *Irish Times*, 24 Mar. 1972.
45. Tim Healy, 'State Gets €6m Boost from 1985 "IRA Cash"', *Irish Independent*, 15 Mar. 2008.
46. National Archives (UK), FCO 87/248; Operation Motorman, the British army's incursion into former nationalist 'no-go areas' took place on 31 July 1972.
47. Patterson, *Ireland's Violent Frontier*, p. 38.
48. Ibid., pp 38–9.
49. Paddy Hayes, *Break-out! Famous Prison Escapes* (Dublin: O'Brien, 2004), pp 118–19.
50. Stephen Collins, *The Power Game: Fianna Fáil since Lemass* (Dublin: O'Brien, 2000), p. 94.
51. Catherine Nash and Bryonie Reid, 'Border Crossings: New Approaches to the Irish Border', *Irish Studies Review*, 18:3 (2010), p. 277.

52. Ó Beacháin, *Destiny of the Soldiers*, p. 365.

53. Anthony Craig, *Crisis of Confidence: Anglo-Irish Relations in the Early Troubles* (Dublin: Irish Academic Press, 2010), pp 156–7.

54. Patterson, *Ireland's Violent Frontier*, p. 59.

55. Paul Bew, Gordon Gillespie, *Northern Ireland: a Chronology of the Troubles, 1968–1999* (Dublin: Gill & Macmillan, 1999), p. 85.

56. Interim Report of the Independent Commission of Inquiry into the Dublin and Monaghan Bombings, Joint Committee on Justice, Equality, Defence and Women's Rights (Barron Report), 2003, pp 275–9.

57. Oireachtas Sub-Committee Report on the Barron Report, 2004, p. 21.

58. Barron Report 2003, p. 75.

59. Ibid., pp 48–9.

60. Ibid., p. 7.

61. Peter Taylor, *Provos: the IRA and Sinn Féin* (London: Bloomsbury, 1997), pp 229–34.

62. Peter Taylor, *Families at War: Voices from the Troubles* (London: BBC Books, 1989), pp 232–4.

63. 'Kieran Doherty', *Elections Ireland*, n.d., ElectionsIreland.org, http://electionsireland.org/candidate.cfm?ID=3268, accessed 18 Nov. 2017.

64. 'Ballsbridge Riot a Watershed in Irish History', *Irish Times*, 17 July 2001; as a *Sunday Tribune* reporter, I had a front-line vantage on the entire Ballsbridge confrontation.

65. *Northern Standard*, 23 July 1981.

66. Ibid., 30 July 1981.

67. Ibid., 6 Aug. 1981.

68. Ibid., 6 Aug. 1981.

69. Ibid., 20 Aug. 1981.

70. 'H-Block Armagh News', *Northern Standard*, 24 Sept. 1981.

71. 'Mullaghmatt Naming Row Goes On', *Northern Standard*, 18 Mar 1982.

72. 'Siege of Clones', *Northern Standard*, 24 Sept. 1981.

73. 'Shocking Emyvale Murder', *Northern Standard*, 8 Jan. 1982.

74. 'Monaghan Youth given Life Sentence for Murder', *Irish Times*, 17 June 1982.

75. Mark Urban, *Big Boys' Rules*, p. 223.

76. Gene Kerrigan, 'Considering the Death of a Man Aged About 25 Years', *Magill*, 1 Dec. 1982.

77. Vincent Browne and Gene Kerrigan, 'They Wouldn't Leave Him Alone: the Death of Michael Lynagh', *Magill*, 1 Oct. 1982.

78. Moloney, *A Secret History*, p. 291.

79. Brian Feeney, *Sinn Féin: a Hundred Turbulent Years* (Dublin: O'Brien, 2002), p. 385.

80. Exodus 15:27.

81. Elim Bible Week Ireland, *Maldwyn Jones Visits Monaghan, the Birthplace of Elim,* 12 Jan. 2015, https://www.youtube.com/watch?v=9vmPoURlsr4, accessed 12 Jan. 2015.

82. Cassells, *The Ulster Canal*, p. 39.

83. Ibid., p. 40.

84. HC Deb., 20 Feb. 1919 vol. 112 cc1116–7.

85. *The Times*, 9 Feb. 1924.

86. Anton McCabe, '"The Stormy Petrel of the Transport Workers": Peadar O'Donnell, Trade Unionist, 1917–1920', *Saothar 19: Journal of the Irish Labour History Society*, 19 (1994), pp 41-51.

87. McCabe, 'Peadar O'Donnell', p. 43, cites *The Voice of Labour*, 15 Mar. 1919.

88. McCabe, 'Peadar O'Donnell', p. 43, cites *Anglo-Celt*, 15 Feb. 1919.

89. *Northern Standard*, 18 Jan. 1919.

90. McCabe, 'Peadar O'Donnell', p. 44.

91. *Derry Journal*, 28 Feb. 1919.

92. McCabe, 'Peadar O'Donnell', p. 44.

93. Ibid., p. 45.

6. Oriel Affairs

1. Edward Longwill, 'The Irish Army and State Security Policy, 1956–74' (PhD, Ulster University, 2009), p. 131; cites MA, SCS 29. CS/111/1. 1970 General Correspondence, Estimates for Defence 1969/70 – Border Activities, Troop Deployments, Section 4.

2. Óglaigh na hÉireann/Defence Forces Ireland, 'Defence Forces in History', n.d., http://www.military.ie/en/info-centre/defence-forces-history/into-the-modern-era-1969-present-day, accessed 18 Nov. 2017.

3. Alison Healy, 'Marching Orders as Monaghan Barracks Shuts', *Irish Times*, 23 Jan. 2009.

4. Joe MacAnthony, 'The Taoiseach's Secret Border Policy', *Sunday Independent*, 19 Dec. 1971; Patterson, *Ireland's Violent Frontier*, p. 35.

5. 'Army May Put Garrison in Clones', *Irish Times*, 3 Jan. 1973.

6. Dick Walsh, 'Local Security Unites Now Unlikely', *Irish Times*, 1 Dec. 1976.

7. O'Halpin, *Defending Ireland*, pp 45–6.

8. Ibid., p. 46; cites an Old IRA questionnaire on 'intelligence', with chief of staff to minister for defence, 24 Nov. 1923, MP, P7/B/195.

9. O'Halpin, *Defending Ireland*, p. 46.

10. Ibid., p. 47; there were also rumours of ex British officers and 'Masonic influences' in the ranks.

11. Ibid., p. 48.

12. Ibid., pp 48–9.

13. Ibid., p. 50.
14. Ibid., p. 57.
15. Ibid., p. 58.
16. Ibid., pp 59–60.
17. Ibid., p. 61–2.
18. Ibid., p. 62–3.
19. Ibid., p. 77.
20. Ibid., p. 305.
21. Ibid., p. 306; cites Bruce Arnold, *Charles Haughey: His Life and Unlucky Deeds* (London: HarperCollins, 1993), p. 55.
22. O'Halpin, *Defending Ireland*, pp 306–7.
23. For a concise overview of this episode and the cover-up, see Steven McCaffrey, "'If It Happened to Us, It Could Happen to You" – a Family Seeking Truth from Government', *Detail*, 3 Mar. 2014, http://www.thedetail.tv/articles/if-it-happened-to-us-it-could-happen-to-you-a-family-seeking-truth-from-government, accessed 18 Nov. 2017.
24. Healy, 'Marching Orders'.
25. 'Castle Leslie Estate – 1,000 Years of Leslie Family History and American-Irish Family History', *Castle Leslie Estate*, n.d., http://www.castleleslie.com/upload/docs/leslie-family-history.pdf, accessed 18 Nov. 2017.
26. B.M. Walker (ed.), *Parliamentary Election Results in Ireland, 1801–1922* (Dublin: Royal Irish Academy), 1978.
27. Seamus McCluskey, *Monaghan's Match GAA Yearbook* (Monaghan: Monaghan GAA County Board, 2004). Reproduced at http://www.irishidentity.com/stories/leslie.htm, accessed 19 Jan. 2018.
28. Brian MacDonald, 'South Ulster in the Age of the United Irishmen' in Thomas Bartlett, David Dickson, Dáire Keogh and Kevin Whelan (eds), *1798: a Bicentenary Perspective* (Dublin: Four Courts Press, 2003), pp 226–42 at pp 238, 240.
29. Dougan, 'Monaghan Unionists'.
30. McGarry, *Eoin O'Duffy*, p. 57.
31. Dougan, 'Monaghan Unionists'.
32. Bardon, *A History of Ulster*, p. 420.
33. London: MacDonald & Co., 1946; London: John Murray Publishers Ltd, 1966.
34. Shane Leslie, *Shane Leslie's Ghost Stories* (London: Hollis & Carter, 1956).
35. 'Celebrated Aristocrat Sir Jack Leslie Dies at the Age of 99', BBC News, 18 Apr. 2016, http://www.bbc.co.uk/news/world-europe-36073642, accessed 18 Nov. 2017.
36. 'Cutting a Rug at the Castle Leslie Club, 1966', RTÉ, n.d., http://www.rte.ie/archives/2016/1108/830060-castle-leslie, accessed 18 Nov. 2017.
37. 'Broadcaster Levin Dies at Age 75', BBC News, 10 Aug. 2004, http://news.bbc.co.uk/1/hi/entertainment/3549674.stm, accessed 18 Nov. 2017.

38. Victoria Mary Clarke, 'Life, Love and the Leslies', *Sunday Independent*, 28 Mar. 2004.

39. Michael Fisher, 'Mushroom Industry in Turmoil Since Brexit Vote', *Northern Standard*, 29 Sept. 2016.

40. 'History', *Monaghan Mushrooms*, n.d., https://www.monaghan-mush-rooms.com/who-we-are/business/history-2, accessed 18 Nov. 2017.

41. Amy Nora Fitzgibbon, 'Mushroom industry "thrown into turmoil" by Brexit', *Irish Farmers Journal*, 27 September 2016.

42. https://www.monaghan-mushrooms.com

43. Monaghan County Council, 'Monaghan Local Economic and Community Development Plan 2015-2021, p. 6-7; https://monaghan.ie/communitydevelopment/wp-content/uploads/sites/8/2016/12/MonaghanLECP2015-2021.pdf, accessed 19 Jan. 2018.

44. 'Pipers Bridge, County Monaghan', *National Inventory of Architectural Heritage*, n.d., http://www.buildingsofireland.ie/niah/search.jsp?type=record&county=MO&regno=41401002, accessed 18 Nov. 2017.

45. Marron, BMS, WS 657, pp 11–16.

46. John McKenna, BMS, WS 552, pp 6–7.

47. *Northern Standard*, 24 Mar. 1922.

48. James Short, BMH, WS 534, p. 7.

49. Terence Dooley, *The Irish Revolution, 1912–23: Monaghan* (Dublin: Four Courts, 2017), pp 116–7.

50. Charlie McGleenan, BMH, WS 829, p. 29.

51. Ibid., pp 29–30.

52. Short, BMH, WS 534, p. 8.

53. McGleenan, BMH, WS 829, pp 28–9.

54. Dooley, *Monaghan*, p. 119.

55. McGleenan, BMH, WS 829, pp 30–1.

56. *Northern Standard*, 11 Sept. 1922; Dooley, *Monaghan,* p. 119.

57. Short, BMH, WS 534, p. 8.

58. McKittrick et al., *Lost Lives*, p. 837.

59. Ibid., p. 737: see Chapter 7 of this book.

60. David Sharrock, 'Family Pray for Peace but Fear for the Future,' *Guardian*, 15 Sept. 1994; Patterson, *Ireland's Violent Frontier*, pp 197–8.

61. Sam McAughtry, *Down in the Free State* (Dublin: Gill & Macmillan, 1987), p. 57.

62. Ibid., p. 60.

63. McKittrick et al., *Lost Lives*, p. 672.

64. Cadwallader, *Lethal Allies: British Collusion in Ireland* (Cork: Mercier, 2013), pp 194–201.

65. Liam Clarke, 'RUC Men's Secret War with the IRA', *Sunday Times*, 7 Mar. 1999.

66. McKittrick et al., *Lost Lives*, p. 511.

67. MacDonald, *The Chosen Fews*, p. 158–84.

68. McKittrick et al., *Lost Lives*, p. 716.

69. Bardon, *A History of Ulster*, p. 767. Other accounts estimate the loyalist numbers as low as 150.

70. Sam McBride, 'RUC Tipped Off the Garda about Robinson's "Invasion" of Clontibret', *News Letter*, 29 Dec. 2014.

71. Sam McBride, 'RUC Tipped Off the Garda about Robinson's "Invasion" of Clontibret', *News Letter*, 29 Dec. 2014.

72. Bardon, *A History of Ulster*, p. 767.

73. Rebecca Black, 'Ian Paisley and Peter Robinson: a Very Public Falling-Out', *Belfast Telegraph*, 11 Jan. 2014.

74. Frank O'Connor, *The Big Fellow: Michael Collins and the Irish Revolution* (London: Corgi, 1965), p. 157.

75. McKittrick et al., *Lost Lives*, p. 163.

76. *Ulster Gazette*, 16 Mar. 1972.

77. 'RUC Name Change 'Insult to Victims', BBC News, 9 Sept. 1999, http://news.bbc.co.uk/1/hi/northern_ireland/442672.stm, accessed 18 Nov. 2017.

78. Murray, *The SAS*, p. 72; John Deering, 'Soldier's Death Raises Fermanagh Suspicions', *Irish Times*, 7 Apr. 1975.

79. Liam Clarke, 'McCoy Won't be Spooked into Revelations', *Sunday Times*, 8 Nov. 2010.

80. Murray, *The SAS*, pp 119–20.

81. Ibid., p. 118.

82. Sidney Lee, 'Stearne, John (1660–1745)', *Dictionary of National Biography* (London: Smith, Elder & Co., 1898), p. 54.

83. 'Man Arrested for Going "Home"', *Manchester Guardian*, 29 July 1938.

84. Sean T. O'Kelly, BMH, WS 1765.

85. Short, BMH, WS 534.

86. 'Eamon Donnelly Remembered', *Newry Journal*, 25 Jan. 2008.

87. Short, BMH, WS 534; Frank Donnelly, BMH, WS 941.

88. De Valera Papers, P150/1381, University College Dublin Archives.

89. Des Fitzgerald, 'Michael Collins in Armagh', *History Armagh*, 1:2 (2005), pp 7–11.

90. Uinseann MacEoin, *The IRA in the Twilight Years, 1923–1948* (Dublin: Argenta, 1997), pp 77–9.

91. Robert Whan, 'Part A: Eamon Donnelly', in *A Catalogue of the Eamon Donnelly Collection at Newry and Mourne Museum* (Newry: Newry and Mourne Museum, 2014), pp 4–12 at p. 6; Dorothy Macardle, *The Irish Republic* (London: Corgi, 1968), pp 786, 788; Eoin Neeson, *The Civil War, 1922–23* (Dublin: Poolbeg, 1989), pp 294–5.

92. 'Eamon Donnelly', *Newry Journal*.

93.   'Mr Eamon Donnelly', *Houses of the Oireachtas*, n.d., http://www.oireach-tas.ie/members-hist/default.asp?housetype=0&HouseNum=8&MemberID=334&ConstID=127, accessed 18 Nov. 2017.

94.   Whan, 'Eamon Donnelly', p. 7.

95.   Stephen Kelly, *Fianna Fáil, Partition and Northern Ireland, 1926–1971* (Dublin: Irish Academic Press, 2013), pp 82–5, 89–90, 95–7; John Bowman, *De Valera and the Ulster Question, 1917–1973* (Oxford: Clarendon/Oxford University Press, 1982), pp 132–5.

96.   Bowman, *De Valera*, pp 14–15.

97.   *Freeman's Journal*, 12 Nov. 1917; *Irish Independent*, 6 July 1917; *Freeman's Journal*, 20 July 1917.

98.   Bowman, *De Valera* (1982), pp 34–6; *Irish Times*, 9 Feb. 1918.

99.   Bowman, *De Valera* (1982), p. 34; *Sligo Champion*, 28 July 1917.

100.   Bowman, *De Valera* (1982), p. 33.

101.   Éamon Donnelly to Cahir Healy, 25 Sept. and 30 Oct. 1936 (PRONI, Healy Papers, D2991/B/10/5–6).

102.   Whan, 'Eamon Donnelly', p. 9.

103.   *Belfast Telegraph*, 28 July 1938.

104.   'Eamon Donnelly', *Newry Journal*.

105.   Whan, 'Eamon Donnelly', p. 9; *Irish News*, 31 Aug. 1938.

106.   Whan, 'Eamon Donnelly', p. 10; *News Letter*, 13 Dec. 1940.

107.   Whan, 'Eamon Donnelly', p. 11; Enda Staunton, *The Nationalists of Northern Ireland 1918–1973* (Dublin: Columba, 2001), p. 150.

108.   Whan, 'Eamon Donnelly', p. 11.

109.   Cahir Healy Papers, PRONI, D2991.

110.   *Newry Reporter*, 2 Jan. 1945.

111.   Brendan Lynn, *Holding the Ground: the Nationalist Party in Northern Ireland, 1945–72* (Farnham: Ashgate, 1997).

112.   Farrell, *Northern Ireland*, p. 178.

113.   Ibid., pp 178–9.

114.   Ibid., pp 181–2.

115.   Ibid., p. 180.

116.   Ibid., p. 180; Parliament of Northern Ireland, Parliamentary Debates: Hansard, House of Commons, vol. 30, col. 2164.

117.   Farrell, *Northern Ireland*, pp 184–5.

118.   Ibid., p. 378 n. 39.

119.   Ibid., p. 198.

7. Dark Edges

1.   McKittrick et al., *Lost Lives,* pp 565–6, 1407–8.

2.   'Club of the Week – Middletown', *Gaelic Life*, 26 Jan. 2012, http://gaeli-clife.com/2012/01/club-of-the-week-middletown, accessed 18 Nov. 2017.

3.   Cassells, *The Ulster Canal*, pp 34–5.
4.   McKittrick et al., *Lost Lives,* p. 849.
5.   Urban, *Big Boys' Rules*, p. 223.
6.   McKittrick et al., *Lost Lives*, p. 849.
7.   Moloney, *A Secret History*, p. 320; McKittrick et al., *Lost Lives,* p. 849; Bardon, *A History of Ulster*, p. 743.
8.   Bardon, *A History of Ulster*, p. 478.
9.   Mick Fealty, 'The Price Was Right', *Guardian*, 13 Mar. 2007, https://www.the-guardian.com/commentisfree/2007/mar/13/mandymaynotbewrongbutbla1, accessed 18 Nov. 2017; Quincey Dougan, 'Sir Charles Norman Lockart Stronge', 15 Jan. 2015, http://quincey.info/?p=1042, accessed 18 Nov. 2017, a reference attributing the quotation to Moloney, *A Secret History*, proved erroneous; C.D.C. Armstrong, 'A Super-selective Memory', *The Spectator*, I November 2003, p. 48 http://archive.spectator.co.uk/article/1st-november-2003/48/a-super-selective-memory, accessed 19 Jan. 2018; Samuel Morrison (Traditional Unionist Voice), Will McLaughlin Remember the Stronge Murders?, The NewsLetter, Belfast, 15 January 2015 https://www.newsletter.co.uk/news/your-say/will-mclaughlin-remember-stronge-murders-1-6523311, accessed 19 Jan. 2018
10.   Hansard, House of Commons Debates, 12 Feb. 1981, vol. 998, cols 968–71, http://hansard.millbanksystems.com/commons/1981/feb/12/security, accessed 18 Nov. 2017.
11.   'Stronge Double Murder Detailed in Government Files', BBC News, 28 Dec. 2012, http://www.bbc.co.uk/news/uk-northern-ireland-20854772, accessed 18 Nov. 2017.
12.   McKittrick et al., *Lost Lives*, p. 737.
13.   Jim Cusack, 'Genocidal Killer Who Got "Up Close and Personal"', *Irish Independent*, 9 Nov. 2003, http://www.independent.ie/opinion/analysis/genocidal-killer-who-got-up-close-and-personal-26236831.html, accessed 18 Nov. 2017.
14.   McKittrick et al., *Lost Lives,* 2004, p. 737.
15.   Harnden, *Bandit Country*, p. 191.
16.   *Ulster Gazette*, 2 Mar. 1972.
17.   McKittrick et al., *Lost Lives*, p. 1061.
18.   '"Border Fox" Dessie O'Hare Granted Bail as He Fights Extradition to Dublin', BBC News, 11 Nov. 2016, http://www.bbc.co.uk/news/uk-northern-ireland-37955818, accessed 18 Nov. 2017.
19.   Ibid.
20.   William Reeves, 'The Ancient Churches of Armagh', *Ulster Journal of Archaeology*, 4:4 (1898), p. 213.
21.   Samuel Lewis, *A Topographical Dictionary of Ireland* (London: S. Lewis & Co., 1837), https://www.johngrenham.com/records/lewis.php?civilparish id=403&civilparish=Tynan&county=Armagh&search_type=full, accessed 18 Nov. 2017.

22. Fergus Mulligan, *Irish Railways*, p. 147.

23. Ibid., p. 148.

24. Ibid, pp 101-2

25. Fitz-Simon, *Eleven Houses*, p. 295.

26. Turtle Bunbury, 'Related Families – Strong of Tynan Abbey', http://www.turtlebunbury.com/family/bunburyfamily_related/bunbury_family_related_stronge.html, accessed 18 Nov. 2017.

27. 'Lady Foley', *The Telegraph*, 24 May 2000, http://www.telegraph.co.uk/news/obituaries/1366806/Lady-Foley.html, accessed 18 Nov. 2017.

28. Ian McCabe, 'Surprise Move from Free State Status to Independent Republic', *Irish Times*, 5 Apr. 1999.

29. Ian McCabe, *A Diplomatic History of Ireland, 1948–49: the Republic, the Commonwealth and NATO* (Dublin: Irish Academic Press, 1991).

30. Darach MacDonald, *Blood & Thunder: Inside an Ulster Protestant Band* (Cork: Mercier, 2010), pp 120–44.

31. Ibid., p. 127.

32. Bardon, *A History of Ulster*, p. 182.

33. Ibid., p. 181; Peadar Murnane and James Murnane, 'The Linen Industry in the Parish of Aughnamullen, Co. Monaghan and Its Impact on the Town of Ballybay, 1740 to 1835', *Clogher Record,* 12:3 (1987), pp 334–68 at p. 362.

34. Cassells, *The Ulster Canal*, p. 25.

35. 'Ulster Canal', *Blackwater Regional Partnership*, n.d., http://blackwaterregion.com/ulster-canal, accessed 18 Nov. 2018; *Dublin Mercantile Advertiser and Weekly Price Current*, 16 June 1834.

36. 'Caledon Woollen Mill', *Blackwater Regional Partnership*, n.d., http://blackwaterregion.com/heritage_site/caledon-woollen-mill, accessed 18 Nov. 2018.

37. McCabe, 'Peadar O'Donnell', p. 45.

38. *Derry Journal*, 28 Feb. 1919.

39. *Voice of Labour*, 1 Mar. 1919.

40. McCabe, 'Peadar O'Donnell', p. 45; *Anglo-Celt*, 10 Jan. 1920.

41. McCabe, 'Peadar O'Donnell', p. 46; *Armagh Guardian*, 4 July 1919.

42. *Armagh Guardian*, 18 July 1919.

43. Calton Younger, *Ireland's Civil War* (London: Fontana, 1970), p. 259; Hezlet, *The 'B' Specials*, p. 69, estimated that 8,500 IRA volunteers lived in the six counties and 'they were practically all of the anti-Treaty faction'.

44. Patrick Buckland, *Irish Unionism, 1885–1923* (London: HMSO, 1973), p. 154.

45. Hezlet, *The 'B' Specials*, p. 57.

46. Ibid., p. 60.

47. *Northern Standard*, 24 Mar. 1922.

48. Hezlet, *The 'B' Specials*, p. 58.

49. Allan Preston, 'Nearly a Century on, Slain Catholic B-Special's Grave Finally Given a Headstone', *Belfast Telegraph*, 3 Oct. 2016.
50. *Northern Standard*, 29 May 1922.
51. Lynch, *The Northern IRA*, pp 96, 132.
52. Ibid., p. 97.
53. Cab. 61.25, R.T.121.
54. Cab. 61.25, R.T.138.
55. Farrell, *Northern Ireland*, pp 82–3.
56. Cab. 61.25, R.T.11; Cab. 61.25, R.T.140.
57. *Northern Standard*, 1 May 1925.
58. Ibid., 3 Apr. 1925.
59. Ibid., 15 May 1925.
60. Ibid., 27 Nov. 1925.
61. A.T.Q. Stewart, *The Narrow Ground: Aspects of Ulster, 1607–1969* (London: Faber & Faber, 1977), pp 175–6.
62. Flynn, *Soldiers of Folly*, p. 11.
63. C. 111/3–4, 'Unlawful Occupation of Council Houses in Dungannon and Caledon, Co. Tyrone, an Official Report to Minister for Home Affairs, dated 19 June 1968, signed Sgt R.J. Kerr D.I. for Inspector General.' Copyright filed as PRONI HA/32/2/27 and posted on CAIN archive at Ulster University, http://cain.ulst.ac.uk/proni/1968/proni_HA-32-2-27_1968-06-19.pdf.
64. Currie, *All Hell*, pp 90–1.
65. Ibid., p. 92.
66. Ibid., p. 94.
67. Barry McCaffrey, 'Family's Bid for Justice that Changed the North Forever', *Irish News*, 11 June 2008.
68. A year later, on 18 June 1970, McRoberts got 27,451 votes, but lost to incumbent Republican Labour candidate Gerry Fitt, who polled 30,649; 'West Belfast, 1950–1970', *Northern Ireland Elections*, n.d., http://www.ark.ac.uk/elections/dwb.htm, accessed 18 Nov. 2017.
69. Currie, *All Hell*, p. 96.
70. Ibid., p. 97.
71. Ibid., p. 98.
72. Glenn Patterson, *The International* (London: Anchor, 1999).
73. Austin Currie, 'Caledon Was About Forcing British to Address Injustices in the North', *Irish News*, 21 June 2008, 'Caledon Was About Forcing British to Address Injustices in the North', *Northern Ireland Civil Rights*, 23 June 2008, http://www.nicivilrights.org/caledon/caledon-was-about-forcing-british-to-address-injustices-in-the-north, accessed 18 Nov. 2017.
74. John Monaghan, '50 Years On: the Official Formation of the Northern Ireland Civil Rights Association Recalled', *Irish News*, 7 Apr. 2017.

75.   Currie, *All Hell*, p. 108.

76.   *Disturbances in Northern Ireland: Report of the Commission appointed by the Governor of Northern Ireland* (Cameron Report) (Belfast: HMSO, 1969), http://cain.ulst.ac.uk/hmso/cameron.htm#chap3, accessed 18 Nov. 2017.

77.   Graham Gudgin, 'Discrimination in Housing and Employment under the Stormont Administration' in Patrick J. Roche and Brian Barton (eds), *The Northern Ireland Question: Nationalism, Unionism and Partition* (Aldershot: Ashgate, 1999), http://cain.ulst.ac.uk/issues/discrimination/gudgin99.htm#chap5, accessed 18 Nov. 2018.

78.   Cunningham, *Monaghan*, p. 6.

8. A Maimed Capital

1.   James MacKillop, *Dictionary of Celtic Mythology* (Oxford: Oxford University Press, 1998), p. 282.

2.   Colin Johnston Robb, 'Astronomy in Armagh', *Seanchas Ardmacha: Journal of the Armagh Diocesan Historical Society*, 1:1 (1954), pp 65-66 at p. 65.

3.   Patrick Moore, 'Armagh Observatory, 1790–1967', 16 Nov. 2009, http://star.arm.ac.uk/history/moore, accessed 18 Nov. 2017.

4.   Todd, Dennis, 'St André, Nathanael (1679/80–1776)', *Oxford Dictionary of National Biography* (Oxford: Oxford University Press, 2004).

5.   See Chapter 2.

6.   Arthur P. Wilson, 'Armagh District Lunatic Asylum: the First Phase', *Seanchas Ard Mhacha: Journal of the Armagh Diocesan History Society*, 8:1 (1975–6), pp 111–20 at p. 112; approximate population figures today for the five counties are: Armagh, 175,000; Monaghan, 60,500; Tyrone, 178,00; Donegal, 160,000; and Fermanagh, 62,000.

7.   *Mad or Bad: an Exhibition about Crime, Gender and Mental Health in Victorian Ireland* (Armagh: Armagh County Museum, 2016), p. 23.

8.   Frank McNally, 'A Murder Cover-up Most Foul', *Irish Times*, 25 July 2014.

9.   Morton, *Come Day*, pp 39–40.

10.   Kevin Quinn, 'Mill Row Memories, 1914–1970', *History Armagh*, 2:1 (Winter 2008), p. 13.

11.   John Montague, *Time in Armagh: Selected Poems* (London: Penguin, 2001), p. 180.

12.   Patsy McGarry, 'C of I provides stage for theatre of the absurd', *Irish Times*, 6 July 2002.

13.   Cassells, *The Ulster Canal*, pp 23–4.

14.   Ibid., p. 29.

15.   *Frontier Sentinel*, 19 Nov. 1920.

16.   Ibid., 19 Mar. 1921.

17.   John McAnerney, BMH, WS 528, p. 2.

18. Donnelly, BMH, WS 941, p. 6.
19. McAnerney, BMH, WS 528, pp 3–4.
20. Short, BMH, WS 534, p. 4.
21. McAnerney, BMH, WS 528, p. 3.
22. Des Fitzgerald, 'Michael Collins in Armagh', *History Armagh*, (Vol. 1, No. 2, 2005), pp 7-11.
23. Eamonn Phoenix, 'Michael Collins and the Northern Question, 1916–22', in Gabriel Doherty , Dermot Keogh (eds), *Michael Collins and the Making of the Irish State* (Cork: Mercier, 2006), pp 94–118 at p. 97.
24. McGarry, *Eoin O'Duffy*, p. 79.
25. Ibid., p. 80.
26. Ibid., p. 81.
27. Fitzgerald, 'Michael Collins', p. 11.
28. Ibid., p. 10.
29. McAnerney, BMH, WS 528, p. 6.
30. Short, BMH, WS 534, p. 8.
31. Farrell, *Northern Ireland*, pp 24–5.
32. Ibid., p. 83.
33. Eda Sagarra, *Kevin O'Shiel: Tyrone Nationalist and Nation Builder* (Dublin: Irish Academic Press, 2013), pp 206–7.
34. Ibid., p. 209.
35. Other centres for hearings were Rostrevor, Enniskillen, Omagh and Derry city.
36. Stephens Papers, TCD 4239, Box 6, File 2, 'Reports on Visits to the North for Sittings of Boundary Commission (Extracts and Summaries).
37. A.C Hepburn, *Catholic Belfast and Nationalist Ireland: in the Era of Joe Devlin, 1871–1934* (Oxford: Oxford University Press, 2008), pp 256.
38. *Northern Standard*, 23 Mar. 1925.
39. Roy Bradford, *The Last Ditch* (Belfast: Blackstaff, 1981), Epigraph; in his second novel, the former unionist minister quotes William, prince of Orange, rejecting the peace terms of the English invaders in 1672: 'My Lord, my country is indeed in danger, but there is one way never to see it lost and that is to die in the last ditch.'
40. *Northern Standard*, 17 July 1925.
41. Quinn, 'Mill Row Memories', *History Armagh*, Vol 2, No. 1 (Winter 2008), pp 13–18.
42. Ibid., p. 17. The article adds in a footnote that the boys from Armagh landed on 7 June 1944, which was 'D-Day plus one', missing the carnage of the first day.
43. Michael H.C. Baker, *Irish Railways since 1916* (London: Ian Allan, 1972), pp 153, 207.
44. Amanda Ferguson, 'Armagh Rail Disaster: Sunday School Outing to Seaside in 1889 Ended in Horror with Loss of 89 Lives', *Belfast Telegraph*, 13 June 2014.

45. Alan Preston, 'Frustrated Bus Commuters Want Armagh Rail Link Reopened', *Belfast Telegraph*, 21 Mar. 2017.

46. Ibid. A statement from one of the campaigners reflects the bizarre geography of Northern Ireland to cope with partition, with a reference to Armagh service for the 'south west'!

47. Flynn, *Soldiers of Folly*, p. 27.

48. Ibid, p. 23.

49. Ibid., p. 26.

50. Ibid., p. 26–7.

51. Ibid., p. 37.

52. Ibid., p. 37.

53. Ibid., p. 38.

54. Ibid., Pp 27-8

55. Ibid., p. 69–71.

56. The Motorway Archive: Online encyclopedia of UK motorway heritage, https://web.archive.org/web/20071009142931/http://www.iht.org/motorway/m1ni.htm, accessed 19 Jan. 2018

57. *Ulster Gazette*, 10 Feb. 1972.

58. Ibid., 19 Dec. 1974.

59. Tim Pat Coogan, *The Troubles*, (New York: Palgrave, 1995) p. 50.

60. Brian Dooley, *Black and Green: The fight for civil rights in Northern Ireland and Black America* (London: Pluto, 1998), p. 35.

61. C.E.B. Brett, *Housing a Divided Community* (Dublin: Institute of Public Administration, 1986), p. 64.

62. John Whyte, 'How Much Discrimination Was There under the Unionist Regime, 1921–68?' in Tom Gallagher and James O'Connell (eds), *Contemporary Irish Studies* (Manchester: Manchester University Press, 1983).

63. Sean O'Hagan, 'The day I Thought Would Never Come', *Observer*, 6 May 2007.

64. Colman Doyle, *People at War,* (Dublin: F.D.R. Teoranta, 1975), p.10.

65. Bew & Gillespie, *Northern Ireland*, p. 8.

66. *Ulster Gazette*, 2 Mar. 1972.

67. McCluskey ended up mutilated and murdered by the Border Fox in 1987.

68. *Ulster Gazette*, 9 Mar. 1972.

69. Ibid., 16 Mar. 1972.

70. Ibid.

71. Sean O'Hagan, 'An Accidental Death', *Observer*, 21 Apr. 2002.

72. 'Ensor, George: Co. Armagh, Armagh, English Street Lower, No. 045–55 (Seven Sisters)', *Dictionary of Irish Architects, 1720–1940*, n.d., http://www.dia.ie/works/view/5953/building/CO.+ARMAGH,+ARMAGH,+ENGLISH+STREET+LOWER,+NO.+045-55+(SEVEN+SISTERS), accessed 18 Nov. 2018.

73. Brett, *Housing*, p. 100.
74. Peter Taylor, *Beating the Terrorists: Interrogation in Omagh, Gough and Castlereagh* (London: Penguin, 1980), pp 237–49.
75. Chris Ryder and Ian Cobain, 'Bertie Irwin Obituary: Forensic Surgeon Who Took a Stand Against Interrogation Methods During the Troubles in Northern Ireland', *Guardian*, 19 Mar. 2015; https://www.theguardian.com/uk-news/2015/mar/19/bertie-irwin, accessed 18 Nov. 2017.
76. Eamon Phoenix, '"Misgivings" over Growing Evidence of RUC Brutality', *Irish Times*, 2 Jan. 2009.
77. Taylor, *Beating the Terrorists*, p. 248.
78. Ibid., p. 251.
79. Ibid, p. 253–4.
80. Ibid., p. 259.
81. Ibid., p. 260.
82. Ibid., p. 268.
83. Ibid., pp 271–3.
84. Ibid., pp 287–8.
85. Fionnuala O'Connor, 'Appalling Treatment of Doctor Who Told Truth', *Irish News*, 10 Mar. 2015.
86. Taylor, *Beating the Terrorists*, pp 300–1.
87. http://cain.ulst.ac.uk/proni/1980/proni_HSS-32-1-15-6A_1978-08-14.pdf, accessed 18 Nov. 2017.
88. Niall Vallely, from Prison Memory Archive, a series of recordings between 2006 and 2007, directed by Cathal McLaughlin, held at Queen's University Belfast, and available online at http://prisonsmemoryarchive.com/armagh-stories, accessed 19 Jan. 2018
89. Suzann Buckley, Pamela Lonergan, 'Women and the Troubles, 1969–1980' in Yonah Alexander and Alan O'Day (eds), *Terrorism in Ireland*, (London: Croom Helm, 1984) p. 80.
90. Raymond Murray, *Hard Time: Armagh Gaol, 1971–1986* (Cork: Mercier, 1998), p. 31.
91. Murray, *Hard Time*, p. 33.
92. Murray, *Hard Time*, p. 12.
93. David McKittrick and David McVea, *Making Sense of the Troubles* (London: Penguin, 2001), pp 123, 171.
94. Murray, *Hard Time*, p. 11.
95. McKittrick et al., *Lost Lives*, p. 782.
96. Murray, *Hard Time*, p. 68.
97. McKittrick et al., *Lost Lives*, p. 738.
98. Murray, *Hard Time*, p. 12.
99. Nell McCafferty, *The Armagh Women* (Dublin: Co-op Books, 1981), p. 9.
100. Bew & Gillespie, *Northern Ireland*, p. 145.

101.   Murray, *Hard Time*, p. 84.
102.   McKittrick et al., *Lost Lives*, pp 1112-5.
103.   Ivan Little, 'The Real Inside Story of Life Behind Bars for These Four Women', *Belfast Telegraph*, 27 July 2012.
104.   Murray, *Hard Time*, p. 117.
105.   Barron Report, 2003.
106.   Murray, *The SAS*, p. 116; Taylor, Brits, pp 143-5; Desmond Hamill, *Pig in the Middle: The army in Northern Ireland 1969-1985* (London: Menthuen, 1985), p. 271; John Parker, *Secret Hero: The life and mysterious death of Captain Robert Nairac* (London: Metro, 2004), pp 79-80, 90-104.
107.   MacDonald, *The Chosen Fews*, pp 158–84.
108.   Cadwallader, *Lethal Allies*, pp 54–5, 332.
109.   McKittrick et al., *Lost Lives*, p. 929.
110.   Urban, *Big Boys' Rules*, p. 152.
111.   McKittrick et al., *Lost Lives*, p. 920.
112.   Ibid., p. 926.
113.   Peter Taylor, *Stalker: the Search for Truth* (London: Faber & Faber, 1987), pp 79–80.
114.   Urban, *Big Boys' Rules*, p. 153.
115.   Ibid., p. 153.
116.   Taylor, *Stalker*, p. 83.
117.   Ibid.
118.   McKittrick et al., *Lost Lives*, p. 943.
119.   Ibid., 1210–11.
120.   John Montague, *History Walk: Selected Poems* (London: Penguin, 2001), p. 182.
121.   Mary Cartmill, 'Your Place and Mine: A. Lennox & Sons', BBC, July 2014, http://www.bbc.co.uk/northernireland/yourplaceandmine/armagh/lennox_sons.shtml, accessed 18 Nov. 2018.
122.   'Shortage of Students Forces Queen's to Leave Armagh', *Irish Times*, 23 June 2004.

9. O'Neill Country

1.   Lewis, *A Topographical Dictionary*.
2.   McKittrick et al., *Lost Lives*, pp 555–8.
3.   Cadwallader, *Lethal Allies*, pp 37, 39, 59, 60, 65, 74-5, 79-80, 99, 101-2, 109, 192, 224, 268, 330-1, 335.
4.   McKittrick et al., *Lost Lives*, p. 556.
5.   Stephen Travers and Neil Fetherstonehaugh, *The Miami Showband Massacre: A Survivor's Search for the Truth* (Dublin: Hodder Headline Ireland, 2007), p. 66.
6.   Cadwallader, *Lethal Allies*, p. 100.

7. Travers, *The Miami Showband*, pp 81–2.
8. McKittrick et al., *Lost Lives*, p. 555.
9. Ibid., p. 557.
10. Travers, *The Miami Showband*, pp 119–30.
11. McKittrick et al., *Lost Lives,* p. 1357.
12. Susan McKay, *Northern Protestants: An Unsettled People* (Belfast: Blackstaff, 2005), p. 199.
13. Ibid., p. 216.
14. Mervyn Jess, *The Orange Order* (Dublin: O'Brien, 2007), pp 17–19.
15. Patrick Tohall, '*The Diamond Fight of 1795 and the Resultant Expulsions,*' *Seanchas Ard Mhacha*, Vol. 3, No. 1 (1958), pp 19–22, (Armagh: Armagh Diocesan Historical Society); Bardon, *History of Ulster*, pp 225-7.; Jess, *The Orange Order*, p. 20.
16. Jess, *The Orange Order*, p. 20.
17. Ibid., p. 18.
18. Bardon, *A History of Ulster*, p. 172.
19. 'Attack on Orange Hall Condemned', *Portadown District LOL No. 1*, 15 Jan. 2008, http://www.portadowndistrictlolno1.co.uk/15-01-2008.htm, accessed 18 Nov. 2017.
20. *The Report (– fifth Report) of the Hibernian Sunday School Society, for the Year 1810 (– Year Ending April 1815), with a List of Subscribers and Benefactors, Printed by J. Parry, No. 33 Anglesea Street, Dublin, 1811*, Appendix VII, p. 31.
21. Ruth Dudley Edwards, *The Faithful Tribe: an Intimate Portrait of the Loyal Institutions* (London: HarperCollins, 1999), p. 13.
22. Ibid., p. 135.
23. Dudley Edwards, *The Faithful*, p. 33.
24. Steve Bruce, 'Unionists and the Border' in Malcolm Anderson and Eberhard Bort, *The Irish Border: History, Politics and Culture* (Liverpool: Liverpool University Press, 1999), pp 127–37 at p. 133.
25. Bruce, 'Unionists', p. 135.
26. Ibid., p. 131.
27. 'Traditions Maintained at Border Twelfth', *News Letter*, 13 July 2016.
28. 'Unionists Unhappy at Road Blueprint', *News Letter*, 1 Aug. 2012.
29. Richard Froggatt, 'James Young Malley (1918–2000): RAF Officer; Civil Servant', *Dictionary of Ulster Biography*, http://www.newulsterbiography.co.uk/index.php/home/viewPerson/1854, accessed 19 Nov. 2017.
30. McKittrick et al., *Lost Lives*, p. 354–5.
31. Ibid., p. 400.
32. Ibid., pp 536–7.
33. Ibid., p. 417.
34. John Potter, *Testimony to Courage: the History of the Ulster Defence Regiment 1969–1992* (Barnsley, Yorkshire: Leo Cooper, 2001), p. 123.

35. McKay, *Northern Protestants*, p. 216.
36. Tommy McKearney, *The Provisional IRA from Insurrection to Parliament* (London: Pluto, 2011), pp 117–18.
37. McKay, *Northern Protestants*, p. 213.
38. Darach MacDonald, 'UDR: Too Many Bad Apples', *Hibernia*, 3 Dec. 1976, pp 6–7.
39. McKay, *Northern Protestants*, p. 214.
40. Currie, *All Hell*, pp 146–8.
41. McKittrick et al., *Lost Lives*, p. 128.
42. Ibid., p. 416.
43. 'Two of 30 Border Shootings Verified', *Belfast Telegraph*, 31 Dec. 2009.
44. McKittrick et al., *Lost Lives*, p. 1110–1.
45. McKittrick et al., *Lost Lives*, p. 1111.
46. Eamonn Baker (ed.), *To Tell You the Truth: Lived Experience of the Troubles* (Derry/Londonderry: Towards Understanding and Healing, 2015), pp 184–95.
47. 'Decision Not to Prosecute Soldier over Killing to Be Reviewed', BBC News, 21 Jan. 2016, http://www.bbc.co.uk/news/uk-northern-ireland-35369890, accessed 18 Nov. 2017.
48. Flynn, *Soldiers of Folly*, pp 11–12.
49. Flynn, *Soldiers of Folly*, p. 12
50. Doyle, *People at War*, p. 112.
51. Moloney, *A Secret History*, p. 385.
52. Ibid., p. 386.
53. McKittrick et al., *Lost Lives*, p. 385; Patrick Mulroe, *Bombs, Bullets and the Border: Policing Ireland's Frontier: Irish Security Policy, 1969–1978* (Dublin: Irish Academic Press, 2017).
54. McKittrick et al., *Lost Lives*, p. 384.
55. Letter from Professor Bob Eccleshall, Department of Politics, Queen's University, to John Gormley, Lower Ormeau Concerned Community, 30 Mar. 1998.
56. Darach MacDonald, 'Secrets and Lies? The Strange Story of Vincent McKenna', *Irish Voice*, 8–14 Sept. 1999.
57. Beatrix Campbell, 'Exposed: the Dark Side of an Irish Peace Hero', *Independent on Sunday*, 26 Sept. 1999; I was credited on the story, with two others, for 'additional reporting'.
58. Steven McCaffrey, 'McKenna Hits Out at 'Smear of Sex Abuse', 27 Sept. 1999.
59. Author's copy of letter from J.C. Taylor and Co. to the editor, *Independent on Sunday*, dated 1 Oct. 1999.
60. John Mullin, 'Balance of Terror', *Guardian*, 21 Oct. 1999.
61. See also, 'The Rise and Fall of Vincent McKenna', BBC Spotlight, 20 Nov. 2000.

62. Simon Hattenstone, 'I Don't Think of Him as My Father Anymore', *Guardian*, 27 Nov. 2000.

63. 'Criminal Appeal Court Doubles McKenna Sentence', *Irish Times*, 9 May 2002.

64. Press Association, 'Sex Offender Vincent McKenna Freed from Jail', *Irish Times*, 10 May 2005, http://www.irishtimes.com/news/sex-offender-vincent-mckenna-freed-from-jail-1.1312254, accessed 19 Nov. 2017.

65. *An t-Óglách*, 11 Nov. 1922, http://antoglach.militaryarchives.ie/PDF/1922_11_11_Vol_IV_No_22_An_t-Oglac.pdf, accessed 19 Nov. 2017.

66. O'Neill Country Historical Society/Cumann Staire Dhúiche Néill, 'Battle of Benburb 1646: the Last Great Victory of a Native Irish Army', http://oneillcountryhistoricalsociety.com/history/battle-of-benburb, accessed 19 Nov. 2017.

67. Darach MacDonald, 'Brantry's Pride Laid to Rest', *Ulster Herald*, 11 Mar. 2004.

10. Friend or Foe

1. Cassells, *The Ulster Canal*, p. 31.
2. Ibid., pp 33–4.
3. Jack Shields, BMH, WS 928.
4. Ibid., p. 12.
5. Ibid., p. 17.
6. Ibid., p. 20.
7. McGleenan, BMH, WS 829, p. 27.
8. Shields, BMH, WS 928, pp 22–3.
9. Bowyer Bell, *The Secret Army: a History of the IRA, 1916–1970* (London: Sphere, 1972), p. 88.
10. Shields, BMH, WS 928, p. 26.
11. Ibid., pp 29–30.
12. McGleenan, BMH, WS 829, p. 33.
13. Father of Erskine Childers, who was Fianna Fáil TD for Monaghan and later president.
14. McGleenan, BMH, WS 829, p. 34.
15. Ibid., pp 36–7.
16. Ibid., p. 36.
17. Ibid., pp 37–8.
18. Ibid., pp 38–9.
19. *Northern Standard*, 16 Jan. 1925.
20. A.C. Hepburn, *Catholic Belfast and Nationalist Ireland in the Era of Joe Devlin, 1871-1934*, (Oxford: Oxford University Press, 2008), p. 256.

21. Hezlet, *The 'B' Specials*, pp 107–8.
22. B. Walker, A Political History of the Two Irelands: From Partition to Peace (London: Palgrave MacMilllan, 2012), p. 68.
23. Bryan A. Follis, *A State Under Siege: the Establishment of Northern Ireland, 1920–1925* (Wooton-under-Edge: Clarendon Press, 1995), p. 100.
24. McGleenan, BMH, WS 829, pp 21–4.
25. Hezlet, *The 'B' Specials*, pp 10, 19.
26. Hezlet, *The 'B' Specials*, pp 50–2.
27. Bardon, *A History of Ulster*, p. 490.
28. Bew et al., *The State*, pp 57–8.
29. Ibid., pp 57–8.
30. Ibid., p. 58.
31. Ibid., p. 58
32. Keith Jeffery, *Field Marshal Sir Henry Wilson: A political soldier* (Oxford, 2006), pp 281-3, 284-96
33. T. Ryle Dwyer, *The Squad* (Cork, 2005), pp 256-258.
34. Mike Cronin, *Maguire, Samuel [Sam] (1877–1927), Irish republican and promoter of Gaelic sports*, Oxford Dictionary of National Biography, online edition; http://www.oxforddnb.com/view/10.1093/ref:odnb/9780198614128.001.0001/odnb-9780198614128-e-92335?rskey=RLOKBM&result=1, accessed 19 Jan. 2018.
35. PRONI 7G/26; Bew et al., *The State*, p. 62.
36. Hezlet, *The 'B' Specials*, p. 106.
37. Ibid., p. 103.
38. Ibid., p. 104.
39. Farrell, *Northern Ireland*, p. 79; Hansard, House of Commons, 8 December 1925, vol. 189, col. 361.
40. Hezlet, *The 'B' Specials*, pp 108–9.
41. Farrell, *Northern Ireland*, p. 79.
42. Hezlet, *The 'B' Specials*, p. 109–10.
43. Farrell, *Northern Ireland*, p. 80.
44. Frank Gallagher, *The Indivisible Island* (London: Gollancz, 1957), p. 177; *News Letter*, 13 July 1922.
45. Hansard, Northern Ireland Debates, 19 Feb. 1936, vol. 17, cols 208–9.
46. Gallagher, *The Indivisible Island*, p. 179; *Irish Press*, 31 May 1947.
47. Hezlet, *The 'B' Specials*, p. 226.
48. *Report of the Advisory Committee on Police in Northern Ireland* (Hunt Report) (Belfast: HMSO, 1969), para. 163, http://cain.ulst.ac.uk/hmso/hunt.htm, accessed 19 Nov. 2017.
49. Johannes Steffens, *The Police Forces of Northern Ireland – History, Perceptions and Problems* (Munich: GRIN Verlag, 2007), p. 5.
50. Tim Pat Coogan, *The IRA* (London: Palgrave Macmillan, 2002), p. 37.
51. McKittrick et al., *Lost Lives*, p. 36–8.

52. Sean O'Hagan, 'The Troubles Are Past but That Doesn't Keep the Fear at Bay Now', *Observer*, 15 Mar. 2009.
53. McKittrick et al., *Lost Lives*, p. 423–4.
54. Ibid., p. 424.
55. Cadwallader, *Lethal Allies*, p. 57.
56. Ibid., p. 58.
57. Ibid., p. 59.
58. McKittrick et al., *Lost Lives*, p. 831.
59. Edgar Graham, *Ireland and Extradition: a Protection for Terrorists* (Belfast: European Human Rights Unit, 1982), p. 14.
60. McKittrick et al., *Lost Lives*, p. 966–7.
61. Tom Connolly, *Detective: a Life Upholding the Law* (Dublin: O'Brien, 2015).
62. Cassells, *The Ulster Canal*, p. 40.
63. John Mulgrew, 'Moy Park Sell-off "Worrying" with Brexit Around Corner', *Belfast Telegraph*, 21 June 2017.
64. Margaret Canning, 'Brexit: Europe Is Our Market, Insists Moy Park Boss,' *Belfast Telegraph*, 1 Mar. 2016.
65. Hansard, House of Commons, 13 Mar. 2017, vol. 623, https://hansard.parliament.uk/Commons/2017-03-13/debates/1703144000002/LeavingTheEUPoultryProducers#contribution-3E1263C8-72A0-4DF1-9B99-DB3CE5FD3101, accessed 19 Jan. 2018
66. McKittrick et al., *Lost Lives*, p. 381–2.
67. Cadwallader, *Lethal Allies*, p. 34.
68. McKittrick et al., *Lost Lives*, p. 588–9.
69. Coogan, *The IRA*, p. 461; Taylor, *Families at War*, p. 156.
70. McKittrick et al., *Lost Lives*, p. 645.
71. Ibid., p. 649.
72. Cadwallader, *Lethal Allies*, p. 175.
73. Ibid., pp 177–80.
74. McKittrick et al., *Lost Lives*, p. 647.
75. Ibid., p. 1263.
76. Ibid., p. 1267.
77. Ibid., p. 1285.
78. Ibid., pp 446, 1080.
79. Ibid., p. 1296.
80. 'HET Report on Moy Murders Slammed as "Slovenly and Speculative"', *Tyrone Times*, 13 Oct. 2012.
81. McKittrick et al., *Lost Lives*, p. 854–5.
82. Dominic Bryan, 'Drumcree and "the Right to March": Orangeism, Ritual and Politics' in T.G. Fraser (eds), *The Irish Parading Tradition: Following the Drum* (London: Menthuen, 2000), pp 191–207 at p. 199.
83. Ibid., p. 204–5.

84. Dudley Edwards, *The Faithful*, p. 315.
85. McKittrick et al., *Lost Lives*, pp 1395–6.
86. Ibid., pp 1406–7.
87. Ibid., p. 1467.
88. 'It's Ten Years Since the Death of the Quinn Boys', *Ballymoney Times*, 24 July 2008, http://www.ballymoneytimes.co.uk/news/it-s-ten-years-since-the-death-of-the-quinn-boys-1-1825131, accessed 19 Nov. 2017.
89. Laura Friel, 'Three Little Boys Were Dead', *An Phoblacht*, 16 July 1998.
90. McKittrick et al., *Lost Lives*, p. 1435
91. Anne Henderson, 'Foreword by the Chair', *Parades Commission for Northern Ireland Annual Report and Accounts, 2015–16*, p. 4, https://www.paradescommission.org/getmedia/0022c84a-6b95-4239-ad80-3cdc1da26a49/NorthernIrelandParadesCommission.aspx, accessed 19 Nov. 2017.
92. Parades Commission of Northern Ireland, *Annual Report 2007*, at http://www.paradescommission.org/getmedia/c90461b0-31ef-4ea3-8eb2-12bf35d4d6d2/NorthernIrelandParadesCommission.aspx, accessed 19 Jan. 2018
93. McKittrick et al., *Lost Lives*, pp 1077–80.
94. Ibid., p. 1080.
95. Murray, *The SAS*, p. 379.
96. Moloney, *A Secret History*, pp 306–8.
97. Murray, *The SAS*, p. 378.
98. Urban, *Big Boys' Rules*, p. 223.
99. McKearney, The Provisional IRA, pp 117–8.
100. Jack Holland and Susan Phoenix, *Phoenix: Policing the Shadows* (London: Hodder & Stoughton, 1996), p. 141.
101. William Matchett, *Secret Victory: the Intelligence War that Beat the IRA* (Belfast: 2016), p. 12.
102. Urban, *Big Boys' Rules*, p. 223.
103. Murray, *The SAS*, pp 390–1.
104. Moloney, *A Secret History*, p. 307.
105. McKittrick et al., *Lost Lives*, p. 685.
106. McKittrick et al., *Lost Lives*, pp 1026–7; Holland, *Phoenix*, p. 140; Urban, *Big Boys' Rules*, p. 221.
107. Urban, *Big Boys' Rules*, p. 222
108. McKittrick et al., *Lost Lives*, pp 1073–4; Holland, *Phoenix*, p. 141.
109. Holland, *Phoenix*, p. 142.
110. Murray, *The SAS*, pp 380–1.
111. Holland, *Phoenix*, p. 143.
112. Murray, *The SAS*, p. 382.
113. Holland, *Phoenix*, p. 143.
114. Murray, *The SAS*, pp 382–3.
115. Urban, *Big Boys' Rules*, p. 230.

116. Connla Young, 'IRA Man Tells the Inside Story of the Loughgall Attack and the SAS Ambush', *Irish News*, 8 May 2017.
117. McKittrick et al., *Lost Lives*, p. 1186.
118. Matchett, *Secret Victory*, p. 24.
119. Justice Minister Gerry Collins, 'Statement on Incident in Emyvale, County Monaghan', Dáil Éireann, 13 May 1987, http://oireachtasdebates.oireachtas.ie/Debates%20Authoring/DebatesWebPack.nsf/takes/dail1987051300004, accessed 19 Nov. 2017.
120. Aaron Edwards, *The Northern Ireland Troubles: Operation Banner, 1969–2007* (Oxford: Osprey, 2011).
121. Matchett, *Secret Victory*, p. 12.
122. Ibid., p. 23.
123. Darach MacDonald, 'Proud to be Prod: Music Memory and Motivation in an Ulster Loyalist Band' (PhD, Ulster University, 2015), p. 76.
124. Dominic Bryan, *Orange Parades: the Politics of Ritual, Tradition and Control* (London: Pluto, 2000), p. 94.

11. The End Is Neagh

1. John Laverty, 'Remembered... the Captain of Chivalry', *Belfast Telegraph*, 27 Feb. 2012.
2. World News Briefs, *New York Times*, 20 June 1979, http://www.nytimes.com/1979/06/20/archives/world-news-briefs-syrians-and-iraqis-establish-joint-political.html, accessed 19 Jan. 2018
3. McKittrick et al., *Lost Lives*, p. 784.
4. W.A. McCutcheon, The Canals of the North of Ireland (Exeter, Devon: David & Charles, 1965), pp 65-9.
5. Barbara Freese, *Coal: a Human History* (London: William Henemann, 2005), p. 88.
6. Irish Waterways Association of Ireland website, http://www.iwai.ie/coalisland-canal/
7. 'Parades and Marches – Chronology 2: Historical Dates and Events', *CAIN Web Service*, n.d., http://cain.ulst.ac.uk/issues/parade/chpa2.htm, accessed 19 Nov. 2017.
8. Emma Blee, 'Lough Neagh's Troubled Waters', *AgendaNI*, 3 Nov. 2010, http://www.agendani.com/lough-neaghs-troubled-waters, accessed 19 Nov. 2017.
9. Noel McAdam, 'Lough Neagh's Future Still Up in Air After Owner Meets Minister', *Belfast Telegraph*, 10 Apr. 2014.
10. Marc Mulholland, 'Prime Minister Terence O'Neill's Bizarre Plan to Drain Lough Neagh to Create a New County', *Belfast Telegraph*, 4 Nov. 2013.

11. John Hewitt, 'Regionalism: the Last Chance' in John Hewitt, *Ancestral Voices: the Selected Prose*, ed. Tom Clyde (Belfast: Blackstaff, 1987), p. 122.
12. John Hewitt, 'Freehold', *Lagan*, 2:1 (1946), pp 37–9.
13. Frank Shovlin, *The Irish Literary Periodical, 1923–1958* (Oxford: Clarendon Press, 2003), p. 165.
14. Ibid., p. 169.
15. John Hewitt, 'Ulster Names' in John Hewitt, *Selected Poems*, ed. Michael Longley and Frank Ormsby (Belfast: Blackstaff, 2007), pp 135–7.
16. Hewitt, 'From Conacre' in Hewitt, *Selected Poems* (2007), p. 6.
17. Paul Muldoon, 'Third Epistle to Timothy', *Poems, 1968–1998* (London: Faber & Faber, 2001), pp 451–5.
18. Muldoon, *Poems*, p. 12.
19. Ibid., p. 19.
20. Ibid., pp 82–3.
21. Ibid., p. 83.
22. Ibid., p. 341.
23. Paul Muldoon, 'Unapproved Road' in Paul Muldoon, *Moy Sand and Gravel* (London: Faber & Faber, 2002), pp 4–7.
24. Paul Muldoon, 'Rita Duffy: Watchtower II' in Paul Muldoon, *One Thousand Things Worth Knowing* (London: Faber & Faber, 2015), pp 30–1.
25. Muldoon, 'Dirty Data' in *One Thousand Things*, p. 111.
26. Sam McBride, 'MEPs Cheer Jim Nicholson and Reject NI Special Status After Brexit', *News Letter*, 6 July 2017.
27. Northern Ireland House of Commons Official Report, vol. 34, col. 1095. Sir James Craig, Unionist Party, then prime minister of Northern Ireland, 24 Apr. 1934.
28. Oscar J. Martinez, *Border People: Life and Society in the U.S.–Mexico Borderlands* (Tucson, AZ: University of Arizona Press, 1994), p. 5.
29. Ibid., p. 5.

Sources

Primary sources
National Archive, London (NA)
Irish Boundary Commission 1924/25: I began research on the border as a Masters history student in the mid-1970s, shortly after the report and documents had been released to the Public Records Office at Chancery Lane, London. Now held at the National Archive in Kew, a simple online search saves weeks of hit-and-miss delving, but they are still filed under the familiar CAB 61, 24 etc. references. Documents from the Foreign Office Ireland Desk pertaining to the Irish border are available for inspection. They include reports on border closures, letters to and from the NIO and Dublin embassy.

National Archive, Dublin (NAD)
State papers include Free State Cabinet minutes, correspondence from the Home Affairs department.

Public Records Office Northern Ireland (PRONI)
Files include the Northern Ireland Cabinet Minutes and correspondence, the papers of former Fermanagh MP Cahir Healy (D2991) and Madden papers (1610-1935) from Hilton Park, Clones.

Bureau of Military History (BMH), Dublin
This invaluable online archive of first-hand accounts of the War of Independence and its aftermath, includes testimonies of volunteers from Clones, Newbliss, Roslea, Monaghan, Armagh and Benburb/Blackwatertown companies with insights into the impact of partition from both sides of the new border, especially tensions and confusion between pro-Treaty 5th (Monaghan) Northern Brigade and neighbouring 4th (Armagh) Northern Brigade. The archive also yielded poignant correspondence regarding the pension claim of the Fermanagh mother of slain Free State commander Matt Fitzpatrick.

University Archives

University College Dublin: Collins Papers include intelligence reports (UCDAD P7/A/39) relating to the IRA Ulster Council's border war, as well as DeValera Papers (P150) and O'Malley Notebooks (P17b). Aiken Papers (P104) provide insights on Armagh 1920-23 and anti-Partition leagues.

Trinity College Dublin: The Stephens Papers (4238-4240) contain the correspondence and journals of E.M. Stephens, secretary of the North Eastern Boundary Bureau with invaluable insights from his visits to the North before during and after the Boundary Commission debacle.

Queen's University Belfast: QUB hosts the online archive (www.http://prisonsmemoryarchive.com), directed by Cathal McLoughlin, of filmed recordings of the prison memories of Northern Ireland combatants from both sides of the recent conflict, as well as relatives, prison staff, teachers, etc.

Ulster University: CAIN (Conflict Archive on the InterNet) is a rich and generous online repository of myriad documents, tribunal and other reports, testimonies and observations of the recent conflict in Northern Ireland. Starting from the police report on the unlawful occupation of houses in Caledon in June 1968 (http://cain.ulst.ac.uk/proni/1968/proni_HA-32-2-27_1968-06-19.pdf), it is a documentary window on the descent into violence and chaos.

Parliamentary debates/reports

Northern Ireland: The Northern Ireland Parliamentary Debates are available online through an archive created by Queen's University Belfast at http://stormontpapers.ahds.ac.uk/index.html, as are ongoing Hansard reports of the Assembly http://www.niassembly.gov.uk/utility/search/?q=hansard.

Westminster: Both historic and contemporary debates in the Houses of Commons and Lords are available through www.parliament.uk.

Dáil Éireann/Seanad Éireann: Online official records of historic and recent debates as well as committee deliberations and Dáil Divisions are available at http://oireachtasdebates.oireachtas.ie/.

Newspapers/magazines

If journalism is the 'first rough draft of history', in the phrase attributed to former *Washington Post* publisher Philip Graham, then contemporaneous reports have been too often neglected. While they sometimes do not bear up to academic scrutiny with its benefit of hindsight, newspapers and other ephemeral literature have been pivotal in forming collective memories of events and episodes. In archives held by Libraries NI, at the Monaghan County Library in Clones, the British Library and the National Library of Ireland, as well as in the dusty basements of local newspaper offices, I have delved into the past for an idea of what it was like on the ground. My research has included the following newspapers, magazines, websites and other sources:

Local
The Anglo-Celt, Cavan
Armagh Guardian
Frontier Sentinel, Newry
Impartial Reporter, Enniskillen
Newry Journal
Northern Standard, Monaghan
Tyrone Constitution, Omagh
Tyrone Times, Dungannon
Ulster Gazette, Armagh
Ulster Herald, Omagh

Regional (Northern Ireland)
Belfast Telegraph
Fortnight
Gaelic Life
Irish News
NewsLetter
Northern Whig

National (Dublin)
Farmers Journal
Freeman's Journal
Hibernia

Magill
Irish Times
Irish Independent
Irish Press
Sunday Tribune
Sunday Independent

National (London)
Daily Sketch
Daily Telegraph
Guardian/Manchester Guardian
Independent/Independent on Sunday
Observer
Sunday Times
Times
The Spectator

International
New York Times
NthWORD
Irish Voice (New York)

Websites
RTE.ie
BBC.co.uk
Thedetail.tv
Thebrokenelbow.com (Ed Moloney)
cain.ulst.ac.uk/
AgendaNI.com
Newulsterbiography.co.uk
oxforddnb.com (biographies)
military.ie (Irish military archives)
ElectionsIreland.com
ark.ac.uk/elections

buildingsofireland.ie
turtlebunbury.com (historic houses)
archiseek.com (built heritage)

www.dia.ie (Irish architecture)
workhouses.org.uk
motorwayarchive.ihtservices.co.uk

Hoganstand.com (Gaelic games)
http://www.sseairtricityleague.ie (soccer)
The42.ie (GAA)

Bygonedays.net (loyalist history)
Ulster-Scots.com
Borderroadmemories.com
Castleleslie.com
Irishidentity.com
Askaboutireland.ie

Theses (unpublished)

Longwill, Edward, 'The Irish Army and State Security Policy, 1956–74' (PhD, Ulster University, 2009).

MacDonald, Darach, 'The Irish Boundary Commission and the Wishes of the Inhabitants of West Ulster' (M.A., UCD, 1976).

MacDonald, Darach, 'Proud to be Prod: Music Memory and Motivation in an Ulster Loyalist Band' (PhD, Ulster University, 2015).

Secondary Sources
Articles in academic journals/periodicals, chapters

Bruce, Steve, 'Unionists and the Border' in Anderson, Malcolm; Bort, Eberhard, *The Irish Border: History, Politics and Culture* (Liverpool: Liverpool University Press, 1999), pp 127–37.

Bryan, Dominic, 'Drumcree and "the Right to March": Orangeism, Ritual and Politics' in T.G. Fraser (ed.), *The Irish Parading Tradition: Following the Drum* (London: Menthuen, 2000), pp 191–207.

Buckley, Suzann; Lonergan, Pamela, 'Women and the Troubles, 1969–1980' in Alexander, Yonah; O'Day, Alan (eds), *Terrorism in Ireland*, (London: Croom Helm, 1984).

Curran, Joseph M., 'The Anglo-Irish Agreement of 1925: Hardly a "damn good bargain"', pp 36-52, *The Historian* 40:1 (1977).

de Breffny, Brian, 'The Paternal Ancestry of Oscar Wilde', *The Irish Ancestor*, 2 (1973), pp 96-99.

Dooley, Terence, 'From the Belfast Boycott to the Boundary Commission: Fears and Hopes in County Monaghan, 1920–25', *Clogher Record*, 15:1 (1994), pp 90–106.

Dooley, Terence, 'Protestant Migration from the Free State to Northern Ireland, 1920–25: a Private Census for Co. Fermanagh', *Clogher Record*, 15:3 (1996), pp 87–132.

Edkins, Jane, 'Introduction: Trauma, Violence and Political Community' in J. Edkins (ed.), *Trauma and the Memory of Politics* (Cambridge: Cambridge University Press, 2003), pp 1–19.

Fitzgerald, Des, 'Michael Collins in Armagh', *History Armagh*, 1:2 (2005), pp 7–11.

Fitzpatrick, David 'The Orange Order and the Border', *Irish Historical Studies*, 33:129 (2002), pp 52-67.

Greene, Sarah, (2012), 'A sense of border,' pp 573-592 in Wilson, Thomas M.; Donnan, Hastings (eds), *A Companion to Border Studies*, Wiley-Blackwell, Chichester.

Gudgin, Graham, 'Discrimination in Housing and Employment under the Stormont Administration' in Patrick J. Roche and Brian Barton (eds), *The Northern Ireland Question: Nationalism, Unionism and Partition* (Aldershot: Ashgate, 1999).

Hall, Donal, 'Partition and County Louth,' *Journal of the County Louth Archaeological and Historical Society*, 27:2 (2010), pp 243–83.

Hewitt, John, 'Regionalism: the Last Chance' in Clyde, Tom (ed.) *John Hewitt, Ancestral Voices: the Selected Prose*, (Belfast: Blackstaff, 1987).

Hewitt, John, 'Freehold', *Lagan*, 2:1 (1946).

Hughes, John, 'Frank Kitson in Northern Ireland and the "British way" of counterinsurgency', *History Ireland*, 22:1 (Jan./Feb. 2014).

Johnston Robb, Colin , 'Astronomy in Armagh', *Seanchas Ardmacha: Journal of the Armagh Diocesan Historical Society*, 1:1 (1954), pp 65-66.

Loughlin, James, 'Parades and Politics: Liberal Governments and the Orange Order, 1880–86' in T.G. Fraser (ed.), *The Irish Parading Tradition: Following the Drum* (New York: Palgrave Macmillan, 2000), pp 25–43.

Lynch, Robert, 'The Clones Affray, 1922 – Massacre or Invasion?', *History Ireland* 12:3 (Autumn 2004).

MacDonald, Brian, 'South Ulster in the Age of the United Irishmen' in Bartlett, Thomas; Dickson, David; Keogh, Daire; Whelan, Kevin (eds), *1798: a Bicentenary Perspective* (Dublin: Four Courts Press, 2003), pp 226–42.

McCabe, Anton, '"The Stormy Petrel of the Transport Workers": Peadar O'Donnell, Trade Unionist, 1917–1920', *Saothar 19: Journal of the Irish Labour History Society*, 19 (1994), pp 41-51.

McMahon, Theo, 'The Tragic Deaths in 1871 in County Monaghan of Emily and Mary Wilde – Half-Sisters of Oscar Wilde', *Clogher Record*, 18:1 (2003), pp 129–45.

Murnane, Peadar; Murnane, James, 'The Linen Industry in the Parish of Aughnamullen, Co. Monaghan and Its Impact on the Town of Ballybay, 1740 to 1835', *Clogher Record*, 12:3 (1987), pp 334–68.

Nash, Catherine; Lorainne, Dennis; Bryan, Graham, 'Putting the Border in Place: Customs Regulation in the Making of the Irish Border, 1921–1945', *Journal of Historical Geography*, 36 (2010), pp 421–31.

Nash, Catherine; Reid, Bryonie, 'Border Crossings: New Approaches to the Irish Border', *Irish Studies Review*, 18:3 (2010).

O'Leary, Brendan, (2012), *Partition*, 29-47 in Wilson and Donnan, Hastings, (eds), A Companion to Border Studies, Wiley-Blackwell, Chichester

Phoenix, Eamonn, 'Michael Collins and the Northern Question, 1916–22', in Doherty, Gabriel; Keogh, Dermot (eds), *Michael Collins and the Making of the Irish State* (Cork: Mercier, 2006), pp 94–118.

Quinn, Kevin, 'Mill Row Memories, 1914–1970', *History Armagh*, 2:1 (Winter 2008).

Reeves, William, 'The Ancient Churches of Armagh', *Ulster Journal of Archaeology*, 4:4 (1898).

Todd, Dennis, 'St André, Nathanael (1679/80–1776)', *Oxford Dictionary of National Biography* (Oxford: Oxford University Press, 2004).

Tohall, Patrick, 'The Diamond Fight of 1795 and the Resultant Expulsions,' *Seanchas Ard Mhacha* Vol. 3, No. 1 (1958), pp 19–22

Rankin, K.J., 'The Role of the Irish Boundary Commission in the Entrenchment of the Irish Border: from tactical panacea to political liability', *Journal of Historical Geography*, 34 (2008), pp 422–47.

Ryan, Paddy, 'So Little Time and So Much to Do: the setting up of the Border from the Customs' Point of view' in Mary Harkin (ed.), *It's Us They're Talking About*, v: *Borders, Boundaries and Divisions: Proceedings from the McGlinchey Summer School 2002* (Clonmany: McGlinchey Summer School Committee, 2003), pp 39–44.

Ryan, Desmond, 'Sinn Féin Policy and Practice (1916–1926)' in Williams, T. Desmond (ed.), *The Irish Struggle, 1916–1926* (London: Routledge & Kegan Paul, 1966).

Staunton, E., 'The Boundary Commission Debacle 1925: Aftermath & Implications', *History Ireland*, 4:2 (1996) pp 42–5.

Wall, Maureen, 'Partition: The Ulster Question', pp 79–93 in Williams, T.Desmond, (ed.), *The Irish Struggle, 1916–26* (London: Routledge Kegan Paul, 1966).

Walsh, Aidan, 'Excavation at the Black Pig's Dyke', *Clogher Record,* 14:1 (1991), pp 9–26.

Whan, Robert, 'Part A: Eamon Donnelly', in *A Catalogue of the Eamon Donnelly Collection at Newry and Mourne Museum* (Newry: Newry and Mourne Museum, 2014).

Whyte, John, 'How Much Discrimination Was There under the Unionist Regime, 1921–68?' in Gallagher, Tom; O'Connell, James (eds), *Contemporary Irish Studies* (Manchester: Manchester University Press, 1983).

Wilson, Arthur P., 'Armagh District Lunatic Asylum: the First Phase', *Seanchas Ard Mhacha: Journal of the Armagh Diocesan History Society,* 8:1 (1975–6), pp 111–20.

Wilson, Thomas M.; Donnan, Hastings (1998), 'Nation, State and Identity at International Borders', pp 1-30 in Wilson, Thomas M.; Donnan, Hastings (eds) *Border Identities: Nation and State at International Frontiers (*Cambridge, Cambridge University Press, 1998).

Books

Anzaldúa, Gloria , *Borderlands/La Frontera: The New Mestiza* (San Francisco: Aunt Lute Books, 2007).

Arnold, Bruce, *Charles Haughey: His Life and Unlucky Deeds* (London: HarperCollins, 1993).

Baker, Eamonn (ed.), *To Tell You the Truth: Lived Experience of the Troubles* (Derry/Londonderry: Towards Understanding and Healing, 2015).

Baker, Michael H.C., *Irish Railways since 1916* (London: Ian Allan, 1972).

Bardon, Jonathan, *A History of Ulster* (Belfast: Blackstaff Press, 1992).

Bell, J. Bowyer, *The Secret Army: a history of the I.R.A., 1916–1970*, (London: Sphere Books, 1972).

Bew, Paul; Gibbon, Peter; Patterson, Hugh, *The State in Northern Ireland: Political Forces and Social Classes* (Manchester: Manchester University Press, 1979).

Bew, Paul; Gillespie, Gordon, *Northern Ireland: A Chronology of the Troubles, 1968-1999* (Dublin: Gill & Macmillan, 1999).

Blair, May, *Once Upon the Lagan: Story of the Lagan Canal* (Belfast: Blackstaff Press, 1981).

Blair, May, *Hiring Fairs and Market Places* (Belfast: Appletree Press, 2007)

Bowman, John, *De Valera and the Ulster Question, 1917–1973* (Oxford: Clarendon Press/Oxford University Press, 1982).

Brett, C.E.B., *Housing a Divided Community* (Dublin: Institute of Public Administration, 1986).

Bryan, Dominic, *Orange Parades: the Politics of Ritual, Tradition and Control* (London: Pluto, 2000).

Buckland, Patrick, *Irish Unionism, 1885–1923* (London: HMSO, 1973).

Cadwallader, Anne, *Lethal Allies: British Collusion in Ireland* (Cork: Mercier, 2013).

Cassells, Brian, *The Ulster Canal* (Donaghadee: Cottage Publications, 2015).

Collins, Stephen, *The Power Game: Fianna Fáil since Lemass* (Dublin: O'Brien, 2000).

Connaughton, Shane, *A Border Diary* (London: Faber & Faber, 1995).

Connolly, Tom, *Detective: a Life Upholding the Law* (Dublin: O'Brien, 2015).

Coogan, Tim Pat, *The IRA* (London: Palgrave Macmillan, 2002),

Coogan, Tim Pat, *The Troubles*, (New York: Palgrave, 1995).

Craig, Anthony, *Crisis of Confidence: Anglo-Irish Relations in the Early Troubles* (Dublin: Irish Academic Press, 2010).

Cunningham, Michael, *Monaghan: County of Intrigue* (Tantallon, County Donegal: privately published, 1979).

Currie, Austin, *All Hell Will Break Loose* (Dublin: O'Brien, 2004).

Day, Angélique; McWilliams, Patrick (eds), *Ordnance Survey Memoirs of Ireland*, iv: *Parishes of County Fermanagh I, 1834–5, Enniskillen and Upper Lough Erne* (Dublin: Institute of Irish Studies in Association with the Royal Irish Academy, 1990).

Delaney, Ruth, *Ireland's Inland Waterways* (Belfast: Appletree Press, 2004).

Denton, Gilbert; Fahy, Tony, *The Northern Ireland Land Boundary, 1923–1992* (London: H.M. Customs & Excise, 1993).

Dewar, Lt Col. Michael, *The British Army in Northern Ireland* (London: Arms & Armour Press, 1985).

Dooley, Brian, *Black and Green: The fight for civil rights in Northern Ireland and Black America* (London: Pluto, 1998).

Dooley, Terence, *The Irish Revolution, 1912–23: Monaghan* (Dublin: Four Courts, 2017).

Doyle, Colman, *People at War,* (Dublin: F.D.R. Teoranta, 1975).

Dudley-Edwards, Ruth, *The Faithful Tribe: an Intimate Portrait of the Loyal Institutions* (London: HarperCollins, 1999).

Dwyer, T. Ryle, *The Squad* (Cork: Mercier, 2005).

Edwards, Aaron, *The Northern Ireland Troubles: Operation Banner, 1969–2007* (Oxford: Osprey, 2011).

Fanning, Ronan, *Independent Ireland* (Dublin: Helicon, 1983).

Farrell, Michael, *Northern Ireland: the Orange State*, London: Pluto, 1980).

Farrell, Sean, *Rituals and Riots: Sectarian Violence and Political Culture in Ulster, 1784–1886* (Lexington, KY: University Press of Kentucky, 2015).

Feeney, Brian, *Sinn Féin: a Hundred Turbulent Years* (Dublin: O'Brien, 2002).

FitzGerald, Garret, *All in a Life: an Autobiography* (Dublin: Gill & Macmillan, 1991).

FitzGerald, James, *What Disturbs Our Blood: a Son's Quest to Redeem the Past* (Toronto: Random House, 2010).

Fitz-Simon, Christopher, *Eleven Houses: a Memoir of Childhood* (London: Penguin, 2007).

Flynn, Barry, *Soldiers of Folly: the IRA Border Campaign, 1956–1962* (Cork: Collins Press, 2009).

Follis, Bryan A., *A State Under Siege: the Establishment of Northern Ireland, 1920–1925* (Wooton-under-Edge: Clarendon Press, 1995).

Freese, Barbara, *Coal: a Human History* (London: William Henemann, 2005).

Fuller, Louise, *Irish Catholicism Since 1950: The Undoing of a Culture* (Dublin: Gill & Macmillan, 2002).

Gallagher, Frank, *The Indivisible Island* (London: Gollancz, 1957).

Graham, Edgar, *Ireland and Extradition: a Protection for Terrorists* (Belfast: European Human Rights Unit, 1982).

Hamill, Desmond, *Pig in the Middle: The army in Northern Ireland 1969-1985* (London: Menthuen, 1985).

Harbinson, Robert, *Song of Erne* (Belfast: Blackstaff Press, 1987).

Harnden, Toby, *Bandit Country: the IRA and South Armagh* (London: Hodder & Stoughton, 1999).

Harvey, Brian; Kelly, Assumpta; McGearty, Sean; Murray, Sonya, *The Emerald Curtain: The social impact of the Irish Border* (Carrickmacross: Triskele, 2005).

Hayes, Paddy, *Break-out! Famous Prison Escapes* (Dublin: O'Brien, 2004).

Henry's Upper Lough Erne in 1739 (Whitegate, Co. Clare: Ballinkella Press, 1987).

Henshaw, Richard, *The Encyclopaedia of World Soccer* (Washington, DC: New Republic, 1979).

Hepburn, A.C., *Catholic Belfast and Nationalist Ireland in the Era of Joe Devlin, 1871-1934*, Oxford University Press, Oxford, 2008.

Hezlet, Arthur, *The 'B' Specials: History of the Ulster Special Constabulary, 1914–2007* (London: Tom Stacy, 1972).

Holland, Jack; Phoenix, Susan, *Phoenix: Policing the Shadows* (London: Hodder & Stoughton, 1996).

Jarman, Neil, *Material Conflicts: Parades and Visual Displays in Northern Ireland* (Oxford: Berg, 1997).

Jeffrey, Keith, *Field Marshal Sir Henry Wilson: A political soldier* (Oxford, 2006).

Jess, Mevyn, *The Orange Order* (Dublin: O'Brien Press, 2007).

Kelly, James, *Orders for the Captain?* (Dublin: privately published, 1971).

Kaufman, Eric, *The Orange Order: a Contemporary Northern Irish History* (Oxford: Oxford University Press, 2007).

Kelly, Stephen, *Fianna Fáil, Partition and Northern Ireland, 1926–1971* (Dublin: Irish Academic Press, 2013).

Laffan, Michael, *The Partition of Ireland, 1912–1925* (Dublin: Dublin Historical Association, 1983).

Leary, Peter, *Unapproved Routes: Histories of the Irish border, 1922-1972* (Oxford: Oxford University Press, 2016).

Lewis, Samuel, *A Topographical Dictionary of Ireland* (London: S. Lewis & Co., 1837).

Livingstone, Peadar, *The Fermanagh Story: a Documentary History of the County Fermanagh from the Earliest Times to the Present Day* (Enniskillen: Cumann Seanchais Chlochair, 1969).

Lynch, Robert, *The Northern IRA and the Early Years of Partition*, 1920–1922 (Dublin: Irish Academic Press, 2006).

Lynn, Brendan, *Holding the Ground: the Nationalist Party in Northern Ireland, 1945–72* (Farnham: Ashgate, 1997).

Macardle, Dorothy, *The Irish Republic* (London: Corgi 1968).

McAughtry, Sam, *Down in the Free State* (Dublin: Gill & Macmillan, 1987).

McCutcheon, W.A., *The Canals of the North of Ireland* (Exeter, Devon: David & Charles, 1965),

MacEoin, Uinseann, *The IRA in the Twilight Years, 1923–1948* (Dublin: Argenta, 1997).

MacDonald, Brian, *A Time of Desolation: Clones Poor Law Union, 1845–50* (Enniskillen: Clogher Historical Society, 2001).

MacDonald, Brian, *The 'Pitchfork' Murders: Uncovering the Cover-up* (Newtownbutler: privately published, 2013).

MacDonald, Darach, *The Chosen Fews: Exploding myth in South Armagh* (Cork: Mercier, 2000).

MacDonald, Darach, *Blood & Thunder: Inside an Ulster Protestant Band* (Cork: Mercier, 2010).

MacKillop, James, *Dictionary of Celtic Mythology* (Oxford: Oxford University Press, 1998)

Martinez, Oscar J., *Border People: Life and Society in the U.S.–Mexico Borderlands* (Tucson, AZ: University of Arizona Press, 1994).

Matchett, William, *Secret Victory: the Intelligence War that Beat the IRA* (Belfast: self-published, 2016).

Minto, Susie (ed.), *The Forgotten People of Ulster: Stories of Orangeism South of the Border* (Kesh: CADOLEMO, 2013).

Morton, Robin (collated), *Come Day, Go Day, God Send Sunday: the Songs and Life Story, Told in His Own Words, of John Maguire, Traditional Singer and Farmer from Co. Fermanagh* (London: Routledge & Kegan Paul, 1973).

McCabe, Ian, *A Diplomatic History of Ireland, 1948–49: the Republic, the Commonwealth and NATO* (Dublin: Irish Academic Press, 1991).

McCafferty, Nell, *The Armagh Women* (Dublin: Co-op Books, 1981).

McGarry, Fearghal, *Eoin O'Duffy: Self-Made Hero* (Oxford: Oxford University Press, 2007).

McGoff-McCann, Michelle, *Melancholy Madness: a Coroner's Casebook* (Cork: Mercier, 2003).

McKearney, Tommy, *The Provisional IRA from Insurrection to Parliament* (London: Pluto, 2011).

McKittrick, David; McVea, David, *Making Sense of the Troubles* (London: Penguin, 2001).

McKittrick, David; Kelters, Seamus; Feeney, Brian; Thornton, Chris; McVea, David; *Lost Lives: The Stories of the Men, Women and Children Who Died as a Result of the Northern Ireland Troubles* (Edinburgh and London: Mainstream, 2004).

Moloney, Ed, *A Secret History of the IRA* (London: Penguin, 2002).

Mulligan, Eamonn; McCluskey, Fr Brian (compiled), *The Replay: a Parish History* (Monaghan: privately published, 1984).

Mulligan, Fergus, *One Hundred and Fifty Years of Irish Railways* (Belfast: Appletree Press, 1983).

Mulligan, Fergus, *William Dargan: an Honourable Life, 1799–1867* (Dublin: Lilliput Press, 2013).

Mulroe, Patrick, *Bombs, Bullets and the Border – Policing Ireland's Frontier: Irish security policy, 1969-78* (Dublin: Irish Academic Press, 2017).

Murray, Raymond, *Hard Time: Armagh Gaol, 1971–1986* (Cork: Mercier, 1998).

Raymond Murray, *The SAS in Ireland* (Cork: Mercier, 2004).

Neeson, Eoin, *The Civil War, 1922–23* (Dublin: Poolbeg, 1989).

Ó Beacháin, Donnacha , *Destiny of the Soldiers: Fianna Fáil, Irish Republicanism and the IRA, 1926–1973* (Dublin: Gill & Macmillan, 2010).

O'Brien, Justin, *The Arms Trial* (Dublin: Gill & Macmillan, 2000).

O'Brien, Mary, *Not a Leg to Stand On* (Cambridge: Vanguard Press, 2013).

O'Connor, Frank, *The Big Fellow: Michael Collins and the Irish Revolution* (London: Corgi, 1965).

O'Day, Alan, *Political Violence in Northern Ireland: Conflict and Conflict Resolution* (Westport, CT: Praeger, 1997).

O'Faolain, Nuala, *Are You Somebody?* (Dublin: New Island, 1996).

O'Halpin, Eunan, *Defending Ireland: the Irish State and Its Enemies Since 1922* (Oxford: Oxford University Press, 1999).

O'Malley, Ernie, *On Another Man's Wound* (Dublin: Anvil Books, 1979).

O'Shiel, Kevin (ed.), *Handbook of the Ulster Question: issued by the North Eastern Boundary Bureau* (Dublin: The Stationery Office, 1923).

Parker, John, *Secret Hero: The life and mysterious death of Captain Robert Nairac* (London: Metro, 2004).

Patterson, Henry, *Ireland's Violent Frontier: the Border and Anglo-Irish Relations during the Troubles* (Palgrave Macmillan, 2013).

Pearson, Hesketh, *The Life of Oscar Wilde* (Twickenham: Senate, 1998).

Potter, John, *Testimony to Courage: the History of the Ulster Defence Regiment 1969–1992* (Barnsley, Yorkshire: Leo Cooper, 2001).

Sagarra, Eda, *Kevin O'Shiel: Tyrone Nationalist and Nation Builder* (Dublin: Irish Academic Press, 2013).

Saunderson, Henry, *The Saundersons of Castle Saunderson* (privately printed, 1936).

Shea, Patrick, *Voices and the Sound of Drums* (Belfast: Blackstaff, 1981).

Shirley, F.P., *History of the County of Monaghan* (London: Chiswick Press, 1877).

Staunton, Enda, *The Nationalists of Northern Ireland 1918–1973* (Dublin: Columba, 2001).

Steffens, Johannes, *The Police Forces of Northern Ireland – History, Perceptions and Problems* (Munich: GRIN Verlag, 2007).

Stewart, A.T.Q., *The Narrow Ground: Aspects of Ulster, 1607–1969* (London: Faber & Faber, 1977).

Taylor, J. Wallace, *The Rossmore Incident: an Account of the Various Nationalist or Counter-Nationalist Meetings Held in Ulster in the Autumn of 1883* (Dublin: Hodges & Company, 1884).

Taylor, Peter, *Beating the Terrorists: Interrogation in Omagh, Gough and Castlereagh* (London: Penguin, 1980),

Taylor, Peter, *Brits: the War Against the IRA* (London: Bloomsbury, 2001).

Taylor, Peter, *Provos: the IRA and Sinn Féin* (London: Bloomsbury, 1997).

Taylor, Peter, *Families at War: Voices from the Troubles* (London: BBC Books, 1989).

Taylor, Peter, *Stalker: the Search for Truth* (London: Faber & Faber, 1987).

Tóibín, Colm, *Bad Blood: a Walk along the Irish Border* (London: Picador, 1994).

Travers, Stephen; Fetherstonehaugh, Neil, *The Miami Showband Massacre: A Survivor's Search for the Truth* (Dublin: Hodder Headline Ireland, 2007).

Urban, Mark, *Big Boys' Rules: the SAS and the Secret Struggle against the IRA* (London: Faber & Faber, 1992).

Walker, B.M. (ed.), *Parliamentary Election Results in Ireland, 1801–1922* (Dublin: Royal Irish Academy, 1978).

Walker, Brian W., A Political History of the Two Irelands: From Partition to Peace, Palgrave MacMillan, London, 2012.

Walsh, Liz, *The Final Beat: Gardaí killed in the line of duty* (Dublin: Gill and Macmillan, 2001).

White, Heather, *Wildfire: the Story of Oscar Wilde's Half-Sisters* (Drumskinny: Principia Press, 2002).

Wilson, T.G., *Victorian Doctor: Being the Life of Sir William Wilde* (Wakefield: EP Publishing, 1974).

Younger, Calton, *Ireland's Civil War* (London: Fontana, 1970).

Books (fiction and poetry cited)

Connaughton, Shane, *The Run of the Country* (London: Penguin, 1992).

Hewitt, John, *Selected Poems*, ed. Michael Longley and Frank Ormsby (Belfast: Blackstaff, 2007).

Leitch, Maurice, *Poor Lazarus* (Belfast: Blackstaff, 1985).

McCabe, Patrick, *Carn* (London: Picador, 1993).

Montague, John, *Selected Poems* (London: Penguin, 2001).

O'Faolain, Sean, *The Heat of the Sun* (London: Penguin, 1983).

Muldoon, Paul, *Poems, 1968–1998* (London: Faber & Faber, 2001).

Muldoon, Paul, *Moy Sand and Gravel* (London: Faber & Faber, 2002).

Muldoon, Paul, *One Thousand Things Worth Knowing* (London: Faber & Faber, 2015).

Acknowledgements

The author wishes to acknowledge permissions to quote from poems:

Lines from 'Freehold' in *The Collected Poems of John Hewitt*, ed. Frank Ormsby (Blackstaff Press, 1991) and from 'Ulster Names' from *John Hewitt Selected Poems*, ed. Michael Longley and Frank Ormsby (Blackstaff Press, 2007) reproduced by kind permission of Blackstaff Press on behalf of the Estate of John Hewitt.

Extracts from two poems by John Montague, 'History Walk' and 'Time in Armagh', are both included in the collection, *Time in Armagh* (1993), reproduced by kind permission of www.gallerypress.com on behalf of the author.

Extracts from works of Paul Muldoon reproduced under licence P171205/069 from his publisher, Faber and Faber Ltd.